Organization and Organizing

This timely collection addresses central issues in organizational communication theory on the nature of organizing and organization. The strength of this volume is its contribution to the conception of materiality, agency, and discourse in current theorizing and research on the constitution of organizations. It addresses such questions as:

- To what extent should the materiality of texts and artefacts be accounted for in a process view of organization?
- What part does materiality play in the process by which organizations achieve continuity in time and space?
- In what sense do artefacts perform a role in human communication and interaction and in the constitution of organization?
- What are the voices and entities participating in the emergence and stabilization of organizational reality?

The contributors to this volume represent scholarship based in North America and it features contributions that overcome traditional conceptions of the nature of organizing by addressing in specific ways the difficult issues of the performative character of agency; materiality as the basis of the iterability of communication and continuity of organizations; and discourse as both textuality and interaction.

The contributions laid out in this book also pay tribute to the work of the organizational communication theorist James R. Taylor, who developed a view of organizations as deeply rooted in communication and language. Contributors extend and challenge Taylor's communicative view by tackling issues and assumptions left implicit in his work.

Daniel Robichaud is Associate Professor in the Department of Communication, Université de Montréal, Canada.

François Cooren is Full Professor in the Department of Communication, Université de Montréal, Canada. He is past president of the International Communication Association.

Organization and Organizing

Materiality, Agency, and Discourse

Edited by

Daniel Robichaud and François Cooren

Routledge
Taylor & Francis Group

NEW YORK AND LONDON

First published 2013
by Routledge
711 Third Avenue, New York, NY 10017

Simultaneously published in the UK
by Routledge
2 Park Square, Milton Park, Abingdon, Oxon OX14 4RN

Routledge is an imprint of the Taylor & Francis Group, an informa business

© 2013 Taylor & Francis

The right of Daniel Robichaud and François Cooren to be identified as the authors of the editorial material, and of the authors for their individual chapters, has been asserted in accordance with sections 77 and 78 of the Copyright, Designs and Patents Act 1988.

Library of Congress Cataloging in Publication Data
Organization and organizing : materiality, agency, and discourse / edited by Daniel
    Robichaud and Francois Cooren.
    p. cm.
    Includes bibliographical references.
    1. Communication in organizations. 2. Organization. 3. Organizational behavior.
    I. Robichaud, Daniel. II. Cooren, François.
    HD30.3.O717 2013
    302.3'5dc23
    2012035524

ISBN: 978-0-415-52931-0 (pbk)
ISBN: 978-0-415-52930-3 (hbk)
ISBN: 978-0-203-09447-1 (ebk)

Typeset in Garamond
by EvS Communication Networx, Inc.

Printed and bound in the United States of America by
Walsworth Publishing Company, Marceline, MO.

To our students

Contents

List of Figures and Tables

Introduction

The Need for New Materials
in the Constitution of Organization

Daniel Robichaud and François Cooren

Over the past 20 years or so, organization studies have witnessed the emergence of new directions and research agendas coming from a wide range of disciplines and theoretical commitments. In the field of organizational communication, for example, debates and discussions around the idea that "communication is constitutive of organizations"—aka the communicative constitution of organization (CCO) perspective—have been increasing (Fairhurst & Putnam, 2004; see also Lawrence, Zelber, & Leca, 2011; Monge & Poole, 2008; Putnam & Nicotera, 2009; Taylor & Van Every, 2000). On a different front, in the constellation of studies published on organizational discourse or fostering discursive views of organizing, there has been much discussion since the mid-1990s about the "discursive" vs. "not-so-discursive" nature of organizations (Alvesson & Kärreman, 2000a; Fairclough 1995, 2005; Reed, 2000). Others have also taken the route of so-called postmodernist thought for the way we conceive of organization and organizing (Chia, 1996), while many scholars coming from various backgrounds and following the lead of Karl Weick (1979, 1995), urge us to think in terms of *organizing* where sometimes even the very notion of organization loses its analytical relevance (Tsoukas & Chia, 2002). The studies of science and technology have also had a significant impact on the theory of organization, not least through the influence of actor-network theory (Czarniawska & Hernes, 2005; Latour, 2005; Law, 1994).

A common thread to most of these developments is a call to reassess the basic nature of organization from a process standpoint. In one way or another, all developments involved implicit or explicit assumptions about the processual nature or mode of being of organization. With a view to unpacking the various ways in which a process ontology of organization might be translated and put to work both in theoretical and empirical research, this book brings together leading and promising young scholars who were asked to lay out their perspectives on the basic question: What *is* an organization? Contributors to the book come from various fields of the social sciences (management, sociology of science, anthropology, discourse analysis, and semiotics, among others), as well as from diverse countries and intellectual backgrounds. They offer new metaphors and constructs to recast the reality of contemporary organizing and organization in different realms: time, space, action, and performativity; interaction, text, and meaning; materiality and artifacts.

New Construction Materials for Organizations

Maybe the most notorious attempt at deconstructing the classical notion of organization is the pioneering work of Karl Weick. In his 1969 book, he wrote:

> The central argument is that any organization *is* the way it runs through the process of organizing. [...] Organization is fluid, continually changing, continually in need of reaccomplishment, and it appears to be an entity only when this fluidity is frozen at some moment in time. This means that we must define organization in terms of organizing. (pp. 90–91, emphasis in the original)

In spite of the wide spectrum of influences and theoretical resources he mobilized over the following 40 years, Weick kept defining the basic problem of organizing in terms of the links agents collectively tie and untie between action and meaning. From the outset, and including his "Organizing and the Process of Sensemaking" paper (Weick, Sutcliffe, & Obstfeld, 2005), he has insisted that organizations come to exist in the activities of agents as they take on a collective meaning. Organizing, in his view, is basically our answer to the inherently equivocal nature of our world, and thus to the infinite punctuations and meanings we can make out of it. Organization may be said to emerge when minimal interaction patterns and collective rules take shape to reduce such equivocality, hence his frequent reliance on the metaphor of a grammar. Organizing occurs, according to Weick, in the tension and ongoing movement between enactment, where the raw data of experience and organizing are literally produced, and retention processes where interpretive causal maps making sense of experience are stabilized as collective sensemaking devices. The nature of organizing is all about the back and forth movement and translations between action and interpretation.

Following Weick (1979), and also incorporating assumptions drawn from ethnomethodology and interactionist sociologies, a growing tradition in organization theory experienced an interpretive turn (Putnam & Pacanowsky, 1983). Activities, communication, interaction, and discourse came to occupy a significant place in the study of organizing, since these were the places where the organization was thought to be "constructed." As insightful, provocative, and empirically illuminating as it might be, this shift of perspective came, however, with a heavy price tag: the logic of the argument entailed that the nature of an organization could not be anything but conceptual, or ontologically *ideal*. All the rest—infrastructures, money, laws, resource distribution, technology, to name but a few—were not so much denied reality, to be sure, but from now on had to be analytically treated as consequences and a product of the ultimate explanatory realm: that of meaning.

Organizations were now made of conceptual, or symbolic material. Notions such as "typifications" (Berger & Luckmann, 1966), mental cognitive "frames" (Fairhurst & Sarr, 1996), "representations" (Tsoukas, chapter 4), "interpretive schemes" and "memory traces" (Giddens, 1984), symbols, in sum, came to occupy the front seat of the way we conceived of organizations. Concepts and types, because of their capacity to create generality out of the particularities of experience, and to feed back into actors' choices and decisions, provided the basic idealist explanations pushing aside the objectivism and materialism inherent in the dominant functionalist view. Weick (1995) illustrates this view when he argues that organizing expands in time and space because local intersubjective constructions translate into "generic subjectivities" which account for the fact that understandings "can be picked up, perpetuated, and enlarged by people who did not participate in the original intersubjective construction" (p. 72). Hence the continuity of organization in time and space depends first and foremost on "interpretive schemes," "retention," or "memory traces," to take Giddens's (1984) structuration theory vocabulary. In sum the interpretive turn led us to focus on the conceptually constructed reality of organization. Foregrounding organizing in organization research more often than not has amounted to a displacement of the reality of organization from the materiality of classic conceptions to the idealism of much contemporary thinking advocating notions of "construction" (Ashcraft, Kuhn, & Cooren, 2009).

For most contributors to this book, these conceptions convey a far too weak version of the very idea of construction. In order to account for the durability that contemporary organizations sometimes achieve, contributors advance many more displacements in our traditional ways of conceiving of agency, materiality, communication, time, and space. They suggest various detours, whereby revisiting these basic issues, we end up with different versions of "organizing" and "constitution" grounded in performativity, according to a redistributed notion of agency, and a renewed version of materialism.

Performativity and Agency

One of the analytical challenges taken up more or less explicitly in the various contributions to this book is to recognize the performativity of organizing as its mode of being. Certainly, most interpretive scholars would reply that, of course, organizations have to be constantly reaccomplished, performed, or enacted. But in most cases this means that performance is thought to be crucial to nourishing the symbolic and conceptual reality of organization so to speak. We need to keep going so the Golem doesn't die (Czarniawska, chapter 1)! Performance, according to some interpretive thinkers, is important because it is what keeps something deeper alive and real. But what if, as Bruno Latour forcefully argues in chapter 3, "there is never anything deeper than what is in its actuality" (p. 43)? What if "essence is existence" as he argued elsewhere (Latour, 1996)? Then the performative dimension of organizing, instead of being the Golem's slave, would be elevated to the mode of being of organization.

From an ontological standpoint, an organization is thus brought into being as it is performed, acted out, as it becomes literally an event. Resources and competencies can only be postulated afterward, in retrospect, in those moments when, thanks to numerous calculation devices, we can so to speak freeze the flow of events, just as an accountant freezes the constant circulation of funds at the end of the year (which she could not have done, by the way, without the compiling of a great number of inscriptions, books, calculating machines, pens, forms, and their categories). Critics of such a position would say that this sounds a lot like a reduction of the organization to its activities, that is, to the level of its actions and operations (since to them reality has a great number of levels, not just our analysis of it). But it only looks like a reduction to those who conceive of action as a strictly local phenomenon and with a very limited scope in time and space. That of course seems incompatible with the reality of an organization that extends in time and space. For such an extension to be possible, one might think, something has to be added to action; that is, structure.

However, as a number of contributors to this book will argue in various ways, action at-a-distance is not a special case of action requiring that something be added to an act. There is a distal quality inherent in any action (Vasquez, chapter 8). Action at-a-distance (i.e., tele-action; Cooren, 2006) might be the general model from which meaningful and situated action is derived, not the other way around. This is why, as Michel Callon puts it, an actor is always a network (Callon, 1991). Such a view informs more or less explicitly a number of modes of contemporary thought (see Czarniawska, chapter 1; Latour, chapter 3), but finds philosophical foundations in the pragmatic tradition, going back to Charles S. Peirce's conception of action as a triad (Peirce, 1960; Robichaud, 2006). In other words, the *translocal* quality we were accustomed to attribute to the phenomenon of organization or structure has always already been inherently involved in what it means to act, in the very nature of action but on various levels.

Organization as Distributed and Plural Agency

In the process of redefining action as a process that is always shared, the problem of agency acquires a brand new dimension: performance does not index inherent or potential competences or capacities, but actual and situated connections, that is, other performances, and definitely performances of many others, which is one of the most fundamental tenets of actor-network theory. As students of organizations, we have only timidly started to explore the implications of such a perspective for our theories of organizing. We have given so much importance to notions such as "typifications," "roles," or "institutions" that we have completely forgotten that these realities do not have any force of inertia on their own. Instead they borrow their impetus from other entities, from other ontologies. It is always by their translation into other matters, other bodies, belonging to other agents that they get to play a part in a course of action, since it is indeed what action is all about.

Organizations in this perspective, can be said to be constituted in communication and interaction, but are definitely not reducible to symbols and meanings, since communication itself would not survive such a reduction. Any action is the deed of numerous agents tied to each other and translated into each other through interaction and communication. Czarniawska (chapter 1) develops this same idea in terms of what she refers to as an "action net":

> Network assumes the existence of actors, who forge connections. Action net reverts this assumption, suggesting that connections between and among actions, when stabilized, are used to construct the identities of actors. (p. 14)

It is inevitable that mobilization of multiple entities from multiple spatiotemporal horizons and ontologies shows up at the forefront of the analysis once action is given analytical priority. The extension in time and space of organization is no longer a mystery, and one realizes that nothing has to be added for such an extension to be accounted for. There are differences in degrees to be sure, not in nature. This in turn leads to the recognition of the fundamentally distributed character of agency. As Taylor says, in concluding this book: "An organization … is a frozen configuration of agency" (p. 386).

A Renewed Version of Materialism

One last consequence of the redistribution of action and agency in our theories of organizing and organization is another displacement, toward a renewed version of materialism. There are strong symbolic relations between an agent and an action, but these relations also have a material and tangible character that sometimes supersedes any other. That is why Czarniawska insists (chapter 1) that both virtual and actual/concrete connections have to be described in our analysis of organizations. The continuous work of organizing is not only interpretive/immaterial/intangible. It is translated into the materiality/durability/body of artifacts that become full-fledged agents contributing the way of being and acting of an organization (Cooren, 2010).

As actor-network theory has been argued for 30 years now, we cannot reduce the participation of artifacts to mere tools carrying our human intentions without deformation and transformation. Just as a translation is always also a form of treason, the translation of intents into artifacts always escapes the control of their creators, in the same way that a text distances itself from, and acts beyond, its author (Derrida, 1988; Ricoeur, 1973). According to this perspective, materiality is not any longer inert and soulless; it is, on the contrary, an irreducible dimension of organization and organizing.

Organizational Communication at the Center

The prelude to this collection of essays was a 2008 conference held on the work of the organizational communication theorist James R. Taylor. For over three decades, Taylor developed a view of organizations as deeply rooted in communication and language, as an ongoing flux of interaction from which stabilized patterns of relations and meanings emerge which, in turn, feed back into the interactions and joint activities of organizational members. His work found an audience among students of organizational communication in search of an analytical apparatus to describe the constitutive role of communication in the emergence and maintenance of organizational realities. It also appealed more broadly, however, to a larger audience, both in North America and Europe, of organization studies scholars with a *process orientation* toward organizations (Tsoukas & Chia, 2002). The conference paid tribute to the 30-year commitment of James R. Taylor to the development of organizational communication as an intellectual site to address the issue of the nature of organizations. His work is not only an outstanding example of an attempt at a synthesis of various trends (Taylor & Van Every, 2000, 2011), but has been throughout the years explicitly driven by the same question that animates this volume: What is the fundamental nature of organization and organizing?

Taylor's key concept is that the organization, to exist, must be authored. Until it has been authorized it has no identity, and can exert no authority. Authoring of identity is accomplished as an act of narrativization (Taylor, 1993c; Taylor & Van Every, 1993, 2000): establishing what the context is, who the actors (including the organization) are, how they relate to each other, what is right and what is wrong. In sum, what's the story (Latour, chapter 3; Weick, 2006).

An organization, however, once constituted, incorporates multiple practices, each of which is grounded in its own distinct logic of materiality. Practices link to each other, communicatively, as mutually defining dualisms (Taylor, 1993c): an indispensable complementarity that is the foundation of all collectively grounded identity (Sacks, 1992): accountant/accountee, software/hardware centers of development, manager/managed, program organizer/professional resource person, technology implementer/user, company/client (Taylor & Van Every, 2011). Since sensemaking is inevitably tied to practice, and since every community of practice authors the text of the organization from its own grounded-in-practice perspective, the establishment of the narrative of the organization as such is inherently problematic. Other than by institutional practice or brute force, it must be continually reconstructed in and through communication.

The establishment of organizational authority thus supposes an interplay of text (that which is to be authored) and conversation (where the authority of the organization's text, as well as those of its members, is negotiated). It emerges in a search for a narrative that can transcend the particular interests of members and their communities, by incorporating the latter into a tolerable metanarrative. The proper object of organizational communication research is precisely this process of negotiation, with the goal of understanding the empirical dynamic leading to a collectively sanctioned authorization, however imperfect, of the organization itself. Organizational communication must thus be clearly distinguished from interpersonal communication: it is a composition of interrelated practices that encounter each other in the interactive talk of individual members, but has its own practice-grounded imperatives.

Contributors to this volume, however, extend Taylor's ideas in many ways, by introducing developments on issues left more of less implicit in his work. To what extent ought the materiality of texts and artifacts to be accounted for in a process view of organization? Do they perform anything in the constitution of organization, and if so, in what ways? What does it mean to act, or display *agency*? What are the voices and entities participating in the emergence and stabilization of organizational reality? Can discourse be a construct both flexible and strong enough to account for the ontology and durability of organization? The present volume was built around such questions as they are addressed by organization and organizational communication scholars both extending and challenging Taylor's communicative view.

The Organization of the Book

This book is divided into two parts. The first part assembles essays by eminent scholars who lay out the conceptual challenges we face as we attempt to develop a way of conceiving of organization that avoids the pitfalls of two traditional solutions; that is, the materialist and idealist perspectives. In chapter 1, Barbara Czarniawska opens the discussion with a historical overview and a pragmatic exploration of the uses of the concept of organization as it reveals intricacies of organizing that have previously been obscured. Linda Putnam (chapter 2) addresses the multiple ways in which contradictions and dialectical tensions are played out in James Taylor's work. Bruno Latour (chapter 3) then describes organizing as a specific mode of existence of organization in the movements of actors as they successively write and live the scripts of organizing.

In chapter 4, Haridimos Tsoukas makes explicit his own view on the processual nature of organization based on Cornelius Castoriadis's concept of "ensemblization" as an organizing process by which ensembles are constituted within practices out of indeterminate possibilities. Building on Tsoukas and on Taylor's work, Anne Nicotera (chapter 5) then unpacks in a systematic fashion the notion of "communication as constitutive of organization" and examines its implication for understanding the "entitative being" character of organization as it transcends and eclipses individuals by both identity and authority being attributed to it. Dualism and duality in contemporary thought and theory building forms the topic addressed by Boris Brummans (chapter 6) as he reflects on the tension between the idea of ongoing processes and the notion of identity as a stabilized "thing." In closing this first part of the book, Robert McPhee and Joel Iverson (chapter 7) focus on the processes of coordination of activities as a central feature of organizing and dwell on the contribution to this issue of the Montreal School of organizational communication.

This book would not be complete without a body of empirical research illustrating in various ways how new assumptions on the nature of organization lead to new ways to problematize organizational processes. The second part of the book thus offers a sampling of research as illustrations, most of them conducted by young, promising scholars.

Chapter 8, by Consuelo Vasquez, addresses the problematic of space and spatialization in a case study where "spacing practices" of organizational agents play a crucial role in the evolution of a particular organizing episode she studied. In chapter 9, Isabelle Piette takes up the issue of identity change in a study where multiple stakeholders of a single industry are led to reassess their identity as an industry as they become involved in a legislative reform process. Mathieu Chaput's study (chapter 10) of the birth of a political party lays a particular focus on discourse and rhetorical argument as organizing devices. It dwells on the key role argumentation plays as a constitutive aspect of organization and organizing. Finally, in chapter 11, Viviane Sergi investigates the role played by documents and various textual artifacts in the organizing of projects in a software company. Based on her ethnographic case study, she offers a repertoire of the ways documents shape both the coordination of work and the connections between organizational actors.

Such studies, in turn, should lead us to rethink our assumptions and theories. As Bruno Latour once put it, the outcome of research should be the dismantling of all theories (personal communication). So the contributors to the second part of the book do far more than merely show us how to conduct research with new analytical devices in mind or, even worse, how to "apply" such devices. Indeed, they push us to move forward on the thin line between a comforting but heuristically moribund reliance on traditional views, and the risky, costly, and exhausting work innovations and new insights demand of us if we are to understand the changing world of contemporary organizing.

Last but not least, James Taylor (chapter 12) closes the book with his concluding remarks and reactions to the preceding contributions, insisting on the challenges of the road yet to be traveled.

Unlike other social and organizational theorists, James Taylor cannot think of an organization as a phenomenon made of a single matter, be it objectified social relations (i.e., structures), or a flow of ongoing interactional processes. He argues that social interaction and activities, or conversation, do lead to the emergence of more or less stabilized social relations that extend their scope in time and space because actors translated them in texts that form the basis of further collective action. The originality of his work lies in his understanding of communication and language as the locus of the basic processes allowing such translation of conversation into texts, and texts into conversation. He provided a conceptual framework that cast both sides of organizations as communicative accomplishments (see also Taylor & Van Every, 2011).

Contributors to this book take up this dual character of organizational processes, by not only describing processes through which organizing emerges from actual actions and interactions, but also showing how the various products of these activities come to act back, so to speak, on their producers, thus rendering problematic conventional views of agency, materiality, and discourse. By translating Taylor's work in a much broader research agenda, they all contribute to celebrating his insights by showing why we should never have to choose, practically *and* theoretically, between the eventfulness and the iterability of organizational life. As Taylor has shown us for the past 30 years, organizations and societies, as forms of life, always navigate between the deadly chaos of smoke and the fixed order of crystal (Taylor & Van Every, 2000; see also Atlan, 1979), a difficult balance that has to be continuously redefined and reachieved.

It is our hope that this book will help theoreticians, researchers, and practitioners navigate in this turbulent world, the only one we have.

About the Authors

Boris H. J. M. Brummans (PhD, Texas A&M University, 2004) is an Associate Professor in the Département de Communication, Université de Montréal, Canada. His research looks at Buddhist organizing in various parts of Asia.

Mathieu Chaput (PhD, University of Montreal, 2012) is a postdoctoral fellow in the Department of Business Administration, Lund University. His research and teaching interests include the communicative constitution of organizations, the rhetoric of political parties, and the analysis of interactions. His work has appeared in such forums as *Management Communication Quarterly, Réseaux, Commposite,* and *The Handbook of Business Discourse,* as well as in numerous national and international conferences.

François Cooren, PhD, is a professor and Chair of the Department of Communication, Université de Montréal, Canada. His research interests lie in organizational communication, language and social interaction, and communication theory. He is the author of two books, close to 20 book chapters, and more than 40 articles published in international peer-reviewed journals. He is the past president (2010–2011) of the International Communication Association (ICA) and the current president of the International Association for Dialogue Analysis (IADA).

Barbara Czarniawska holds a Chair in Management Studies at GRI, School of Business, Economics and Law, University of Gothenburg, Sweden. Doctor *honoris causa* at Stockholm School of Economics, Copenhagen Business School, and Helsinki School of Economics; she is a member of the Swedish Royal Academy of Sciences, the Swedish Royal Engineering Academy, the Royal Society of Art and Sciences, Gothenburg, and Societas Scientiarum Finnica. She takes a feminist and constructionist perspective on organizing, recently exploring the connections between popular culture and practice of management, and the organization of the news production. Her interest in methodology focuses on techniques of fieldwork and the application of narratology to organization studies. Her recent books in English includee *Shadowing and Other Techniques of Doing Fieldwork in Modern Societies*, (2007), *A Theory of Organizing* (2008), and *Cyberfactories: How News Agencies Produce News* (2012).

Joel O. Iverson (PhD Arizona State University, 2003) is an Associate Professor in the Communication Studies Department at the University of Montana. His research interests include organizational communication and structuration theory, particularly in the areas of organizational knowledge, mission, volunteers, and risk.

Bruno Latour is a French philosopher and a very influential theorist in the field of science and technology studies (STS). He is a Professor and Vice-President for Research at Sciences Po, Paris (since 2007). He has authored close to 125 articles and 15 books, translated into several languages.

Anne Maydan Nicotera (PhD, Ohio University, 1990) is an Associate Professor and Associate Chair of the Department of Communication, George Mason University, where she teaches courses in organizational and interpersonal communication. Her research is grounded in a constitutive perspective and focuses on culture and conflict, diversity, race and gender, and aggressive communication, with a particular interest in healthcare organizations and institutional forms. She has published her research in numerous national journals, has published five books, and is a frequent contributor to edited volumes. She has developed a theory and associated measurement tool for a construct called structurational divergence, which describes the intractable organizational conflicts that can result from the simultaneous application of multiple meanings in intra- and interprofessional interactions. She is also an experienced organizational training and development consultant.

Robert McPhee (PhD, Michigan State University, 1978) is a Professor in the Hugh Downs School of Human Communication, Arizona State University. He has published theory and research articles on organizational and group communication in journals including *Management Communication Quarterly, Organization, Communication Monographs, Quarterly Journal of Speech, Human Communication Research,* and the *Communication Yearbook.*

Isabelle Piette is a PhD candidate in strategy at HEC Montreal. She holds a master's degree in management from HEC Montreal and a master's degree in literary studies from the University of Quebec at Montreal. Her research focuses on interorganizational collaboration, organizational identity, and narrative approach.

Linda L. Putnam is Professor of Communication, University of California, Santa Barbara. Her research focuses on negotiation and organizational conflict, organizational discourse, and gender in organizations. She is the coeditor of *Organizational Discourse Studies* (2011), *Building Theories of Organization: The Constitutive Role of Communication* (2009), *The Sage Handbook of Organizational Discourse* (2004), and *The New Handbook of Organizational Communication* (2001). She is a Fellow of the International Communication Association and a Distinguished Scholar of the National Communication Association.

Daniel Robichaud, PhD, is Associate Professor, Département de Communication, Université de Montréal, Canada. His research focuses on the role of communication, discourse, and narratives in constituting organizational identity, managing organizational change, and achieving interorganizational collaboration. His work has been published in numerous international journals and he is currently Associate editor of *Communication Theory*.

Viviane Sergi is Assistant Professor, Université du Québec, Montréal, Canada. She was previously a postdoctoral fellow at the Royal Institute of Technology, Stockholm (Sweden) and at the Canada Research Chair in Strategic Management in Pluralistic Settings, HEC Montréal (Canada). She holds a PhD in administration from HEC Montréal. Her research interests include project organizing, leadership, materiality, and methodological issues related to the practice of qualitative research. She has conducted qualitative fieldwork in various settings, including public organizations (hospitals, universities and arts organizations) and an IT company. She is currently exploring project organizing and leadership from a practice perspective.

James R. Taylor, PhD, FICA, is the author, coauthor, or editor of eight books, including *The Emergent Organization: Communication as Its Site and Surface* (2000) and *The Situated Organization: Case Studies in the Pragmatics of Communication Research* (2011). He is the author of more than 90 scientific articles, and has received several "best paper" awards at ICA and NCA. He is a fellow of the International Communication Association, an Emeritus Professor and "Pioneer" of the Université de Montréal, and has also been voted outstanding member of the Organizational Communication Division of the International Communication Association.

Haridimos Tsoukas holds the Columbia Ship Management Chair in Strategic Management at the Department of Public and Business Administration, University of Cyprus, and is professor at the Warwick Business School, University of Warwick. He received his PhD from the Manchester

Business School. His research interests include knowledge-based perspectives on organizations, organizational becoming, practical reason in management, and epistemological issues in organizational research.

Consuelo Vásquez, (PhD, Université de Montréal, 2009) is Assistant Professor, Département de Communication Sociale et Publique, Université du Québec, Montréal, Canada. Her research looks at the constitutive role of communication in spacing and timing.

Part I

Theoretical Developments

1 Organizations as Obstacles to Organizing

Barbara Czarniawska

"What Is a Necessary Step in the Construction of Knowledge at One Moment Becomes an Impediment at Another"

In this introductory section, I wish to return to a statement that I have made on various occasions (e.g., Czarniawska, 2006; but see also Shenhav, 2003): in the late 1960s, organization theorists changed the dominant meaning of the term *organization* so as to be able to import systems theory. Here, I repeat my argument in brief.

In 1961 Dwight Waldo, then a central figure in administration theory, wrote a review essay titled "Organization Theory: An Elephantine Problem." It was published in *Public Administration Review*, at the time a leading journal in the field. Waldo's review encompassed six books, most of which were edited volumes. Among the most frequent contributors were Herbert Simon, James G. March, Richard Cyert, Chris Argyris, Mason Haire, Anatol Rappaport, Jacob Marshak, Rensis Likert, Peter Blau, William Foote Whyte, James Thompson, and Kurt Lewin. Waldo noted:

> [N]early all the pieces printed or reprinted are the product of the past ten years; and … a high proportion of the authors are in their early professional years. In short, … there is no doubt that organization theory and research are in a boom period. (1961, p. 212)

In his review, Waldo discussed what he saw as the main trends in this boom. One was a transition from administration theory to organization theory. This shift resulted from an emergent paradigm in social science methodology—behaviorism (which we now include under a broader label of positivism)—introduced under the banner of an emulation of the natural sciences. Such an approach did not sit well with the notion of administration, which was "an applied science—if it is not indeed a profession, an art, or something less. 'Administrative theory' suggests an engagement with the world, a striving after values" (Waldo, 1961, p. 217). Organization theory was, on the other hand, a theory not of action, but of a unit existing "out there."

What, then, was the object of "organization theory"? In his thorough etymological investigation of the meaning of the word, William Starbuck (2003) discovered that:

> The word "organization" derives from an ancient Indo-European root that also spawn[ed] the words "organ" and "work." The Roman verb *"organizare"* meant initially "to furnish with organs so as to create a complete human being," but later Romans gave it the broader meaning "to endow with a coordinated structure." *Organizare* migrated from Latin into Old French. In 1488, the French language included the word "organization," which an ancient dictionary defined self-reflectively as "the state of an organized body." ... Although dictionaries published between 1750 and 1840 do not mention this usage explicitly, around 1800 some writers began to use "organization" to describe a property of societies. (p. 156)

This last usage persisted for another 150 years; *organization* was employed as a noun denoting a state of being organized and was used in the plural only to denote voluntary associations, as distinct from firms and public service offices. Thus Weber spoke about "the modern organization of the civil service," which was "monocratic" (Weber, 1920, p. 656). This interpretation of the term—as a label for a state achieved by actions of organizing—was of no use for joining the major research fashion of the 1950s: systems theory (von Bertalanffy, 1950, 1951). The application of systems theory required a creation of "organizations"—separate units divided by "boundaries" from their "environments" and related to them by "adaptation."

One can construct a strong counterargument to my thesis, or at least to my dating, in the form of one of the classics of organization theory, *The Functions of the Executive* by Chester I. Barnard (1938/1968). Barnard clearly spoke of "organizations," sometimes adding the adjective *formal* or *business*. But he had obviously also read Talcott Parson's *The Structure of Social Action* (1937/1968), in which Parsons had already applied systems theory, translating into its terms the classic works of sociology by Durkheim, Weber, and Pareto. Also, as Parson himself wrote in an introduction to the paperback edition of his book, "just under 1200 hard cover copies were sold in the year 1966, some eighty per cent of the number in the original McGraw-Hill edition, which was exhausted only after approximately 10 years" (1937/1968, p. v). Clearly, the time for this idea has come.

This conceptual move must have seemed appealing in the 1960s, as it provided a kind of middle ground between mechanistic Taylorism and idealist administration theory, and permitted close bonds with the most attractive branch of science at the time—cybernetics (Wiener, 1948). It must also have been a relatively easy conceptual move, because it imitated a much earlier step made by Darwin. Lewontin (1995) pointed out that by introducing "organism," "environment," and "adaptation," Darwin sought to mechanize biology, which was still all too prone to mystification and idealism. Alas, as suggested in the quote that became the heading of this section, this loan has become a burden both for organization theory and for biology.

Indeed, at the present time, in the second decade of the 21st century, this set of metaphors is not providing good service to either human biology or organization theory. The environment is not a preexisting set of problems to which an organism, or an organization, must find solutions: these organisms or organizations created the problems in the first place. The environment of organisms consists largely of other organisms, and the environment of organizations consists almost entirely of other organizations (Perrow, 1991). By the same token, the notion of adaptation is misleading as a tool for understanding the relationship between an organism and its environment. And although it can be claimed that organisms have boundaries separating them from their environments, it is much more difficult to apply the notion of preexisting boundaries to organizations; mergers, acquisitions, transnationals, and networks make such an idea appear highly tenuous. New concepts and metaphors are constantly being sought, and administration theory has been revisited, together with many other forgotten ancestors. After all, as Waldo (1961) pointed out, while dutifully noting the triumphant entry of "the scientific study of the American business organization," the beginnings of organization theory could be found in Plato and Aristotle, and could be traced through Machiavelli and Hobbes to Fayol and Urwick.

I do not wish to imply that the presence of systems theory was a 50-year mistake, a hiatus in the development of the body of organizational knowledge. On the contrary, systems theory, and cybernetics in general, has been and remains the main inspiration for organization theory. But if organization theory itself was shaped to fit systems theory 50 years ago, at present it is systems theory that is adapted and selectively used by organization theoreticians. And returning to forgotten roots takes place on another, more sophisticated plane, and adduces more interesting results. It could be that after a half-century foray into systems theory, organization theory may return to administration theory (now called "management," however), not so much contrite as wiser.

By the 1990s, the idea of an organization/environment dichotomy was one of the many received dichotomies to collapse, due (among other reasons) to the observation that the environment of organizations primarily comprises organizations (Perrow, 1991). "Internal and external factors" were revealed as the epiphenomena of the activity of border making, and "macro- and microsystems" as products of scientific epistemologies. The new economy turned out to be one in which workers own the means of production (through their pension funds) but do not control them (O'Barr & Conley, 1992), one in which organizations are born and die at the rate of the banana fly, and the Web is the market. New questions have been posed, two of them especially pertinent and provocative. If organizations are rational tools for the realization of collective interests, why are there so many different types of organizations? Michael Hannah and John Freeman (Hannah & Freeman, 1989) drew freely on evolution theory, taking populations of organizations as their unit of analysis. Walter W. Powell and Paul J. DiMaggio, and many other new institutionalists represented in the edited volume, *The New Institutionalism in Organizational Analysis* (Powell & DiMaggio, 1991), asked the opposite question: if organizations are rational tools for realization of collective interests, why are there so few kinds of organizations? Why are organizations increasingly similar?

Perhaps, said James G. March and Johan P. Olsen in *Rediscovering Institutions* (1989), organizations are best considered neither as "rational tools" for the realization of collective interests nor as "natural and organic systems," but as modern institutions. Their conceptualization changes, as do the practices and normative justifications of their existence change.

In what follows, I first ask if the changes in organization theory influenced the practice of organizing; that is, I try to evaluate the performativity of organization theory. Then I present a brief overview of theories that maintain a focus on organizing rather than on reified "organizations." Within this frame, I formulate two provocations vis-à-vis traditional organization theory, claiming that artifacts can liberate and discourses can imprison. In the end, I review several ways in which organizations can be obstacles to organizing.

Building a Golem: How Organization Theorists Helped to Reify Organizations

The readers will easily recognize in this heading an allusion to the by-now classic 1981 article of Michel Callon and Bruno Latour, "Unscrewing the Big Leviathan." Their claim was, in short, that the difference between micro-actors and macro-actors is due not to their "nature," but to the negotiations (including wars) and associations that built them. However, the process of creating the alliances that eventually form macro-actors is poorly understood because macro-actors obliterate any traces of their construction, presenting themselves through their spokespersons as being indivisible and solid. Social scientists contribute, often unwillingly, to this construction process, by increasing this solidity and consistency in their descriptions.

McKenzie, Muniesa, and Siu (2007) expanded this thought, claiming a strong performativity of economics. In their view, it is the science of economics that creates markets. Do organization theorists create organizations? Perhaps they do create (certain types) of organizations, but no doubt in association with some macro-actor: industry or the state.

This phenomenon can be seen in Philip Selznick's book on the Tennessee Valley Authority, published in 1949—before the boom of systems theory—but already preparing a transfer from administration theory to organization theory. This "scholarly study of a complex organization" represents, on the one hand, everything from which the natural science-oriented researchers attempted to cut themselves free: a value-laden theory of (democratic) administration and an inductive methodology. On the other hand, it announces all the major trends to come: structural functionalism, behaviorism, and reification of organizing.

The TVA—the complex organization under study—was conceived as a rational tool, implanted in the midst of institutional fields: a revolutionary, planned intervention against an evolutionary tradition of the place. In order to survive, said Selznick, the TVA had to co-opt local forces and adapt itself to them. Selznick's study remained unique for a long time, in its simultaneous focus on an "organization" and its "environment," and its interest in both intra- and interorganizational processes. At the same time, it became a marketing device for TVA, leading, as Albert Hirschman (1967) pointed out, to a situation in which, for a number of years after World War II, any country that had a river valley *had to* have a copy of TVA.

In Great Britain after the war, the government promised expert support to any company that needed help in restructuring. The Tavistock Institute of Human Relations was given the task of collaborating "with Management and workers in an attempt to solve the social and psychological problems which faced them through changes in methods of work or of management" (Rice, 1958/1987, p. 6). A large team of researchers would approach the company in question, study it, and deliver an exhaustive report, diagnosing its problems and suggesting solutions (thus the idea of "company doctors," which additionally strengthened the conceptualization of a company as an "organism," a natural system). The leading names were Eric Trist, Albert K. Rice, Elliot Jaques, and Wilfred R. Bion.

The Tavistock Institute continued the Elton Mayo tradition (the Human Relations School) and combined it with an open system theory as represented by Von Bertalanffy. The concept of sociotechnical systems assumed that every production system contained a technological organization (equipment and process layout) and a work organization (people and their tasks). The two must fit together to fulfill their function, as judged by the economic viability of the production system. "Each system or sub-system has ... at any given time, one task which may be defined as its primary task—the task which it is created to perform. Thus the primary task of private enterprise in a Western economy is to make profits, while that of public utility is to give services" (Rice, 1958/1987, p. 32). Consequently, the environment blurred into a generic provider of energy in return for fulfillment of the primary tasks, defined by the same environment. Yet within this frame, "organization" is still a *state* of a system or a subsystem, such as "enterprise" or "utility."

In 1958, James G. March and Herbert Simon published *Organizations*. The first edition of the book begins as follows:

> This book is about the theory of formal organizations. It is easier, and probably more useful, to give examples of formal organizations than to define the term. The United States Steel Corporation is a formal organization; so is the Red Cross, the corner grocery store, the New York State Highway Department. The latter organization is, of course, part of a larger one—the New York State government. But for the present purposes we need not trouble ourselves about the precise boundaries to be drawn around an organization or the exact distinction between an "organization" and "nonorganization." We are dealing with empirical phenomena, and the world has an uncomfortable way of not permitting itself to be fitted into clean classifications. (1958/1993, p. 20)

By the second edition, they changed their minds about definitions: "Organizations are systems of coordinated action among individuals and groups whose preferences, information, interests, or knowledge differ" (1993, p. 2).

By that time it was too late. The "coordinated action" part has been omitted by most of their followers, with the exception of J. R. Taylor and Van Every (2000). Organizations were seen as systems of mechanical or organic parts, in which people were either cogs or body parts (heads and hands). March and Simon were primarily interested in brains, and reached out to the growing wealth of artificial intelligence studies to create a theory of decision making as attention allocation; the conceptualization of an organization as a computer (an information processing machine) came close.

Then and later (see e.g. W. R. Scott, 1987), there was a lively debate between the two schools as to whether organizations were more like machines (technical systems) or more like organisms (natural systems); but nobody seemed to question the proposition that organizations had to be seen as systems. The idea of "sociotechnical systems" mentioned above was a compromise, as was Tom Burns and G. M. Stalker's *The Management of Innovation* (1961), a book that reviewed 20 cases of postwar Scottish and English firms (15 in the growing electronics industry), and arrived at the conclusion that "mechanistic" organizational structures were appropriate and effective in stable, simple environments, whereas dynamic and complex environments call for "organic" structures, flexible and self-adaptive. A work that strongly supported Burns and Stalker's thesis, although it had been developed independently, was Joan Woodward's *Industrial Organization* (1965).

By the 1960s, the idea launched by Burns and Stalker had developed into what was later called a contingency theory. By then it had been forgotten that Burns and Stalker's notion of a sociotechnical system was grounded in the observation that "the social structure of the factory interlocked with, and often mirrored, that of the small isolated town in which it was situated" (1961, p. 1).

Contingency theory, in all its variations, matched some attributes of the internal organization with those of the environment. Paul R. Lawrence and Jay W. Lorsch (1967) took up this thread in the United States; and because it was easy to operationalize, it lent itself readily to empirical studies and intellectual cooperation. The British Aston Group became a paragon for collective research on organizational structures. It is noteworthy that, having reified "organizations" into "objects" with "attributes," they needed new terms for the activity of organizing. Thus the Aston Group studied the "organizational functioning" (Pugh & Hickson, 1964/1996) and "the way in which an organization is set up and run" (p. 11).

Contingency theory ran out of power by the end of the 1970s, however, for at least three reasons. First, all environments seemed to be "turbulent," demanding innovation and experiencing rapid change. "Mechanistic" organizations and "stable environments" became counterfactuals, or remnants of the past. Second, the oil crisis galvanized the turbulent Western economies. As Burns and Stalker commented in a preface to the 1994 edition of their book,

> The high-road of successful entrepreneurship led to takeovers rather than to the cultivation of effective organizations, and this, in turn, led to the diversion of profits to dividends which would boost share-prices and fend off corporate raiders, rather than to investment of money and time in technical or organizational innovation. (Burns & Stalker, 1994, p. xix)

Third, numerous studies revealed structures to be a result of processes; an epiphenomenon produced by static research methods.

In 1967 James D. Thompson's *Organizations in Action* was published, a book that is still enormously popular in fields outside organization theory; and through its use as a teaching text, it has likely influenced succeeding generations of practitioners. This book can be seen as the opposite of March and Simon's *Organizations* (1958/1993). Both works are "propositional inventories," to use March and Simon's term from the introduction to the second edition, but whereas *Organizations* set an agenda for research in the years to come, Thompson's book attempted to close it, by presenting the "final theory of organizations." Aiming to be exhaustive, to combine the incompatible (the rational tool vs. natural open systems approaches), embracing an impressive range of schools and sources, this book is a striking example of how an assumption that knowledge is accumulative achieves the closure of an intellectual field. Such closure, if taken seriously, could put an end to a discipline. Teachers from other disciplines are seduced by the simplicity and the transparent structure of the book, which seems to incorporate the ideal of a theory.

In the practice of organizing, the conceptualization of organizations as "open systems" (be they artificial or natural) is still dominant (unlike economics, organization theory seems to be able to exert its performative capacity only with a delay of 20 to 30 years). Among theorists, however, there is an increasing feeling that if organization theory intends to maintain its objective of reflecting and explaining the actual practice, it must resign from the ambition of simplicity and dedicate itself to complexity (Thrift, 2005).

Breaking Golem into Pieces: The Garbage Can, the Net, and Other Fragmented Theories

Garbage Can and Loose Couplings

By the 1960s, Richard M. Cyert and James G. March's *A Behavioral Theory of the Firm* (1963) had taken yet further the notions present in Organizations, and portrayed firms as coalitions of multiple, conflicting interests. In 1972, Michael D. Cohen, James G. March, and Johan P. Olsen published an article titled "A Garbage Can Model of Organizational Choice," soon to be followed by March and Olsen's *Ambiguity and Choice in Organizations* (1976), featuring the simulation tests of the garbage can model. Some readers suspected a hoax, a joke, but the garbage can model was seriously intended to be a model of decision making in "organized anarchies"—organizations where preferences are problematic, the technology is unclear, and participation in decision making is fluid. Until the present day, readers are divided between those who believe that this description fits all actual organizations, and those who believe that only universities and such other half-professional and half-political organizations can be accommodated under that label. March and his collaborators, insisting on the earlier assumption that it is the *allocation of attention* that explains actual decision making, posited formal organizations as garbage cans in which accessible problems, solutions, decision-making opportunities, and participants meet randomly, producing outcomes/decisions. One of the concepts they introduced was that of *loose couplings*, a notion that was developed simultaneously by other scholars.

The idea of *loosely coupled systems* was first borrowed from cybernetics by psychologist Robert B. Glassman (1973). It was then introduced to organization theory by Karl E. Weick, who originally applied it as a tool for understanding the erratic organizing typical of educational institutions (1976), and later for grasping the occurrence of disasters in high-reliability organizations that tend toward tight coupling (Weick, 1990). As the attention of organization researchers turned from hierarchies toward networks, many researchers studying various organizational contexts adopted the idea. Its attraction lies in allowing for the simultaneous existence of rationality and indeterminacy in the same system.

Legitimacy and Institutions

On the other side of the Atlantic, David Silverman was trying to develop a version of organizations in his *The Theory of Organizations* (1970), "not as some clear, fixed reality, but as a set of legitimated rhetorics" (1994, p. 2). Thus the authors who perhaps contributed the most to problematizing the notion of "organizations" as separate entities—March, Simon, and Silverman—simultaneously did the most to stabilize the concept, not least by the titles of their successful books.

The 1970s witnessed another pivotal event—the publication of *Markets and Hierarchies* by Olivier E. Williamson (1975). Inspired by Ronald Coase's famous 1937 article, "The Nature of the Firm" (Coase, 1937), Williamson suggested that economic institutions such as the firm "have the main purpose and effect of economizing on transaction costs" (1985, p. 1). This was a critical reminder, not least because it made it obvious that organization theory cannot focus on either intraorganizational or interorganizational processes, but needs to address both, simultaneously, and in connection with one another. Yet the move accomplished by Williamson was even more important to the history of science. He was the first to use the phrase "new institutionalism," and he used it to characterize his approach, thereby legitimizing the return of interest in "old institutionalist" works by Veblen, Polanyi, and Selznick (G. Hodgson, 1996). This interest developed throughout the 1980s and continues until now, with the exception of the UK organization theory, still firmly devoted to the idea of "organizations" and ignoring, by and large, the notion of "institutions," unless the term denotes public-sector organizations.

Organizing

Among the works that borrowed extensively from systems theory, one was especially prominent: Daniel Katz and Robert L. Kahn's *The Social Psychology of Organizations* (1966). Rather than an original contribution, it was a summary of all systems theory inspired work and therefore an enormously popular textbook. In 1969, Karl E. Weick published a book titled *The Social Psychology of Organizing*. The book remained unknown, and misunderstood, until its republication in 1979 (Weick, 1969/1979), when it became a bestseller (Lundberg, 1982).

In this book, Weick returned to the ideas of social psychologist Floyd Henry Allport (Allport, 1954, 1962) in his notion of organizing as "a consensually validated grammar for reducing equivocality by means of sensible interlocked behaviors" (Weick, 1969/1979, p. 3). Weick pointed out that "the substance of organizing, the raw material that supplies the stable elements for the grammar, is interlocked behavior.... This interlocking is circular and was described by Allport" (Weick, 1969/1979, p. 4).

Weick's title clearly announced the book's links to open systems theory, as well as his intention to advance beyond this perspective. The concept of open systems became the mainstay of organizational analysis, but remained underdeveloped. Weick undertook its development while simultaneously transcending it through the adoption of concepts related to autopoietic, that is, self-regulating and self-reproducing systems (Luhmann, 1995; Maruyama, 1974; Seidl & Becker, 2005). He argued that the focus of organization theory must be situated in the *process of* organizing, in the process of assembling "ongoing interdependent actions into sensible sequences that generate sensible outcomes" (Weick, 1969/1979, p. 3). The result of organizing is interlocked *cycles*, which can be represented as causal loops rather than as a linear chain of causes and effects.

Organizing runs through stages reminiscent of biological evolution, and is triggered by a change in environment followed by an enactment: organizational actors bracket a certain segment of their environment for active treatment. This stage corresponds to variation. The subsequent treatment consists of selection—attempts to reduce the ambiguity of ongoing events by applying accessible cognitive schemes to them, which makes it possible to (temporarily) assemble them. This step is then followed by retention—storing the successful results of such sensemaking, which enlarges and renews the repertoire of cognitive schemes, but paradoxically limits the possibility of noticing subsequent changes in the environment. Bracketing at first reveals but later obscures, when the resulting insights begin to be taken for granted.

Organizing is thus an ongoing encounter with ambiguity, ambivalence, and equivocality, part of a larger attempt to make sense of life and the world. It is this assumption that sets Weick's theorizing apart from the rest of the field that evolved around the notion of "uncertainty," a negative state that must be eradicated in order for organizing to take place. Weick, like March, cherishes ambiguity and gives it a central place in evolutionary processes. Although organizing is an effort to deal with ambiguity, it never completely succeeds. Furthermore, the ordering it involves does not consist merely of imposing the rules of rationality on a disorderly world; it is a far more complex and inherently ambiguous process of sensemaking (Weick, 1995).

Action Nets

You can define a net in one of two ways, depending on your point of view. Normally, you would say that it is a meshed instrument designed to catch fish. But you could, with no great injury to logic, reverse the image and define a net as a jocular lexicographer once did: he called it a collection of holes tied together with a string. (J. Barnes, 1984, p. 38)

Karl Weick's theory of organizing has inspired me to proffer the idea of an action net (by action, I mean an event to which it is possible to attribute purpose or intention; Harré & Secord, 1972). Another inspiration has been provided by the new institutional theory (Powell & DiMaggio, 1991), which suggests that at each place and time one can speak of an *institutional order*—a set of institutions (not necessarily coherent) that are recognized as prevailing at a specific time and place. Such institutions determine organizing in the sense that certain connections between actions are legitimate while others are not—or not yet. In the contemporary institutional order of Western economies, those who produce sell their products, and those who own money invest it. In earlier institutional orders, those who produced could be consuming their products or bartering them; those who had money could put it under a pillow. Such people still exist, of course, but they no longer prevail; in fact, they are considered eccentric.

I have no analytical ambitions for the term *action net*; to the contrary, it minimizes the a priori assumptions before the study can begin. Many studies begin with the location of actors or organizations; what I wish to emphasize is that such entities are outcomes rather than inputs of organizing.

The notion of action nets goes beyond new institutionalism, however. When Powell and DiMaggio (1991) compared the "old" institutionalism (represented by Selznick, 1949) to their new variation, they noted that Selznick intended the term *interorganizational field* to cover all actual connections between the Tennessee Valley Authority and all other organizations. DiMaggio and Powell (1983/1991) borrowed their concept of organization field from Pierre Bourdieu (who in all probability borrowed it from Kurt Lewin, 1951), and endowed it with a more symbolic significance—rightly so, as information technology now plays an important role in creating virtual organization fields. They ceased to speak about organizations having relationships with other organizations; instead, they noted that a frame of reference is shared by organizations dedicated to the same type of activity—including the consulting and normating organizations that advise them. These different actors need not know each other or meet in reality in order to be models, competitors, or idols for one another.

DiMaggio and Powell's contribution is valuable because they made it clear that ideal images play a significant role in organizing. Yet they lost one aspect that Selznick was able to capture: actual connections, occurring in a concrete place and at a specific time. A university must contract one or several cleaning firms; but although cleaning firms do not belong to the organization field of higher education, a cleaning firm on strike will seriously disturb the functioning of any university. The notion of action net permits the capture of both actual and virtual connections; there is no reason to differentiate between them a priori.

Why a net rather than a network? The difference between action net and network lies not in space but in time. Network assumes the existence of actors, who forge connections. Action net reverts this assumption, suggesting that connections between and among actions, when stabilized, are used to construct the identities of actors. One becomes a publisher when one starts to publish books or journals, which means that connections have already been made with such actions as writing and printing.

The affinity between the notion of action net and actor-network theory is much stronger than the affinity between action net and institutional theory. Actor-network theory does not share the assumption of network theories; to the contrary, one of its main tenets is that connections create actors—not the other way around. But because of its original purpose—to show how the winning scientific theories and technologies gained their advantage—the studies that take this approach have not focused on organizing processes that did not construct macro-actors. The focus of attention in studies employing the perspective of action nets should be different: organizing may or may not lead to a construction of macro-actors, depending on the degree to which the connections between actions become stabilized and whether or not there is a legitimate spokesperson to represent such an actor-network. During the reform of the Swedish health service in the 1980s, there was an attempt to assemble various providers within the municipalities (Czarniawska, 1997). A few organizational forms were tried; some proposals were conceived centrally and others arose spontaneously, but this connection has never been properly stabilized. It survived in some municipalities and vanished in others. Ten years later, the Central Health Agency still presents diverse ideas about forms of cooperation among various organizations (see Erlingsdottir & Lindberg, 2005), but no macro-actor has emerged, in spite of many connections and many organizing attempts.

The concepts prevailing within organization theory are those of "actors and their networks" (nothing in common with actor-network theory)—some version or another of network theory. The picture that results from such an approach lacks explanation for the existence of these actors and not others, and for the connections they have with one another. Are they in the same network by design or by default or because they were forced to connect, or simply because they liked one another?

It is much easier to begin a study with such a picture as a starting point, because the actors are clearly visible. It is easy to find a City Hall and the mayor's office. It is more difficult to assume that city management consists of a complex action net in which the mayor's actions are taken among those of many others. One way out of this difficulty is to study progressively an action net that is being connected, or, to use Foucault's term, to do a genealogy of an existing action net. In the latter case, one must go from an existing actor-network back in time, when there was nothing more than some tentatively connected actions. Yet another possible study, joining the insights of the actor-network approach and the action net approach, could start disassembling an actor-network: How many connections must dissolve in order for a macro-actor to disintegrate into micro-actants and separate actions? All these approaches give no special status to the existing organizations, treating them as stabilized fragments of wider action nets.

Studying organizing as the construction, maintenance, and destruction of action nets can lead to conclusions that go against much of the conventional theory of organizations. Here are some examples.

Discourses Can Imprison ...

In an earlier article, we focused on the emergence of discourse communities as a byproduct of organizing (Bragd, Chistensen, Czarniawska, & Tullberg, 2008). We borrowed the concept from the field of education where, following Foucault's suggestions, the scholars pointed out that a discourse not only creates its object, but also constructs (or reconstructs) the identities of its users: thus the notion of *discourse community*. We applied this notion to the results of three field studies of organizing.

The Joint Team

The first case was an example of a planned construction of a discourse community. Swedish Rail engaged UK consultants to aid in its restructuring (Tullberg, 2000). The consultants did not speak Swedish, so the community of reformers became the same as an English-speaking community. The self-defined identity of the so-called Joint Team has spread widely within Swedish Rail, whether the reaction was derision or admiration. The team itself worked hard to circulate an image of "those who know, and who are able to introduce new ways." A counterimage of "the others" helped to construct their own difference: "The old guard, other managers, are old-fashioned and keen on protecting their own domains. We are different: we collaborate and help one another." There was also some irony and distancing with which their self-promotion was met, but such ironic comments were unofficial and were made in private.

The members themselves were fully aware of the fact that the Joint Team was constructed to serve as a symbol and a model for the "new" Swedish Rail: a Model Discursive Community. The change of language—where the literal change of language solved a practical problem and served a symbolic function—was strengthened and accompanied by changes in style: the style of the meetings, the style of the surroundings, even the dress code (the British consultants favored a formal code). The symbolic utterances had a ritual character; that is, their contents were not relevant. What mattered was that the members of the team felt that they belonged to a community. Connerton (1989) claimed that social memory resides in rituals and bodily practices, not in individual heads or collective minds. All revolutions start with a change of ritual and the introduction of a dress code. What is said is not as important as how it is said.

The Car Project

The second case is similar to the first; and although a creation of a discursive community was not the goal of the project studied, it was considered to be the important means. This time, it wasn't English: English had been Volvo Car Corporation's official language for many years, and they had settled into a comfortable "Swenglish" that might be difficult for foreigners to understand (including those from the new owner, Ford), but not for Volvo natives. A new discourse community has been created around a project creating a new SUV (Bragd, 2002). In one sense, this community was relatively inclusive: the Volvo employees who were not members of this project did not differ much from project team members. Those "others" were people who had worked with similar projects in the past, and their teams actually served as analogies, as reference points. Also, these "aliens" could well be involved in the next project. The created discourse community was new, but not exceptional.

Indeed, the much-advertised "newness" of the project team discourse did not reach the sediments of the inherited discourses: military, male, hostile to women, and incomprehensible (rather than ambiguous) to newcomers and strangers. Whereas new ways of inclusion were carefully constructed, the old means of exclusion were unreflectively in place. New discourses always feed on old discourses or, as Latour (2005) put it, local interactions are always distributed. This picture was corroborated in the third study, where "the project" concerned the acquisition of one company by a company from another country.

The Swedish-Danish Corporation

The third case differed from the other two in that there existed a project of bridging cultural differences, which revealed only an existing discursive community. The study (Christensen, 2007) was a part of a bigger project following the acquisition of a 150-year-old Danish company by a Swedish competitor. From the beginning, the integration of the two nationalities within the new company was an explicit goal. Seven project teams were built "across the border" to function as integrators. Top management was intent on constructing "fireproof walls" (field metaphor) to protect them from intrusions from outside. Team members were not supposed to talk with outsiders about their project work; eventually, the seven teams were to become "mothers" (field metaphor) to 50 cross-border projects in both companies.

One of the early measures consisted of hiring consultants whose role was to "educate" the employees about the differences between the Swedish and Danish cultures. However, neither set of employees thought that their cultures differed greatly. Indeed, the Swedes and the Danes mixed well, not because of the similarity of their languages, but because the majority of participants were already members of the same discursive community—the community of male managers. This case highlights well the difference between language communities and discourse communities. Men conversed well in spite of language differences, but women did not feel that they "fit in" (all the "mothers" were male).

Conclusions (Reaching Beyond Organizational Borders)

These cases have all demonstrated that discourse is an important resource in the purposeful creation of new communities. Be they "new and desirable" as opposed to "old and undesirable"—new in the sense of coalescing around a new product or new in the sense of joining two previous communities—the creation of a "new discourse" is among the chief means of achieving the community renewal.

But no new discourse smoothly replaces the previous ones. It must be translated, domesticated. In the process, what was a pure language may become a pidgin or a Creole, a parody or pastiche; it may be translated with passion or with distance and derision. Nevertheless, the style of discourse is also a style of action, and although a change of discourse is rarely of the type desired by those who introduced the change, the changes are usually more profound than the most hard-bitten skeptics would allow.

As usual, the unintended consequences tend to be more puzzling than intended ones, at least to an observer. No discourse can be new in the sense of being created from a void; it can only be new in the sense of being constructed from material at hand. Thus, however new the new discourse, it always employs elements of old discourses.

The elements that were especially visible in the two last cases were elements of "old exclusions." Although the main purpose of new discourses was new communities and therefore inclusion, they inadvertently excluded the same "outsiders"—women and strangers—as did the previous ones (see also Acker, 1994).

In the present context, it is important to point out that "formal organization" was not the right entity for studying this phenomenon. The communities created in Swedish Rail were constructed from among some SR employees, and the UK consultants. In the case of VCC, the new discursive community, although it did have predecessors and will have followers, was a temporary creation resulting from a project. In the case of the Swedish-Danish Corporation, two formal organizations and two linguistic communities were involved.

... While Artifacts Can Liberate

Metaphorical Artifacts: The "Iron Cage" of Institutions

It has been suggested that a formal organization is a modern institution (March & Olsen, 1989), but before examining organization as an object, one could look at institutions in general. The dominant metaphor is that of an "iron cage," launched by Max Weber and "revisited" by DiMaggio and Powell (1983/1991). The connotations are negative: a cage "imprisons" its inhabitants, and the iron bars prevent them from escaping or breaking it. However, the same metaphor can be interpreted differently, and DiMaggio and Powell's analysis corroborates this deviant interpretation.

In the first place, cages not only imprison, but also protect. In a zoo, the cages protect the visitors from the wild animals, and no less importantly, they protect the animals from the visitors. A cage gives safety, and so does following institutional patterns of behavior.

Second, a cage, especially if made of iron, offers support: one can lean against it. Again, the normative justification of existing institutions gives support to those who conform to such institutions, a backing that daring entrepreneurs and other deviants decline to use.

Thus, if formal organization is seen as a modern institution, it follows that it, too, can be used both ways. But whereas the negative sides of institutions are often discussed, the negative sides of (the existence) of organizations are less often under scrutiny. I try to counteract this disequilibrium later; at this point I adopt a positive connotation of seeing organizations as objects, one that has also been often neglected.

Virtual Artifacts: Organizations

> An organization does not exist in the realm of the physical: It can be neither seen, or heard, touched nor smelled—directly. (Taylor & Gurd, 1994, p. 56)

Although this obvious dictum is often forgotten, even the most ardent "reifiers," when brought back to their senses, must admit that organizations are virtual objects. Virtual or not, their "nature" (or kind of virtuality) is constantly debated. The "mechanistic" conceptualization of organizations has been a standard target of attack, even from systems theoreticians, who favored biological systems. But this is because organizations were mostly seen as factories rather than machines (I will return to this metaphor). If, however, Perrow's (1986) suggestion that organizations should be treated as tools is taken seriously, then they can be seen as machines, most closely resembling robots. An organization in such a perspective is a combination of a dispatcher (Latour, 1998) and a translator—a machine that is given a legal personality (Lamoreux, 2004), thus acquiring the right to an identity, a will, and an image. Humans are not "cogs" in this machine anymore than they are chips in their computers (although a poetically minded writer may choose to metaphorize them as such). They constructed this machine, but once constructed, the machine continues to construct them (Kunda, 1992). The two main parts, a dispatcher and a translator, are dependent upon one another. To be able to send objects and humans to the right places at the right time, the dispatcher must know how to contact them; the dispatcher depends on translator services. The translator is needed because there is a movement of people and objects; had they stayed at the same place, there would be no need for translation, as (supposedly) there was in the Tower of Babel before its fall.

In such a perspective, organizations are literally instrumental: either they work, or they do not. If they don't, they should be repaired or exchanged (possibly dropped). No "survival" comes into question. Consequently, they can be designed better or designed worse, but they cannot be designed perfectly.

The Ambiguity of Design or, the Arc of Reciprocation Is Always Bigger that the Arc of Projection

A large part of traditional organization theory has been dedicated to "organizational design," on a firm but not always acknowledged assumption that if the structure is right, the right processes will follow. My knowledge, gathered during many years of studying organizing prevents me from sharing such a belief. A structure may facilitate processes, but guarantees nothing. Only processes can control processes; that is, a regulation must be constant.

Furthermore, even the best designed rules may not function in practice. This defect can be counteracted by flexibility (dropping one's tools, to use Weick, 1996 metaphor), but also by an unprejudiced observation of spontaneous practices, with a goal of stabilizing and making permanent those that seem promising. In other words, design must be seen as a neverending process.

To argue for my stance, I rely on the theory offered by Elaine Scarry in *The Body in Pain* (1985). Her basic claim was that an artifact's "reciprocation" (the ways in which it can be used) always exceeds the designer's projection. How is this possible? Well, for one thing, the context of use is always richer than the context of design; or, put differently, the contexts of use are many, the context of design only one. Here, among other things, lies the strength of open source, as it combines the stances of the designer and the user—as does, at least in principle, participatory design. But one can also say that the uses tend to surprise the designers because designers project more than they intend. They project ideas inculcated in them by the institutional order of which they—and the users—are a part.

It is therefore safe to conclude that designers cannot control the arc of projection because they say more than they know (the institutional order speaks through their work); and that designers cannot control the arc of reciprocation because they cannot foresee the contexts of use. Contrary to the much-quoted saying of poet Audre Lorde ("The master's tools will never dismantle the master's house"; 1979/1981), the tools of the masters were often used to destroy various masters' houses.

Objects of Many Uses: Computers

Taylor and Gurd (1994) said that the existence of an organization is made known through its artifacts. Indeed, what more typical artifacts than computers, and what better examples for the thesis that the arc of reciprocation is always wider than the arc of projection. Here is a tentative list of the uses of computers in the workplace: some reported in official surveys, some observed:

- elements of decoration
- surfaces on which to place decorative elements
- notice boards (outside and inside)
- computation devices (including household bills)
- communication devices (including private e-mails, chatting, and looking for a partner)
- graphic art creation devices (including subversive art)
- video/audio composition devices (including subversive music and videos)
- video/audio reproducing devices (TV, DVDs)
- word processing (including private texts),
- desktop publishing
- scheduling (calendars)
- programming devices
- doors to virtual worlds
- picture frames (screens)
- weapons
- objects for unloading agressive feelings
- half-products for hard covers and folders
- beds for growing grass (other people's keyboards)

Not only are these uses not specific to organizations; but as often as not, they can be used both for construction and destruction. Although formal organizations try to domesticate their computers (sometimes even binding them with chains), they will always remain beyond total control.

How Organizations Hamper Organizing

> All organizations are drags. (Sampson, 1995, p. 232, quoting from an interview with Christopher Hogg, Chair of UK corporation Courtaulds)

The list of positive uses of an organization-as-object was grounded primarily in the unexpected uses of such tools. In this section, I list and discuss several negative aspects of relatively conventional and expected uses of organizations.

The first problem has been well illustrated by the Golem legend. The threatened Jews of Prague built a golem to defend themselves; the clay monster fulfilled its purpose, but then turned against its creators. Sometimes this is literally so, as Gideon Kunda (1992) showed in his study of Tech, where the engineers created an "organizational culture" that turned hostile toward them. A less drastic but perhaps more common situation occurs when the creators of a tool do not wish to relinquish it, even when the original purpose is no longer relevant. I once interviewed the General Director of the Swedish Agency for the Protection of Environment who told me that his goal was to make the Agency superfluous. I was rendered speechless, so unusual was this utterance. In contrast, there are a great many examples of temporary organizations being kept alive by their creators at virtually any price (e.g., Pipan & Porsander, 2000). The biological system theory helps to justify such behavior by speaking of the survival instinct. Thus means become goals, tools become objects of cult, and survival replaces service.

It is also taken for granted that organizations have borders, although, as March and Simon (1958/1993) said in their original text, an attempt to establish with any exactness how these borders lie can be complicated. Borders must exist, however, or it will not be certain what an "organization" is or what its "environment" is. This assumption, however, hides a phenomenon known in peace studies: it is not that borders happen to run through conflict-ridden territories, but that the drawing of borders creates conflict in a territory. Thus, as Cyert and March (1963) have noted, the very creation of organizations and the concomitant drawing of borders provokes conflicts, which the conventional theory of organizations hides. Furthermore, the constant redrawing of borders in mergers and acquisitions should make the organization theorists stop and reflect. Indeed, boundary-setting is becoming a distinct area of interest, but even so, as in the volume edited by Paulsen and Hernes (2003), both boundaries and organizations exist, and boundaries have to be managed from inside.

This persistent focus on "inside" and "outside" can be explained, in my view, by the fact that behind all mechanical and organic metaphors hides one that is most persistent if often implicit: that of a building (in Italian, a building is called *struttura*). Either the focus on structural aspects evokes this image, or a historical image of a factory directed the focus of research that way.

One could argue that the metaphor of a building, even more than that of a cage, has a strong positive connotation—that of a shelter. Do organizations not provide shelter, in the sense of employment? Alas, not all of them do. Anthony Sampson, who portrayed "the fall of the company man" through periods of downsizing and layoffs, quoted Neil Millward, a UK ex-civil servant, as saying "Employees in Britain, unlike those in virtually every other European country, just do not have the mechanisms to bring their influence to bear" (Sampson, 1995, p. 231). For this, quite another kind of organization is needed—that of the original meaning, a trade union, or a professional association.

In the previous discussion, all the problems caused by taking the existence of formal organizations for granted are possibly hampering the work of researchers. Does it matter at all to the practitioners? In a collection of studies of organizing caused by situations of threat and risk (Czarniawska, 2009), we have shown that a common impulse is to build a structure—an organization—comprising existing networks. In most cases, however, this strategy misfires, and proves to be inferior to a spontaneous construction of an action net following the idea of what needs to be done. Thus, changing the focus of organization theory from organizations to organizing may not only refresh the theory, but also be of use to practitioners.

2 Dialectics, Contradictions, and the Question of Agency

A Tribute to James R. Taylor

Linda L. Putnam

The fields of organizational communication and organizational studies have changed dramatically in the past several decades. The growth
of postmodern thinking, extensive work on discourse approaches, and
theory development on the links between communication and collective
action typify some of the changes during this period. Clearly, James Taylor has made an indelible imprint in shaping the terrain and contours of
this landscape. While most scholars were just beginning to talk about discourse in the early 1990s, Taylor was writing the first of his two books that
set forth his initial ideas about organizations as conversations and texts
(Taylor, 1993c; Taylor & Van Every, 1993).[1] Today, this work is referred to
as the Montreal School, a unified yet differentiated group of scholars who
pursue a related theoretical perspective. The Montreal School has produced five books and numerous articles and chapters with rich and complex theory development, multiple constitutive views of organizations,
and empirical research that illustrates this perspective. The influence of
this work is evident in its application to essays on coordination (Quinn &
Dutton, 2005); discourse and institutions (Phillips, Lawrence, & Hardy,
2004); self-organizing systems (Taylor & Giroux, 2005); communication
technology (Taylor, Groleau, Heaton, & Van Every, 2001; Taylor & Van
Every, 1993); collaborative action (Güney, 2006; Saludadez & Taylor,
2006); and a host of other topics, as this book so aptly illustrates.

This chapter embraces the Montreal School and pays tribute to Taylor's landmark contribution to organizational communication. It does
so through adopting a view that has its basis in dialectics and using it
to examine theory building in the text–conversation approach to what
an organization is. Thus, this chapter has two functions: (a) to tease out
choices that Taylor et al. make in managing dialectics in the text-conversation approach and (b) to use these choice points to highlight the robust
nature of this theory, areas for future development, and ways to extend
this theory. This paper begins with a discussion of a metaphor for organizing known as dialectics or the management of tensions among opposites. It then provides a brief overview of some key tenets in the Montreal
School. The bulk of this talk focuses on teasing out how dialectics serves

as a source of theory building in this approach and how it can aid in pinpointing areas for future development. Thus, drawing from the work on paradox as a form of theory building (Poole & Van de Ven, 1989), it shows how dialectics can aid in unpacking, extending, and refining aspects of this theory. In doing so, it demonstrates in a reflexive way how dialectics infuses theory building and how the text-conversation perspective infuses dialectical notions of organization.

Overview of Dialectics

For this analysis, dialectics functions as a broad-based lens or metaphor that refers to using the tensions among opposites to examine the relationship between communication and organization (Putnam & Boys, 2006). Dialectics highlight the tensions and struggles involved in holding opposites together or managing the "both-and" of bipolar pairs. As a perspective for examining organizational communication, it focuses on the dynamic interactions or push-pulls between opposing forces that enact social reality (Bakhtin, 1981; Baxter & Montgomery, 1996). Scholars who embrace this perspective have examined how incompatibilities or tensions among opposites influence theory building (Poole & Van de Ven, 1989; Seo & Creed, 2002; Seo, Putnam, & Bartunek, 2004), how primary and secondary contradictions enact dialectics of control (Fairhurst, Cooren, & Cahill, 2002; Howard & Geist, 1995; Papa, Auwal, & Singhal, 1995), and how organizational participation programs invoke paradoxes such as becoming empowered by giving up individual rights or having the top of the organization order the bottom to participate (Carroll & Arneson, 2003; Stohl & Cheney, 2001; Wendt, 1998). Researchers also examine how change evolves through the continual interplay of interdependent forces such as autonomy and connectedness (Jameson, 2004); solidarity and division (Rudd, 1995, 2000); and emancipation and control (Vaughn & Stamp, 2003). Working from postmodern approaches, research on the dialectics of control and resistance reveal how control is rarely absolute, how the interdependence of the two surfaces through overt and covert practices, and how change and resistance often lead to unintended consequences (Mumby, 2005; Real & Putnam, 2005; Sotirin & Gottfried, 1999; Tracy, 2004; Trethewey, 1999).

Only a few studies in the Montreal School focus directly on the management of dialectical tensions in understanding what an organization is. Specifically, Katambwe and Taylor (2006) examine a leadership succession discussion in which organizational members mix both integration and differentiation in the everyday practices of running a business. By analyzing what was said and what was done, they show how organizational members simultaneously include one another (integrate) while distancing themselves from each other (differentiate). Thus, this study represents a direct focus on the management of differentiation and integration and inclusion and exclusion in constituting the organization. I contend that dialectical thinking, however, underlies much of the theory building in the text–conversation approach and serves as a lens for developing conceptual relationships.

In many ways, dialectics functions as a form of Janusian thinking in that Taylor, Cooren, Giroux, and Robichaud (1996) and Taylor and Van Every (2000) bring together two heads facing in different directions through tensions between text and conversation, the unitary–pluralistic nature of organization, a flatland conception of micro–macro, and the mediation of subject and object. This paper draws on the idea that language contains the seeds of its opposite (R. H. Brown, 1977; Burke, 1950/1969) and that the material and social world spiral back and forth among an array of antithetical forces. Thus, one of the fundamental properties of language is opposition and this property can serve as a means for understanding the nature of an organization. Through a brief review of the text–conversation theory, I argue that Taylor and Van Every (2000) use conceptual tensions among opposites to build theory, contrapose antithetical views, and transcend incompatibilities in developing notions of what constitutes an organization.

To begin this project, I provide a brief and simplistic overview (and clearly Putnam translated and appropriated) of the general constructs and tenets of the text–conversation theory. Even though it is almost ludicrous to boil down this approach into a "nutshell" (I am a "nut" for trying to do so and no nutshell is big enough or complex enough to house this perspective), this overview seems necessary to unpack the role of dialectical thinking in this theory. Providing a synopsis of this approach is almost an impossibility, given the interwoven nature of the theory or what McPhee (2008) refers to as the spaghetti-strand position. That is, threads of the theory are intertwined reflexively in each other and cannot easily be separated. Thus, this brief overview is clearly a simplification of the essence of the Montreal School's arguments.

Synopsis of Conversation–Text and the Montreal School

Taylor, Cooren, et al. (1996) treat conversation as interactive, situated events in which organizing occurs. Conversation is the site of organizing through coorientation in which humans and nonhumans form a relationship as they orient around something to be done and how to do it (the triad as a communication unit). Coorientation embodies the action nature of organizing. The recursivity of language through grammar, syntax, speech acts, and texts conveys the attitude and orientations of actors and implicates them in substantive and relational aspects of messages (Taylor, 1999; Taylor, Cooren, et al., 1996; Taylor & Van Every, 2000). That is, language not only aligns humans and nonhumans in organizing but it also conveys attitudes and relational messages that connect actors in particular ways.

Texts reflect what was said and provide a record of past conversations; thus, conversations move through time and space in the form of texts. Written and oral texts become abstracted and removed from situated interactions and become the basis of future conversations. Texts then mediate conversations through reflexively conveying orientations and attitudes from a previous exchange that become the subject of future interactions. As tacit understandings from the past become explicit in the future, actants create a metatext in which the previous relation of the speaker to the spoken becomes the focal point of new conversations and the "us-ness" that forms a collective (Taylor & Cooren, 1997).

From this relationship, a macro-actor emerges as a spokesperson or a collective voice for the "us." Macro-actors translate what other actors want, reference other actors, speak for the silent and absent, and redirect individual sensemaking into a larger collective narrative. In this narrative, distinctions among actors emerge, new rules and contracts take shape, and roles emerge. Through referencing others who are often removed from interactions and putting them in collective narratives, the spokesperson reconstructs the entity as an organization that becomes the source for future conversations (Taylor, 2009).

The translation of individuals to collective agency, therefore, occurs through metaconversations in which local conversations become the subject for global collective interactions or communities of practice. The successive embedding of one conversation into another and one text on another (metatext) with sensemaking creates a new collective that reframes and brings a form of closure to previous conversations (Robichaud, Giroux, & Taylor, 2004). Metaconversations form a loosely coupled self-organizing system in which multiple types of coorientations (conversations, practices, and actions) come together as individuals make sense of ongoing activities (Taylor & Giroux, 2005). Thus, the constitution of the organization as an entity develops recursively from metaconversations of multiple communities of practice. As these metaconversations interface with a material and social world, an "organization" emerges that is larger than any one community of practice (Taylor, 2009).

Dialectics and Theory Building

As this overview suggests, Taylor's work (Taylor & Van Every, 2000) has left a true legacy in the field and he has contributed more than any other scholar to unpacking the notion of an organization and the role of language and communication in constituting what an organization is. It seems fitting on this occasion to reflect on the theory building in this approach and to use this reflection as a way of extending key constructs and charting directions for future development.

In theory building, dialectics provides a lens for discovering assumptions, shifting perspectives, and posing problems differently. Poole and Van de Ven (1989) describe how theorists can look for the tensions among oppositions in their fields of vision and use them to develop more encompassing theories. They urge theorists to focus on the theoretical debates around the issues, to identify and compare them with similar theories, and to set forth counterintuitive explanations. Clearly, Taylor and Van Every (2000) have embraced this logic and in examining such constructs as enactment, rules and resources, and performative views of organizations they have engaged in dialogue with Giddens (1979, 1984), Latour (1987, 1994), and Weick (1979). But Taylor and colleagues have also consciously pursued theoretical oppositions as puzzles to discover ways of relating, contraposing, and integrating them.

A dialectical lens posits five ways to deal with oppositional tensions in puzzle solving: (a) selection, in which the theorist obscures the oppositions, selects one pole and ignores the other side of the dichotomy; (b) separation recognizes both sides of the pole, but separates them into different levels; (c) integration combines oppositions through neutralizing them and thus creates a forced merger; (d) transcendence represents a synthesis or reframing that transforms the dichotomies into a new reformulated whole; and (e) connection embraces the oppositions, respects and privileges both of them, seeks energy from them, preserves and celebrates their tensions to generate new constructs. The first four approaches stem from traditional dialectical approaches and the fifth one, connection, grows out of the notion of dialogue that purports the simultaneity of unity and difference in social forces (Bakhtin, 1981).

The first option, selection, entails denial in which parties ignore the opposite poles and choose one side of the dichotomy over the other. This approach is the most typical way that theorists manage oppositional poles, say between action and structure; however, it tends to produce specialized versions of theories; that is, ones that disregard key elements of the theory and their interrelationships or ones that ignore dynamic patterns embodied in systems of oppositional tensions. Separation, the second approach, differs from selection by working with both poles of the opposition, but treating them as independent rather than interdependent and tightly related. Thus, the opposite poles remain self-contained. The classic example in many traditional organizational communication theories is the separation between the micro- and macrolevels of organization as different spatial levels or at different times, such as stage or temporal models of development; or on different topics such as segmenting the internal from the external communication and vacillating back and forth between them. Separation, then, works with both sides of the bipolar opposites, but on different levels, at diverse times, or as different discrete topics.

The third approach, integration, addresses the tensions in oppositional pulls through merging them or neutralizing them, such as a compromise or arraying them in a relationship that splits the difference. Neutralization is a balance in that both ends of the opposite poles are legitimated, but they remain unfulfilled in their totality. For example, the "meso" level of organizations represents an integrationist view of the micro–macro oppositional pulls. Rather than vacillating between micro and macro, meso approaches merge the two and locate them in a "middle of the road" view of organization. Since the oppositional tensions are compromised, this approach is a less stable way to manage dialectics in that it forces a merger in theory building, one that sometimes replicates selection or privileges one pole over the other (Baxter & Montgomery, 1996).

Transcendence, also known as reframing or synthesis, grows out of the classic thesis, antithesis, and synthesis views of dialectics rooted in Hegel (1807/1949). This approach manages the tensions in bipolar constructs through transforming opposites into a new perspective or a reformulated whole. The emergence of a new concept recasts the opposite pulls through developing a new way to conceive of their relationship. Even though transcendence recognizes and embodies both sides of the pole, the tensions that generate energy between the opposites are channeled and emerge into a new form that transcends the two opposite pulls.

Connection legitimates oppositional forces through treating both poles as mutually beneficial and mutually privileged (Bakhtin, 1981). For Bakhtin, dialogism as a way of managing dialectics does not presuppose any form of transcendence or synthesis to some higher order of development. It results from a perpetuation of ongoing forces of unity and difference. Thus, it connects the push-pull of opposite forces and uses the tension between them to generate new insights and open ideas to multiple and evolving interpretations. Connection, then, rejects teleological change in favor of indeterminacy.

These five modes function as topoi or standard forms of inventions in theory building and aid in deciphering options for theory development (Poole & Van de Ven, 1989). A dialectical lens suggests that the most robust and generative theories employ transcendence, reframing, and connection as ways to manage oppositional tensions rather than relying on selection, separation, and integration. The role of dialectics in theory building provides a way to examine key contributions of the Montreal School, to tease out how bipolar tensions pose puzzles in this approach, how scholars have addressed these puzzles, and which oppositional tensions are ripe for further development. This analysis also points to new directions for theory development and ways to create space between the opposite poles rather than to close off options. Overall, the goal of this paper is to use dialectics as an analytical tool to tease out theory development in Taylor, Cooren, et al.'s (1996) approach to what is an organization.

Managing Dialectical Tensions: The Montreal School

Although numerous oppositional tensions underlie key concepts in the Montreal School, this paper focuses on five major categories and the subdialectics within them: (a) text and conversation as the durable and the fleeting, (b) the organization as both univocal and multivocal, (c) the flatland of the micro and macro, and (d) the mediation of subject and object.

The Text–Conversation Dialectic

Clearly, the most familiar and widely used pair of oppositional tensions in the Montreal School is the text–conversation dialectic. Embraced by both management and communication studies (Ashcraft, 2004; Kuhn & Ashcraft, 2003; Phillips, Lawrence, & Hardy, 2004), the text–conversation dialectic has come to symbolize the recursive interplay between organizing as conversation and organization as text. Conversations produce texts and texts mediate conversations; thus texts transcend the saying and the said, the past and the present, and the here and now.

The significance of this dialectic is the way that Taylor, Cooren, et al. (1996) connect or hold the two constructs in play, continually linking them in a recursive process that avoids a separation, selection, or privileging of one of them in the theory. Implied in this relationship is the dialectic of durability and fleeting. As Taylor and Van Every (2000) note, texts are like crystals with forms and patterns that can be stored and displayed while conversations are random, chaotic, and fleeting like smoke that dissolves fast.

Thus, the text-conversation dialectic reframes the age-old tensions between stability and change by situating both constructs as continuous and evolving yet as having staying power that spans time and space. In true theory-building form, the text-conversation dialectic also produces a new and significant construct through teasing out the role of imbrication in this relationship. Imbrication draws from the discursive properties of language and refers to the emerging structures and routines that surface from the ways that conversation and text interface. It occurs when order emerges from traces of past conversations that change or reproduce them. The tensions between coorientation in which actants engage in dynamic interactions to get something done and imbrication in which patterns of communication (texts) become unquestioned build on this interplay between stability and change.

The link between coorientation as action and imbrication as structure offers potential for future theory development. Specifically, some actions may become stable and imbricated over time while others may become disorientated and unstable. For example, Dionysiou and Tsoukas (2008) report on an ethnographic study of TELCO, a corporation characterized by disruptions and instability despite multiple efforts to coorient around specific actions. They conclude that organizational members were unable to "take the roles of others" or to abstract and generalize from specific practices in ways that would help them coorient. Thus, future work might focus on the stable and unstable dialectic and particularly the times when coorientation leads to disorientation and when actors resist or disrupt imbrication. Thus, the subdialectics of coorient-disorient and stable-unstable provide options for extending theory building and unpacking the text–conversation relationship in critical ways.

Through using connection to manage the text-conversation dialectic, Taylor and colleagues generate significant concepts and subsequent entailments that continue to enrich this approach, including such notions as tightly coupled activity coordination and loosely coupled organizational self-structuring. Text–conversation has become one of the most significant features of this theory, in part from the ways in which these tensions are continually held together between the fleeting and the durable aspects of organization.

The Univocal–Multivocal Dialectic

The next dialectic, multivocal and univocal, is managed through transcendence which positions the "many in the one" and aligns these oppositional tensions into a new concept. Metaconversation, as the site where organization occurs, is the "us-ness" that emerges from multiple conversations. It is produced through the recursive property of language and the successive embedding of conversations in texts and texts in texts to create a new form which transcends the pluralism of many voices, the networks of local conversations, and the multiple communities of practice. As conversations are embedded in one another, the processes of orienting to do something begins to close out or blackbox previous conversations (discursive closure) and create a new "us-ness" that has an entity status. The entity is larger than any one community of practice or set of conversations. As Robichaud et al. note (2004, p. 621), this process is the place where "the unitary and the pluralistic worlds of talk encounter each other on a single plane."

Metaconversation as a way to manage the pluralism-unity dialectic transcends both poles in a recursive way; that is, it holds them together while it simultaneously privileges both of them. Similarly, Katambwe and Taylor (2006) show how the concept of *interactive ambiguity* holds together the internal contradictions between unity and diversity and between competing texts of family and professional management in a leadership succession. Thus, concepts such as *metaconversation* and *interactive ambiguity* transcend being plural and diverse by simultaneously existing as one and unified. These concepts channel the tensions between opposites into new forms rather than merging, abandoning, or reducing them.

Central to the construct of metaconversation is a macro-actor, or a spokesperson who emerges to speak on behalf of a collective, to translate what other actors say and want, and to reference actors who are absent or silent. Macro-actors represent collectives and intercollectives that are held intact through linking conversational domains to each other in multiple communities of practice. It is through the macro-actor that metaconversation holds the univocal and the multivocal in play. The spokesperson connects and preserves these tensions through narratives of struggle in which stories play out recursively amid the unitary and multiple voices that connect them. Thus, a macro-actor speaks as a collective by simultaneously embracing voices in narratives that depict opposing sides and play out the drama of the unitary and the multivocal.

Of significance, is the recent work on organizational presence or the way that an organization is made present through representatives that invoke it in ongoing interactions (Brummans, Cooren, & Chaput, 2009; Cooren, 2006; Cooren, Brummans, & Charrieras, 2008). This work holds together the unitary and multivocal in a recursive interplay through examining the presence (and to some extent the absence) of naming, representation, and enactment of the organization in routine conversations.

Narratives of sensemaking also create metaconversations in light of struggles—casting players as villains, opponents, and allies. These contests or moments of struggle among the unitary and the competing communities of practice also give rise to new collectives and macro-actors. This conception also locates power not as a property of the macro-actor but in the network of people or in the alliance for which the actor speaks.

While Taylor and Van Every (2000) have been reluctant to use the term *power*, the notion of contestation or struggle gives rise to subdialectics embedded in treating metaconversations as both univocal and multivocal. Two pairs of subdialectics that offer potential for additional theory development are consent and dissent and legitimate and delegitimate. The polemic character of narrative suggests that contesting agencies play out the drama of the unitary and the multiple voices through simultaneously engaging in consent and dissent. The tension between consent and dissent emerges discursively as part of coorientation and sensemaking activities. Unpacking how this struggle occurs and how consent and dissent are intertwined would aid in understanding the nature of contestation and its role in constituting the organization. Narrative theory suggests that these moments of struggle unmask stable relationships and produce new forms of organization, therefore, exploring consent and dissent would help scholars uncover how this occurs (Greimas, 1987; Robichaud et al., 2004).

In like manner, the notion of legitimate and delegitimate underlies struggles over the authority of texts that feed into the dialectic between consent and dissent. Both Taylor (2009) and Kuhn (2008b) examine issues of authority and what brings authoritative texts into existence. For Kuhn, texts become authoritative through imbricating them; validating them; and making them valued knowledge for specific activities and outcomes. Various actors and macro-actors vie for authorship, speak in the name of the organization, inscribe boundaries, and become a reference point for the organization. Kuhn illustrates how some actors' efforts to author texts rest on the relationship between consent and dissent that leads to challenging the authority of a text (contestation). He refers to

Freeland's (2001) description of GM's efforts to inscribe multidivisional forms, pricing policies, and standardization as a new organizational text, but one without a clear vision of the whole. In the absence of this vision, conversations became stifled, meaningful dissent was absent, and the texts that executives developed failed to infuse routine practices and activities. Thus, dissent seems intertwined with the legitimacy of texts and provides a basis for analyzing authority in the interplay between unitary and multiple voices.

In general, Taylor and colleagues employ both transcendence and connection to manage the tensions among the unitary and the pluralistic. The organization is simultaneously one and many and continually plays out the tensions between these opposites through spokespersons who represent both the unitary and polemic quality of narratives, the struggles among actants, and the contestations between multiple communities of practice. Investigating the role of consent and dissent in these struggles and the process of legitimating texts provides a way to build on these dialectical tensions and to extend the role of metaconversation in this theory.

The Micro–Macro Dialectic

The third dialectic, micro–macro, emerges in Taylor's work through dissolving the duality between the two poles and creating a flatland. Typically, theorists who favor macro-orientations to organizations engage in separation and treat the organization writ large as distinct from and dominant over local interactions while those who favor microinteractions employ several options: (a) separation by collapsing the macro into the micro or (b) vacillation by moving between the two poles in stages or on different levels (a selection approach to managing the dialectics).

Rather than operating from two levels of organizational reality (organization as entity and individuals as components), Taylor and Van Every (2000, p. 143) treat the macro–micro as a flatland that is "invariably situated, circumstantial, and locally realized in a finite time and space." Other grounded-in-action theorists such as Weick (1979), Boden (1994), and Giddens (1984) also question the micro–macro duality, but often through favoring one pole over the other (Fairhurst & Putnam, 2004). For Taylor and Van Every (2000) and Latour (1987) social reality does not happen at different levels—it takes place on the same plane in that the organization manifests itself in the day-to-day interactions of its members. Even though some scholars see this stance as favoring the local over the global (McPhee, 2004; McPhee & Trethewey, 2000), I think the situation is more complex.

Taylor and colleagues make a concerted effort to hold the tensions between micro–macro together and to reframe them in a meaningful way. Specifically, they recast them as scaling up and scaling down the organization. This reframing drops the notion of levels and focuses on how bottom-up processes link with top-down practices and vice versa. Yet, the idea of scaling up and scaling down still invokes a metaphor of levels which makes it difficult to connect or hold these bipolar opposites together. For example, Cooren and Fairhurst (2009) employ a bottom-up approach to show how scaling up from micro-associations and moving downward through hybrid actions can string these micro-associations together. Scaling up produces a hybrid from many different interactions and scaling down contributes to stabilizing future micro-interactions.

For Taylor (2009), bottom-up and top-down organizing are tied together through coorientation; that is, social interactions aimed at getting something done. These coorientations form different communities of practice that lead to intercommunity activity coordination among groups of actants. The difference in bottom-up and top-down is not in one of levels but of different types of coorientations among communities. As Taylor (2009) notes, organizations relate to other agencies through coordinated activities or coorientations among collective actors. This reframing also embraces both inductive and deductive approaches to theory building, although more work has progressed inductively than deductively.

Yet, both theorists and researchers have to stake out a point of entry into these processes, which creates a conundrum in determining how scaling up and down work. To begin deductively and scale down or inductively and scale up makes it difficult to hold tensions from both orientations together. Specifically, to focus on coorientations among communities of practice situates texts and conversations as researchers move within or across these domains.

As I struggle with these ideas, I concur that organizing and organization do not exist on different levels. Organizing takes place through social interactions, conversations, and coorientations that produce different types of texts. Ultimately, though, the point of entry still makes it difficult to hold the bottom up and top down together; hence, research as well as theory development inadvertently lapses into segmentation rather than connecting these polar opposites.

The micro-macro dialectic, then, may remain a conundrum or an undeniable paradox. One idea for rethinking it might be to focus on multiple points of entry. Thus a researcher might collect conversations and texts at multiple points in the process, for example, of intercommunity coorientations, macro-actor representations, and interactions among micro-actors. Theory development might extend constructs through multiple points of entry. For example, how do coorientation and imbrication play out at different points of entry into the text-conversation dialectic? Adopting multiple points of entry for the actants, theorists, and researchers may help unravel the micro–macro paradox.

The Subject–Object Dialectic

The final dialectic, subject and object, becomes managed through integration or a balance between the two that at times seems like a forged merger. Rather than privileging humans or material constraints, agency mediates the subject–object tension. The subject as intentional actor is transformed by the object into a synergistic agency (Brummans, 2006). Drawn from Latour's (1994) work, this marriage of subject and object both enables and constrains as it spans time and space. As a hybrid between the two, agency emanates externally in networks as opposed to internally in intensions or motives of individual actors. Subjects appropriate objects to get things done and objects respond to subjects; the two are recursively intertwined. Objects have built in properties or affordances that exert influence in the absence of and independent of a subject's goals. Latour's (1994) example of the public debate over gun control illustrates this recursive relationship. Gun advocates argue that guns don't kill by themselves, people kill. Yet, the gun adds something and is clearly not neutral in the act of killing. That is, people can be transformed by carrying a gun and can execute the actions that the object allows them to do (Taylor & Van Every, 2000). Thus, the humans and guns are recursively related through action. Through casting both the subject and the object in praxis, the two become intertwined.

Integration becomes the mode for managing this dialectic as the two are married through agency. This dialectic also embodies a relationship between the social and material. To their credit, Taylor and Van Every (2000), Cooren (2001, 2004), and Latour (1994) avoid treating the material and the natural worlds as passive, inert, and insignificant. They also avoid collapsing the material into the discursive—a critique that Reed (2000) and other scholars levy at many discourse approaches. Through granting nonhumans agency, Taylor and Latour focus on the interactions between humans and nonhumans.

Yet, I sense in the way that action mediates this dialectic that nonhumans emerge as malleable for human use, an orientation that implicitly privileges the social over the material world. This privileging stems from two concerns: (a) a theory of meaning rooted in signs and (b) a tendency to ignore the unpredictability of objects. The first concern draws from Latour's (1994) inclination to root the relationship between humans and nonhumans in signs as the foundation for meaning in the subject–object interaction. For example, a red light signals stop, a speed bump slows down traffic like a silent policeman, and a machine that detects metal signals a security breach. In each of these examples, the theory of meaning between humans and nonhumans seems governed by signs in which the humans give meaning to objects rather than meaning emanating from features or characteristics of the material. Thus, "when we see an object, we see it through the screen of language, and hence what we "see" is the meaning [that we impose]. The object itself becomes a sign; it appears to 'stand in' for meaning" (Rogers, 1998, p. 248). Treating the object as a sign mediated through language tends to preserve the socially constructed meanings of the body, nature, and matter (often arrayed hierarchically through human-based sign systems).

Environmental scholars, who are also struggling with how to manage the social-material dialectic, urge us to enter into a partnership in which the social is not privileged nor does the material world dominate the social, rather the two are grounded in a relationship that respects the interdependence of both (Merchant, 1995). Rather than presuming that objects are signs mediated through humans, theorists need to examine each in its own right, especially in the way that the characteristics of objects (affordances) produce fluidity rather than predictability of practices. Thus, one area to extend theory development would be to focus on the dialogue or interplay between subject and object, especially how these interactions construct boundaries between them. This exploration might attend to the degree of permeability of boundaries between the social and the material. In some situations, conversations construct boundaries in fluid and permeable ways while in other instances, interactions close off boundaries and the two poles are less permeable. Unpacking this recursive relationship through preserving the uniqueness and privilege of both the social and material would move the management of this dialectic from integration to connection.

A second area of concern in the marriage between the subject and the object is the unpredictability of the material. For example, what happens when a signal system fails, if a traffic light is not working or the security mechanism is broken? No doubt a different type of organization emerges to accommodate this type of subject–object relationship. Thus, theory development in this area might explore the predictable-unpredictable dialectic. Both the social and the material operate within these tensions, but scholars often treat nonhumans as always predictable; for example, the speed bump always slows down traffic. Discourse studies of the environment point out how nature and the material often function in unpredictable ways and reveal a multiplicity of forces that shape the relationship between humans and nonhumans (Rogers, 1998). The multiplicity of forces calls attention to intertextuality or ways to analyze objects and texts outside a specific organizational situation that invokes other metaconversations and communities of practice.

Cooren and Fairhurst (2009) begin to address these concerns in a study that tracks how a decision to install a security system in an apartment complex grows out of multiple meetings, conversations that span time and distance, and objects that invite visitors to check in at the front desk as opposed to entering without being identified. What seems missing in this analysis, however, is how the object alters the nature of organizing in unpredictable and nonlinear ways and how the security system interfaces with other material features in the process. For example, what back-up features exist for the security system? What happens when actors ignore and alter the human and nonhuman interface; for example, shifting the camera out of focus? What type of organizing occurs when the mechanism malfunctions or if the alarm produces false signals because of bad weather or strong winds? Exploring unpredictable and nonlinear relationships between the subject and object would help in deciphering optional ways of organizing, both predictable and unpredictable ones.

Summary and Conclusion

In closing, Taylor and colleagues have developed one of the most comprehensive, generative, and robust theories of what an organization is. Grounded in communication, rooted in characteristics and features of language, this approach provides sophisticated ways in which metaconversations connect, transcend, and reframe the dialectical tensions between text–conversation, organizing–organization, and the univocal and multivocal. The theory addresses ways in which these tensions are interdependent, recursively related, and invoke an array of other bipolar tensions, such as stability–change, fleeting–enduring, integration–differentiation, and presence–absence. As it provides a masterful view of theory building through teasing out and preserving the interplay among dialectical tensions, it exposes conundrums, puzzles, and arenas that need extension. This analysis calls attention to developing the concepts of struggle, legitimacy, and authority as salient features in the text-conversation approach, attending to scaling up and down as multiple points of entry, and focusing on the interdependence of a multiplicity of material forces, especially in privileging subject–object equally, in unpredictable ways, and linked to the social construction of permeable and impermeable boundaries.

Thus, this paper pays tribute to Jim Taylor, the founder of the Montreal School, for the depth, richness, and expansiveness of this theory. It has evolved over time, taken on inconsistencies, and continues to wrestle with new puzzles as any good theory should. We are indebted to him for the heuristic value of this work. As it lives on and through scholars, it will be applied, appropriated, translated, and misinterpreted—as any good theory should be. Its fertile ground is unsurpassed and it will give rise to provocative insights on "what is an organization" for many generations of scholars to come.

3 "What's the Story?"

Organizing as a Mode of Existence[1]

Bruno Latour

> To focus on sensemaking is to portray organizing as the experience of being thrown in an ongoing, unknowable, unpredictable streaming of experience in search of answers to the question "what's the story." (Weick, Sutcliffe, & Obstfeld, 2005)

As Weick and many others have excellently shown (Taylor & Van Every, 2000; Czarniawska, 1997), one of the difficulties of grasping an organization is that it is impossible to detect its type of agency without defining the ways in which we speak of and in it. As soon as you speak about an organization, you lose the specific ways in which it would have appeared had you attempted to participate in its organizing by telling and retelling its story (Cooren, 2001, 2010).

I am not alluding here to the classical and in my view largely spurious distinction between "theory" and "practice," I am referring to a much more troublesome obstacle: Agencies are visible only if grasped in the right key. Such an obstacle is common to all agencies that do not resemble the "middle sized dry goods" which are supposed to populate the world of "common sense."

I have shown elsewhere that the same difficulties arise when trying to speak of religious beings, political representation, legal reasoning, psychological entities, and, of course, scientific objects themselves (Latour, 2007b, 2009, 2010). You may add the word *God* to a sermon a hundred times and yet fail to carry even the beginning of what it is to speak in a "religious" fashion (Latour, 2011); you may complain about all the political issues of the time, and yet not even start to make the political enunciation move in such a way as to generate a Body Politic.

Speaking religiously requires the present conversion of the speaker as well as those he or she addresses, a feat rarely seen these days, when sermons are confused with the expression of vague certainties about some faraway "elevated" matters, eyes piously turned to heaven. Speaking politically means that you are ready to abandon your own certainty about issues so as to produce the subtle alchemy between what you say—representation—and what you are told to do—obedience—(the autonomy and tautology of political speech acts) a feat utterly distinct from the lazy way in which we most often perform "issue-dropping" (as in name-dropping) and display all the outward emotions of indignation and protest (Latour, 2003). I think that we could easily agree that the same is true in the matter of organizing: There is a huge, an abyssal difference between speaking about an organization and talking or acting organizationally.

The highly specific type of agency vanishes every time because it is being measured up against a type of information transfer that I have called "double click" and in comparison with which it is always found wanting. One of the ways to overcome such an obstacle is to shift from an ostensive definition to an *adverbial* form and to accept speaking *religiously* (and not about religion), *politically* (and not about political issues), *legally* (and not about law), *psychologically* (and not about emotions or psyches), *scientifically* (and not about science). In every case, an inquiry into the type of agency is more fecund when taking it as an adverb. As soon as you fall back onto an ostensive definition—"what is" religion, law, psyche, science?—each of those agencies takes up a ghostly character which is due to double click's ill-adjusted demands: "How much do you resemble the matters of fact of 'common sense'?" Answer: "Not in the least! You tried to grasp us with the wrong hand."

In this chapter, I wish to show that it might not be impossible to avoid the same pitfall when dealing with organizations. Instead of trying to define "what is" an organization and lose the agency, I wish to grasp it *along the ways* in which we speak *organizationally* (horrible word, I agree, but this is a little price to pay to try to hear its tune in the right key).

It is of course awkward to write a chapter in the organizing mode that is necessarily disengaged from the practical task of deciding upon some real state of affairs, but I will try nonetheless thanks to two tricks: I will speak not as a scholar but as the dean of my school, and I will do it as if I were giving a lecture about it, which will allow me to designate the readers as the "you" assembled in the lecture hall and pressed for time because of what I will define as a *script*. Those two tricks will allow me to somewhat imitate the type of problems I wish to share with you in the little time "we have together," thus giving us a chance to agree on what sort of agency will appear when we find ourselves in the sort of situation Weick has described: When we try, somewhat desperately, to answer the question "what's the (organizational) story?"

Speaking *about* Organization or Speaking *to* Organize

So many scholars have linked organization and discourse analysis that I would feel very foolish in once again surveying the same ground if I did not want to insist on a peculiar trait of what, with François Cooren, we could call the "organizational speech act." If the answer to the question "What's the story?" is so complicated it's because this is not a story in the usual sense of the word because its listeners are *its authors as well as its characters*. When we engage in organizing, we are simultaneously *above* the story and *under* it—but never *completely*, and never at exactly *the same time* and in the same *capacity*. It's such a strange situation that I will designate it by the word *script*. Let me exemplify this definition with a typical example taken from my life as a dean.

This morning we are in a crisis and the board of directors has assembled to decide what strategy to follow and which other dean to hire to hold the helm of our School more firmly. As one director has just argued, an administrator would certainly be more in our tradition, but it might also be more suitable this time to fall back, at last, on some sort of academic. "Fine," one of us says, "but if we look back to Emile Boutmy's original 'blueprint' for our institution, such a choice would mean that we forget that our founder always showed the utmost diffidence toward straight academics." And he adds: "It's in the DNA of our institution to hire only hybrids and never to confide anything to scholars"—by which he means the professional profiles of "universitaires" who have brought French universities to their dire present state. He then proceeds to suggest the name of a hybrid character who is neither a straight professor nor an administrator, he is a sort of "acade*mix*." It is at this moment that, following his gesture, we all turn to the bronze bust of Emile Boutmy, the founder of our school, which sits on a shelf above the fireplace in the room where we are meeting.

At this point, naturally, no one expects the energetic head on its pedestal to nod in approval or to react indignantly like the statue of Don Juan's father whose iron grip drags the womanizer to Hell. We are all aware that the allusion to the "essence" of our school is not something that can be proven beyond any doubt: no one actually demands that the blueprint be unfolded or the DNA code be decrypted for us. It is perfectly plausible to imagine that we would have all turned our heads toward the bust even if the speaker had made a completely opposite claim and had said that "because times have changed, now is the time to *depart* from Boutmy's diffidence regarding academics and to hire at last a true *universitaire*."

We are all well aware that talking of "the DNA of the institution," a biological metaphor, or of "a blueprint," a technical metaphor borrowed from the world of engineers and architects—are only ways to designate the *continuity in time* of our school; that is, its series of *discontinuities* that we could call its heritage. And we all know that when we say that our school possesses an "essence" that should "dictate" our present choice, this essence is so little assured and commands our behavior with so little clarity and so weak a pressure that we simply don't know what to do.

That's exactly what Weick tried to capture by the notion of "sensemaking." The "essence" will not carry us on any more than Boutmy's ancestral head, with its late 19th century hairdo, will show the direction we should pursue. Essence, in other words, does not flow *from* Boutmy's time to this very morning as some irrepressible river in the stream of which we would just have to swim, but, so to speak, *backward from* our crisis meeting *to* the bust of our founder. The best proof of this retrograde movement is that the three solutions (an administrator, a straight academic, a hybrid) could all as well be "attributed" to our founder's approbation. The "essence" goes from the present moment back to the past, and then from the past to the present; it begins to be insured by our founder's stamp of approval—but only *after* our decision has been settled.

But then why do we turn to the bust? Are we really serious? Of course, we smile slightly while doing this. It is simultaneously an automatism—we all turn our heads to follow the finger of our fellow director pointing at it—and somewhat of a theatrical gesture: Each of us smiles in a different way—from outright irony to deference, with many nuances in between. And yet, it would be entirely false to say that "turning toward the founder's effigy in a moment of crisis" is useless, entirely satirical, or even clearly seen as a mere retrograde movement from the present to the past, as I suggested a minute ago. Yes, we "attribute" to Boutmy our own decision; yes, we all say that "it is in the blueprint" and in the "DNA" of our school only "after" we have decided what to draw from this heritage, and yet there is no question that we are really in search of an answer to the present crisis by going back to what our institution "really means"—yes, exactly: "What's the story?"

The best proof that this is not an ironic or amusing moment is that we rarely do it and only when the continuity of our school or its overall "architectonics" or "architecture" is at stake. So, in fact—and contrary to what a superficial observer might think—there is something deadly serious in looking back to what our school means in order to decide *which past to inherit*. Not only that, but after having settled the matter, we are all satisfied that we have been faithful to an instruction that we *did not know* before was really part and parcel of what had been bequeathed to us. We now feel that, thanks to our decision, we prolong a history which remains (which we have situated ...) "in the line" of this history and which would have met the founder's approval—even though we know it would be ludicrous to check for such a continuity in this gentleman's exact words.

What is binding us then? It would be totally false to say that we are not bound at all and that we can "freely" modify at will the genealogy, history, and development of our school without any reference to what it is now, what it has been, and the reason why it was founded in the first place: an antiuniversity to resist French academic corporatism and archaism. But it would be just as silly to claim that its past and present reality is so assured that we just have to follow what it is at *time t*, to be certain of what it will be at *time t + 1*.

The best proof that it is a highly peculiar type of situation is that we have assembled in the council room to decide how to carry on the *same* organization to *time t + 1*. You don't usually do that for stones, for mugs, or for mats. There is such a *hiatus*, such a *gap* in between *time t – 1, time t* (the reference point of the present), and *time t + 1* (tomorrow) that we are meeting in order to carry the school one step further, *beyond* the gap, *beyond* the hiatus. It won't go by itself. It won't jump the gap because of the force of its own *inertia*. Contrary to the nature of celestial bodies, there is no inertia at all in an organization. But if you stop carrying it along: it drops dead. As Garfinkel has shown so well, you have to *achieve* it, so that it goes to what he marvelously called "the next first time"—it repeats itself until the next time, which is always the first time (Garfinkel, 2002). Repetition, in other words, is never repetitive (Butler, 1878/2009).

This is what makes the life on our board of directors so hard: We simultaneously have the feeling that this school is as solid, weighty, obdurate, obstinate, as a hundred ton pyramid that sits on our weak shoulders paralyzing and stifling us; and that, at the same time, or in the next moment, it could dissipate like a flock of sparrows—we have to work hard to bring it together so that it can last for another span of time, the duration of which remains totally unpredictable (the next crisis could be tomorrow, tonight, or in 10 years) (Powers, 1998).

If we have some difficulty in answering the question "what's the story," it's thus because it is not all a story but a highly specific type of entity whose continuity does not resemble that of stones, mugs, or mats more than it does novels or fables. One of its many peculiarities is that we are simultaneously under its enormous weight as well as above it so that it remains weightless in our hands. It has its own consistence, its own resilience, its own obdurate presence to which we can point with a gesture just as *ostensive* as when we point at stones, or mugs, or cats, or mats, and yet if we are no longer *performing* it, the whole organization will come to a halt.

This is why, in the thick of being an organizer, it is utterly impossible to distinguish organization and *dis*organization. There is no way to make a distinction between being organized and being disorganized, or between being well-organized and badly organized—which has no meaning for those who are in the middle of it. The state of crisis where you catch up and patch up one crisis after the other is the *normal* state of affairs, as Weick et al.'s quote at the beginning of this chapter points out so well. They might not all lead to a crisis meeting in the council room and to soul searching inquiries as to what Emile Boutmy "really wanted." But they are crises all the same, for a simple reason that is directly linked to one of the features of the scripts: they have *variable deadlines* so that, even in the best of times, at any given moment some may require you to shift from being now "under" them to being now "over" them, while at the same time you are still "under" many other scripts and are ready to "launch" still some other new ones coming to fruition at different times.

So even when everything works "according to plan," chaos follows necessarily from the many "roles" you have to fulfill: playwright, actor, character, rewriter, shadow writer, props, accessories, stage, all at once. But this "normal" state of chaos is always compounded by the fact that since there is no such thing, as we shall see, as a superorganism, most if not all of the scripts will be at worst contradictory, and at best ambiguous or incomplete (remember Wittgenstein's demonstration that it is impossible to make a rule completely explicit).

It would already be bad enough to have to answer many different scripts with different end points in different capacities; but in addition, you have to deal with incompatible instructions that are targeting many possibly opposite *personae* in you, some utterly implausible. The battle of Borodino described by Tolstoy in his masterpiece *War and Peace* is probably the most realistic description of the essence of any organization. Things can get worse, of course, but can they be any better? Now that I am also a dean (after having been somewhat of a recluse and irresponsible academic for 40 years) I very much doubt it. And this is not, I hasten to say, because I have fallen into a badly organized school.

To put it in less dramatic terms and to take stock of the obvious fact that the field of battle is not always littered with dead bodies, we could say that to organize is always to *reorganize*. The little prefix "re" is there to remind us of the gap which is always yawning (or smiling) at us between *time t* and *time t + 1* and that no momentum will ever allow us to cross without pain. There is the same difference between organizing and reorganizing as between "the first time" and "the next time." A description should be careful to avoid the false transcendence of superorganism, but just as careful to avoid ignoring that tiny little transcendence, that little cleft through which any organization should, so to speak, *gain* its subsistence. To act organizationally (horrible word I know) is to situate oneself at this growth point: that's where the obstacle lies over which the horse should learn to jump. Either you recognize it and you act as an organizer or you don't recognize it and then you simply talk "about" an organization.

This is well-known even in the analysis of a very menial job: constant adjustments have to be made for any course of action to be carried through to its completion; but it is exactly as true at the top (except of course an organization has no "top" but only *rooms* in which the buck sometimes stops) where "constant adjustments" are now called, depending on the characters of the leaders, "innovation," "flexibility," "charisma," "improvisation," "arcane," or "outright mess." There might be no real difference between organization and disorganization—contradictory scripts come to maturity at any time and under any shape—but there is a huge difference between taking up again the task of organizing and *ceasing* to do so: in this case the institution dissolves for good. No substance will come to its rescue. As to the essence, it will fade away. Whatever he said in his time, Emile Boutmy will be betrayed; that is, translated.

To sum up this first section, organizations possess an original *mode of existence*—a term that I use to point out the various types of agencies that circulate in the multiverse (James, 1909/1996). When you use the ontology of one mode as a touchstone to evaluate the agency of another, it produces *category mistakes* as if you wanted nature to speak directly without the institutions of science or flowers being delivered directly through the Wi-Fi (Latour, 2010). Organizing might generate strange beasts but it is not a reason to exaggerate their strangeness.

The Whole Is Always Smaller Than Its Parts

Using the example above, I now wish to show that clarifying some of those category mistakes might help us listen to the specific tune of organizations. I have to begin by pointing out that their originality does not depend on having to pay for their existence, so to speak, through constant reinvention and retelling. The existence of a hiatus, of a gap, between two instants of time is not what is so strange in the organizational mode of existence. This is a general feature of all "actual occasions," to use Whitehead's terminology (1929/1978). To last in time requires additional work and cannot be just confided to some "sub-stance" which, as the etymology indicates, would "stand beneath" a given entity in order to insure its continuity, so to speak, for free and without extra trouble.

Even though common sense seems to impose the view that, when faced with any state of affairs, one should look for an essence, foundation, or substance to explain what something is and why it lasts, it requires no immense ingenuity or deep metaphysical insights to realize that there is never anything deeper than what is in its actuality (never, that is, once James, Whitehead, and Dewey have done the job!) (Debaise, 2006). "Under," "above," "beneath," "beyond" the actual occasions there is nothing that explains them or that would last longer than they do. What lasts manages to do so on its own by *inheriting* from other occasions. For the continuity of its existence, each essence has to pay the price in the hard currency of change.

Although this point might seem too broad, it is important to make it general enough to cover all types of bodies, including biological entities to which organizations are so often compared. All organisms are in the same boat; to subsist, none of them may rely on an already existing substance, program, structure, or blueprint. Literally, *everybody* has to overcome this hiatus between two moments of time: my school yes, to be sure, but also my own body, the cat on the mat, the mat too, and even the pavement on which they all lie at rest. Seen at the microscopic level, the slabs of stone are in a more permanent state of crisis than my school will ever be. They would need infinitely more jumps from one quantum state to the next in order to resist disintegration than my institution will ever need overhauls, coup d'états, palace revolutions, reengineering, and downsizing so as to last a few more decades. As to biological bodies, it is enough to read Darwin to begin to measure the number of gaps one organism has to jump over in order to remain in existence a little bit longer.

Remember that when we turned toward Emile Boutmy's bust, one of us alluded to "what dictates," as he put it, "the DNA of our school." A metaphor, I know—a rather crude borrowing from the highly contested field of molecular biology. But that's just the point: When we appeal to the "DNA of an institution," we believe that we designate a sub-stance (a genetic blueprint) which is just as assured, stable, and predictive as that of the DNA directing the "programs" in the cells of organisms. What is fascinating, when one considers the biological literature, is on the contrary, how badly predictive the DNA blueprint is of which proteins will be encoded and which tertiary or even secondary structure they will fold into (Fox-Keller, 2000). If there is a hiatus that every organism has to overcome to last a little bit longer, this is surely even truer of a swarm of selfish genes competing for their inheritance. This is why this expression of a "DNA blueprint" is so telling: it does exactly the opposite job for which it is intended since it permanently destroys any notion of a superorganism not only in the easy case of human organizations but *also* in the very case of biological organisms for which there is no question, nonetheless, that they "generate themselves."

Essence is the consequence and not the cause of duration. Thus such a risky, fragile, provisional character is not what is so strange in an organization since all entities run the same risk and pay for their continuation in the same small change: namely, *alterations*. Or, to say it in still other words, *subsistence* is never caused by some underlying substance.

Is it now possible to extract organizations from the idea that they somehow form a "collective body" that would be more than the sum of its parts? So entrenched is this idea, that it seems silly to want to fight against it. And yet, I think we should follow Gabriel Tarde's original insight and consider that the whole is always *smaller* than its parts and that this is why organizing is never provided with its right sort of agency (Candea, 2010; Tarde, 1895/1999, 1899/2000). I know this is a difficult point because it is perilously close to the tired old clichés that some relations should exist between the "individual actors" and the "structure" or "system" "inside" which he or she "acts."

And yet, I think it is important to show that from the point of view of organization practice, there is never an inside or an outside, there is never a small and a big, it is some entirely different puzzle that organizing has to solve, and to solve again and again. It is precisely at this point that we might finally distinguish organizing—as a mode of existence with a specific type of agency—and *organizations* as what is talked "about" when we *stop* organizing (using the apt distinction made by Czarniawska between "theories of organization" and "organization theory"). Organizations—the things—are the phantoms that appear when organizing—the mode—disappears. Hence the constant misunderstanding in organization studies between objects and processes (Weick, 1995).

This misunderstanding might be lifted once we accept foregrounding the curious "flip-flopping" of scripts that generates organization in their wake instead of asking the question of how we could reconcile "individual action" and the power of structures. The "deep" question raised by so much social theory—"How can we simultaneously be the authors and the children of the same overarching society?"—is just the question that should *not* be answered. The point for me here is that, contrary to the idea of a superorganism, we are never *simultaneously* under and above an organizational script. We are *never simultaneously* but always *sequentially* fabricators and fabricated, and we shift roles at specific *deadlines* that are themselves scripted. While being simultaneously authors and children of "the Body Politic" is an essential feature of the *political* existence, this is never the case in the organizational mode: we are "under" or "above" but *never at the same time*, and—especially important—*never in the same capacity.* As I will try to make clearer below, organizations as things are *the spurious image* produced by conflating two types of agencies, the political and the organizational modes of existence. Everything happens as if social theory, because it could not differentiate the two, had tried to make sense of an artifact: the whole is apparently superior to its parts because of a *suspension* of organizing practices.

This is actually quite easy to show. When we live under the script we are the ones *to whom* the script delegates instructions to be carried out. This is often called "roles" by sociologists of a Goffmanian persuasion, except this is a misleading metaphor since, at the deadlines, the situation changes completely and we are suddenly made to be the ones who insert instructions *into* the script. When we assembled with the chairman to discuss this session (remember I am imitating the lecture mode here), we burned into the timetable that I would speak 50 minutes but we could have said 60; now that we are both "under" the script, it is the timetable that is attributing *to me* a slot to which I should be faithful—except if, through a sort of grand Derridian gesture, I decide to speak for 3 hours. The theatrical notion of "roles," like the literary metaphor of "text" both run into the danger of missing exactly the turning point that is the specific feature of organization: we are the role followers at 10.30 but we were the playwrights at 10 and we will be it again at 11; we were the speech writers at 11 and we will become the *characters* in the speech at 11.30. And in addition, each of us is designated as characters in multiple contradictory stories, all of which come to an end at different deadlines and with different sanctions (Greimas, 1987). What sort of theater is this? What kind of text is that?

You could argue that the difference is tiny between being simultaneously authors and children of some overarching order and being sequentially scriptwriters and *characters written* inside some organizational injunction. The impression that I am splitting a hair at this point could be all the more correct, since in practice, I agree: we are never completely "under" nor completely "above" a script. No matter how "free" we might have been to change the schedule, the chairman and I were also under some other instructions that we also had to respect. Conversely, while you carry a course of action that has been written for you by a script—and thus when you live "under" the script that seems to be "above" your head—you nonetheless keep a floating attention to where it is leading you—you remain also "above" it. In other words, you are never "slavishly following an order" without some sense, however vague of the "meaning of the whole goal."

And it is true that this experience is common enough: Even when you are driving and following the sturdiest in-board GPS road instructor, you remain aware that the sweet female robot voice may lead you astray. To be sure, you are "under" its (or her) set of instructions—but something remains attentive to where it is leading you, thus you remain somewhat "above" her scripted trajectory even while you "follow" her. And yet, there is clearly a difference when, after having reached a part of town that is clearly not the one you intended, you decide to switch off the GPS and to go back to a good old street map or maybe, relying on an even older practice, you get out of your car to ask a passer-by for a fresh set of oral instructions (November, Camacho, & Latour, 2010). You are clearly "above" the script there in a different sense than when you were simply double-checking that you were not "slavishly" following the automaton. The breakdown has obliged you to flip over much in the same way as our discussion in the council room has forced us to shift from being the unconscious followers of Emile Boutmy's "blueprint" to the cautious rede-signers of that very same (well, now slightly different) set of injunctions. I hope I have made clearer why this flip-flopping has nothing to do with the right link to be made between "individual actors" and the "structure" of which they are a part. There is no individual to begin with but many different characters inscribed into many contradictory scripts with different deadlines (for instance the "same" dean might be expected to sit in four meetings at the same time); as to the structure it is never more than what has been inscribed in the script by various authors (the dean and his secretary meet over the schedule to try to clean their common agenda by rewriting it somewhat). This is precisely why, in organizing, the whole is always *smaller* than the parts—as long as we are in the act of organizing. It should be clear by now that I am trying to replace the individual versus system dichotomy by another *rhythmic* variation, the one between residing above or under a script.

No wonder it is so difficult to answer the question: "What's the story?" With the traditional idea of individuals "inside" a bigger collective entity of some sort, the nature of the story, of the recipients, and of the authors is entirely lost from view (Latour, 2005). Whatever the metaphor or the concepts put to work to follow organizations, they remain useless if they don't manage to register this flip-flopping of positions distributed in time

and varied in capacity. In my view, this flip-flopping is not well understood by saying that there exists a dialectical tension between tradition
and innovation, order and disorder, actor and system, and so on. As soon
as you lose the rhythmic pulsation of the scripts, the spurious afterimage
of an organization as a whole "inside" which "we" as individuals try to act
jumps at you.

This definition of organizations seems to me a good way to make sense
of the mass of work which had to be done in the field of organization
studies to redescribe each of the notions that were connected with that of
collective entities. It is now possible to follow the precise *tools* that allow
the organization to shift from one sequence where we *insert* instructions
into a script to the next sequence where we *follow* those same instructions
all the way to still another sequence where, often in a state of crisis, we
verify whether or not we will have satisfied the conditions.

If the study of organizations has been submitted to such a radical
change in recent times, it is precisely because attention has shifted from
general arguments about institutions as superorganisms or individuals
endowed with limited rationality (March & Simon, 1958/1993) to the
practical tools allowing for those bizarre sequences of trajectories stitching
together moments when actors are "above" and when actors are "under"
scripts of many descriptions and incarnated in many different types of
material. I am thinking of course of the transformation of organization
into writing devices, or of the study of organizational speech and writing
acts, or of the new attention to instruments, to accounting, to auditing
(Hopwood & Miller, 1994), or again of the social study of finances (Callon, Millo, & Muniesa, 2007). In that sense, it has become clear from
all these studies that we are never "in" an organization, no matter how
"gigantic": rather, organizational scripts *circulate* through a set of actors
that are either attributed some tasks or are in a momentary state of crisis
to reinstruct the scripts with new instructions for themselves or for others. In brief, "inside" and "outside," "big" or "small" do not qualify the
envelope of the organizational agency. Those adjectives do not grasp its
peculiar ontology.

On the other hand, it is precisely because organizational studies have
been thoroughly "*descaled*" that the specificity of organizations has begun
to shine through. If IBM were to be considered as "bigger" than its constituents, Jim Taylor's and François Cooren's work on how to achieve bigness by speaking in a certain way would only deal with a superficial and
irrelevant feature of institutions (Cooren, 2010). The same thing applies to
Paolo Quattrone and Chris McLean's careful study of accounting instruments: if the organization were *already* big and *already* overarching, there
would be no function whatsoever for all those trivial tools (Quattrone,
Thrift, McLean, & Puyu, 2010). And the same could be said of all the
other discoveries made about the technologies of public or private management (Chandler, 1990; Lascoumes & Le Galès, 2002). It is because

organizations are never "big" and that no one lives "in" them that the organizational work relies so much on the flip-flopping circulation of so many of those humble tools. The study of organization has really advanced once the phantasmagoria of size has been put aside—and this is why it has been, from the start, a tenet of actor network theory that scaling up and down should remain in the hands of actors themselves (Callon & Latour, 1981).

A Secular Definition of Organization

Can we go a little further and begin to use this redefinition of the organization to shed some light on the reason why it is so often missed? It would be moot to speak of a category mistake if we could not begin to compare agencies—or, to use my vocabulary, their different modes of existence—in order to account for why it is that organizations look so different when seen from another vantage point. Why is it that the clear recognition of a trait specific to the organizational mode of existence is blurred into a mystery once it is metamorphosed into a dialectical miracle through which the "same persons" would simultaneously be the authors of organizations and those who are defined by the organizations as if there existed a system or a structure into which human actors fit? Since we are now aware that this vicious or virtuous circle renders organizations totally opaque, is it possible to detect where it comes from? Well, as I said above, my hunch is that living under and above a script is easily confused with another type of *circularity*: that of politics. Everything happens as if we had attempted to study a *chimera*—in the biological sense of the word—obtained by the unfortunate fusion of the *political* and of the *organizational* modes of existence.

The creation of a path that links the parts and the whole is a crucial feature of the political regime, what I have called, for this reason, the circle of representation and obedience (Latour, 2003). "Are we one or many? Is the whole more than the sum of its parts? Should the whole really consist of its constituents?" Those are some of the essential questions for making the Body Politic continue its existence one more turn. Here too, I agree, there is a hiatus to be overcome—a gigantic gap that the whole of political philosophy has tried to fathom (Latour & Weibel, 2005).

That the two processes can be distinguished may be exemplified by the small crisis that made us bow to the bust of Emile Boutmy. For once, this time it is not political at all: There is no question inside the board that we are a coherent bunch of codirectors; that we agree on who is the leader; and that we belong to the same ensemble. In brief, we know the assemblage that is designated when we say "we"—"we should," "we don't know," "we have to decide," and so on. And yet, while the composition of the "we" is not in question, *we* have no idea what *we* should do! In other words, the political assemblage is not in crisis, while the organization is very much in trouble; proof enough that the two regimes can and should be distinguished. This does not mean, of course, that the organizational crisis, were it to last, would not begin to corrode the political ensemble just as well—but this is not the case now, the leadership is not in question, the mereological question has been sufficiently stabilized.

But no matter how important, these questions have nothing to do with the gap over which the organizational regime has to learn how to jump. The confusion is clearly detectable by a shift from Greek to Latin: the political circle that was called *autophuos* by Plato in the *Gorgias* (Latour, 1999), has become sui generis. The two expressions are exactly similar except one means the political question of bringing the parts into a whole, while the other designates the mystifying invention of a social entity *above and beyond* its ingredients. While the first clarifies the political mode of existence, the second obfuscates the organizational regime! There is never any sui generis corporate body in an organization: and that's exactly where the difficulty lies. Organizations, in other words, remain always *immanent* to the instrumentarium that brings them to existence—this is why I call them *flat* (Latour, 2005).

It is not because both regimes are concerned with complex questions of composition that they should be mixed up. By inventing the notion of a society on the one hand, and of individuals on the other, and then wondering how the two are related, we would make the detection of the paths through which organizations trace their zigzagging patterns very difficult. Our moral and political obsession for the composition of the whole would have blinded us to the type of composition that comes from submitting and being submitted to scripts. The shadow cast by the Body Politic has made monsters of organizations.

We may thus advance the suggestion that when Durkheim (and so many social scientists after him) had invented the notion of a "society" which is at once what is above us and what we have internalized, he tried to register the organizational mode of existence but had forgotten its peculiar rhythm: When we are "under" scripts, we are not individual actors but are trying to follow the many contradictory characters delegating us to do many different things at once; and when we are "above" scripts, we are simply rewriting highly localized instruments in order to reshuffle characters and deadlines. In other words, the real collective experience is never that of being an individual in a society (Dewey, 1927/1954). Sociologists have taken the notion of organized actions for the whole of the collective (Thévenot, 2006).

So how can we detect the oddity without additional mystery? We can do so, first by putting aside the collective body artifact: An organization is not and will never be a superorganism, a whole superior to its parts, a corporate body, a moral entity made up of its many individual constituents. The addition of any concept of "society" to the inquiry will only blind us. Second, we can detect the oddity by accepting the metaphysical evidence that no entity lasts by having a substance on which to rely, a foundation on which to rest, or an essence to carry it further in time. When, during another episode, our unquestioned leader makes a moving speech about the school that we have inherited and the new school that "we should be ready to deliver to the hands of our successors once our transitory bodies will have turned as much into dust as Emile Boutmy's bones," we know perfectly well that what is *passing* from our present team to the next is not like the baton of a relay race but rather like *the whole race*—stadium, television rights, car lots, illicit drugs, and hotdogs included. What passes is not a stable fixture but a whole moving assemblage of disconnected parts.

There is nothing above us, the superorganism; there is nothing below us, the foundation, there is nothing before us, the "blueprint," the "DNA"; there is nothing after us, the goal we pursue in the dark; and yet *there is an essence*: the school to which we are attached and whose precise trajectory we scrutinize with agonizing anxiety. This is the oddity that we should consider without adding to it any other parasitical transcendence. There is no transcendence (the whole) except this tiny transcendence, namely this tiny gap we manage to overcome this morning in the council room. By contrast with its mystical version—the chimera of the political fused with the organizational whole, this is what I call the *secular* definition of organization.

In order to conclude this lecture (and to respect the script "under" which my chairman and I are still living so as to avoid receiving a string of more and more comminatory slips of papers, you know: "5 minutes," "2 minutes," "1 minute," "STOP," "dismissed!") I want first to come back to the point I made at the beginning: Types of agency appear only when taken in their right key, that is, the subtle but essential difference between talking *about* an organization and talking in an organizational *way* or, even better, *as* an organizer. I have reminded you that organizing shares with all other actual occasions the same general pattern. To use again Whitehead's terms: what lasts (the essence of the school) is generated by what does *not* last (the constant work of taking it up again). That is just the paradox that is missed by supposing the existence of a macro-actor. To use this marvelous English intransitive verb: organizations *obtain*.

Second, I have shifted attention from a dead alley—organizations as sui generis meta- or macroentities "inside" which social theorists always try to put the little, puzzled, limited human actors as if they were another doll in another Russian doll—to a very different phenomenon: a fully "flattened" process of circulation of scripts. If you take the organization for a big animal, this instrumentarium is irrelevant. But if you know there is no "big" organization to begin with, then this instrumentarium is the only thing there is to trace and thus to track organizations.

Third, I have pointed out that whatever concepts we use to follow the tasks of organizing, it is essential to check whether they can register the strange flip-flopping that is their main feature: we live sequentially under and above those sets of inscriptions as if we were walking on a tightrope while being attached to it.

Well, where do we go from here? Time is now too short (and my chairman, with an eye fixed on his watch, is showing signs of growing impatience ...) but it would surely be worthwhile to draw the felicitous and infelicitous conditions of this highly specific mode of existence. Austin's term (Austin, 1962) is especially useful here since, as François Cooren has argued, many of his examples actually come from organizational speech acts when they do not come from law. Even though these truth conditions will be wildly different from those in scientific, legal, religious, or political regimes, they are nevertheless extraordinarily precise: we seem to have an unlimited bag of tricks to detect how our organization should behave and be led. If in doubt, record in any office the conversations around the coffee pot.

To conclude, organizing is a much more ubiquitous phenomenon than what happens in corporations, ministries, or gangs. And yet, no matter how widespread it is, it remains a very specific one which generates a very peculiar range of agencies when contrasted with other modes of existence: agencies where we learn to live sequentially, from crisis to crisis, under and above scripts that are providing us with completely opposite personae. By taking organizing as a mode of existence, I hope to have somewhat clarified the answer to the question: "What's the story?"

Note

1. This chapter is based on a talk given at the Université de Montréal in May 2008 to honor the work of Professor Jim Taylor. I thank the participants for their remarks. This version was published in Passoth, Jan-H., Peuker, Birgit, & Schillmeier, Michael (2011). *Agency without actors? New approaches to collective action* (pp. 163–177). London: Routledge. Reprinted with permission.

4 Organization as Chaosmos

Haridimos Tsoukas

What is is not ensemble or system of ensembles. What is is not fully determined.

What is is Chaos, or Abyss, or Groundlessness. What is is Chaos with nonregular stratification.

What is bears with it [comporte] an ensemblistic-identitary dimension—or an ensemblistic-identitary part everywhere dense. Cornelius Castoriadis (1997, p. 307)

There is a sense in which we cannot think without the concept of "organization." This is not only because we impose our Kantian thought categories on the world but also because the world lends itself to being perceived as organized or, at least, organizable. "The idea of absolutely formless matter," notes Castoriadis (1975/1987), "is unthinkable, for it amounts to an absolute indifference of matter with respect to the form 'imposed' on it, which would entail that the imposition of various forms on matter would be equally indifferent among themselves, and nothing in relation to experience could be either true or false" (p. 342). Human consciousness meets the thus-being of the world. The idea of coherent discourse and action would vanish unless our thinking about the world and the world itself could be seen as somehow *organized*.

Organized does not mean *fully* determined. It rather means that the operations (or the constitution) of an entity thought to be (or become) organized can be partly subsumed under the ensemblistic-identitary (henceforth: ensidic) logic; namely, they can be seen as an ensemble of distinct and well-defined elements, referring to one another by means of well-determined relations, which follow the categories of symbolic logic (e.g., the categories of class, relations, properties, and the principles of identity, noncontradiction, and the excluded middle). The underlying schema of ensidic logic is that of *determinacy* (Castoriadis, 1997, p. 293). Singling out, labeling, and categorizing are important operators that necessarily are put to work when ensidic logic applies.

Without ensidic logic, as well as the ontological stratum of the social-historical world (including language) that lends itself to ensemblization, there is no organization. An activity becomes organized insofar as *types* of behavior in *types* of situations are systematically connected to *types* of actors. An organized activity provides actors with a given set of cognitive categories and a typology of actions. In an organized activity objects and behaviors are singled out, labeled, defined, abstracted, and connected.

A process view of organization brings this out more clearly (Cooren, Taylor, & Van Every, 2006; J. R. Taylor & Van Every, 2000). Weick (1979, 1995) has been convincingly arguing for years that organizing is a process of generating *recurrent* behaviors through drawing on consensually validated cognitive categories. Action is undertaken, which is subsequently reflected upon (punctuated); namely, experiences are singled out, labeled, and connected, thus removing equivocality from individuals' interactions, and, finally, a stock of knowledge emerges and is retained—equivocality has been removed, the activity is organized. Weick illustrates this process of organizing with an ecological analysis of his provocative statement: "How can I know what I think until I see what I say?"

"What I say ..." is the generation of raw data—enactment. "Until I see ..." is the process of selection and involves punctuating a stream of experience into sensible and nameable units, and connecting them through imputed causal relationships. Through selection, the raw data are turned into information—they are made sense of. "Know what I think ..." is the outcome of the effort of sensemaking. This outcome is stored in the retention process in the form of an enacted environment (Weick, 1977, pp. 279–281, 1979, pp. 130–145). In short, an entity enacts equivocal raw talk; the talk is viewed retrospectively and sense is made of it; this sense is stored as knowledge in the retention process. The result of the process of organizing is the reduction of equivocality and a sense of what has occurred. The activity of *seeing* what one has said implies organizing raw data in meaningful ways. Organizing is in-formation, the creation of form (J. R. Taylor, 2000a, 2000b).

Thus, at the core of organizing is punctuation of an "environment," which the actors have brought about through acting, and coherently relating its elements. The role of singling out, labeling, categorizing, and connecting is essential in this. Organization is possible only insofar as what initially looks undifferentiated and opaque is turned into something sensible (representable) by applying the operators of ensidic logic. Organization entails representation (Cooper & Law, 1995; Robichaud, Giroux, & Taylor, 2004). This is nicely illustrated by Weick (1977, pp. 291–292) in his example of a group of musicians who gradually become organized into an orchestra:

> The environment that the orchestra members face is not simply the composition placed in front of them, but rather what they do with the

composition when they play it through for the first time. The musicians don't react to an environment, they *enact* the environment. In the credibility study the enacted environment available to the musicians after their first play was an undifferentiated "soup." As observers we might label this soup with nouns such as "sounds," "tempos," "themes," "shadings," and "errors." The first play-through of the composition could be made sensible by participants in a variety of ways. The crucial point is that the play-through, not the sheets of music, was the environment the musicians tried to make sensible.

Once musicians enact an environment, they then punctuate or break that environment into discrete events that are available for relating (e.g., "those twelve notes are thrilling," "those six bars are impossible," "that portion is ugly," "the notes are hard to read," "the tempo at which we start seems to be crucial." Essentially, the musicians punctuate the stream of enacted music into reasonable nouns and then try to relate or connect the nouns in a reasonable manner.

Signification within the ensidic logic concerns inclusion in classes (categories), identification of properties, insertions within relations, and combinations of categories. However, the operators of ensidic logic work on something that is made available to them. Classes, properties, and relations are possible insofar as certain demarcations are carried out, or, to put it slightly differently, certain categorical distinctions are established. What are such distinctions made *on*? Ensidic logic operators operate *on* an ontological stratum (that of social imaginary significations) that is indeterminate—*apeiron*—inexhaustible, and originary. Social imaginary significations are "arbitrarily" posited that *constitute* the domains of classes, properties, and relations. Equivalences and relations are established *from* the originary constitution of certain "arbitrary" points of view.

Castoriadis (1997) calls the positing of social imaginary significations "radical imaginary," meaning

> the *positing, ex nihilo*, of something that "is" not and the connection (without previous determination, or "arbitrarily" made) between this something that "is" not and something that, in another sense, "is" or "is not." Every signitive relation and every language obviously *presupposes* this positing and this connection. The latter thereby are founders of the ensemblistic-identitary domain, as well as of every other humanly conceivable domain. (p. 305)

For example, following Castoriadis's (1997, p. 305) argument, to say "0101 = The cost code for this component" presupposes the positing of what "is"; namely, material objects in the shape of rounds, bars, and other figures (identical to themselves) as signs (which, as such, "are" not naturally); the positing of what "is" not, namely concepts, such as zero, one, equals, and English-language words, and the connections between them. The statement "0101 = The cost code for this component" *signifies* insofar as one has the capacity to see in it what "is" not there, namely *numbers, words,* and *equivalences*, where there are only rounds, bars, and other figures.

Castoriadis calls the inherently indeterminate being *magma* from which ensidic organizations may be derived. Magma is a mode of being that gives itself prior to ensidic logic being imposed on it. Here is how he defines magma: "A magma is that from which one can extract (or in which one can construct) an indefinite number of ensemblist organizations but which can never be reconstituted (ideally) by a (finite or infinite) ensemblist composition of these organizations" (Castoriadis, 1975/1987, p. 343). Magma is an indefinite multiplicity such as, for example, all the significations of the English language, or all the representations of one's life. The components of magma are indeterminate, they blur into one another, and, although they can be marked out, they cannot be rigorously separated and enumerated. It is impossible, for example, to rigorously separate out those representations that "refer to my business" from those that do not. It is always possible for some representations that seemingly do not refer to my business to form chains of associations that eventually connect with it. The magmatic mode of being is inherently indeterminate, it constitutes an undifferentiated "mass," consisting of diverse components linked in multiple, indeterminate ways with one another, which can never be exhaustively singled out and defined. In his effort to describe magma through the inevitably ensidic logic that characterizes definitional language, Castoriadis (1975/1987) observes, somewhat poetically: "[To think of magma is to think] of an indefinitely blurred bundle of conjunctive fabrics, made up of different cloths and yet homogenous, everywhere studded with virtual and evanescent singularities" (p. 344).

Notice the similarities in the language of Weick and Castoriadis, despite their different disciplinary points of departure as well as their divergent intellectual concerns. For Weick (1977, p. 284), enactment, namely the generation of raw data through the undertaking of action to bracket and single out some portions of a stream of experience for further examination, leads to an "undifferentiated 'soup'" (p. 291), which is then punctuated into nameable units that are causally related to one another. Thus, in organizing, the raw data are turned into in-formation. Similarly, Castoriadis begins with the positing of magma (indeterminate being) from which an indefinite number of ensemblist organizations may be derived. An indeterminate and fuzzy multiplicity may be marked on, or, in Spencer-Brown's (1979) language, distinctions may be drawn, in an indefinite number of ways and, thus, ensemblist organizations may come about. In other words, *organization is the ensemblizing of magmatic being.* The latter is the *apeiron*, the gaping Chaos, from which form may emerge. Chaos and Cosmos are mutually constituted. To organize means to put the ensidic operators to work; namely, to single out, label, categorize, and connect. Ensidic operators may be explicitly articulated or take the form of a taken-for-granted norm.

To put it differently, to organize is to create, explicitly or tacitly, an ensemble of distinct and well-defined elements that are logically related to one another. What organization achieves is the creation of quasi-stable representations, concerning, for example, markets, technologies, or human behaviors, and their translation into habitual modes of acting (routines) (Cooper & Law, 1995; Kallinikos, 1996). Without such representations, a hospital cannot treat patients, a school cannot educate students, McDonald's cannot make and sell hamburgers, and photocopier technicians cannot repair photocopiers. Concerning the latter, for example, repair manuals issued to technicians contain canonical images of what a broken machine is and how it may be repaired (Orr, 1996). For the designers of such manuals, photocopiers are abstractions, whose reliable operation can be statistically described. The role of engineers is to investigate patterns in machine breakdowns, codify them, relate types of breakdown to types of repair action, and incorporate the relevant information in the manual. Without turning the photocopiers into abstract representations, organized action by the repair technicians cannot be undertaken (Tsoukas, 2005, p. 78). This applies even in cases in which there is a tacit body of knowledge concerning how work is to be carried out, as in the case of the flute making companies described by Cook and Yanow (1996). Although there is a paucity of explicit representations to guide the work of flute makers, nonetheless, in the course of time, generic notions of what a good or a "clunky flute" is have arisen that guide flute making work. Singling out, labeling, categorizing, and connecting are necessary components of the collective effort to carry out work in both cases. The prototypical example of ensemblizing human action is, of course, the assembly line (Ritzer, 2008), where every aspect of work is sought to be explicitly represented, codified, and, ideally, quantified.

Mintzberg (1989, p. 176) has alluded to the systematic ensemblizing of human action carried out by bureaucracies by suggesting that the latter tend to have standardized programs that are applied to standardized situations. The world is reduced to certain predetermined contingencies, which are matched with certain predetermined responses. Referring to professional bureaucracies, Mintzberg describes the representational aspect of organizing that turns a portion of the world into an ensemble to be processed for the sake of obtaining certain outcomes. He notes (1989):

> [T]he professional has two basic tasks: (1) to categorize, or "diagnose," the client's need in terms of one of the contingencies, which indicates which standard program to apply, and (2) to apply, or execute, that program. For example, the management consultant carries a bag of standard acronymic tricks: MBO, MIS, LRP, OD. The client with

information needs gets MIS; the one with managerial conflicts, OD. (p. 176)

Similarly, Feldman and Pentland have alluded to the ensemblizing of human action in their study of routines, the building blocks of organizational behavior. Organizational routines are repetitive, recognizable patterns of interdependent actions, involving several actors. They consist of two aspects: the ostensive and the performative. The ostensive aspect is the schematic form of a routine, while the performative is the actual carrying out of a routine by specific individuals in specific contexts (Feldman & Pentland, 2003, p. 101). The ostensive aspect singles out, names, and connects types of activities to deal with generic phenomena. Thus, for example, the hiring routine involves attracting, screening, and choosing applicants. Each one of those activities involves, in turn, procedures and templates of how an organization goes about recruiting applicants of a certain kind, in particular labor market segments, and criteria of assessment.

All such procedures, templates, and criteria are representations, namely abstract generalizations, concerning how multiple actors are to coordinate their efforts to deal with an issue at hand, in this case hiring suitable candidates. The ostensive aspect is the routine-in-principle (the routine-in-abstracto)—the abstract schema of how diverse individual behaviors are to be connected to address a generic issue. Unless there are quasi-stable schemata (representations) of types of activities, involving types of multiple actors, there can be no repetitive patterns of activities, hence no routines. It is through those schemata that a phenomenon such as *hiring* is cognitively represented and individual or departmental roles are delineated—that hiring itself is turned from an *opaque need* to hire employees to a *particular form* of handling it. This is more clearly shown when compared to situations in which organizational routines are underdeveloped (Dionysiou, 2007). There abstraction is low, who-takes-part-in-what "routine" is not clear, decision criteria are not articulated, procedures and templates remain unspecified, what the "routine" aims to achieve is unclear. In such cases, the ensemblizing of human behavior is weakly achieved, indeterminateness is more pronounced.

The ensemblizing of human behavior, namely the turning of a fuzzy multiplicity to an ensemble consisting of abstract representations, makes it possible for rules of action to be established—for types of behavior in types of situations (conditions) to be connected to types of actors. Rules are prescriptive statements or informal norms that take the form of propositional statements: "If the type of conditions X obtains, then behavior of type Y ought, or ought not to be, engaged by actors of type Z." "If X ..." is the "factual predicate" of a rule, which is derived either from events that occurred in the past or from some abstract, canonical image of the activity at hand "... then Y" is the "consequent"; namely, the consequences that follow when the conditions specified in the factual predicate obtain. The factual predicate is a generalization selected because it is thought to be causally relevant to the achievement of a goal or the fulfillment of "justi-fication" (Schauer, 1991, p. 27). A justification determines which gener-alization will constitute a rule's factual predicate and is *implied*, it is not explicitly contained in the rule.

Rules do not apply themselves; they are applied by concrete people, sit-uated in specific contexts (Gadamer, 1980; Tsoukas, 1996; Wittgenstein, 1953). Individuals must share an interpretation as to what the components of a rule (the factual predicate, the consequents, and the actors) mean as well as what the rule aims to achieve (its justification), in order to apply it. As B. Barnes (1995, p. 202) remarks, "nothing in the rule itself fixes its application in a given case, ... there is no "fact of the matter" concerning the proper application of a rule, ... what a rule is actually taken to imply is a matter to be decided, when it is decided, by contingent social processes." Since rules necessarily generalize, an individual following a rule needs to learn to act in *proper* analogy with previous examples. To follow a rule is, therefore, to extend an analogy. Barnes (1995) has put it as follows:

> To understand rule-following or norm-guided behavior in this way immediately highlights the normally open-ended character of norms, the fact that they cannot themselves fix and determine what actions are in true conformity with them, that there is no logical compulsion to follow them in a particular way. Every instance of a norm may be analogous to every other, but analogy is not identity: analogy exists between things that are similar yet different. And this means that, although it is always possible to assimilate the next instance to a norm by analogy with existing examples of the norm, it is equally always possible to resist such assimilation, to hold the analogy insufficiently strong, to stress the differences between the instance and existing examples. If norms apply by analogy then it is up to *us* to decide where they apply, where the analogy is sufficiently strong and where not. (p. 55)

Notice that, on this Wittgensteinian view, the proper application of a rule is not an individual accomplishment but is fundamentally predicated on *collectively* shared meanings: rule followers "must be constituted as a *collective* [emphasis added] able to sustain a shared sense of what rules imply and hence an agreement in their practice when they follow rules" (Barnes, 1995, p. 204,). Shared meanings are embedded in *practices*.

For example, abstract terms such as *faulty photocopier* (Orr, 1996), *path-ological change* (Polanyi, 1962, p. 101), or *clunky flute* (Cook & Yanow, 1996), derive their meaning from the way they have been *used* within the respective practices. One learns to recognize a, say, "clunky flute" and, therefore, to apply relevant rules, because one has been taught to *use* the category "clunky flute" in practice, within a practice. To be a member of a practice is to act within a teleologically structured, cooperative activity, bound by rules, whose identity is constituted through the key distinctions articulated (or manifested) in the normative use of language, body, and equipment (Dreyfus, 1991, ch. 5; Hardy, Lawrence, & Grant, 2005, p. 61; Harré & Gillett, 1994, pp. 28–29; MacIntyre, 1985; C. Taylor, 1985a, pp. 54–55, 1985b, p. 27). The distinctions constituting a practice are related to basic tasks, notions of competence and quality, orientation to time, understandings of reciprocity and authority, and are self-descriptions that situate the members of a practice relative to some standards of excellence and obligations (MacIntyre, 1985, pp. 187–194; C. Taylor, 1991, p. 305). The activities carried out within a practice are teleologically structured insofar as they are oriented toward attaining certain ends that determine it as the activity it is (e.g., teaching, nursing, flute making, photocopier repairing).

Through their participation in a practice, actors such as, for example, flute makers gradually learn to relate to their surroundings "spontaneously" (Wittgenstein, 1980, p. §699). In the case of the flute makers, the flutes and the material they are made from, their shapes and their sounds, as well as the flute makers' relationships to one another in the practice and the goal of flute making (the justification behind the rules), are not explicit objects of thought for individual flute makers but "subsidiary particulars" (Polanyi & Prosch, 1975, pp. 37–38)—taken-for-granted aspects of the normal setting in all its recognizable stability and regularity. The taken-for granted aspects of a work activity constitute what Wittgenstein (1979, p. §94) calls the "inherited background," against which practitioners make sense of their particular tasks (Shotter & Katz, 1996, p. 225; J. R. Taylor, 1993a, p. 325, 1995a, p. 69). Practitioners are aware of the background, but their awareness is largely "inarticulate" (C. Taylor, 1991, p. 308) and implicit in their activity (Ryle, 1963, pp. 40–41). The background provides the frame that renders their abstract representations comprehensible (Dreyfus, 1991, pp. 102–104; Kögler, 1996, ch. 3; J. R. Taylor, 1993a, pp. 327–328, 1995a, pp. 69–70).

In other words, if the abstract generalizations implicated in rules are seen as the syntax, they can be applied only after their semantics have been specified. The semantics are established within a practice. The ensemblizing of human behavior can be carried out insofar as ensidic operators are applied at the ontological stratum provided by the magmatic being, as the latter is *self*-constituted in particular practices. Notice, however, that, insofar as any entity enters human discourse, it enters the realm of *signification*, hence the realm of *indeterminacy*. "Being in language is accepting to be in signification" remarks Castoriadis (1975/1987). "It is accepting the fact that there is no determined response to the question: what is Socrates and who is Socrates?" (pp. 350–351). Naming (representing) helps to mark, to distinguish, to demarcate—it determines. At the same time, any representation is a signification and as such it refers to indefinite other significations depending on the language game it enters. The meanings underlying the *sensus communis* of a practice are not fixed but essentially changeable, depending on the language games within which they are expressed, itself a contingent matter. Barret, Thomas, and Hocevar (1995), for example, have shown how meanings of total quality in the U.S. Navy changed over time, from narrowly focusing on process improvements (initially) to extending to task design, management style, and broader issues of organizational culture (later). The values of the total quality program (empowerment, participation, and continuous improvement) turned out to be indeterminate: they had their meanings extended as the organizational experience of "total quality" accumulated.

In light of the above, therefore, the original definition of organization can be restated as follows: *organization is the ensemblizing of magmatic being as the latter is self-constituted within practices.*

Whereas rules consist of abstract representations, which are meant to apply across contexts, insofar as rules have a bearing on experience, they must be related by their users to the complexities of the real world, namely they must be related to *context* and *time*. This is as true of relatively simple representations, such as geographical maps, as it is of the extremely abstract formalisms of astrophysics. For example, take the use of geographical maps. A map is a representation of a particular territory. As an explicit representation of something else, a map is, in logical terms, not different from that of a theoretical system, or a system of rules: they all aim at enabling purposeful human action; that is, respectively, to get from A to B, to predict, and guide behavior. I may be very familiar with a map per se but to *use* it I need to be able to *relate* it to the world outside the map through my cognition and my senses (Polanyi, 1962, pp. 18–20; Polanyi & Prosch, 1975, p. 30). Given that the map is a representation of the territory, if I am to be successful in reaching my destination, I need to be able to match my location in the territory with its representation on the map.

In other words, an actor needs to fill in the "phronetic gap" (J. R. Taylor, 1993b, p. 57) that inescapably exists between a representation and the world encountered. The circumstances that confront an actor always have an element of uniqueness that cannot be specified by a rule. The "interaction order" (Goffman, 1983/1997), in which rules are enacted, is infinitely richer than the synoptic order, in which rules are formulated. Since, like most categories, representations have a radial structure, they consist of a stable part made up of prototypical (central) members and an unstable part made up of nonprototypical (peripheral, marginal) members radiating out at various conceptual distances from the central members (Johnson, 1993; Lakoff, 1987). Patterns of action stemming from acting on central cases tend to be carried out by the rule book (e.g., repairing a typical fault in a photocopier). But the world also throws at actors peripheral cases in which they are, in varying degrees, puzzled as to what to do and how to respond. The customer, for example, may have been using the machine in idiosyncratic ways, leading to a somewhat unusual pattern of faults (Orr, 1996). As a result of the radial structure of categories, there is an intrinsic indeterminacy when organizational members interact with the world—hence the need for them to fill in the phronetic gap by imaginatively extending a category beyond prototypical cases to peripheral ones (Johnson, 1993; Lakoff, 1987; Tsoukas & Chia, 2002).

The effort to close the phronetic gap inherently leads to improvisation. Orr (1996) reports how repair technicians improvise as they go about doing their work. Orlikowski (1996) shows how specialists enact ongoing situated accommodations, adaptations, and alterations in response to previous variations, while anticipating future ones. Weick (1998) talks about how jazz musicians constantly improvise as they listen to themselves and to each other. Improvisation is ever present (Fairhurst & Putnam, 2004). At the same time, all this flow of tinkering, accommodating, and adapting is not incoherent. On the contrary, it is usually *patterned*, as a result of individuals acting from within the same inherited background that teleologically shapes their actions and makes individuals interrelate their actions with those of others (Weick & Roberts, 1993). Organization, thus, is the patterned unfolding of human action. Boden (1994) aptly remarks: "What looks—from outside—like behavior controlled by rules and norms is actually a delicate and dynamic series of interactionally located adjustments to a continual unfolding and working out of 'just what' is going on and being made to go on, which is to say, the organizing of action" (p. 42). Organization is immanent in human action.

In the interaction order, time never goes away, and this is an additional reason why actors are required to close the phronetic gap in action. Time is not included in the logic of propositional statements. As Bateson (1979) insightfully noted, "the *if … then* of causality contains time, but the *if … then* of logic is timeless" (p. 63). For example, the "if … then" in "If the temperature falls below 0 C, then the water begins to freeze" is different from the "if … then" in "If Euclid's axioms are accepted, then the sum of all angles in a triangle is 180 degrees." The first statement makes reference to causes and effects, whereas the second is part of a syllogism; the first includes time, the second is timeless (Prigogine, 1992, pp. 23–25). When causal sequences become circular, as is always the case in interactive systems (von Foerster, 1981, p. 103), their description in terms of logic becomes self-contradictory—it generates paradoxes (Bateson, 1979, p. 61; Beer, 1973, p. 199; Capra, 1988, p. 83). Exclusive reliance on ensidic logic as a guide for action turns out to be impossible because the ensidic logic underlying propositional statements follows the rules of symbolic logic and, therefore, requires consistency and noncontradiction.

The unfolding of actions undertaken in response to the particularities of context and time is captured in narrative accounts. Actors, situations, and actions are placed in a sequenced, contextualized statement with a plot. Features of reality that are dropped from the abstraction process characterizing ensemblization (e.g., particular purposes and relationships, emotions, nuances of context, etc.), are recovered in a narrative. Reality is rendered historical and specific, not general and contingent: "I did this, the machine reacted in that way and I carried on doing this," as opposed to "If the following conditions obtain, do this." In the former case one looks for particular connections over time, whereas in the latter case one searches for universal truth conditions (Bruner, 1986, p. 11). Whereas in the ensidic logic, context is treated as a contingency, in the practical logic underlying situated action, context is treated as situation and circumstance, which crucially shapes the unfolding of events (Pepper, 1942; Sawyer, 2003). In a narrative account there are multiple links between events, not just causal in a logical sense. In narrative, events can be connected by cooccurrence, spatial proximity, formal similarity, or metaphor, all types of association that are not allowed in ensidic logic.

Narratives not only allow for multiple connections among events across time, they also preserve multiple temporalities. As well as being linked to clock time, narrative time is first of all humanly relevant time (Ricoeur, 1984): its significance is not derived from the clock or the calendar, but from the meanings assigned to events by actors (Bruner, 1996, p. 133). In this sense narrative time is asymmetrical. The moment, for example, after the death of a loved one is qualitatively different from the moment before her death. It is this asymmetry of time (powerfully argued in the sciences by Prigoine; see Prigogine, 1992, 1997; Prigogine & Stengers, 1984) that gives narrative its dynamic texture. By accommodating multiple temporalities, narratives are far more complex than propositional statements in which, as we saw earlier, time is absent (Tsoukas & Hatch, 2001).

In light of the above, therefore, the latest definition of organization can be restated as follows: *Organization is the patterned unfolding of human action in the effort of actors to reconcile the ensemblizing of magmatic being, as the latter is self-constituted within practices, with an infinitely complex reality.*

*   *   *

I have argued here that, in a broad sense, organization is an ever incomplete effort to shape chaos and formlessness. More specifically, organization consists of three ontological components, all necessary although not equally present in practice, each one of which points to a different function (see Table 4.1). Organization as the ensemblizing of magmatic being underlines the representational dimension of organizing. Without representation, there is no organization. Portions of the world need to be re-presented in terms of the ensidic logic for an entity to be seen as organized. Through ensemblization portions of the world are labeled, described, classified, and connected, and human action is made possible across contexts. Organization implies generalization and renders human action able to transcend contexts. The generic categories and the associated

Table 4.1 Organization as Chaosmos

	The Three Ontological Components of Organization		
	Organization as Ensemblization (syntax)	Organization as a Nexus of Practices (semantics)	Organization as Emergent Patterns of Action (pragmatics)
Logic	• Ensemblistic-identitary (ensidic) • Decontextual-ization • Closure	• Cultural • Contextualization	• Situational • Re-contextual-ization
Main features	• Categories • Generalizations • Rules • Routines	• Intrinsic good • Standards of excellence	• Overcoming of "phronetic gap" • Interlocked behaviors
Knowledge	Propositional	Tacit	Narrative
Process	Representation	Meaning-making	Improvisation
Action	Instrumental	Appropriate	Practical

rules constitute the syntax of organization. The semantics that must be in place for the syntax to work are underlined by organization as culture. The meanings generic categories have and the justifications rules aim to achieve are established in the context of social practices. Participants in practices must share the meanings of the key categories involved in the practice for them to be able to carry out their tasks and apply the rules. Through representation human action is sought to be decontextualized and, thus, rendered operative across contexts, and insofar as representations are significations, they are necessarily rooted in the practice of a particular community, through which they acquire collectively shared meanings. Decontextualization is possible provided its contextual roots are acknowledged. Insofar as meanings and justifications are coached in language, they enter signification—hence they are open-ended. Although a practice is teleologically structured and grounded on particular values, it is also indefinite in the sense that the significations through which its values and ends may be expressed are indefinite and indefinitely linked. A practice, at its roots, is magmatic—it constitutes an indefinite multiplicity. Both syntax (rules) and semantics (meanings) are applied by concrete people in a concrete world, which is infinitely more complex than its representations. There is always a phronetic gap between representations and the world, which is filled in through actors improvising. Representations and meanings are instantiated through the pragmatics of human action. Insofar as patterns of actions emerge, the organization emerges through the interrelating of human actions.

A perspective, therefore, that takes human agency seriously as this one does, views organization as consisting of three processes: a process of representation, a process of meaning-making, and a process of improvisation. Take any of these processes out and you have no organization. Disorganization occurs when any of these processes displace the others. In excessively bureaucratized environments, for example, failure of organization may come about because of the very limited scope for improvisation (excessive rigidity, meaning excessive adherence to rules losing sight of their tacit justifications), or because of the underdevelopment of the *sensus communis* which animates generic categories and rules. In underorganized environments (such as "organized anarchies"), failure of organization may come about as a result of the insufficient development of representations to guide human action, which leads to particularistic standards and excessive improvisation. Human action is bound to particular contexts, unable to operate *trans*contextually.

In practice there are occasions in which the three processes of organization overlap considerably. Yet even in such cases it is worth analytically separating the three processes out. For example, in craft-based work, representations tend to be tacit and deeply interwoven with the *sensus communis* of the practice. Yet the self-interpretations through which the practice is constituted are analytically different from the representations underlying practitioners' work. The practice is more likely to be developed and sustained if it refines its representations so that it enhances its transcontextual effectiveness. In cases in which improvisation seems to dominate, a closer look reveals a developed set of representations or a common culture underlying improvisational acts. For example, for theatrical improvisation to be effective, certain principles must be followed by those involved, such as actors should accept the offer made by another in the previous turn and add something new to the developing dramatic frame ("yes and" principle) or an actor should not reject what another actor has just introduced to the dramatic frame ("no denial" principle) (Sawyer, 2003, pp. 95–96). Similarly, Brown and Eisenhardt (1998) have underlined the working out of improvisation in organizations operating in high velocity environments on the back of rich shared meanings and organizational rules (albeit kept to the minimum and focused on the essentials).

In conclusion, while for a long time organization has been approached from the spectator's view and, as a result, only the representational (i.e., formal) dimension of organization has been most visible, if organization is approached from a process-based ontology that takes human agency seriously, we are able to appreciate the complexity of organization. The latter is not just *representation* (although this is important). It is also self-constituting *meaning-making* and patterned *action-taking* in the face of inherently incomplete knowledge. Without both of them there cannot be organization. Whenever there is organized action, there is a constellation of processes of representation, self-interpretation, and improvisation in action. When a human system is said to be organized, all of those processes must be in place, although in what proportion is a contingent matter. When a human system is thought to be disorganized, it is because one or more of those processes has been underdeveloped. Organizational failures typically stem from either one or more of these processes being weak, or the links among them being underdeveloped. And vice versa, as Weick and Roberts (1993) have shown, albeit by drawing on a different vocabulary, when there is organizational excellence, it is typically due to the way the three processes are interwoven to constitute a dynamically self-correcting and self-renewing whole. Good organization, when encountered, is nothing short of a little miracle—the fine balancing of *cosmos* and *chaos* over time.

5 Organizations as Entitative Beings
Some Ontological Implications of Communicative Constitution

Anne Maydan Nicotera

Defining the Task: Defining "An Organization"

A central task of answering the question "what is an organization?" is determining the ontological status of the organization-as-entity. As suggested by Fairhurst and Putnam's (2004) analysis of discursive approaches, organizations are simultaneously systems of material constraints, cycles of patterned regularities, and entities emergent from interaction. Although the third is most central to the present question, the others must not be lost because an organization is clearly all of these things. Most scholars would agree that "an organization," while associated with materiality, is not a material "thing." But beyond this, we usually fail to explicitly recognize "an organization" as a type of socially signified entity unless we have a concrete case before us, at which point we merely implicitly consider the organization as the context for our research, so the question of what it *is* becomes invisible. In short, we have failed to adequately confront the question of defining organizations as socially signified entities, although we routinely treat them as such (Kuhn & Ashcraft, 2003; J. R. Taylor & Cooren, 1997). In fact, Czarniawska argues that organizational theorists have actually created an unproblematic presumption of entity. But discussions of "organization as entity" typically turn to the "we"—to a discussion of collective agency (Cooren & Fairhurst, 2009; J. R. Taylor & Cooren, 1997) or collective identity (Cooren & Fairhurst, 2009; McPhee & Iverson, 2009; J. R. Taylor, 2009), losing the questions of what such an entity *is*, and how it has come to be.

Agency

Thinking of organizations as social actors is not a novel idea, although Latour prefers the term *actant* for nonhumans (see Coleman, 1982; Kuhn & Ashcraft, 2003; Latour, 1994, 1999; Robichaud, Giroux, & Taylor, 2004; J. R.Taylor & Cooren, 1997, for examples of very different ways of approaching this notion). The concept of "corporate citizenship" popular in the 1980s (e.g., Kocolowski, 1986; Melville, 1987; Peach, 1985; Spooner, 1986) is testament to the ease with which we presume organizations have such agency. However, with our current focus on organizational and textual *agency* (e.g., Cooren, 2008; Cooren & Fairhurst, 2009; Robichaud, 2006; J. R. Taylor & Cooren, 1997), we have not taken the time to ontologize the organization as a socially signified *entity*. What I mean by this is that in our focus on the "we" (agency), we have glossed over the "it" (entity). Clearly, for Cooren and his colleagues, organizational agents, or as Latour (1994) prefers *actants* (whether viewed as collective or hybrid), are presumptively entities, but the nature of "entity" is backgrounded as they foreground "agency." This paper proposes that our thinking will be enriched by problematizing "entity"—specifically by seeking its genesis—switching figure and ground, to put agency in the background and to foreground entity.

Collectivity

The fundamental notion of organizations as social collectives accomplished by communication is in itself a rich idea, the kernel of complex and stimulating theoretical discussions of networks and communicative structures that represent an enormous literature of their own (e.g., Krippendorff, 2008; Mayer, Grosjean, & Bonneville, 2008; Monge & Contractor, 2003). For the present purpose, it is important to note that notions of organizations as social collectives implicitly assume these collectives have agency and are communicatively constructed. It has long been habitual to call "an organization" a social collective (e.g., Hawes, 1974) or a communicative construction, but these terms do not get at the heart of the matter because they are mere descriptors rather than uniquely defining features. Multitudes of social collectives (e.g., "my family," "the neighbors") and communicative constructions ("my marriage," "voters") are entities but are *not* organizations, whereas others may be (e.g., "my family business," "the neighborhood association," "Worldwide Marriage Encounter," "the League of Women Voters"). Clearly, organizations are *both* social collectives *and* communicatively constructed, but they are also something else, something that goes even beyond such things as boundary recognition and formalization (see Czarniawska, chapter 1, this volume, for a thoughtful treatment of both). Three distinct features define "an organization." These are the things that are communicatively constructed: (a) the collectivity, (b) the social signification of the collectivity as an entity whose interests are represented in individual and collective activity, and (c) the distinct *entitative being* that transcends and eclipses any individual and the collective itself as it is attributed both identity and authority.

Representation

The organization exists in the communication (J. R. Taylor & Robichaud, 2004), is made present in interaction (Brummans, Cooren, & Chaput,

2009), and human (and nonhumans; see Cooren, 2006) agents incarnate it as they act in its name (Brummans, Cooren, & Charrieras, 2007). Moreover, an organization is socially signified in the third person as an independent recognizable entity in whose interests an individual or a collective may act. Following Tsoukas's (chapter 4) logic, this feature may be seen as *representation*. But representation as a socially signified entity is not enough to make that entity "an organization." For example, a human or nonhuman agent (such as a document) can act in the name of a committee, presentifying and incarnating (see Cooren, 2006) the committee, but the committee is not an organization because it is not working on its own behalf, but on behalf of yet another nonhuman entity in which is it embedded. In other words, it is not an organization because its primary mission or raison d'être is not to further its own interest, but to act in the interests of another entity. *It is not an organization because it does not have primary authority and its identity and authority do not transcend and eclipse that of the human(s) who comprise its collective.*

A collective embedded in an organization may itself become an organization, as when a collective of speech teachers embedded in the National Council of Teachers of English (NCTE) became the National Association of Academic Teachers of Public Speaking (NAATPS), now the National Communication Association. This collective of speech teachers ceased to make their own interests secondary to the interest of the NCTE. When the primary interests of the speech teacher collective superseded the interest of the NCTE (organization as entity), the NAATPS was born—incarnated as an association (Gray, 1964) that was attributed its own identity, agency, and authority. In other words, an organization does not act *primarily* on behalf of and in the name of another entity (collective or not), but is attributed the authority to compel others (individual and collective actors and actants) to act on *its* behalf, which leads us to the final defining characteristic.

Entitative Being

In the genesis of organization-as-entity, the notion of incarnation/presentification allows for the conceptualization of two defining characteristics: representation and *being*, respectively the representation of the interest and the identity of the socially signified entity whose interest is represented. (This is deeply embedded in the process-product duality of organization.) A socially signified entity can be said to have *entitative being* (or to *be* an entitative being) when, by virtue of authority attributed to it, its identity *transcends and eclipses any human individual or human collective*. The entitative being, though it emerges from a human collective, is itself a nonhuman. Not all socially signified and presentified entities have *entitative being*, which exists when the socially signified entity is attributed not just agency and attitude, but also *authority*. This concept explains how we can blithely say such things as *"universities* hire *cleaning firms"* (see Czar-niawska, chapter 1, this volume, and below). It is also why, even though it is a subset of the New York State government, the "New York State Department of Transportation" can be defined as an organization, but "the curriculum committee" in my academic department cannot. Organizations can be embedded in larger organizations, and not all collectives that are signified as entities are organizations.

For example, my university department curriculum committee has collectivity and representation. Its members come to general meetings and present reports *on behalf of* (representing) the curriculum committee. But that committee does not have entitative being because it does not have an identity that is attributed agency, attitude, and authority that transcends and eclipses the human beings who comprise its collective. People are said to be "on" the committee or to be "a member of" it. If I am said to be "on" or "a member of" something, this recognizes me as a member of a collective—but my identity is neither transcended nor eclipsed. Nor do its members *work for* the committee. The committee, rather, is a vehicle by which its members collectively *work for* the university. The curriculum committee is not "an organization." "The university," on the other hand, *is* an organization because it is an entitative being. As a member of *its faculty* (note the use of possessive), I have authority only insofar as I occupy a position that is granted authority by that entitative being. Even the highest ranking authority figure, the university's president, *acts for* the university. Note the language: he or she is the *university's* president—she or he "belongs to" the entitative being, not vice versa. "The university" has the authority, through individual and collective human agents acting on its behalf, to grant and limit the authority of its members. When I am presenting information in the classroom, I often say to my students, "Write this down," and most of them do—without question because that is something I get to do by virtue of the authority granted me by "the university." I would be outside the realm of that authority if, when presenting information in a committee meeting, I turned to my university president and said, "Write this down." In fact, it would not occur to me to do such a thing, as it so violates the attributions of authority dictated by the university as the entitative being. And, outside the context of the entitative being, I would be thought quite odd were I to go around spouting information and instructing people to write it down. Here, we quite easily attribute agency, identity, and authority to "the university."

Furthermore, organization, as a *state* of being, is not entitative. In other words, not all that is organized is "an organization." For example, note the clear differences between an individual medical practice and a group practice. The group practice is an organization with an authority that transcends that of the individual physicians. When confirming appointments, the office staff refers to the *practice* by *its* name: "This is Mary, calling from Golem Gastroenterology to confirm your appointment tomorrow." The name "Golem Gastroenterology" transcends and eclipses the physicians as individuals and as a collection of individuals. Even when the entity's name appropriates the names of the doctors, such as if the practice were named "Jones, Smith, and Carter," when invoked as the name of *the practice*, that entity eclipses the individuals whose names are thus appropriated by the "it." If Dr. Carter dies, the practice may or may not change its name.[1] And even though Drs. Jones, Smith, and Carter are humans, "Jones, Smith, and Carter" is not. The practice is an organization because it has all three: collectivity, representation of its interests (e.g., the phone calls are made on *its* behalf), and *entitative being*—an identity and authority that eclipses even the individuals whose names it bears. Contrast this example with the individual physician practicing alone. He has the institutional artifactual accoutrements that go with the practices of the profession (office space, files, equipment), and he may even have several employees. Clearly, this is a business: services are rendered; invoices are delivered; payments are made; employees are hired and paid. Clearly the business is organized: tasks are identified, roles are assumed, and activities are coordinated. It may even be formally signified as a legally recognized entity through incorporation. But without an "it" that transcends the human(s), it is not "an organization." The employees work for the doctor, not a nonhuman being that transcends him. When the receptionist calls a patient she may say, "This is Mary from Dr. Smith's office." Dr. Smith never ceases to be an individual. "Dr. Smith's office" here specifies a place or a context, not a thing. Mary works for Dr. Smith, not for an entitative being. Interestingly, individuals may assume the nonhuman identity of "the office" as a *thing with agency*: Mary may sometimes say, "This is Dr. Smith's office calling." By representing herself as a nonhuman thing that belongs to Dr. Smith, she anthropomorphizes "the office" and dehumanizes herself. But even here Dr. Smith, a human individual, does not cease to be primary. He is never eclipsed by a nonhuman entitative being; quite the contrary, he remains primary, in ownership of the represented "it" with authority over it. So whereas his practice is a socially signified and represented entity (a business), perhaps even a legally recognized entity, it has no entitative being and is thus not understood to be "an organization" or treated as such in the language of those who speak of it.

Relations among the Three Defining Characteristics

Collectivity, representation, and entitative being are definitionally interdependent and recursive, linked by presentification/incarnation. A collectivity has to be recognized by its linguistic representation, or social signification, through presentification/incarnation. Representation, in turn, depends on both the understanding of the interest that is represented and the socially signified entity whose interest it is. That socially signified entity has *entitative being* when it is represented as a collectivity whose existence and authority transcends and eclipses the *human* being(s) who comprise it. Entitative being can exist without collectivity only in linguistic simulation. In actuality, entitative being cannot exist without collectivity and representation, but the appearance of entitative being is easily achieved linguistically. This can be illustrated by showing how the illusion of "organization-ness" is commonly used as a small business strategy.

I have an acquaintance, "Dr. Leviathan," with a very successful public relations agency. For her business, operated out of a home office, she employs one full-time employee (herself), a part-time assistant, and the occasional student intern. For the sake of image and legitimacy, she needs her clients and potential clients to see her business as "an organization"— a represented, collective, entitative being—of which she is the CEO. She needs a Golem to transcend and eclipse her (see Czarniawska, chapter 1, this volume). The business is represented as an entitative being named "The Leviathan Group." Note the use of plural noun. There is no actual "group," just the illusion. She hires other individuals on an ad hoc basis as she needs them for contracts. Those individuals function as subcontractors, are not named by her in any promotional material as "members" of the "group," and are not given titles. The agency website allows it to easily masquerade as an organization because it creates the illusion of collectivity. Clickable links include "About Us" and "Contact Us." On the "Contact Us" page, no individual is named. The mailing address begins with "The Leviathan Group, LLC," and the e-mail address is info@thelevia thangroup.com. On the "About Us" page, representation, entitative being, and collectivity can all be seen in phrases like "At the Leviathan Group, we believe...." The use of a plural noun and plural pronouns is a rhetorical device that creates the appearance of collectivity. In actuality, collectivity is but an illusion. Aside from the CEO, no other individual's name can be found. The group is identified only as "a group of multitalented, experienced consultants." None of this is factually inaccurate. Dr. Leviathan does indeed subcontract to many such individuals, and their talents are crucial to the success of her business. But that "group" is not a collective. They do not interact with one another, do not identify themselves as associates of the agency, and do not even know who all the others are. Those with first-hand knowledge of the agency do not refer to the agency as "an organization." Because its interests are represented in individual actions, the agency can be defined as a socially signified entity. Moreover, as an LLC (limited liability company, a common form of incorporation in the United States for small businesses), the agency is also a legally signified entity. And because it is presentified and incarnated as having identity and authority that transcends the individual, the agency has *the appearance of* entitative being. But because its apparent entitative being has not emerged from actual collectivity, it is not genuine. And because of that, in its day-to-day operations and the language used there, it is not understood to be "an organization." Pronouns used in everyday language are singular and refer to the individual human who owns the agency.

But we must not be distracted by size as it is displayed in a small number of full-time members. For example, I once was employed on a contractual basis as an associate with a very similar consulting firm that employed only three people full-time and whose office space comprised less than 100 square feet. Undoubtedly, the firm was an organization, but the social collective that it sprang from consisted of a dyad. Only after the firm existed as a corporation did it hire the third full-time employee. The firm contracted dozens of associates, distributed all over the world, a social collective that continually and recursively presentified and incarnated the firm and acted on its behalf—and as individuals far outnumbered the collective that comprised the full-time employees of "the organization." These associates were listed in the firm's promotional literature by name, and each carried the title "associate." None were on salary, but some carried business cards bearing the firm's name and logo. Although they did not interact with one another or work on behalf of the firm full-time, all considered themselves "members" of the firm, providing it with a very real, albeit distributed collectivity. Unlike Dr. Leviathan's agency, this firm had all three distinguishing characteristics of an organization. And in everyday conversation, the firm's name was casually used—transcending and eclipsing the human(s).

Communicative Constitution

Having made these distinctions, it is important to find a theoretic ground to support this line of thinking. Communicative constitution of organization (CCO) represents a theoretic approach with great potential to explicate the question, "What is an organization?" and thus my question of its genesis. The driving question herein is more than the question of how an organization that is preexisting in the discourse is constituted in and by communication. Herein, we must find the ground upon which to base an understanding of communicative constitution that will account for the emergence of an organization from nothing. How does communication bring an entity into being? How do we get from an idea to entitative being—"an organization?" Two enterprising Steves building and selling personal computers together is not an organization. But it can become one: How do we get from these humble beginnings to something as iconic as Apple and Mac?[2]

J. R. Taylor, Cooren, Giroux, and Robichaud (1996) best summarize two central conceptual dilemmas answered by CCO, calling into direct question the implicit assumption in most organizational communication research that organization can exist independently of communication and the implicit essentialization of organization and formalization. These implicit assumptions set the ground for implicit container metaphors of organization (Smith, 1993) and for the treatment of communication as a variable. "We err in thinking of communication as a transparent window on organizations; the properties that we recognize as organizational are *in the communicational lens* [emphasis added], not in the object they are focused on" (J. R. Taylor, Cooren, et al., 1996, pp. 2–3). Yet still, while undoubtedly "communication" is more than a variable or an element of organization, and just as clearly organization cannot exist apart from communication, the broad claim of CCO is also a dangerous essentialization of both "organization" and "communication." To assume that organization is constituted by (or "made of") communication is to broadly assume that "communication" and "organization" are mutually constitutive. This is an attractive philosophical position that makes for engaging classroom discussion exercises—but it takes on the overly generalized and thus pedantic function of explaining nothing by explaining everything. And by studying, almost exclusively, formal organizations and institutions, we go blithely on in the practice of our scholarship with the contradictory implicit assumption that "organization" means "formalization" (J. R. Taylor, Cooren, et al., 1996).

Although the process-product duality of organization is a well-accepted and relatively noncontroversial idea (see Cooper & Law, 1995; Tsoukas & Chia, 2002; Van de Ven & Poole, 2005), discussions of organizational ontology generally focus not on organization-as-entity, but on organization-as-process (e.g., Brummans et al., 2009; Czarniawska, chapter 1, this volume; Robichaud et al., 2004). Like our focus on agency, our focus on *process* ("organization" as a verb) has glossed over *entity* ("organization" as a noun), as well. We have become so accustomed to treating "organization" as a verb synonymous with "organizing" (à la Weick) that when we consider (an) "organization" as a noun, we usually treat it merely as a state of being organized (which is not entitative) or, at best, as a formalized product of "organizing." Depending on one's purpose this is more or less problematic. For example, for Czarniawska (chapter 1, this volume) a process emphasis is essential. The very purpose of her "action net" approach is to move beyond an implicit presumption that organization springs from actors forging connections (attributed to network theory) to make *organizing* a primary focus—resting on the observation that organizations, as well as the identities of actors, are products of organizing.

> The process of creating the alliances that eventually form macro-actors is poorly understood, as macro-actors obliterate any traces of their construction, presenting themselves through their spokespersons as being indivisible and solid. Social scientists contribute, often unwillingly, to this construction process, by increasing this solidity and consistency in their descriptions. (p. 4)

She eschews a focus on entity because it gets in the way of understanding process. Switching figure and ground, the present purpose rests on a parallel claim: A focus on process gets in the way of understanding entity. What is interesting is the way in which even Czarniawska seems to unselfconsciously lapse into language that does not problematize the primacy of the "it." "A university must contract one or several cleaning firms; but although cleaning firms do not belong to the organization field of higher education, a cleaning firm on strike will seriously disturb the functioning of any university" (p. 13). Here she seems to implicitly invoke the Golem she so disdains. Do "universities" contract with "cleaning firms" or do university-representing individual actors negotiate contracts with cleaning-firm-representing individual actors for the labor of individual actors who then do the cleaning? Czarniawska's own languaging illustrates that an unquestioned presumption of the preexistence of the "it" is insidious to our scholarly consciousness, but she also poses a solution to this problem: "One way out of this difficulty is to study progressively an action net that is being connected, or, to use Foucault's term, to do a genealogy of an existing action net" (p. 14). I do not see this as a focus on process to the neglect of product, but a focus on the connection between them, starting with process as the entry point.

Likewise, the present purpose is to problematize neither the process (organizing) nor the product (the organization) but what happens in between. The purpose in the present analysis is to begin to unpack the "how" of that process-product relation—to problematize the hyphen between "process" and "product" (see also Marroquín & Vásquez, 2008, for an analysis of how this process-product dynamic unfolds in communication on a daily basis). That an organization (entity) is the product of organizing (process) is, of course, a key assumption upon which this analysis rests. But it is also the entrée to the central question, which is to understand the nature of the organization as an "it" and to understand how "it" comes to be in the first place, and how not all "its" come to be organizations.

James Taylor (see chapter, 12, this volume) cautions that "an organization is not 'out there'" (p. 212). According to Taylor, an organization is a feature of communication, and as a result it is grounded in patterns of exchange, the negotiation of transactions, and the formation of relationships. Neither does this analysis deny Latour's assertion (chapter 3, this volume) that "an organization is not and will never be a superorganism, a whole superior to its parts, a corporate body, a moral entity made up of its many individual constituents" (p. 49). But an organization is something different, if not more than a social collective: It has, as described previously, *entitative being*. As such, organizations-as-entities are routinely ascribed agency; actions, attitudes, and authority are daily unproblematically attributed to such entities.

In today's newspaper, on one page alone, I read that *Washington* has "snubbed" Ottawa, that the *US Securities and Exchange Commission* has "announced" talks, that *it* has "chosen" Australia over Canada, that *it* does not "want" to try forging an agreement, that *the world's biggest banks* have "rebuffed" calls for stricter rules, and so on and on. Thus organizations are actants in a way that objects like guns are not. In the case of an organization it is the people who *represent* it who are the affordances. This is true even though there is no real entity—and here I am in total agreement with Bruno Latour—that we can ever point to and say that's it, *there* is the organization. *Unlike* the gun it is an entirely fictitious, totally immaterial construction. It just happens, however, that it is a powerful actant *because we attribute an attitude to it*. (Taylor, chapter 12, this volume, pp. 214–215)

Agency and collective identity are promising directions in pursuing a focus on "organization as entity," but they are just the first step; a focus on "we" is not enough in the search for the birth of organization-as-entity. *And so, I envision herein our most pressing task to be determining the ontological status of the "it."* In so doing, we should seek to locate the conception and birth of the organization-as-entity. A modest proposal of a model to trace this process is presented herein.

We-to-It to Organization

In the search for this transition from *"we"* to *"it,"* we lack a conceptual connection between micro- and macroprocesses. What really is the process by which individual conversations become an organization-as-entity? How does the entitative being come into that being in the first place? Even CCO theory has not answered this question. We have become adept at theorizing organization as the collective *"we,"* but not at theorizing the *"it,"* although Cooren's notions of hybrid agency (Cooren, 2006; Cooren & Fairhurst, 2009), presentification (Brummans et al., 2009; Brummans, Cooren, & Charrieras, 2007; Cooren, 2006), and incarnation (Brummans et al., 2007; Cooren, 2006) are an extremely promising start. Despite our best previous explanations of the connection between localized interaction and organizational entities, such as "lamination" (Boden, 1994) or "imbrication" (J. R. Taylor, 2000b), we persist in implicitly conceiving of the micro and macro as separate existences—despite J. R. Taylor and Van Every's (2000) "flatland" view; see Cooren (2006), for a thoughtful discussion of this problem. Clearly, we must begin with the "micro" or localized because human interaction is so obviously necessary for the birth of an organization rather than vice versa. Therein lies the very foundation of the term *CCO*.

Unfortunately, it appears that the coining of the term CCO has been treated as the explanation, rather than the question. And so, the key issue remains mysterious: our conceptual disharmony between the micro- and macro-levels. Our own discourse stubbornly persists in the conceptual divide between the local processes of individuals interacting in dyads and small groups and the global processes of systemic operations and organizations as collective and hybrid agents. It seems to be in this conceptual space between micro and macro, local and global, individual/dyad/group and systemic—*we* and *it*—that the CCO process might reside. If organization is communicatively constituted, the central question seems to be "how do we get there from here?"—"there" being an entitative being (product) and "here" being a human conversation (process). We do agree that we must travel through collectivity, but the latter part of the trip is heretofore unmapped. Robichaud et al.'s (2004) concept of the metaconversation provides an exciting set of propositions, claiming in part that "organization as a single entity is constituted in one sense by its emergence as an actor in the texts of the people for whom it is a present interpreted reality" (pp. 630–631). The function of the metaconversation is double. First, it situates collective actors in "narratively grounded texts through which the conversation is mediated" (p. 631); second, it instantiates individual actors as representatives of those collective actors.

Conception: We to It

As argued above, a collective agent (*we*) is not necessarily an organization (*it*), but an organization (*it*) must necessarily be a collective agent (*we*). So clearly, a sense of collectivity must precede the birth of an organization-as-entity: there has to be a "*we*" before there can be an "*it*." It seems, then, that "organization" as a "thing" is conceived in *self-conscious* collectivity—in the moment the "*we*" refers to the "*it*"—when members of the collectivity refer to the collective in the third person in the present tense. This might be seen as the most fundamental form of presentification—making the organization present in interaction (Brummans et al., 2009). If the organization exists in communication (Taylor & Robichaud, 2004), and is made present in interaction (Brummans et al., 2009), then its moment of conception is the first moment that communication presentifies the entity.

When the collectivity is recognized *by* the collectivity as an existing recognizable entity in its own right, independently from individuals, the organization is conceived, and once the "*it*" exists, the "*we*" persists so that "*we*" and "*it*" are sometimes treated as the same entity, but sometimes considered to be separate. Treatments of organizational identification reflect this observation (Cheney, 1983a, 1983b; Cheney & Tompkins, 1987; Scott, Corman, & Cheney, 1998). When identified with the organization, members invoke collectivity, using first person reference (*we*); when not identified, members presentify the organization, using third person reference (*it*). For example, two comments on campus recently overheard: "I like the way *we* are starting to integrate writing instruction across the curriculum" vs. "I don't get why the university [*it*] wants me to teach composition." The first speaker casts herself as a member of a collective agent; the second makes the organization present, separating herself from it—but note that she ascribes agency and attitude to the "*it*" *and* casts it as authoritative, dictating to her what she must do. Brummans et al. (2007) examine this very concept; in their study of "incarnation" they are tracing the ways in which the "it" is incarnated or made present through interaction. Taylor (see chapter 12, this volume) points out that what is crucial in this turn of pronoun from first to third person is in the *dissociative* properties of the latter.

> We use pronouns such a *I* , *we, you, it, he, she*, and *they* with great skill to communicate to others our associative and dissociative preferences. As we do, we are continually establishing our own identity, as well as that of the actants we relate to, *including that of the organization*. (p. 216)

It is the *dissociation* that is the crucial issue, not the existence of the organization as an actant. A social collective, the "we," is an actant. The notion that an organization is an actant is not incommensurate with my purpose, but it also does not distinguish the organizational "it" from the organizational "we." The ability to dissociate from the organizational entity, while attributing to it agency, attitude, and authority is the crucial illustrative point. This is what creates the entitative being that can then be made present through representation of its interests. Only once we have dissociated from the "it" and attributed to "it" attitude, agency, and authority do we unproblematically create the *entitative being*, by allowing "it" to transcend and eclipse the human being(s).

Birth: It to Organization

With the moment of conception thus located, I turn now to the birth. Brummans et al.'s (2009) insightful study of organizational naming implicitly recognizes the importance of understanding the "organization as entity." "*It*" becomes an organization as it is "presentified," or made present. This process of "presentification" (see also Cooren, 2006) is obviously a crucial part of organizational birth. However, just as not all that is organized is an organization, not all social collectives that are presentified are organizations, so this is not a sufficient condition for organizational birth. To be "an organization," the collective must be presentified as an actant whose existence is independent from other collectives, even as it is related to and interdependent with them, and it must be continually presentified and *incarnated* (Brummans et al., 2007) so that individual and collective actors alike are continually acting on its behalf or, to use

Brummans et al.'s (2007) phrasing, acting "in the name of" *it*. Thus, an organization is born in the moment "*it*" is incarnated by an individual or collective agent acting on its behalf or in its name (Brummans et al., 2007). It is the transcendent *independence of its existence* from other collectives (entitative being) and the *primary nature of its interests* in interaction (representation) that distinguish an organization (such as a company or firm) from other incarnated entities (such as a department or committee). To survive its infancy, then, the organization's raison d'être must remain primary in the agentic activities of the individuals, collectives, and non-human agents that continually and recursively presentify and incarnate it (representation), attributing authority to it and relinquishing individual authority to it. Through this recursive incarnation, "it" (with its attributed authority) becomes reified: "It" develops entitative being, thus becoming "an organization." Robichaud et al. (2004) mark this same discursive process as the birth of organization, including the notion of representation. The organization-as-entity is seen as being brought into existence when it is talked of. Further, its identity is seen as "narratively built in its relationships to 'others' … a crucial component of this process [being] the emergence of a spokesperson [who] talks *for* it" (p. 630).

Modeling the Process: I to We to It to Organization

J. R. Taylor, Cooren, et al. (1996) propose a set of six "degrees of separation" between conversation and text that offers an attractive mechanism of getting "there" from "here," and from which my model is constructed. The capsule summaries here appeared in a widely used communication theory textbook (Miller, 2005). Italicized notations are mine.

> *First degree*: intent of the speaker is translated into action and embedded in conversation. *Individual action/agency; speech acts; human interaction*
>
> *Second degree*: events of the conversation are translated into a narrative representation, making it possible to understand the meaning of the exchange. *Collective sensemaking (Weick, 1995); emergence of the social collective (we)*
>
> *Third degree*: the text is transcribed (objectified) on some permanent or semipermanent medium (e.g., the minutes of a meeting). *Creation of Text (J. R. Taylor, Cooren, et al., 1996); hybrid agency (Cooren, 2006; Cooren & Fairhurst, 2009)*
>
> *Fourth degree*: a specialized language is developed to encourage and channel subsequent texts and conversations. *Emergence of a speech community (Philipsen, 1975); precursor to or sign of self-conscious collectivity (it)*
>
> *Fifth degree*: the text and conversations are transformed into material and physical frames (e.g., laboratories, conference rooms, orga-

nizational charts, procedural manuals). *Materialization; creation of artifacts; precursor to or sign of presentification; incarnation then follows presentification* (Brummans et al., 2007)

Sixth degree: a standardized form is disseminated and defused to a broader public (e.g., media reports and representations of organizational forms and practices). *Reification; recursive presentification and incarnation.*

Although this increasingly abstract sequence can occur in the context of a preexisting organization-as-entity, when viewed as a process of organizational conception and birth, these six steps represent a phasic model—a sequence of "states" if you will. They offer a baseline of the mileposts we need to trace the path through from discrete moments of human interaction to "an organization." Grounded in an explicit CCO presumption, this way of thinking may allow us to break the beguiling myopia of "organization is a process" that has led us to treat "organization(noun)" as the product of "organization(verb)," but rarely to problematize "organization(noun)" as a kind of entity. It seems that the organization-as-entity is likely conceived somewhere between the second and fourth degree, with the emergence of self-conscious collectivity, and is born somewhere between the fourth and sixth degrees of separation, with incarnation. A communicative exchange has to be mutually understood for a collective agent to develop and recognize itself, and the organization-as-entity must have existence prior to its being standardized to external audiences.

And so, using this baseline, I propose the following process as a model of the link between micro and macro, the path from human action to organization-as-entity: *I* to *we* to *it* to *organization*.

Individual action/agency; human interaction (I): Human actors engage each other in goal-directed conversation in Taylor, Cooren, et al.'s (1996) sense of the term.

Construction of the social collective (we). Through a process of collective sensemaking (Weick, 1995), a social collective with agency emerges.

Construction of Text (J. R. Taylor, Cooren, et al., 1996): Through the execution of its agency, the social collective generates enduring outcomes of conversation that become the ground for ongoing goal-directed interaction among the collective's members. Hybrid agency emerges (Cooren, 2006; Cooren & Fairhurst, 2009).

Self-conscious collectivity (It: Conception): With the emergence of a speech community (Philipsen, 1975), the collective becomes conscious of its own collectivity as a distinct entity in itself. Perhaps hybrid agency sets the stage for self-consciousness?

Presentification (Brummans et al., 2009; Cooren, 2006): The existence of material frames and artifacts are a sign of presentification, which may be a precursor to or simultaneous with organizational birth.

Materialization may be a precursor to (but not a guarantee of) presentification: A project group, as a self-conscious social collective (*it*), allotted space by an existing organization can use that material frame as the grounds for presentification as an organization whose raison d'être becomes primary in the activities of its agents.

Materialization may be simultaneous with or the mode of presentification: A self-conscious social collective (*it*), may declare itself to be an organization by creating material frames (e.g., business cards, websites, manuals, manifestos, etc.); the material frames then maintain the primary nature of the organization's raison d'être.

Organization (Birth): An organization is born in the moment "*it*" is incarnated by an individual or collective agent acting on its behalf or in its name (Brummans et al., 2007), when its interests are primary, as defined above.

Reification: The organization, once *it* exists as an *entitative being*, is recursively presentified and incarnated in standardized form as those forms are disseminated to broader publics and audiences external to the organizational boundaries. To be an organization, this form must be reified as an entitative being—an independent entity upon whose behalf and in whose name individuals and collectives continually act such that those interests remain primary and the *it* transcends and eclipses the humans comprising its collectivity.

That this model begins with "I" or individual action is not subject to Van Every's observation that our "default assumption" (Taylor, chapter 12, this volume, p. 209) is to habitually start with the individual as the basic social unit. It must be understood that the "I" in this model is fully embedded in a complex network of social significations (some of which are entitative beings), so what is already meaningful has not sprung from within the individual, but traces back to her or his social and organizational embeddedness and previous interactions. The "I" is explicitly and self-consciously an arbitrary beginning point because the "I" (the individual actor) is itself socially constructed by organizing processes (Czarniawska, chapter 1, this volume). In short, according to Robichaud et al. (2004) an individual can be seen as a text that has been produced from a previous conversation. Each individual who enters the conversation has been constructed by previous interactions with others, often in the context of another preexisting organization-as-entity. The "I," the "we," and the "it" must be continually defined recursively with one another, just as are collectivity, representation, and entitative being.

Weick (1995) offers an interesting overview of Wiley's (1988) solution to the micro-macro problem that is quite relevant here. Wiley posits several levels of sensemaking. At the individual level, the *intrasubjective* thoughts, feelings, and intentions are the sources of meaning (the "I"). *Intersubjective* meaning (the "we") becomes distinct from intrasubjective as those sources of meaning "are merged or synthesized into conversations during which the self gets transformed from 'I' into 'we'" (p. 71). This is not the creation of norms (social structure), but of *social reality*. The next level is the *generic subjective*; this is where Wiley, and subsequently Weick, locates organizations (the "it"). The notion of entitative being, transcending and eclipsing the human being(s) is apparent: "human beings, subjects, are no longer present.... Social structure implies a generic self, an interchangeable part—as filler of roles and follower of rules—but not concrete, individualized selves" (p. 71): Eclipsed, indeed. Wiley's final level, culture, is *extrasubjective*. Weick likens the extrasubjective to the institutional realm, which may be where the "it" is reified and understood in the stage model proposed herein.

Of course, by its theoretic nature, a phasic or stage model instantly raises questions of why or how movement occurs through the stages, the order and necessity of the stages, and the extent of their normativity and self-recursivity. Stage models in communication have historically been useful tools for framing questions, concretizing abstract processes, and grounding analysis (e.g., models of relational development or organizational socialization). When the research they have generated begins to raise questions too complex for a linear chronologic approach, stage models are abandoned. At this period of exploring the genesis of organization, however, we are in need of the concretization and framing a stage model can provide. Although we already know a great deal about the social construction of collectivity, the questions remain: how does a social collectivity become self-conscious (conception: how does *we* become *it*)? I suspect, as noted above, that hybrid agency plays some part here. How, then, does a self-conscious collectivity become an organization-as-entity (birth: *it* to *organization*)? What processes generate initial and subsequent presentification and incarnation? Does the process unfold differently for organizations that are conceived in preexisting social collectivities and organizations that are quite consciously created, the social collective assembled intentionally as a mode through which to build the new entity? What processes maintain the primary nature of the organization's interests to the extent that it is "acted for" significantly more than it "acts for"? How, then, do we account for things like nonprofit organizations whose raison d'être is precisely to act on the behalf of other collective entities? I do not pretend to suggest answers to these essentially discursive questions. The primary purpose of this paper is to present a model that frames these questions and provides a set of baseline concretized processes to ground our analysis. The secondary purpose is to discuss ontological issues that are brought insight by considering the six degrees metaphor alongside Tsoukas's (chapter 4, this volume) ontological components of organization and Robichaud et al.'s (2004) ontological framework. Having presented the model, it is to this latter task that I now turn.

Ontological Implications

Tsoukas (chapter 4, this volume) defines organization as "the ensemblizing of magmatic being." This definition is ripe for application across the process-product hyphen because of the concept of "ensemblization" from Castoriadis's (1975/1987) *ensemblist-identitary* logic. In Castoriadis's logic, society exists

> [O]nly insofar as it institutes itself and as it is instituted, and that institution is inconceivable without signification…. The institution of society is the institution of social doing and of social representing/ saying. (p. 360)

Inasmuch as organizations can be defined as signified social entities, or entitative beings, the ensemblist-identiary logic is an excellent fit for the present ontological purpose. "Magmatic being" refers to:

> [T]he mode of being of what gives itself before identitary or ensemblist logic is imposed…. A magma is that from which one can extract (or in which one can construct) an indefinite number of ensemblist organizations but which can never be reconstituted (ideally) by a (finite or infinite) ensemblist composition of these organizations. (1975/1987, p. 343)

Although Tsoukas explicitly addresses process, Castoriadis's *ensemblist-identitary* logic easily allows his ontology of organization to be applied to the product—the representation or "imagined" organization or organization-as-entity—because ensemblization is the hyphen in the process-product relation. Ontologically, the phasic model of organizational conception and birth can be seen as a model of ensemblization. The process-product (conversation-text) relation is not linear but recursive, so that the two are seen as mutually constitutive. The relation begins with process; then, we can identify points of conception and birth of an organization as a signified entity as process and product recursively and mutually constitute each other.

The Function of Language

Robichaud et al. (2004) base their analysis in the recursivity of language, conducting a narrative interpretation of sensemaking in language.

Arguing that communities and their narrative compose an organization, they utilize transcripts of public meetings between citizens and city government officials to illustrate the constitution of *metaconversation* as it simultaneously displays and reconstructs local conversations. In so doing, they illustrate the continual (re)generation of organizational identity and transcend the dichotomous ways in which organizations have traditionally been defined.

> Organization, as we usually conceive of it, is simultaneously pluralistic and unitary, multivocal and univocal, polyphonic and monophonic, many and one. If we are to avoid the appearance of paradox, the challenge that confronts us as organizational communication researchers is to identify the process that explains how a multiverse of domains of language use, each grounded in a set of practices, is transformed into a consolidated identity that is recognized as that of a singular actor—the organization. How, we are inquiring, is the multivocal translated into the univocal, and vice versa? (p. 618)

As Czarniawska (chapter 1, this volume) attempts to do with action nets and I attempt to do with the notion of entitative being, Robichaud et al. (2004) are specifically driven to explicate the hyphen in the process-product duality of organization. Using "modality," a property of language that indicates the relationship between the speaker and the utterance, they argue that language recursively produces *metaconversation*, "that is, the conversation in which a collective identity is constituted that is larger than that of the smaller communities of practice making up the organization" (p. 618), a striking parallel to entitative being. Modality mediates the recursive translation of conversation into text and text into conversation. Finally, narrativity is seen as central in such constitution: it helps structure the text used to account for events and informs the interaction that is the context of such accounting. Unlike most previous treatments of CCO, Robichaud et al. (2004) explicitly problematize the duality of organization.

> By "constitution," we mean both how the organization is established or constituted (a process view) and the unspoken set of underlying understandings about rights and responsibilities that characterizes that particular social entity—in effect, a kind of contract that participants have arrived at (a product view of constitution). (p. 624)

In short, we are all, in different ways with different points of entry, attempting to trace for organizations what Castioradis calls "ensemblization" in the construction of society. Robichaud et al. (2004) specifically seek the genesis of what I have called the *entitative being* similarly tracing it through collectivity:

The constitution of organization occurs in a metaconversation [emphasis original], where (1) "organization" refers to a language based social entity composed of multiple communities of practice or cognitive domains and (2) "occurs in a metaconversation" means emerging from the recursive processes of the conversations of the members, where each conversation narratively frames, implicitly or explicitly, the previous one. (p. 624)

Language unites individuals in collaborative activity. Collaborative activity defines collectivity. Collectivity creates the ground for representation and the emergence of an organizational entity: "To the extent that social entities or organizations persist and evolve, they do so through the mediation of language" (p. 619). Their analysis of language offers an enriching set of links between the conception/birth model and Tsoukas's ontological layers grounded in Castioradis's notion of ensemblization. It might be said that both Robichaud et al.'s recursivity of language and Czarniawska's action net have ensemblizing force.

The Components of Organization

Tsoukas (chapter 4, this volume) identifies three ontological "components" of organization: representation, practice, and action. Each is no more important than any other, and overemphasis on one must be avoided so as not to obscure the others.

Representation.   Tsoukas (chapter 4, this volume) specifies *representation* as the process of organization providing syntactic meaning and the bearer of Castioradis's ensemblistic-identitary (ensidic) logic that locates and singles out principles of identity, providing a logic of closure. The main features of organization seen in representation are categories, generalizations, rules, and routines. Knowledge is thus propositional and action instrumental. Representation, or syntactic meaning, thus provides us with the knowledge of the organization's *structure*, how it is "put together" (e.g., who is in charge of whom, what goals are primary, and who does what in pursuit of those goals).

In my phasic model of organizational conception and birth, Tsoukas's representation corresponds directly to my defining characteristic of representation of interests. At each phase, a set of interests is represented, beginning with the individual (preembedded and signified) and evolving through collective to a reified "organization." The key turning point is presentification, where an entitative being begins to emerge as the "thing" whose interests are primarily represented. In pursuit of those interests, individuals and collectives gain, through the representation component, their knowledge of what the entitative being's goals are and what the means are by which they are to be achieved (e.g., identification of specific tasks, division of that labor, and modes of operation by which to accomplish them). As such, individuals forge their identities according to this structure, thus allowing the entitative being to transcend and eclipse the human being(s). The organization-as-entity is thus structured in its representation so that things such as job descriptions, workload, rank, and status that define each person's organizational identity directly depend on the meaning derived from the ontological layer of representation.

According to Robichaud et al. (2004), the recursive embedding of one speech situation within another allows representation. Interestingly, they depict individual speakers as representing other individuals, entitative beings, and previous conversations. In a hypothetical conversation between union representatives *speaking for* strike-threatening employees and a management negotiation team *speaking for* the organization, "What is talked about is previous conversations, and those who are involved speak as representatives of these conversations. The metaconversation they engage in is based on the existence of an implicit canonical script made of social and institutional rules and contracts" (p. 623). This "canonical script" thus provides syntactic meaning and can be seen as constituted by the ensemblistic-identitary (ensidic) logic.

Practice.   Tsoukas (chapter 4, this volume) goes on to describe a nexus of practices providing semantic meaning, the bearer of cultural and contextual logic. Each practice is constituted in terms of three features. First, each involves the cooperative effort of human beings, is bound by rules, and is extended in time. Second, each establishes a set of internal goods—outcomes that cannot be achieved in any other way but through participating in the practice itself. Finally, by participating in a practice, each individual must necessarily attempt to achieve the standards of excellence operative in the practice at the time. In short, the nexus of practice provides tacit knowledge of what our behavior means in the context of the organization-as-entity and the commensurate ability to act appropriately in that context.

In the phasic model of organizational conception and birth, this practice component corresponds directly to my defining characteristic of collectivity. Tsoukas's "nexus of practices" strongly resembles Czarniawska's (chapter 1, this volume) action net. At each phase of the CCO model of conception and birth, the collective can be seen as forming from interaction that stems from a nexus of practices, or action net. As the organization-as-entity emerges, its own action net is assembled, linked to existing ones.

Why a net rather than a network? The difference between action net and network lies not in space but in time. Network assumes the existence of actors, who forge connections. Action net reverts this assumption, suggesting that connections between and among actions, when stabilized, are used to construct the identities of actors. One becomes a publisher when one starts to publish books or journals, which means that connections have already been made with such actions as writing and printing. (p. 14)

It is Czarniawska who points out that the crucial connections in the ontology of organization are not between *individuals* but between their *practices*, and once established these practices preexist any given individual's engagement in them. But the action net cannot spring fully formed from nothing. The model of conception/birth begins to show how an organization-as-entity emerges from the collectivity as interaction takes the form of a nexus of practices that recursively define that collectivity.

Robichaud et al. (2004) are likewise committed to an understanding of organizational communication as grounded in communities of practice. Communication both occurs in and is about a material and social world. Like Czarniawska (chapter 1, this volume), they point out that the essential component of collective identity is to be found in practice. "Salespersons are salespersons because they sell, computer programmers are programmers because they write software code, and so forth. But there is a consequence. To be recognized as an authentic member of such a community, one must display its practices" (p. 620). Practice, as an ontological layer, thus defines collectivity. Further, the development of self-consciousness of the collective (from *I am* a programmer to *we are* programmers), so crucial for the emergence of the *it* in the conception/birth model, is dependent on Robichaud et al.'s premise that "the primary function of language is to support collaborative activity, typically associated with some common field of practice" (p. 619). Organizations as entities are thus established from coorietational relationships among collectivities. These coorientational relationships are understood through a "quasi-contractual" set of understandings. Coorientation thus is more than a set of mutual orientations: The respective orientations are not between individual actors, but between categories of actor (Robichaud et al., 2004). Finally, these communities are multiple. An organization can be defined as

> [A] diversity of communities of practice engaged (or failing to be engaged) in the metaconversation, through their representatives. It is in this way that the structures of power, legitimation, and meaning are worked out over time, as Giddens (1984) has argued. Organization is thus simultaneously singular and plural—a universe and a multiverse. (p. 631)

Action. Using the term *action* quite differently from Czarniawska, Tsoukas (chapter 4, this volume) describes emergent patterns of action providing pragmatic meaning, the bearer of situational and recontextualized logic. It is here where organizational members improvise, interlocking their behaviors according to their narrative knowledge to accomplish practical things. Here, we might locate Searle's (1969) speech act: Human actors *do things with words* according to the knowledge they possess about how their actions can and cannot be coordinated with the actions of others. One of our basic assumptions in organizational communication is that organization is accomplished through, and can be described by, the coordination of human actions (March & Simon, 1958/1993).[3] Underlying this basic assumption is the implicit presumption that human actions are goal-directed. Most organizational communication scholars would reject a definition of "an organization" that described all organizational members as united by "common goals." We do, however, embrace the notions of interdependence and multiple goals, and most would agree that "an organization" could be described as a system of coordinated action, and that whether the coordination is intentional or not, the human action is rooted in agency. My contention here is that to examine the conception and birth of organization, we should particularly narrow the focus on agency to self-conscious collective agency.

In the organizational conception/birth model, Tsoukas's emergent patterns of action corresponds directly to my defining characteristic of the entitative being. Action here works in two important ways. First, individual actors move from acting for *themselves* to acting for *the emergent collective* to acting for *the emergent entitative being*. At each iteration, the individual relinquishes authority until she or he is eclipsed by the entitative being. As the collective emerges from those interlocked actions, it becomes an actant, acting first for itself but moving in the direction of acting, again, for the entitative being, increasingly relinquishing authority until it is eclipsed. As the entitative being is incarnated from interlocked collective actions, it takes the shape of these emergent patterns of action, transcending and eclipsing human individuals and collectives. This takes place on Wiley's (1988) *generic subjective* level of sensemaking (Weick, 1995, p. 71). Second, those emergent patterns of action function to reify the entitative being, representing it to external audiences as "the organization" and thus fortifying its ability to transcend and eclipse the human being(s) from which it came. And thus, a university can hire a cleaning firm, with both "universities" and "cleaning firms" understood as specific institutional types on Wiley's *extrasubjective* level of sensemaking (Weick, 1995, p. 72). The entitative being can be unquestionably said to *act*, regardless of the fact that, in Castioradis's terms, it is a wholly *imaginary* being. Through these emergent patterns of action, classes are taught, students earn credentials, research is accomplished, grants are funded and rejected, and all the while the floors get mopped, all of this imagined without regard to any individuals because these patterns of action have allowed the entitative being to transcend and eclipse the human being(s).

Robichaud et al. (2004) view the successive embedding of one text within another text, each with its own context of enunciation, as the site of recursions organizing implications. They describe it as climbing a ladder rung by rung to produce metanarrative. "This is how the FBI gets to 'be frustrated,' how the department 'is forced to admit,' how the Senate comes 'to approve'" (p. 623), just as universities hire cleaning firms. Whereas my emphasis is on the entity, theirs is on the action, but the observation is the same. Furthermore, as previously noted, narrativity has a central role in Robichaud et al.'s treatment of constitution. Narrativity allows individual actors to interlock their behaviors and account for the products of those interconnected actions. It is from the unfolding of such interlocked activities that identities emerge, linking individuals to communities and entitative beings. The community's sensemaking activities are seen as narratively based and assymetrical, emerging from a "complementarity of social activities; there is no selling without buying and no heroic actions without menacing ones" (p. 620). It is this very assymetrical structure of interlocking actions and meanings that allows for ensemblezation.

Conclusion

Following Tsoukas's (chapter 4, this volume) logic, the three components of organizational ontology are the very stuff of ensemblization. The three efforts to unpack the process-product hyphen highlighted here, my own model of organizational conception and birth, Czarniawska's (chapter 1, this volume) action net theory, and Robichaud et al.'s (2004) theory of metaconversation, can all be seen as efforts to trace ensemblezation. Once the organization-as-entity is defined as a specific kind of socially signified entity—one whose interests are primary and represented in the actions of individual and collective agents, a collective nonhuman entitative being—the "degrees of separation" metaphor allows a unique way to concretely map ensemblezation as the development of a "we" from an "I," an "it" from a "we," and the subsequent reification of that "it." Both Czarniawska's action net (chapter 1, this volume) and Robichaud et al.'s (2004) metaconversation offer unique opportunities to explore the many questions raised by this conceptualization of recursive stages of organizational conception and birth. In all, these efforts show clearly that our understanding of organizations as dual (process-product, verb and noun) have led organizational scholars to privilege one ontology over the other, and that the real stuff of organizational ontology lies between them, in the hyphen, where both verb and noun exist recursively with one another.

Notes

1. *Naming* seems to be key to entitative being—once "it" has been brought into being, it must be named (see Brummans et al., 2009). The importance of *naming* to the nature of entitative being is beyond the scope of this chapter, but it is clear that naming is key. In a locally famous court battle in New York State, a vintner

named Walter S. Taylor was enjoined from using the name "Taylor" or any likeness of the Taylor family on his labels. As the story goes, the original Taylor Wine
Cellars was founded in the 1950s at Bully Hill Farms by Walter S. Taylor and his
father Greyton Taylor. Walter was fired in the 1970s for publicly denouncing the
common practice of fortifying New York wines with California wine. He subsequently bottled wine under the company name Bully Hill Vineyards, touting it as
producing "100% New York State wines." Several years later, Taylor Wines was
sold to a corporate interest (famously rumored to be Coca-Cola), which prevailed
in a lawsuit against Bully Hill Vineyards to prevent Walter from using the Taylor
family name. Walter was enjoined to destroy all paintings, artwork, poetry, and
promotional materials that mentioned the Taylor name, described his heritage, or
used likenesses of his ancestors. A talented artist, Walter adopted a sketch of a grin-
ning goat with its tongue sticking out as his company logo with the motto, "They
got my name and heritage, but they didn't get my goat!" a phrase that appeared
on numerous labels t-shirts, and signs. He sold stuffed plush goats in the Bully
Hill gift shop. Also, he adopted many other creative practices of resistance. For
example, he used "Walter S. blank" with the Taylor name blacked out on Bully Hill
promotional materials and labels, and he printed labels bearing unnamed sketches
of his ancestors with heavy black lines over their eyes or wearing a "Lone Ranger"
mask. Because of these acts of resistance (called "the antics of Walter S. Taylor" by
the presiding judge), the original order was declared to be overly restrictive; today,
Bully Hill promotional materials clearly proclaim the Taylor family heritage (see
www.bullyhill.com). The winery also publicly displays a sign proclaiming, "A product is the extension of the human soul." (The court order documenting this story is
available online from volume 590 of *The Federal Reporter*, 2nd edition, December,
1978–March, 1979 at http://legal.rights.com/F.2d/590/590.F2d.701.78-7272.272.
html)
2. Apple Computer, Inc. began with the partnership of Steve Jobs and Steve Wozniak
assembling and selling one of the first preassembled personal computers, the Apple
I (a reference to Sir Isaac Newton) initially to hobbyists and then to retail stores.
The Macintosh, or Mac, was introduced after the corporation was well-established.
3. Although Czarniawska (chapter 1, this volume) claims that "the 'coordinated
action' part has been omitted by most of [March and Simon's] followers, with the
exception of J. R. Taylor and Van Every (2000)" (p. 8), I disagree. This may be the
case in the international multidisciplinary arena of organizational studies in general, but it is my observation that, at least in the United States where my experience
is based, organizational communication scholars are quite careful to maintain a
focus on the ways in which communication functions to coordinate human action.
This is the way many of us were trained in the discipline of communication, and
I continue to observe that this basic idea is customarily taught in organizational
communication courses in the United States. Another difference is in her observation that as a whole we focus too much on "organizations" and not enough on
"organizing." It is my observation that in the communication corner of organizational studies, we overfocus on "organizing," consistently teaching the Weickian
notion that "organization" is a process and losing any sense that "organizations"
are reified entities. It is, in fact, my frustration with this observation that initially
inspired this piece.

6 What Is an Organization? Or: Is James Taylor a Buddhist?

Boris H. J. M. Brummans

An infinite time has run its course before my birth; what was I throughout all that time? Metaphysically, the answer might perhaps be: I was always I; that is, all who during that time said I, were in fact I. (Jorge Luis Borges citing Schopenhauer, 1999, p. 8)

Those things of which I can perceive the beginnings and the end are not my self. (Jorge Luis Borges citing Grimm, 1999, p. 8)

I

For many centuries, people in various parts of the world have examined the nature of the universe and the human mind, resulting in numerous philosophies. In this essay, I will describe the Tibetan Mahayana Buddhist philosophy of *sunyata* and use its claims about the universe and the mind to provide a new lens for reading James Taylor's ideas about the communicative constitution of organizations. As I will show, Taylor's outlook invites this kind of Buddhist reading because it focuses on the ways in which actors jointly embody and enact the world. While Weick and others have recently started to explore Buddhism to rethink our understanding of processes of organizing (see Weick & Putnam, 2006; Weick & Sutcliffe, 2006), I will attempt to show how a Buddhist interpretation of Taylor's ideas not only can be used to develop a more communicative view of the processes these authors describe, but a different way of looking at organizations altogether. Since my thinking is so deeply steeped in Tibetan Mahayana Buddhism, I will start by explaining this philosophy, trying to be as precise as possible within the scope of this text and the limits of my own understanding.

II

Tibetan Mahayana Buddhism, with the notion of *sunyata* at its heart, poses an outlook that at first may seem far-fetched. The Sanskrit word *sunyata* stands for "emptiness" or "voidness," yet it is not meant to imply "nothingness" (Vimalamitra, 2000). Rather, it is said to be equivalent to the idea of "dependent origination" or the "interdependent arising of conditions" (see Keown, 2004, p. 282), which entails that things (plants, animals, human beings, artifacts, etc.) do not have an inherent, permanent existence, but arise (and subside) because their condition depends on (is interdependent with) other conditions (see also Gyatso, 1982/2005; Shantideva, 1997/1999). Thus, Mahayana Buddhists do not claim that nothing exists (which would imply nihilism), but that the concepts used to define phenomena with a seemingly intrinsic, independent, permanent nature ("myself," "this tree," "that house," "we," "they"), which are intimately connected to, influenced by, and embodied through perceptions, feelings, impulses, habits, and actions, are "empty" or "void" (i.e., only impermanent, interdependently arising conditions).[1] In turn, the realities in which people find themselves "enmeshed" (Rosch, 2007, p. 259) are generally perceived and experienced as inherently real, a mode of seeing and being that, Buddhists believe, induces "ego attachments," the clinging to one's own sense of self and the selves of others (i.e., the individual identities of things and people). These attachments are consequently presumed to create three interrelated forms of suffering: hatred (symbolized by a snake), desire (cock), and ignorance (pig) (see Keown, 2004, p. 31).

By becoming mindful of *sunyata* (through discussion and debate, the study of Buddhist sutras or canonical scriptures, meditation, and a disciplined lifestyle, all guided by a trusted teacher), Mahayana Buddhists claim that it is possible to liberate oneself from these "Three Poisons." This does not imply trying to suppress one's feelings in a cold, detached manner, but fostering awareness about the interdependent arising of conditions and letting the wisdom and feelings of compassion yielded by this awareness guide one's actions in the world.[2] Mahayana Buddhists suppose that any human being has the ability to develop this kind of mindfulness, since it is not believed to come from without but to be always already within the mind, like a mirror hidden underneath layers of dust (see Evans-Wentz, 1954/2000, p. 3). Hence, anybody can "access" the mentioned wisdom and compassion within him- or herself, and thus advance great happiness for all sentient beings.

III

Several scholars have thought about what Buddhist mindful organizing might look like, and what its advantages might be. In 1973, for instance, the British economist and philosopher E. F. Schumacher argued that organizing in view of Buddhist philosophy might promote the well-being of an organization as well as society and nature at large. More recently, Kernochan, McCormick, and White (2007) argued for the importance of compassion, mindfulness, and selflessness in management education by reflecting on their own Buddhist practices. In addition, Weick and Putnam

(2006) presented an intriguing look at the role of Buddhist mindfulness in processes of organizing, grounded in the philosophy of *sunyata* (see also Weick & Sutcliffe, 2006). According to these authors, mindful organizing involves "diminished dependence on concepts, increased focus on sources of distraction, and greater reliance on acts with meditative properties" (p. 275). Hence, those who engage in this form of organizing presumably face a paradoxical challenge: "Attempts to increase mindfulness in an organizational context are complicated, because organizations are established, held together, and made effective largely by means of concepts" (p. 281). Investigating this issue more deeply is important, because it may show how people "keep reaccomplishing the coordination and interdependence associated with collective action" and deal with "the inevitability of suffering" involved in trying to reaccomplish order as it "keeps rising and falling, appearing and disappearing, forming and dissolving" (p. 283). In other words, understanding mindful organizing may help people enact organizations by taking impermanence as a point of departure rather than something to combat and thereby alleviate "stress, tension, and anger" (p. 276).

A question that has received little attention so far but might advance the study of Buddhist organizing is this: How does communication figure into organizing processes that are grounded in the Buddhist philosophy of dependent origination? To develop a response to this question, I turn to James Taylor's work.

IV

Through personal conversations, e-mail correspondence, and reading most of his published (and unpublished) work, it has become clear to me over the past years that James Taylor will never want to wed himself to a particular movement, let alone a religion or spirituality. He thus remains "uncornerable"—and thankfully so. In spite of this, Taylor seems driven by something, namely the pursuit of understanding how organizations are constituted within ongoing cycles of interaction between networks and subnetworks of interdependent human and nonhuman agents:[3] atoms are composed of +/– relationships between electrons and protons; farmers work their lands together with their oxen, who arguably collaborate as much as they resist the farmers' efforts; reporters and cameramen work in tandem, yet with different objectives in mind (reporters intend to give a good account of what is going on, while cameramen aim to shoot the event in the best way possible). Through pushing and pulling, engaging and disengaging, competing and collaborating, different types of agents constitute connections that fold into each other or "imbricate," scaling up and down, and thereby create the ongoing dynamics of what people call "organizations" (see esp. Taylor & Van Every, 2000).

More often than not these dynamics seem messy. Yet as Taylor has shown, there is an underlying orderliness to them, at least as far as they are grounded in patterns of human communication. According to Taylor and Van Every (2011), human agents play out "language-games" (Wittgenstein, 1953) that follow a particular "form," which is not to say that the paths of agents are always already predetermined. Indeed, texts act upon human agents by confronting them with previous ways of operating, sensemaking, and so on, yet human agents also define, question, and redefine the meaning of the texts that guide and structure their interactions by engaging in ongoing conversations[4] (see Robichaud, Giroux, & Taylor, 2004; Taylor, 2001a; Taylor, Cooren, Giroux, & Robichaud, 1996; Taylor & Van Every, 2000). For example, members of a reputable accounting firm may try to change a specific costing procedure (text) they have used for years through various meetings and informal discussions (conversation), even if this brings about resistance from certain colleagues who do not see the need for change. For Taylor, the interplay between text and conversation lies at the heart of the language-games that motor processes of organizing, but what exactly does he have in mind when he speaks of these language-games having a certain form? What generates or fuels these games? To answer this question, Taylor's concept of "worldview" needs to be introduced—a notion he has tried to explicate in several texts (see Groleau & Taylor, 1996; Taylor, 1995b, 2000a, 2001a, 2005, 2011; Taylor & Cooren, 2006; Taylor, Gurd, & Bardini, 1997) but, in his own opinion, "never been able to get quite right."

V

Perhaps the difficulty with the idea of worldview is that it is a little awkward as a communication term because it suggests that an individual agent simply "sees" the world in a particular way—Merriam-Webster refers to the German *Weltanschauung*, "a comprehensive conception or apprehension of the world especially from a specific standpoint." Nothing could be farther from Taylor's conception, though, since for him the transaction between two agents (A and B) is the point of departure; not the individual entities themselves. Both are bound together by being oriented toward a common object of value (X), yet construct its meaning in an opposing way during their ongoing interactions because they do not share the same feelings, perceptions, bodies, histories, identities, modes of operating, and social/organizational roles or positions. Hence, their communication encounter implies that they "coorient" (a term Taylor has appropriated from Newcomb, 1953) toward the object by "worldviewing" in opposing ways.

To give an example, an accountant (agent A) and her client (agent B) may engage in interaction to resolve a particular tax issue (object X) with the Internal Revenue Service (IRS) (collective/macro agent C). The relation between accountant and client can be represented in simplified form as: A-X-B. In this situation, A enacts her role as accountant on behalf of her accounting firm (which we could call collective/macro actor D). Her string of activities consists of discussing the issue with her client, investigating the issue based on her accounting expertise, filling out specific forms, representing the client to the IRS in meetings with IRS agents, and so on. B acts out his social role as a client, "in his own name." His activities involve explaining his problem to A, signing the forms A has prepared, paying A for her services, etc. While A and B are joined in their orientation toward X, for A, it constitutes an integral part of her profession. It allows her to enact a specific role and generate income for her company and, via the company, for herself. In turn, successfully resolving the issue also helps to corroborate her expertise to the company that employs her and to her client with whom she has built a trustful relationship over the years. For B, X simply constitutes a nuisance he hopes to clear away as soon as possible. Nonetheless, resolving the issue is important for him because it keeps him out of legal trouble and corroborates his identity as a "good U.S. citizen who pays his taxes" to the federal government, to his family and friends, and to others.

Even an everyday example like this illustrates that any communication situation is always enacted through transactions between two parties engaged in a different way of "worldviewing." Taylor argues that looking at these differences can help us explain, for an important part, how human interactions are enacted, whether involving sellers and buyers, husbands and wives, or former U.S. President Jimmy Carter and former Israeli President Menachem Begin; in fact, in several recent conversations Taylor even voiced the belief that the principle of worldview may pertain to human-nonhuman (e.g., farmer and ox) and nonhuman-nonhuman interactions (e.g., ape 1 and ape 2 or a set of electrons and protons), since they all involve situations in which each party is "embedded in their own socially [or naturally] defined space-time envelope" (Taylor, 2011, p. 14).

VI

Taylor and Van Every (2011) draw on Bateson (1972) to deepen their explication of worldview, arguing that differences in worldview lead to the enactment of different kinds of relationships. "Symmetrical differentiation" occurs when two parties/agents "have the same aspirations and the same behavior patterns, but are differentiated in the orientation of these patterns" (Bateson, 1972, p. 68). Hence, in this case, two agents rival each other in trying to achieve a goal (X) by engaging in win-lose interactions. This kind of interaction can be seen in the competition between athletes or the rivalry between nations: A pushes B, B pushes back, which stimulates A to push even harder. Unless checked, this mode of interaction may lead to aggressive behavior, which may ultimately destroy the relationship—a

process Bateson called "schismogenesis." "Complementary differentiation" occurs when "the behavior and aspirations of the members of the
two groups are fundamentally different" (p. 68); they complement rather
than oppose each other: If A pushes B, B gives in. This kind of interaction can be found in interactions between different classes or castes, or
in colonizer-colonized interactions. Also here, schismogenesis may result,
if pushed too far. A third type of relationship is possible, which Bateson
called "reciprocity." If a reciprocal relationship is enacted, agents' asymmetrical moves balance each other out, leading to a situation in which
neither party engages in a destructive tug of war or entirely dominates or
submits to the other. "The reciprocal pattern ... is compensated and bal-
anced within itself and therefore does not tend toward schismogenesis"
(p. 69).

These ways of viewing human (and perhaps also nonhuman) interactions are indicative of Taylor's belief that two agents cannot worldview in
the same way because they are differently positioned historically, socially,
and materially in a given context—just like two fermions (electrons, protons, or neutrons) cannot simultaneously occupy the same space according to the Pauli exclusion principle in physics. As Taylor writes, using a
buyer–seller relationship as an example,

> Each partner to the transaction, seller and buyer, is embedded in their
> own socially defined space-time envelope. Each belongs to its own
> community of practice. Each has its own purposes, its own sched-
> ule and its own modes of sensemaking. Buying and selling are thus
> perceived by those involved through different lenses, coming from
> different experiential worlds.... Worldview is thus a property of rela-
> tionship. There are always, and only ever, two worldviews exemplified
> in any bilateral transaction. The relationship establishes a distinction
> of worldview. To the extent that people enter into a transaction, they
> inherit a point of view that it, by definition, establishes. But of course,
> the converse is also true. As ethnomethodologists have consistently
> argued, it is the transaction that reflexively constitutes the roles of
> buyer and seller, and thus confers identity on the agents who embody
> those roles. There is thus an inherent tension in the enactment of
> organizational process. Communication is not neutral. True, you and
> I together compose a we: a fusion of two into one. But we err if we
> forget that every we is also decomposable into an I and a you. An
> organization is both a we and yet simultaneously a collection of I's,
> we's, and you's. (p. 112)

So for Taylor, "because all transactionally based communication is an
encounter of worldviews it implies differences. Communication engenders
asymmetric, complementary relationships" (p. 19). His world is inherently
dualistic in the sense that it is composed of continuously opposing, yet

interdependent forces. It is here, I believe, where the links between Taylor's vision and Tibetan Buddhist philosophy start to show in particular.

VII

As I have explained, the Buddhist philosophy of dependent origination posits that nothing exists independently; all things, whether rocks, plants, animals, or human beings, exist as interdependently arising conditions. What I also explained was that many human agents (and possibly many nonhuman ones as well, although this is hard to prove) conceive of and experience themselves as independent entities with a more or less unique identity or self. What I did not explain yet is the idea that this way of experiencing occurs, according to Mahayana Buddhists who follow the Vajrayana Dzogchen teachings[5] because agents embody and enact the world based on a "dual mind." This specific kind of mind zooms in on the dual nature of things (I–you, we–they, this–that, good–bad, etc.). However, it is also possible to embody and enact the world based on "nondual mind," a form of awareness that centers on nonduality and that is said to arise by itself, to appear spontaneously without the efforts, control, or will of a self, and to be always already within us—albeit often overshadowed by the dual mind.

Buddhist scholar Henry Vyner (Vyner, 2002, 2004a,b, 2005) describes the difference between dual and nondual mind as follows: When the mind operates in dualistic mode, it experiences itself as being two minds; one is the stream of consciousness, which presents meanings to the mind's awareness in the form of a temporal sequence of fleeting thoughts, impressions, feelings, words, and emotions; the other is the observer or watcher of this stream, which either responds to the stream or just watches (see also Rosch, 1999, 2008). The experience that some entity monitors the mind is what gives people the impression that there is a duality between subject (watcher) and object (stream of consciousness). What distinguishes dual from nondual mind is the awareness with which the watcher operates: The "conceptual ["ordinary"] mind" (see also Thondup Rinpoche, 1995/2001, p. 15) acts dualistically, as an ego. In this case, it habitually responds to the meanings presented by the stream of consciousness by accepting, rejecting, or following thoughts, impressions, and feelings (e.g., repressing or acting upon an emotion). This occurs in light of particular "ego-narratives," stories, told, embodied, and acted out, over and over again, which construct the self in a particular way vis-à-vis other selves and filter and influence the experience of self vis-à-vis others. If the watcher is able to observe the stream without accepting, rejecting, or following meanings (which does not happen overnight and may require years of practice under the guidance of a Buddhist teacher), the duality between watcher and stream is said to cease, allowing nondual awareness, to arise spontaneously, by itself.

VIII

Where Taylor's view and ancient Tibetan Buddhist philosophy meet is in their focus on the way dual minds construct and enact their worlds within and without. While Buddhist philosophy expressly centers on an individual human being's delicate thinking, feeling, and acting processes, Taylor adds a detailed explanation of the ways in which connections between dual minds are continuously created through the textual and conversational constitution and reconstitution of systems of embodied concepts, which fuel the dualities within and between individuals and collectivities. Closely following Mead (1934), Taylor's view assumes that living organisms become "minded" through their capacity to creatively use what Mead calls "significant symbols" (language, both verbal and nonverbal) in interactions rather than to simply react in conditioned ways. According to Taylor (and Mead), language enables organisms to reflect on and be conscious of their selves as objects in relation to other selves[6] with whom they constitute a community or society—not unlike Vyner's description of the experiential duality between the watcher and the stream of consciousness. Like Mead, Taylor thus points out that mind and self are part and parcel of communication processes rather than entities which are somehow external to, or independent from, ongoing interactions. Walking in Mead's footsteps, Taylor seems to argue that it is by internalizing/learning a society's language that an organism becomes minded, and that it is by taking particular social roles, defined by and in this language ("child," "parent," "student," "professor," "entrepreneur," "politician," etc.), that a minded individual comes to see itself as "a self" with particular attributes—or a multitude or "parliament" of selves.

While Taylor's view much resembles Mead's, it emphasizes especially the dualistic nature of human life: an I is defined in relation to a me or, as Mead said, a "generalized other." I equals "not-you" (although it is defined in relation to it and can only exist due to this relation) and presupposes a particular relationship between (frequently dualistic) roles, such as "I, the professor; you, the student" or "I, the client" and "you, the accountant." But Taylor and several of his colleagues go further than this (see Cooren & Taylor, 1997; Robichaud et al., 2004; Taylor & Cooren, 2006; Taylor, Cooren, Giroux, & Robichaud, 1996; Taylor & Van Every, 2000), claiming that a group of I's may refer to their collectivity of selves as a we and an us ("we, the United States of America"; "we, the Apple Macintosh Corporation"). In turn, because they have become an entity or "it," they may distinguish themselves from other "it's" or collective actors ("they, the Arab nations"; "they, Microsoft"). Through the use of significant symbols in text and conversation, individual human agents (or selves) consequently allow themselves to speak and act on behalf of a collectivity, whether it is a community, organization, or nation. For example, when Steve Jobs introduced the newest Apple Macintosh gadget to his employees, he was not just speaking on behalf of himself, but also on behalf of his company and, indirectly, on behalf of all the people who constitute it. Thus, "macro-actors" (Callon & Latour, 1981) like organizations act and express themselves through various spokespersons, as can be seen in everyday expressions, such as "the FBI is frustrated," "the university denounced the professor's actions," or "China believes the Dalai Lama has instigated the recent protests in Tibet." However, as one of Taylor's students, François Cooren, has shown, not only human agents help to constitute an organization in this way, but also nonhuman ones, such as texts, machines, artifacts, and so on (see also Brummans, Cooren, & Chaput, 2009; Cooren, 2004, 2006; Cooren, Brummans, & Charrieras, 2008; Cooren, Fox, Robichaud, & Talih, 2005; Cooren, Matte, Taylor, & Vásquez, 2007). Hence, any kind of agent can be mobilized (or mobilize itself) to act on behalf of a collectivity and thereby re-present it or make it present again and again. What Taylor keeps insisting on, though, is the idea that all these agents worldview differently, dualistically, creating ongoing cycles of pushing and pulling, engaging and disengaging, competing and collaborating, which tend to be perceived as the basic dynamics of organizations (and life more generally).

Tibetan Buddhists seek to break these cycles to constitute a way of life in which all sentient beings feel freer, more compassionate, and happier. What is needed for this, they argue, is the cultivation of mindfulness, which liberates oneself from one's self, so to speak; that is, from the dualistic awareness that impedes nondual mind. In other words, according to Mahayana and especially Vajrayana Buddhists, conceiving of and experiencing the world filtered through concepts and significant symbols necessarily forces people to think, perceive, act, and feel dualistically. It encourages putting "things" (ideas, feelings, thoughts, etc.) in "boxes" or category systems to keep the world "orderly," "controllable," "understandable," or "graspable." Note that the Latin root of the word "concept," *conceptum* (from *concipere*), refers to something "taken in and held onto" or "grasped."

This is not very distant from Weick's (and Taylor's) understanding of sensemaking, which entails making the world sensible through ongoing processes of communication. For example, quoting Taylor and Van Every (2000, p. 58), Weick, Sutcliffe, and Obstfeld (2005) argue that communication can be seen

> as an ongoing process of making sense of the circumstances in which people collectively find [themselves] and of the events that affect them. The sensemaking, to the extent that it involves communication, takes place in interactive talk and draws on the resources of language in order to formulate and exchange through talk (or in other media such as graphics) symbolically encoded representations of these

circumstances. As this occurs, a situation is talked into existence and the basis is laid for action to deal with it.

Weick and Taylor see life as consisting of "piles of cues" (Weick, 1999, p. 41) in need of being bracketed. In line with William James's (1890/1950) observations, they perceive it as "a buzzing, pulsating, formless mass of signals, out of which people try to make sense, into which they attempt to introduce order, and from which they construct against a background that remains undifferentiated" (Czarniawska, 1998, p. 1, cited in Weick, 2006, p. 1724). Creating a sensible world through verbal (and nonverbal) language thus "seduces" one to operate dualistically, for it encourages labeling; that is, "differentiation and simple-location, identification and classification, regularizing and routinization [translate] the intractable or obdurate into a form that is more amenable to functional deployment" (Chia, 2000, cited in Weick et al., 2005, p. 411), which is essential for the constitution of individual and collective selfhoods (see Weick et al., 2005). In turn, as can easily be seen in daily life situations (e.g., the interactions between a father and his son, an accountant and her client, Israelis and Palestinians), a particular way of sensemaking implies a particular way of worldviewing, which yields clinging to a particular sense of individual and collective self vis-à-vis individual and collective selves that are seen as separate, independent, or altogether different (see also Rosch, 1999, 2008).

Taylor's focus on the dualistic nature of life becomes even clearer in his writings on narrative, which he believes (as does Weick) plays a pivotal role in the constitution of individual and collective selves. Robichaud et al. (2004) state, for example, that organizational participants are "'role-bearing individuals bound up in processes instantiated as events in mentally projected storyworlds' (Herman, 2002, p. 120)" (p. 619). Here again the close resemblance between Taylor's and Mead's ideas shines through. However, seeing people as being caught up in their own projected narratives also shows a close likeness with the Buddhist philosophy I have explained. As Robichaud et al. note, the use of significant symbols allows human beings to create and enact narratives, including the ego-narratives of which Vyner (2002) speaks: "Narrative is language's natural provision for making sense of both individual experience and social interaction. It establishes the objects and events to which people's attention is directed, and it provides a complex set of identities and roles that individual actors may enact" (Robichaud et al., 2004, p. 619). By keeping up a particular story as part of their ongoing conversations, groups of people also constitute social collectivities, such as organizations, Robichaud et al. claim, which leads to collective (and individual) differentiation: "It is not simply that others are not recognized as being 'in' the conversation of the community; they are constituted narratively as 'out.' A boundary is created, in its most basic form, as an us and a them." (p. 621). It is particularly due to the narrative nature of human sensemaking, then, that social life is constituted dualistically:

> What determines the character of a particular cognitive domain—and its associated community of practice—is how the people who are linked to each other by a common preoccupation with some object *make distinctions*. Narrative theory is precisely concerned with the way distinctions are made: what the objectives are, who the actors are, and what the underlying contractual understandings are and who respects them, as well as who breaches them. Identities emerge out of the unfolding of activities—identities that are specific to the narratively based sensemaking activities of that particular community. The *inherent asymmetry* of narrative sensemaking also emerges from the complementarity of social activities; there is no selling without buying and no heroic actions without menacing ones. (p. 620, emphasis added)

IX

Let me now explain how Tibetan Mahayana Buddhism and in particular the Vajrayana philosophy of nondual mind differs from Taylor's view of the world. I believe Vajrayana Buddhism extends Taylor's vision by showing that the world may seem inherently dualistic to human beings who attempt to make sense of it by using concepts and significant symbols, yet that an alternative, nondual mode of perceiving, being, and operating is possible. Hence, Tibetan Buddhism encourages us to look differently at ourselves as individuals and (organized) collectivities. In what follows, I will develop this alternative view by drawing on Francisco Varela's work, particularly his 1999 book, *Ethical Know-How*, which aligns discoveries made by modern science with insights from Buddhist philosophy (see also Varela, Thompson, & Rosch, 1992). Additionally, I will refer to Eleanor Rosch's Buddhist readings of human perception, conceptualization, and experience, which will be equally helpful in substantiating my ideas (see Rosch, 1999, 2004, 2007, 2008).

In his 1999 book, Varela shows how a society of interacting nonhuman agents, such as a colony of insects or community of apes, acts as a whole that is not only larger than its parts, but actually constitutes an organism in itself that both interacts with and enacts its environment (quite similar to Weick's (1979, 1995) ideas—Varela refers to "enaction" rather than "enactment." Thus, a society of insects or apes constitutes a "selfless self" or "virtual self"; that is, it acts as a more or less coherent whole yet lacks a central agent. To support this claim, Varela (1999) provides the example of a beehive or ants' nest:

The beehive and the ants' nest have long been considered "superorganisms," but this was little more than a metaphor until recently. It was not until the 1970s that detailed experiments were made whose results could not be explained without taking into account the entire colony. In one particularly elegant experiment, the most efficient nurses in a *Neoponera apicalis* colony were removed from a subcolony. These nurses radically changed social status, foraging more and nursing less. The contrary happened in the main colony: formerly low-level nurses increased their nursing activity. The whole colony, however, showed evidence of both configurational identity and memory. When the efficient nurses were returned to the main colony, they resumed their previous status. What is particularly striking about the insect colony is that its separate components are individuals and that it has no center or localized "self." Yet the whole does behave as if there were a coordinating agent present at its center. This corresponds exactly to what I mean by a selfless (or virtual) self: a coherent global pattern that emerges from the activity of simple local components, which seems to be centrally located, but is nowhere to be found, and yet is essential as a level of interaction for behavior of the whole. (pp. 52–53)

Varela's description suggests that what is true for a collectivity of non-human agents like bees is probably true for any society of agents. For example, a human being like, let's say, James Taylor may appear to be a more or less stable self that interacts with the world in which it is situated, yet on a more microscopic level "James Taylor" simply is a name an observer (he himself or someone else) attributes to "a coherent global pattern that emerges from the activity of simple local components," such as the innumerable interacting atoms and molecules that compose Taylor's body, brain, etc. "James Taylor" is thus a virtual self, in Varela's sense, which emerges (and subsides) in actual, concrete contexts enacted through the ongoing interactions between interdependent human and nonhuman agents who together embody or "incarnate" "him." Varela's work suggests, in line with Mead's (1934) ideas, that even Taylor's mind emerges out of the continuous interactions between subnetworks of human and nonhuman agents, turning mind into a dynamic process that, emerges as an embodied aspect "of actual complex situations" (Rosch, 1999, p. 73; see also Rosch, 2004). (Evidently, this view challenges Latour's distinction between humans and nonhumans actors, because it shows that nonhumans are quite essential for the constitution of human ones; see also Brummans et al., 2009).

Particularly interesting about Varela's conception of the world is that it comes close to Taylor's (and Cooren's) conception of organizing, of what it means to be an organization, and of what an organization is. However, while Taylor and Cooren concur that an organization is a virtual self or "fiction" (see esp. Brummans et al., 2009; Cooren & Taylor, 1997), they do not extrapolate this view to individual human agents like organizational employees, let alone nonhuman ones, such as texts or buildings. That is, the individual (esp. human) selves that incarnate a larger, virtual "macro-self" (the organization) are regarded as somehow "nonvirtual," which is untenable not only from a Buddhist point of view, but also, as Varela (1999) shows, from a modern scientific point of view. Varela demonstrates, for instance, that even an individual human being's brain is composed of innumerable agents working together at dizzying speeds, creating the impression of "a more or less coherent brain":

> Nothing … suggests that the brain "processes" information in [an input-processing-output fashion]; such popular, computer-like descriptions of the workings of the brain are simply incorrect. Instead, the architecture of the brain supports a different kind of operation: signals move "back and forth," gradually becoming more coherent until a microworld has been constituted. The entire exercise takes a certain amount of time, which accounts for why every animal exhibits a natural temporal parsing. In this human brain this flurry of cooperation [between societies or subnetworks of agents] typically takes about 200–500 msec, the "nowness" of a perceptual-motor unity. Contrary to what seems to be the case from a cursory introspection, cognition does not flow seamlessly from one "state" to another, but rather consists in a punctuated succession of behavioral patterns that arise and subside in measurable time. This insight of recent neuroscience—and of cognitive science in general—is fundamental, for it relieves us from the tyranny of searching for a centralized, homuncular quality to account for a cognitive agent's normal behavior. (pp. 48–49)

Varela's idea of a virtual self thus invites us to question the notion that human beings are like homunculi running around frantically in a multitude of environments of the world. Additionally, it challenges a whole range of dualities (e.g., between the individual and the collective, the micro and the macro, and the human and the nonhuman), and it suggests that whether one perceives and experiences these dualities depends on the kind of awareness with which one operates, in line with the Buddhist philosophy I have explained. Hence, one may see things (e.g., a beehive, a bee, James Taylor, or the Microsoft company) as more or less stable, individual entities that interact with "the world" and foreground their uniqueness and differences vis-à-vis other entities. Alternatively, one may see an ongoing flow of interacting human and nonhuman agents whose identities can be deconstructed to infinite regress because they are virtual selves composed of "sub" virtual selves and "sub-sub" virtual selves.[7]

If someone operates based on dual awareness, the former mode of perceiving is active. In this case, the interdependencies between agents move to the background and become blurry. It seems as if a composite of nonvirtual selves are enmeshed in interactional games in which they engage by worldviewing differently because they are "embedded in their own socially [or naturally] defined space-time envelope" (Taylor, 2011, p. 14). Selves are seen and experienced as separate things with separate minds and bodies that are separate from their environments (see Rosch, 1999, p. 71; see also Rosch, 2008). As I have explained, through this mode of awareness, individual human agents—and even collective nonhuman ones, as Taylor has pointed out—gain their sense of personal "I" vis-à-vis "me," "us" vs. "them," etc.

If someone cultivates nondual awareness, the selfless nature of selves, whether human or nonhuman, individual or collective, become the center of attention. In this case, one becomes more and more suspicious of one's "feeling of 'I' as a true center" (Varela, 1999, p. 61). One becomes increasingly aware that "I," "we," "they," etc., are ever-changing societies of virtual selves. Hence, "[j]ust as the manifestation of our selves and our knowing minds are an interdependent part of environments, so they are literally interdependent parts of other living beings" (Rosch, 2004, p. 41). In turn, the selves people and things inhabit, embody, enact, narrate, and frequently cling to seem increasingly artificial or "empty."

Thus, from a nondual point of view, an organization(al self) arises and subsides as part of concrete situations that are embodied and enacted through a multitude of interdependent agents, just like an individual human being('s self) or any agent('s self) does, making it increasingly difficult to pinpoint the frontier between the individual and the collective, the micro and the macro, and the human and the nonhuman. This view has important implications for the study of organizations and processes of organizing, as I will discuss next.

X

From a nondual perspective, an organization may be "a [more or less] coherent unity or functioning whole" (Merriam-Webster), but it is questionable to what extent it is an *instrument* (*organum*); that is, a goal-directed, systematically planned arrangement or united effort of one or more centralized selves. An organization emerges in ways that often fly in the face of those who try to manage "the organization" by exerting control over its emergence, frequently creating negative emotions, such as frustration, sadness, and anger. As Weick and Putnam (2006) noted, following Chia (2005), traditionally,

> [a]cts of managing are seen to sort competing demands, prioritize those demands, and create order out of chaos. Sorting and prioritizing

are acts of differentiation and conceptualizing. Demands are a cluster of experiences gathered into a concept. And the creation of order is an act that ignores impermanence, instills a belief in permanence, yields to a craving for predictability, and perhaps produces clinging. Attempts to create order freeze a dynamic reality into something that people then cling to. The ordering and clinging are useful and necessary for managing, but the dominant action is still clinging, and the order is still subject to inevitable rise and fall, and the rise and fall of order is still the occasion for stress, tension, and anger. (p. 276)[8]

The Buddhist view I have described focuses on transforming these occasions for stress, tension, and anger by suggesting that an organization may be "managed" by cultivating awareness (one's own as much as that of others) about the ways in which virtual, selfless selves are embodied and disembodied, arise and subside, as momentary conditions that are inseparable from the ongoing flow of events; meditating or reflecting on the ways in which these selves embody actions that reverberate throughout "the" entire network as it stretches out beyond the artificial confines of "the" organization; and letting the insights or wisdom and feelings of compassion gained from these meditations/reflections guide individual/collective action.

From a nondual point of view, it is understandable why foreseeing or planning the future of any virtual self, whether an organization, human being, or other agent, so frequently fails. As especially moments of crisis show, often in painful ways (e.g., see Weick, 1990, 1993), it seems the dual mind is regularly unable to "keep up" with the speed of actual, here-and-now situations. It is as if the dual mind is too slow in terms of its efforts of trying to make the ongoing stream of experience sensible, always playing catch-up retrospectively, even feeling caught up in its ongoing cycles of sensemaking and sometimes wishing it could stop making sense. In light of the Buddhist view developed here, ways of managing a situation need to take the actual situation into account and thus cannot be imposed on the situation beforehand. It suggests that, indeed, life does "happen to you while you are busy making other plans," as John Lennon said, and that the wisdom to deal with a situation should be "found" in the situation by perceiving the interconnections and interactions between the various agents that embody and enact it, including oneself.[9] As Buddhism shows, these insights hold for routine as much as nonroutine situations. Even the supposedly simple activities of sweeping a shop floor or plowing a field with an ox require attention and, if done mindfully, can lead to feelings of great contentment and happiness. Thus, moments of "being in the moment" need not only happen in "jam sessions," as Eisenberg (1990) suggested, but may occur continuously in organizational settings, if nondual awareness is properly fostered.

Since this more mindful way of managing/organizing focuses on the way interacting agents emerge and subside as parts of concrete everyday situations and actual larger environments, it challenges the human tendency to draw boundaries around things, themselves, others, contexts, and so on. It thereby presents a different *optique* for problematizing the idea that an organization is a relatively stable object (see Fairhurst & Putnam, 2004) with more or less fixed boundaries (see Diamond, Allcorn, & Stein, 2004; Heracleous, 2004; Hernes, 2004) or a cohesive culture (see Martin, 2002). Moreover, it may help us rethink the relationship between individual, organizational, and social identity; organizational identification as organizational attachment or "consubstantiality" (Burke, 1950/1969) rather than the inculcation of decision premises (Cheney, 1983a,b); ways of leading an organization that foreground nonduality instead of duality; and strategies for organizational conflict management that privilege interdependencies over independencies.

XI

A final note of caution is in place before concluding this essay, because my writing may have created the impression that developing nondual mind simply entails an intellectual exercise involving the deconstruction of the virtual, selfless nature of the selves that human and nonhuman agents embody and enact. However, as Varela (1999) has pointed out, for Buddhists exploring "the *sunya*, the virtual nature, of [the] deeply entrenched and continuously active drive for identity constitution is a matter of [lifelong] learning and sustained transformation" (pp. 62–63; see also Rosch, 2008). In this regard, one could say that cultivating nondual mind implies developing awareness of the ways in which the identities of interconnected actor-networks are always already "in deconstruction" (Derrida, 1976); that is, how they exist within and as part of the slipstream of *différance* between what is and what is not, and thus "deconstruct *themselves by themselves*" (Derrida, 1986, p. 132, emphasis added).

According to Derrida, "all" we need to do is to "recall" this deconstruction (p. 123), to bring this ongoing process of deconstruction back to mind, which is much easier said than done. However, Buddhists have developed a number of practices (especially meditative ones) that allow the nondual awareness necessary to recall the deconstructive nature of identities to be embodied and enacted. Explicating these practices would go well beyond the scope of this text, and it is important to point out that the "catch" here is not to get caught up in new webs of dualities during this process of learning, even not dualities presented by Buddhism, such as dual and nondual mind. Hence, Buddhist practice centers on embodying and enacting the awareness that anything known to the mind through the senses, concepts, emotions, even Buddhism, exists as part of the interplay of *différance* and therefore inevitably falls prey to the interdependent arising and subsiding of conditions (see Rosch, 2008; Vimalamitra, 2000). As Rosch (2008) has suggested, in a way, one thus cannot engage in this process with the intent of succeeding. Part of the process is failing to develop nondual mind, which, in turn, tempers or completely extinguishes the will or desire to control the ongoing stream of "arisings." By giving up any attempt to accomplish nondual mind, and enlightenment (nirvana) more generally, which cannot be done by sheer force or will, one's self and one's fixation on the selves of others supposedly is emptied or freed.

It may be difficult to imagine these kinds of moments of complete surrender, especially in a world so focused on control and ridden with concepts. However, even in this world, people experience moments in which they temporarily "forget" themselves; for example, when they are really involved in a particular activity (see Eisenberg, 1990). In hindsight, people often report feeling very connected, unfettered, liberated, or alive, in these instances, and perceiving themselves as being "one" with the moment, with others, and with their surroundings. According to the Buddhism philosophy I have described, these instances can be seen as brief moments in which one realizes one's emptiness, "that one's every characteristic is conditioned and conditional" (Varela, 1999, p. 34). They suggest that any human being has "the ability to know [himself or herself] directly as an interdependently arising part of the energies of nature" (Rosch, 2004, p. 40). Put in another way, in these moments, time and space seem timeless and spaceless, "one is the action" and "no residue of self-consciousness remains to observe the action externally" (Varela, 1999, p. 34). For Mahayana Buddhists, the aim/nonaim is to foster this kind of nondual action without getting attached to this aim (or nonaim), since they believe that "action out of wisdom means action (properly nonaction or spontaneous action) fully in contact with the realties and needs of the situation and unencumbered by the strategies of the self centered ego or by preconceptions or methods" (Rosch, 2008, p. 153). When this kind of "nondual action is ongoing and well-established," they presume, people experience it "as [being] grounded in a substrate" (Varela, 1999, p. 34) that feels at once foundationless and peaceful.

XII

Having realized over these past years that there is no use in trying to pinpoint James Taylor's identity, the facetious subtitle of this essay came to me easily. In a way, Taylor's writing continuously remind us that the labels we attach to our individual and collective selves "never get it quite right." Yet we often pretend they do, and then forget that we were just pretending, which frequently causes all sorts of tensions, struggles, and conflicts. For Taylor, this is a fact of life, the way the world turns, but, as I hope to have shown, at least one alternative view is available for those who doubt that he has it totally right.

One evening, not too long ago, I wrote Taylor an e-mail after we had discussed Buddhist philosophy, asking him (jokingly) whether he considered himself to be a Buddhist.

As usual, his response was striking and put a smile on my face. "Farmer, actually."

Notes

1. As Nagarjuna wrote in his *Fundamental Treatise on the Middle Way*, "What arises in dependence on another, is not at all that thing itself—But neither is it something different: It neither is nor is it not" (cited in Shantideva, 1997/1999, p. 186).
2. As Shantideva (1997/1999) stated in *The Way of the Bodhisattva: A Translation of the Bodhicharyavatara*, "All things…depend on something else; on this depends the fact that none are independent. Knowing this, we will not be annoyed at objects that resemble magical appearances" (p. 82).
3. It is commonly known that Taylor's thinking is, in many respects, influenced by Bruno Latour's (1986b, 1993, 1996, 2005) ideas about actor-networks.
4. In Taylor's view, "[c]onversation refers…to the interactive, situated 'eventfulness' of language use," while "text refers to the semiotic artifact (oral or written) produced in the use of language, which may persist as a trace and record of past conversations" (see Robichaud et al., 2004, p. 621).
5. *Dzogchen* is the term used to describe a body of *Vajrayana* or tantric teachings that signify the most advanced stage of the path of the *Nyingma* lineage, one of the four principal teaching lineages in Tibetan Mahayana Buddhism (the others being *Gelug, Sakya,* and *Kagyü*). *Vajrayana* or tantric Buddhism refers to a "special path which arose within Mahayana Buddhism based on treatises known as *tantras* and, while generally embracing the same aims, claimed to provide a rapid means to accomplish the goal of enlightenment (*bodhi*) by means of its distinctive techniques" (Keown, 2004, p. 292, emphasis added). For in-depth discussions on Dzogchen, see especially Gyatso (2002/2004), Norbu (2000), Thondup (Thondup Rinpoche, 1989/2002, 1995/2001), Urgyen (1995), Vimalamitra (2000), and Vyner (2002, 2004a, 2004b, 2005).
6. While nonhumans may be limited in their capacity to use our human languages to communicate and reflect on themselves and others, scholars in a number of fields are still debating whether they lack the ability to use "significant symbols" (Mead, 1934) and be self-consciousness altogether. Although very controversial, recent research in biology suggests, for example, that some nonhumans may be able to communicate and sense in ways that surpass the capacities of most humans (e.g., see Sheldrake, 1999).
7. For example, a beehive can be perceived and experienced as a virtual self that constitutes an essential part of the larger environment with which it interacts and which it enacts. However, each individual bee can also be regarded as a virtual self composed of uncountable nonhuman agents, such as molecules, atoms, electrons, etc. Note that this view shows great similarities with Gabriel de Tarde's observations (see Latour, 2002), and Latour's (2005).
8. From a traditional point of view, a manager could be said to act like a yeti trying to catch marmots:

   The yeti stands by a marmot hole, waits for one to come out, grabs it, and stuffs it underneath him to wait for the next one—he wants to catch a bunch. Another marmot comes out, and the yeti lunges, grabs it, and sits on it—while the first marmot runs off. The next marmot comes out, and the yeti lunges for it, grabs it—and the marmot he's sitting on runs off. (anecdote recounted by the XIVth Dalai Lama of Tibet, Tenzin Gyatso, see Goleman, 2003, p. 71)

9. As Varela (1999) argued, [T]ruly ethical behavior does not arise from mere habit or from obedience to

patterns or rules. Truly expert people act from extended inclinations, not from precepts, and thus transcend the limitations inherent in a repertoire of purely habitual responses … [I]ntelligence should guide our actions, but in harmony with the texture of the situation at hand, not in accordance with a set of rules or procedures. (pp. 30–31)

7 Activity Coordination and the Montreal School

Robert McPhee and Joel O. Iverson

In organizational theory and organizational communication theory, a number of streams of argument have advanced the position that activity coordination is a primary process and outcome of the communicative constitution of organizations. For instance, the selection phase of Karl Weick's (1979) model of organizing, conversational analysis such as Boden's (1994) work, and the structurational model of four constitutive flows of organizing advanced by McPhee, Zaug, and Iverson all stress activity coordination as one of the main flows of communication sustaining organizational constitution. In short, the phenomenon of coordinated work activity is vital to, perhaps at the heart of, attempts to answer the question "What is an organization?" Thus, it is not surprising to find sustained attention to activity coordination in the work of the Montreal School (TMS), a recent label for the works of Jim Taylor and his collaborators and students (who we will not try to list; many but certainly not all of them are editors and contributors to Cooren, Taylor, & Van Every, 2006).

Our own starting point is the four-flows model developed in McPhee and Zaug (2000) and McPhee and Iverson (2009). In this chapter, we seek to identify some important conceptual resources of TMS and note their potential in particular as contributions to the understanding of activity coordination as conceptualized in the four-flows model. We hope this analysis will help show the potential of TMS conceptual developments, both for the specific phenomenon of coordination, and for a broader range of scholars who may wish to draw on the ideas of TMS without taking on the whole TMS theoretic complex.

Overview

The topic of coordination is of signal importance to students of organizations, as well as of organizational communication. Organizations get their signal power from the coordinated work of multiple people, the coordinated operation of multiple units, the coordinated management of multiple capital flows planning endeavors, the coordinated delivery of products and socialization of employees to timed, controlled operations, and the coordination of organizational outputs with the needs of societies and market customers. The study of coordination ranges from micro- to macroanalysis, both in theory and in research. Analyses also range from approaches that avoid a specific communication focus (as in classic contingency theory (e.g. Hage, 1965) and transaction-cost theory (Williamson, 1975) to those that emphasize communication.

In true communication analyses, whether macro or micro, the analysis of coordination has proceeded on two levels that we might call the pattern level and the interchange level. The pattern level involves study of generalized tendencies in coordinative, or good coordinative, communication. The focus is on communication networks, styles, rules, and shared cognitive perspectives that lead to coordination. For instance, Lewis (2006) reviews a broad range of interdisciplinary work on collaboration and finds research emphasis on the context, skills, and broad process of collaboration. Another example is the work of Malone and Crowston (1994). They examine coordination as "the act of managing interdependencies between activities performed to achieve a goal" (p. 87), a definition that we accept with the caveat that coordination can be a state (harmony among activities) or a process rather than a specific act. They examine general patterns such as the level and kind of interdependence between departments or operations such as supply and manufacturing, and such processes as proposing alternatives, establishing a common language (e.g., programming language), and assigning a common superior to be notified of and resolve problems.

Theorizing and research on the interchange level is more ideographic, and is most inspired by conversational analysis. It often includes a microscopic analysis of a particular coordination situation, or array of situations, to illustrate the workings of a specific interpretive/communicative resource such as a conversational practice. For instance, Hutchins's (1995) work on the adaptive moves of navigators calculating positions when electricity fails on a ship exemplifies this level of work. Interchange studies rarely generalize; one exception is the work of Robertson (1997), who examined *types* of physical and verbal acts taking place during cooperative work in a software company; another is the work of Boden (1994), whose special relevance is noted below.

This distinction is a relatively manifest, even obvious one. We want instead to limit our scope by focusing on one pole of a distinction built into a theoretical perspective that we advocate and have been developing for some time. It could be called the structurational model of the communicative constitution of organizations, or the four-flows model, and we will turn to it next.

Activity Coordination in the Four Flows Model

The four-flows model is rooted in structuration theory (Giddens, 1984, 1987; cf. McPhee, 2004), especially as developed in the field of organizational communication. Structurational studies of organizational socialization/assimilation (Chitgopekar, 2007; Iverson & McPhee, 2008; Myers, 2005; Witmer, 1997), formal structuring (Canary, 2007; Ford-ham-Hernandez & McPhee, 1999; Kirby & Krone, 2002; McPhee, 1985, 1988; McPhee, Habbel, & Fordham Habbel, 1987; Witmer, 1997; Yates & Orlikowski, 1992), and institutional analysis (Browning & Beyer, 1998; Browning, Beyer, & Shetler, 1995; Witmer, 1997) have contributed to growth of an overall model of organizational communication phenomena.

The model is based on assumptions about communication, elaborated from structuration theory. As McPhee and Iverson (2009) elaborate these,

> "[C]onstitution" has (at least) three common meanings—constitution of a sign as meaningful within a system of meanings; constitution of a party as an agent in interaction or communication; and constitution of a social relationship or system as an institution. The first is a matter of practice or language game—a sign or element has been constituted as meaningful if we know how to go on with it in a language-game.... The second meaning of "constitution," constitution of an agent, involves recognition of the powers of the agent to, e.g., make claims or otherwise participate in interaction. (p. 53)

Such powers are dependent on, but irreducible to, history and context. The third meaning is distinct from the first two, since an organization is not reducible to its name or any other semantic-syntactic resource base; nor is it typically reducible to a person or group identifying themselves as part of or spokespeople for an organization. We the authors could call ourselves the "Association of Structurational Researchers," but more would have to happen before we could get the usual suspects to be members of our association or get anything done as a group. Thus, if we are discussing the typical sense of an organization as a system of persons (plus material and other resources) formally designed to achieve an outcome through coordinated work, the first two senses of constitution do not account for the constitution of an organization. Each sense of constitution involves (typically) a different array of communication acts and patterns, with different organization-constituting outcomes resulting from the productive/reproductive force of such interaction. To a certain extent, the model even at this general level emphasizes distinctions that speak against the implicit Montreal School claim, but also the broader claim of social constructionists, that communicative constitution is *equivalent* to organizational constitution.

The basic claim of the four-flows model is that organizations, thought of as systems, are constituted in four irreducible flows of communication. The term *flows* has multiple sources; we mainly want to emphasize the dynamism and turbulence of each flow, but not to imply that such processes are unidirectional, regular, or simple. Flows can overlap, as one communication process enacts and has a place in multiple flows. There is a sense that flows are typically functional in, not just constituting the organization, but also achieving explicit or hidden goals of one or more organization members (or outsiders). But the flows can also involve typical (and of course unique) forms of opposition, conflict, contradiction, and dissemination. If we look closely at typical important processes of/in each flow, we find that different organization-constituting forms prevail and different constitutive outcomes result. Mike D'Antoni, former coach of the Phoenix Suns basketball team, was engaged in constituting the team differently when he coached during games than when he negotiated his departure from the team.

For us, the term *model* is more appropriate than *theory* because the explanatory force of the model, and the empirical claims it makes, are limited. Its content might be summarized as follows:

- it implies that (organizational, but all) communication can be profitably modeled using the concepts of the structurational hermeneutic;
- it implies that organizations cannot be constituted simply through processes that constitute signs and agents;
- it claims that in any organization, you'll find all four flows;
- it claims that the flows constitute the organization in complementary but basically dissimilar ways, so that one model (of, e.g., coorientation) does *not* fit all;
- it claims that the flows (especially reflexive self-structuring) will work in ways distinctive from similar processes in families, mobs, etc.;
- it claims that *some* communicative patterns will typically be present (with atypical cases being worthy of study); and
- it implies that connections among the flows are the *crucial* aspects in the constitution of any specific organization.

One flow that the model discusses is activity coordination. This typically involves interactive episodes during which members integrated in a single organizational locale or working sphere (Gonzalez & Mark, 2005) adapt to situational contingencies and the relevant acts of other members. This flow is very inclusive; for instance, all episodes of engaged interaction are coordinated activity, since the engaged parties are reacting to one another. Here again, we have to resort to prototypes. One well-known example is teamwork, where, for example, a surgical team communicates to conduct an operation effectively. Another is joint authorship, when one author works on a draft, then passes it along for revision by another. Often, the communication process supports mutual reaction to unique exigencies, and there is little likelihood that the same decisions will generalize to a later project in any way.

In some ways, activity coordination is prototypical of organizational communication altogether. You are teaching at a university, walk to the main office, and notice flames—there's a fire. Naturally, you might shout "Is there anybody trapped in there?" or "Dial 911," the standard emergency number in the United States (if you don't have a phone in hand), or "Where's a fire extinguisher?" You are communicating to do your part (and find out what it is), helping cope with the fire. Such adaptive "working together" is on some accounts vital to, perhaps at the heart of, attempts to answer the question "What is an organization?"

But sometimes, definitely, actions, decisions, and communicative patterns generated on the spur of the moment *do* generalize, and become a convention or even a piece of broadly relevant organizational knowledge. This outcome increasingly overlaps into another of the four flows, reflexive self-structuring, because it is no longer merely local adaptation, but has generated an explicitly prescribed interaction structure. Your university holds fire drills, wherein you practice a task to which you are assigned, often involving scripted communication with assigned contacts. Roles, plans, specified interaction patterns—these, too, are the essence of organization, on a different account. But, of course, the scripts rarely work exactly as planned, and members have to adapt them on the spur of the moment—back to activity coordination.

We suggested (in McPhee & Iverson, 2009) that several communication sequences are prototypical in the flow of activity coordination. One is the development of, and reliance on, a joint medium of task representation. People trying to coordinate their activity need a way to do it, and coorient toward such a medium when it is in place. This may be a computer monitor or other display device, a simplified vocabulary, or any way of indicating what the task is and where the group is at in dealing with it. A second process is specific role negotiation as standard roles are adjusted or forsaken when current contingencies require it. Finally, a process with varied but recognizable communicative dimensions is support; that is, a means of indicating that help is willing and waiting.

Studies of activity coordinating communication are legion, though underappreciated in the formal field of communication. In earlier work, we have explicitly recognized, even proclaimed, the different, though often overlapping theories and models of coordination developed by conversation analysts, symbolic interactionists, computer-supported cooperation scholars, social psychologists, organization and education scholars, and communication scholars. However, we haven't actively explored the contributions of the Montreal School to the understanding of activity coordination, assuming that we take it as a delimited phenomenon worthy of focal study, as well as a distinct flow with specific constitutive implications.

The Montreal School

We presume it is uncontroversial to think of the Montreal School as consisting of the works of Jim Taylor and his collaborators and students—who we will not try to list; many but certainly not all of them are editors and contributors to Cooren, Taylor, and Van Every (2006)—as a rigid formalized theory. On the contrary, we certainly detect multiple paths of theoretic development, growth of insights, and movement in focus and centrality of concepts. It is even unclear whether a better name for TMS might be *text-conversation dialectic theory* (stemming from Taylor, 1993c), but as we see it, that is one main line of reasoning but far from the whole or sole originative core of the School's work.

Nevertheless, to be able to write this article at all, we will assume, or (more dangerously) project, a specific centripetality to TMS, and in particular we see it as differing from the structurational account of organizational communication sketched above. First, we perceive that it has quite different assumptions and a different agenda. While not simply accepting the equivalence view of organizational constitution (that *organization* and *communication* are equivalent and simply different terms for the same thing), it explores and occupies the conceptual region around that view, and aims to reveal how the complex of communicative organizing operations is the key to and the means of explaining (the usual sense of) organizational communication phenomena. Second, we would describe its explanatory strategy as an expanded structuralism, drawing strikingly on linguistic and formalistic models such as Greimas's model of narrative, a rule-oriented account of speech-act theory and conversational analysis, and actor-network theory, while explicitly noting their instantiation, production, and productivity in the domain of interaction or conversation (thus the term *expanded structuralism*). Tersely, we see the *primary* explanatory direction of the theory as tending *from* the (a priori or linguistic) formal structures that are the site or canvas of organizational communication, *to* interaction practices and outcomes (the surface), and also to material and other agents of communication, and organization itself (although the constitutive significance of the other dialectical movement is certainly articulated in TMS). Despite (and we recognize that some might say "because of") these differences from our structuration-based treatment, TMS has developed insights and models that have real cross-paradigm utility; we will focus on those and describe some of their uses, especially for understanding the activity coordination flow and its place in the constitution of organizations. TMS has definitely not limited its attention to the category of activity-coordinating communication, but some of its most memorable examples (to us) are examples of activity coordination. To give a very short list, they include

- the example of subordinate agency elaborated by Taylor and Van Every (2000, p. 80), where a principal says to an agent, "Jeff, why don't you take them through the model," with consequent coordinated action by Jeff.
- the "Manhattan skyscraper" cases (Cooren, 2006; Taylor & Cooren, 2006), in which a building manager negotiates and plans actions to satisfy the requests of building tenants.
- the "MR. Sam" analyses (Cooren, 2007; Katambwe & Taylor, 2006) in which executives of a large Canadian corporation negotiate plans for reorganizing.
- The downsizing case (Cooren & Fairhurst, 2002), in which a manager, after listening to employee narratives about the feared effects of downsizing, developed a plan whereby the organization addressed those fears and thereby transformed the employee narratives.
- Among others.

Based on our reading of both TMS theory and the examples of coordination that stand out in their work, the specific constructs of coorientation, narrative, text–conversation dialectic (narrowly considered), as well as the overall TMS scheme, represent distinctive contributions made by TMS. We explore each of those in relation to the flow of activity coordination.

Coorientation

A key contribution made by the Montreal School is its rehabilitation and development of the concept of coorientation. Based on Newcomb's (1953) conceptualization, Taylor contends that coorientation conceptualizes the complex relationships of people to each other (A to B) and a common object (X). At its most basic, two people think, not just about an object X, but about each other's orientation toward X. Communication changes their orientations toward X, typically toward symmetry or similarity. But this social-psychological sense of coorientation, although sophisticated in its day, is, as Taylor warns us, way too simple.

Taylor (2001b; Taylor & Robichaud, 2004) contends that we need to reconceptualize the model in several ways to make it applicable to communication in any sense. He focuses his change on three elements or keywords: *context, interaction,* and *translation. Context* recognizes the situatedness of the communication: that members are in an interactive exchange situation, in juxtaposition with many other relations (to persons, objects, etc.), involved in a larger goal-oriented activity, and also cooriented with groups and larger social agents (in the sense that they are capable of attributed orientation), in an environment that is both material-social and linguistic. Under *interaction,* Taylor focuses on the fact of exchange or interchange that makes the coorientation interesting.

He lauds Newcomb for noting that agents don't just communicate to get agreement in their orientation, but that the coorientation situation may actually tend toward complementarity of view and toward conflict. *Translation* focuses on language used to translate people's attitude to one another. Taylor emphasizes that coorientation usually concerns less the object than the terms and norms of communication (a valuable insight for activity coordination!). A key insight from TMS is that the translation is not merely information transmission from one source (A) to another (B) about X, but it is the interwoven, dialogic theorizing based on communication where each are mutually interacting with one another and in many ways communicatively enacting X in the process as well as X's relationship to A and B in the situated activity. As a result, coorientation provides an understanding of emergent meanings. Moreover, parallel to the relational model that is the surface of coorientation, Taylor employs two very definite communication terms. One is *lamination*, borrowed from Deirdre Boden (1994), which refers to cases where people in Unit A say "Unit B" discussing a unit far away from the episode of communication in Unit A. Obviously, such lamination achieves coorientation on Unit B. Second is the more relational-sounding term *imbrication*: "Co-orientation … is the building-block of all organizational processes and structures. Imbrication is the process by means of which co-orientational systems become translated into infrastructure" (Taylor, Groleau, Heaton, & Van Every, 2001, p. 26). It is the process (and so essentially communicative, not relational/structural) of "tiling" whereby specific local enactments of joint relevances exist within connected arrays of such enactments. Both these conceptions reveal how communication "organizes," creates a communicatively constructed and active patterning of relationships that grounds and guides communication.

In application to our topic in this paper, a state of coorientation can be thought of as coordination achieved, in particular, on a group task representation (cf. McPhee & Iverson, 2006; in the terms of Taylor, 2006, both the "conceptual level" and an aspect of the "social material" level): "Because we all find our full existence in a mixture of material-social and linguistic environments, we confront the continual necessity of translating one to the other" (Taylor, 2006, p. 147). For Taylor, communication is the means for translating in an interactive system with others through coorientation. Taylor states, "Coorientation aims to reconcile the contrasting imperatives of material-social and linguistic constraints and enablements. It is through coorientation that the language-based establishing, person to person, and group to group, of compatible beliefs and coordinated responses to events as they occur, is accomplished" (p. 147). Thus, coorientation is the *mechanism* for enacting and sensemaking in the world on individual and multiple collective levels. Coorientation provides a useful means of conceptualizing the communicative explanation of how activity coordination occurs. Further, coorientation provides a means to move from the social-psychological model to an essentially dialogic model of communication by extending the Newcomb's A-B-X model.

One main implication of the coorientation concept elaborated by Taylor is that it is an excellent baseline model for activity coordination. It says the latter is more than the individual elements (Bs and Xs) in organizations or the isolated (communicative) things people in organizations do. Rather, in the flow of activity coordination communication is emergent context-linkage, recruitment, self-definition, and directionalization, achieved in dialogical, reflexive fashion. Coorientation highlights the ground-level communicative processes that are involved in the everyday actions of activity coordination, and how they are importantly constitutive of organizations in their own way.

The coorientation system allows us to analyze the interrelatedness of linked locales of activity coordination. The imbrication or tiling of a local action on other A-B-X relationships allows for an understanding of how activity coordination may be carried out locally in microinteraction, but have broader relatedness with a coordinated flow of activities. Both imbrication and lamination theorize the connection of activity coordination to self-structuring and reflexivity. The ability, for example, to present a paper to an audience is dependent upon other prior and continuous actions including planning activities, arrangements for rooms, the preconference, and so on. Moreover, the concept of coorientation allows for an account of power differentials and hierarchy to be felicitously embedded in the conceptualization of a social framework for sensemaking.

Narrative

Narrative further extends TMS theorizing of communication by extending Greimas's model of narrative. In this model, narrative is not merely storytelling, but rather is the basis of meaning. Narrative provides connection amongst actions as well as into larger meaning structures. A single action that is not considered in context is difficult to make sense of, but as part of a narrative, discrete actions and communication become more meaningful. In this way, the narrative structure reflects the structurational hermeneutic: meaning for any act of communication is drawn from the whole and the whole gets its meaning from the parts that have and continue to constitute it.

Cooren and Fairhurst (2002) articulate four phases of narrative based upon Greimas's model: manipulation, competence, performance, and sanction. Manipulation "involves the creation of a tension between a subject and an object" (p. 87). This tension, or breach (Taylor & Van Every, 2000) drives the need for action and articulates the reason for action. Next, the competence phase sets up the subject with allies that are considered to be *helpers* and *opponents* that create obstacles for achieving the desired manipulation. Performance "constitutes the main action performed by the subject in her quest" (Cooren & Fairhurst, 2002, p. 87). The final phase creates an exchange or sanction from the sender to the subject. Typically this involves the fulfillment of the quest. Taylor and Cooren (2006) recognize that these phases of the narrative allow for sensemaking of events, but also for understanding how different organizational activities can be organized within different levels of narrative as well as different perspectives. Narrative provides the structure of meaning.

Going through the four phases, each relates in useful ways to understanding activity coordination as does the overall narrative approach. First, manipulation is useful for punctuating and understanding the circumstances leading to the need for activity coordination. An organization is operating smoothly, but then an event occurs, such as a failed delivery of merchandise or, in Orr's (1996) example, a broken photocopier. The manipulation sets up the need for coordination and gives purpose for the activities that ensue, such as fixing the copier. When coordinating activities, the organizational members use their available resources to coordinate and interact with tools, each other, their knowledge, and while the problem in the copier is the opponent. The actions performed for the copier technicians is the improvisational interaction they perform to fix the copier. The sanction is accomplishment resulting in getting to leave the copier in working order and probably the pay they receive. The four phase model in this instance not only provides a detailed way to understand the activity coordination, it also includes the motivation (phase one) for coordinating in the first place.

As an overall approach, narrativity provides a means of understanding and processing the activity coordination for the organizational members. This results not only in several implications for activity coordination. First, narratives provide a schema that's well suited to give a bird's eye view to coordination. Coordination may involve problem-solving that constitutes a narrative in its own right, but typically it is a detour from and back onto the path to some larger, planned or self-structured goal. Coordination includes helpers, opposition, and ties into a meaning network. Coorientation seems to be a smaller unit of analysis; while it involves a social focus on a single object, narrativity gives a larger structure for a sequence of action typically involving multiple parties, multiple objects, and multiple interactions.

Moreover, Cooren and Fairhurst's depiction of a leader as a practical narrator gives the leader the role of dealing with the multivocal, complex landscape of meanings and providing a larger narrative that fits various activities and individual narratives into the larger discourse of the organization. A narrative leader can thus give meaning and satisfaction to members of the organization who would not otherwise understand their experiences and outcomes. This provides ties of narrative to the other flows such as reflexive self-structuring. One can envision an action of activity coordination that is then retold by leaders and members, adopted and established as a way of operating regularly (self-structuring) or as an aberration for an instance, but the normal procedures should remain in place.

Text-Conversation Dialectic

The text-conversation dialectic is the central, even eponymous, conception in the theorizing of Taylor and perhaps the whole Montreal School. The concept seems very clear initially, but subtleties multiply. Probably the easiest way into the dialectic is to consider the movement from conversation to text—the first movement of the dialectic. Conversation is discursive, especially linguistic action, by at least one but typically two (or more) parties. Due to different senses of context, contributions by the parties to the conversation may differ and not be in sync in their interpretive background, but through communication, text emerges, of at least three forms: speech acts that are declarations or have declarative significance (see below); a coorientation pattern revealed in lamination and imbrication; and narrative (see above). Now, there is secondly a movement from text to conversation. One version (the smallest unit of analysis) of this movement is the trajectory of the speech act: language allows us to do things with words by using a conventional procedure in an appropriate context. Taylor, Cooren, et al. (1996) argue that the "appropriate context" is essentially organizational—"the organizational frame" (p. 12). Part of this frame, and perhaps all of it, is the text, and presumably other situational aspects, already generated in conversation. In part, this movement has force because it draws on what Taylor and Van Every (2000) call "a priori forms" of language. For instance, English (and many other languages) include conventions for "declarations," which can have constituting force: "the National Assembly recognizes and proclaims ... the following rights...." Coorientation as expressed in language, and in narrative forms, is also marked by TMS as having constitutive force, as already discussed.

Each direction of movement in the dialectic of text and conversation brings in ideas that can potentially stimulate the analysis of activity coordination. For instance, one theoretic theme in connection with the movement from conversation to text is the idea of mapping (Taylor & Van Every, 2000). In setting up a joint medium for task representation, it's vital to get the rules of representation and manipulation worked out. If a basketball coach is sketching out a play during a time-out, it's vital to *declare* which players will be on the court, which X or O stands for which player. In doing this, one is performing the text-generative operations, in communication, that specifically correspond to the TMS's view of organizational constitution. "Organizations *self*-organize, and they do so as the result of the dynamic of local interaction. The self-organization is a communication phenomenon, and in this sense communication is a meso-level that needs to be theorized if we are to understand the relation of macro (structure) to micro (practice) and vice versa" (Taylor, 2005, p. 215).

Another theoretic theme in connection with the movement from conversation to text, described by Taylor, Groleau, et al. (2001), is the "dance of agency," or "dialectic of resistance and accommodation," first described by Andrew Pickering (1995) in his account of scientific research and discovery. In a sense, Pickering's description fits Karl Popper's notion of "conjecture and refutation" as the scientist comes up with a model or hypothesis for the research object, does an experiment, suffers failure, but learns from it so as to design a better model or experiment, progressing to one that succeeds. But Pickering argued that the experiment can only fail in certain ways, and that that limitation constrains and enables the research object's ability to describe itself by resisting the scientist's conjectures in specifically revealing ways, so that the final scientific model depends both on the (historically contingent) pattern of revealing resistance by the object and the (also historically contingent) sequence of accommodations— newly conjectured models or hypotheses—that between them lead to an objectively supported but partial and accidentally articulated model of the phenomenon.

Just such an image can inform us about activity coordination. This kind of dialectic of resistance and accommodation can relate coordinating parties, as one, then the other, conjectures ways of working together, and encounters resistance that can lead to the next, more accommodated try. For instance, in trying to find the ways TMS most valuably contributes to the four-flows analysis of activity, we found ourselves coordinating our account in just this way. What idea from TMS was most valuable? Where can it be articulated to reveal that value? Well, seeing that option for using it, how can we rephrase our account/interpretation of the idea? This is a very abstract example, but exactly the same thing happens every time Steve Nash dribbles down the floor, looks for openings and advantages, feints to see how the opponents will react, then starts a play that his teammates adjust to.

A third idea within the same conversation-text movement facilitates taking account of multiple agents in the coordination process. One pattern that can emerge in the conversation supporting/enacting coordinated is the coordination of multiple agent goals, perhaps (but certainly not necessarily) in a linear head/complement hierarchy. Given a jointly legitimating account, each agent in a group may accept his or her place in a pattern requiring and guiding service as a complement to the person higher in the chain of support to the person whose purpose is paramount. One basketball (or, in an analogous game, hockey) player, guarded, finds him- or herself able to pass the ball or puck to a second player who, although also guarded, can pass it to a third player who is unguarded and can take the open shot.

On the other hand, the text-to-conversation movement is important because it gives the meaning, the stability, and the resources for activity coordination. In part, this process can be in rapid dialectical interchange with the conversation-to-text movement. As a coach diagrams one play after another, to respond to different contingencies, the earlier plays-as-texts are available as interpretive resources the players use to understand the latest play diagram. At a slower pace, the text (here meaning the consensually available memory stock among agents) is a resource for skillful and political coordination by agents. Cooren (2006) gives one example of a company representative who is talking with a building manager who, as shown be other examples in the TMS 2006 book, is inclined to push clients to do what he wants. One client, Frida, uses reference to shared knowledge to avoid resistance by the building manager:

> Frida: Yah and uh Oscar would like to have also a company name on the door *you know that* [emphasis added].... (p. 88)

This is not a novel idea, but it is definitely related to the overall issue of text as interpretive resource feeding, in nondeterministic ways, into conversation.

Overall TMS Perspective

Finally, the Montreal view of organization as emergent in communicative process (Taylor & Van Every, 2000), taken as contributory to a whole reframing of the understanding of coordination, yields important results. We might diagram the standard, pre-four-flows, and pre-TMS, approach to the analysis of *coordination* this way (see Figure 7.1).

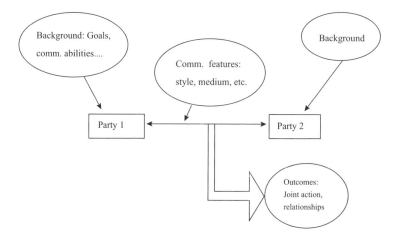

Figure 7.1 "Received" model of coordination process.

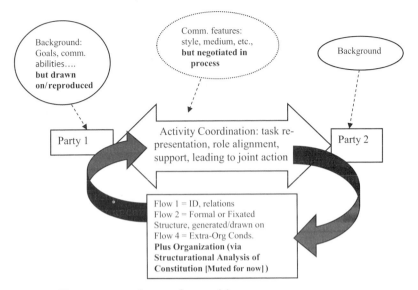

Figure 7.2 The activity coordination flow model.

The four-flows approach perhaps changes our understanding into this different model (see Figure 7.2).

To put some of the new emphases of the four-flows model into words, it notes that occasioned coordinative processes have constitutive force that is vital to the job of coordination itself; they often depend on and have implications for the other three flows; they can help constitute (produce/reproduce) the organization themselves; and they involve specific, prototypical interaction formats. We would argue that a full understanding of activity coordinating communication, from our own theoretic standpoint, would require a satisfactory conception of communication as structurative, which is only adumbrated in this paper.

Moreover, the broader contribution of the Montreal School model lies in the conceptual additions and reorientations they add to the notion of coordination. One more diagram helps to reveal those contributions (aee Figure 7.3). What's striking here, in our view, is the reframing of the phenomenon of coordination, from presentation as a process with specific and delimited constitutive force, to a status as part of a broad dialectical movement of organizational constitution. Coordination processes (such as joint task representation) constantly add to and sustain or transform (that is, reproduce) the communicative resources, contexts, routines, and practices of the organization. TMS would emphasize that the objects of such reproduction include coordinated subjective understandings, emergent macro-agents, and organizational texts. It would make us more aware that such reproduction proceeds in a way that is nonlinear, autopoietic, and contributory to organizational textual resources (if not, as structuration

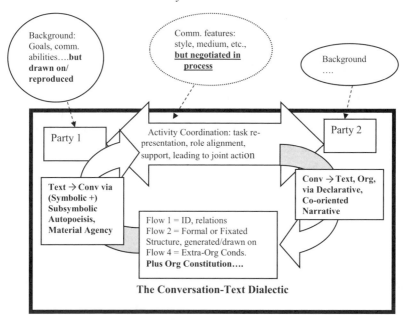

Figure 7.3 Activity coordination as refigured by Montreal School concepts.

theory would urge us to deny, a unitary organizational text). The added textual resources might include, not just successful coordination, but possible coordination steps that were overlooked and realized only in retrospect, multiple coordination steps that got in each other's way and created miscoordination, and coordination steps that, while locally effective, involved long-term commitments that eventually proved damaging (e.g., because too expensive to maintain). Such a collective narrative might lead the organization to pay more attention to coordination efforts and abilities in the future, or it might lead to a turn toward more predictable, preprogrammed domains of work.

The four-flows theory also emphasizes that attempted local coordination can lead to a growth (and perhaps sharing) of local knowledge; rules elaborated in more or less formal organizational self-structuring; or broader coordination efforts that can affect relations with other organizations. Nonetheless, those changes are accompanied by (and perhaps coextensive with) sensemaking conversations which themselves can spur coordination efforts to create unifying narratives as TMS leads us to note.

Conclusion

We contend that this essay is one portion of a constructive conversation amongst theories. The flow of activity coordination is simple to conceive in the abstract, but difficult to visualize and fully characterize in the details.

The constructs of coorientation, narrative, text-conversation dialectic, and coordination in the Montreal School provide a rich resource for theoretical development (about coordination, to say the least), clearly not limited to work inside the school narrowly viewed. It leads us to new insights, even though it has also initiated controversy. A look at the history of ideas tells us that new theoretic complexes usually die or become irrelevant, while adaptable ideas, insights, and arguments are more likely to endure and yield unpredicted intellectual value. Our paper illustrates that TMS has plenty of the latter.

Part II

Empirical Explorations

8 Spacing Organization
Or How to Be Here and There at the Same Time

Consuelo Vásquez

Introduction

Conventional wisdom has it that an entity is either here or there; it cannot be in two places at the same time. But what if an entity were considered to be a collective, made up of various representatives?[1] This would then call into question such a received view, given that representatives are supposed to make present, that is, to re-present, in various space-time configurations, what or who they are said to act for or speak on behalf of. This seems especially true for an organization, which is "identified, defined, and delimited through the different agents that speak or act in its name" (Cooren, 2006, p. 83), these agents being multiple and heterogeneous—CEOs, secretaries, organizational charts, workers, logos, and so on. According to such a view, this spatial/temporal maxim starts to weaken as we accept the organization's "splitting" capacity of being here and there at the same time.

In the last decades, various organizational researchers have addressed this spatial/temporal topic by questioning how these collective forms appear to transcend local practices in terms of space and time. One trend of ideas that has significantly contributed to this discussion draws upon actor-network theory to understand the mode of being and doing of collectivities (see, for instance, Callon & Latour, 1981; Cooper, 1992; Cooren, Brummans, & Charrieras, 2008; Cooren, Fox, Robichaud, & Talih, 2005; Latour, 2005; Latour & Hernant, 1998). However, while these studies mobilize different concepts intrinsically related to notions of space or time, they hardly ever explicitly define or problematize these dimensions.[2] Yet, as Raper and Livingston (1995, cited in Massey, 1999) state, "the way that spatio-temporal processes are studied is strongly influenced by the model of space and time that is adopted" (p. 262). This is an argument for the importance of defining space and time, since how we mobilize these concepts—perhaps in ways we do not intend—has theoretical, social, and political effects (Bannerman et al., 2005).

Thinking space is thus my starting point to understand organizing because it permits us to grasp the complexity of this phenomenon as well as its social and political implications. Following Massey (1993, 2001, 2003, 2004, 2005), the concept of space that I subscribe to is one that considers space as open and dynamic; that is, space as space-time combined in becoming (Crang & Thrift, 2000). This conceptualization of space implies that it is constituted through interaction, rather than pre-existing as a dimension that defines an area within which the social takes place. Furthermore, space is defined by interactions. But what is even more important to understand is that these interactions do not occur *in* space; they create it (Massey, 1993). It is, then, a performative view of space; one based on the interactions that involve heterogeneous actors—human and nonhuman. Space can then be imagined as the coexistence of multiplicity, of heterogeneity, what Massey (2005) terms a coexistence of trajectories as *stories-so-far*.

From this definition of space, I propose in this paper to "space the organization," that is, to explore the various spacing practices of organizational agents in their daily interactions. To do so I analyze a project of science and technology diffusion in a Chilean governmental organization.[3] Through this analysis, I demonstrate how the agents implicated in the coordination of this project expand their organization by enrolling different actors and by intersecting diverse trajectories. These spacing practices are far from being neutral as they respond to specific goals and strategies. Through them the organization can transcend, dislocate, displace itself, or tele-act (i.e., act from a distance). It can, in other words, be here and there at the same time.

Space as Space-Time: Trajectories as Stories-So-Far

Traditionally, space has been defined in opposition to time. It is commonly presented in terms of "absence of" time, "absence of" movement, or "absence of" change. Evacuating movement, dynamism, and temporality from space obstructs the analytical and political force of this concept. If, on the contrary, we consider space and time as interwoven—"that is space and time combined in becoming" (Crang & Thrift, 2000, p. 3)—we incorporate dynamism in space and by doing so, we open the door toward a political application of this concept (Massey, 2004). As Massey (1994) argues, a vision of space as space-time supposes "a configuration of social relations within which the specifically spatial may be conceived of as an inherently dynamic simultaneity" (p. 3). It implies, then, giving up the three-dimensional notion of space (and the one-dimensional view of time) and replacing it by a four-dimensional concept of space-time, in which "space is not static and time is not spaceless" (p. 264). As noted by Massey (1994), the integration of space and time does not mean that we cannot make any distinction between them, but rather that the distinction we make needs to hold them in tension.

Another point related to this notion of space-time is that each definition must be constructed in interrelation. Space-time is, thus, constituted
through interaction, rather than preexisting as a dimension that defines
an area within which the social takes place. Space-time is not absolute; it
is relational. In this sense, Clegg and Kornberger (2006) argue,

> [S]pace is more than an abstract neutral framework filled with objects.
> Human and non human elements constitute the experience of space
> through their forms of occupation, activity and movement as much
> as they are constituted through those spaces that enable and restrict
> certain events. We constitute space through the countless practices of
> everyday life as much as we are constituted through them. (p. 144)

It is, then, a performative (and reflexive) view of space; one based
on the interactions between the various human and nonhuman actors
that participate in organizing practices. Hence this open, dynamic,
and relational space is constantly in the process of being made by those
multiple interactions.

Furthermore, these interactions also involve heterogeneous actors—
human and nonhuman. Space is, thus, created out of the heterogeneous
networks of relations at every scale from local to global (Massey, 1994). The
spatial characteristic of these heterogeneous relations is their simultaneity,
what Massey (2005) calls *coexisting heterogeneity*. It is in the simultaneous
coexistence of sociotechnical relations that movement can be found and
not only in the idea of traveling through space and time. Moreover, and as
a result of this definition of space as *coexisting heterogeneity*, the realm of
the spatial is being (re)politicized.

In this spirit, Massey (2005) proposes to conceptualize space-time as
a coexistence of trajectories as *stories-so-far*. As she affirms, "such a space
is the sphere in which distinct stories coexist, meet up, affect each other,
come into conflict or cooperate" (Massey, 1999, p. 274). She proposes the
concept of trajectories to raise the idea of process and change, of continuous
motion and permanent construction. To illustrate this notion, Massey
(2003) invites us to imagine a journey from Manchester to Liverpool. One
way to characterize it is as moving from one point to another, as traveling
through space and time, what we would commonly call a trajectory.
"You're moving between two places on a map. Manchester and Liverpool
are given; and you, the active one, travel between them" (p. 2). Another
way to picture this voyage is as a meeting of coexisting trajectories as
stories-so-far. The journey here is quite different:

> So, you're barely out of Manchester, approaching the mosses that
> stretch away, flat, on either side, when Manchester itself has moved
> on.... That collection of trajectories that is Manchester is no longer

the same as when you left it…. And Liverpool? Likewise it has not just been lying there, static on the map, awaiting your arrival. It too has been going about its business; moving on. Your arrival in Lime Street, when you step off the train, begin to get into the things you came here to do, is a meeting-up of trajectories as you entangle yourself in stories that began before you arrived. (p. 2)

Space is then a slice through all those trajectories, an encounter of unfinished stories. Consequently, traveling is not only across space (and time) but also across a multitude of stories.

If we go back to the triggering question of this essay, which is how organization can travel/dislocate/transcend to be here and there at the same time, and look at this spacing capacity of organization in terms of intersecting trajectories, new issues and challenges are raised to understand organizing. As mentioned before, thinking of space as space-time implies considering many different aspects when the concept is applied to organizing. First, it raises issues of agency (and coagency) and leads us to mobilize a definition of action and interaction as heterogeneous associations. Consequently, this raises the questions of how and why these associations are made, since these associations are not neutral and respond to specific goals and strategies. Describing the articulation of these associations and their power is then key in understanding the spacing practices of organizational agents (Latour, 1986a). It is through this articulation work of associating heterogeneous actors and diverse trajectories that the organization can move successively and simultaneously.

Second, thinking about space as space-time also raises issues related to mobility and stability, as a dynamic and open view of space supposes an *organization-in-the-making* view. This should, by no means, imply a celebration of process as opposed to effect. Instead, this conceptualization of space should be able to embrace both of these dimensions, "the state of being organized and the act of organizing" (Cooper & Law, 1995, p. 240). In this sense, when I suggest *spacing the organization* I am referring both to the organizational agent's spacing practices—the day-to-day organizational process—as well as to the organization's expected result; that is, to expand itself, to displace itself, to be able to move from one place to another in different moments.

Third, space as space-time questions the notion of boundaries. In a traditional definition of space as a container, a specific area within which interaction occurs, boundaries are fixed and static. Inside and outside are taken for granted as space remains static. Now, in considering a dynamic and open space, boundaries become shifting and fluctuating events. Boundary setting is carried through interaction as it responds to specific criteria of inclusion and exclusion. But even more, if we want to advance Massey's idea of coexistent and heterogeneous trajectories, the sole idea of boundaries does not exist. Boundaries are imposed on spaces and times. There are resources that organizational agents mobilize in spacing their organization. In this sense, boundaries are produced by certain agents, in certain moments, with certain goals. Boundary setting is indeed strategic.

Finally, space as space-time, implies issues of ordering and disordering. The multiplicity of trajectories as *stories-so-far* implies the possibility of multiple *modes of ordering* (Law, 1994), which, in turn, supposes an understanding of organization "as ongoing performances involving heterogeneous modes of action and materialization, both of which must be actively affiliated and aligned across a range of often unruly contingencies" (Suchman, 2000, p. 313). The work of alignment is then key in maintaining the coherence of those multiples and coexistent *stories-so-far.* This is why a main story—what I call a scripted trajectory—is presented, developed, and mobilized in order to align and associate the heterogeneous organizational agents. In acting out this script, organizational agents position themselves and others above/under it, inside/outside, and before/after. This spacing practice of distributing individuals and things in space reminds us of Foucault's (1995) notion of discipline. As he states:

> Each individual has his own place; and each place its individual. Avoid distribution in groups; break up collective dispositions; analyse confused, massive or transient pluralities. Disciplinary space tends to be divided as many sections as there are bodies or elements to be distributed.... Discipline organises an analytical space. (pp. 141–143)

Now, even if Foucault focuses primarily on physical space—as in the Panopticon, an architectural space that created and sustained homogeneous effects of power—we can transpose his arguments to the notion of space-time as elaborated in this section. As we will see in the analysis, it is in the acting out of a scripted trajectory that the exercise of power is being accomplished. The scripted trajectory plays a similar disciplinary role in relation to the Panopticon because it distributes the different organizational agents that subscribe to it over and under, before and after, inside or outside.

Taking these implications into account, I propose to explore the various spacing practices of organizational agents in their daily interactions. To do so, I will devote the next section of this paper to analyzing a project of science and technology diffusion in a Chilean governmental organization named Explora. More specifically, I will focus on a particular activity, 1,000 Scientists, 1,000 classrooms, which consists of encounters between scholars and school students in the context of Explora's National Science and Technology Week. Before starting the analysis, let me present a brief note on methodology and the research site.

A Brief Note on Method and the Research Site

The fieldwork of this case study took place in Explora, a Chilean governmental organization of science and technology diffusion. Using an organizational ethnographic approach (Schwartzman, 1993; Ybema et al., 2009), I analyzed the organizational dynamic of a project of science and technology diffusion. The data collection mainly consisted of shadowing[4] the planning, management, execution, and evaluation activities by which the project came into existence (Bruni, 2005; Fletcher, 1999; Kephart & Schultz, 2001; McDonald, 2005; Sachs, 1993; Vàsquez et al., 2012).

Between July and October 2006, I videotaped a variety of activities; for example, several meetings and numerous telephone calls; I also videotaped events, such as a scientific congress for children, a technology exposition, scientific conferences for youth, and so forth. To complete the shadowing, I collected work documents (e-mails, design materials, organizational charts) and interviewed the members of the project team, as well as those from the central committee in charge of the organization.

From the multiple activities developed by this organization, I specifically shadowed Explora's 12th National Science and Technology Week (NSTW) in Explora Sur, one of Explora's regional branches. The NSTW project is developed every year during the first week of October to promote through diverse activities and events science and technology in the community and especially in the area of scholarship. The most important activity of this annual event, 1,000 Scientists, 1,000 Classrooms, consists of conferences between Chilean academics and students who meet to discuss their research or in terms of the children, their interest in science or a specific scientific topic. 1,000 Scientists, 1,000 Classrooms must be organized in every regional branch, as requested by Explora's central committee (there are also what are referred to as "spontaneous" activities that are presented by each regional branch).

Furthermore, this activity has to be held on the Tuesday of the NSTW—this is said to create synergy and coherence in "every corner of the country"—and must at least amount to one thousand conferences, as indicated in the activity's name. This way, Explora, through its representatives, can proudly affirm that on the first Tuesday of October, 1,000 academics left their universities and headed to 1,000 schools, from North to South[5] to meet with many students and share their knowledge and interest in science. The organization of this activity is, therefore, of great importance for each regional branch as specific standards are prescribed and goals are expected to be met. The episodes that I will analyze next correspond to a series of meetings related to the planning and coordination of this activity in the regional branch I studied. The analysis focuses particularly on the spacing practices of the different agents involved in the organization of 1,000 Scientists, 1,000 Classrooms. We will see how being there at the same time is not only the expected result of the 1000

Scientists, 1000 Classrooms activity but also supposes a general mode of organizing.

Spacing Practices in 1,000 Scientists, 1,000 Classrooms

The excerpts selected for the analysis were chosen as being representative with respect to the overall organizational process of the 1000 Scientists, 1000 Classrooms' activity. They can be understood as different "place-moments" of one of the many stories-so-far related to this activity. It is principally (part of) the story as it is constructed in the interactions between the organizers of this activity and the different agents they enroll in order to space their organization. I have chosen three main episodes to illustrate this spacing dynamic. The first one corresponds to the first meeting between Alexandra, the regional coordinator of Explora Sur and project manager of the NSTW, and Paula, the assistant she hired to coordinate this specific activity (who, incidentally, is also her daughter). The second episode corresponds to an update meeting between Alexandra and Paula that triggers a series of adjustments to the projected plan and the implementation of a new strategy of enrolment. The third episode illustrates this new strategy, namely the "door-to-door" activity by Paula, followed by Andrés, a PhD student in chemistry, as she tries to convince a chemistry professor to participate in the activity. Through these episodes we can actually see Explora traveling from one place to another (sequentially and simultaneously) as it is made present through different agents in a series of interactions. The three episodes are presented in chronological order. The transcripts are an English translation—all interactions took place in Spanish. The passages in bold are the passages considered to be key to the analysis.

The first meeting takes place in Alexandra's office about 2 months before the actual day when this activity has to be completed (the first Tuesday of October). It follows a series of meetings between Alexandra and her staff to kick off the organization of the NSTW. In this context, Alexandra has called Paula to her office to explain the functioning of 1,000 Scientists, 1,000 Classrooms and the specific tasks she has to do as the person responsible for this activity.

1	*Paula:*	(Inaudible) I need you to explain to me, I must
2		leave now.
3	*Alexandra:*	OK, OK. Let's see. **Here is a form for the 1,000**
4		**Scientists**; I am going to send it to you by e-mail.
5	*Paula:*	OK.
6	*Alexandra:*	**This is a form that the scientists fill out.** You must have
7		seen it before.
8	*Paula:*	No, never. I haven't seen it.
9	*Alexandra:*	No? OK, hmm, but I am going to send it by e-mail and

10		in that form they put=
11	*Paula:*	=The topics that they want to speak about.
12	*Alexandra:*	In fact, they put a title to their meeting [with students];
13		they indicate whether they have any preferences. **This is**
14		**something that we try to avoid** because if they say: "Ah,
15		I want, ah, I studied in the F550 school of—I don't know
16		where—I want to go there."
17	*Paula:*	OK.
18	*Alexandra:*	And, what really happens is that in that school=
19	*Paula:*	=Nobody cares.
20	*Alexandra:*	Exactly. Or for us it is suddenly like more complicated.
21		Now, anyway, if somebody wants it, and everything, we
22		do it. But we try that, we hope they will be open and
23		available and in in in the letter that I—because **this form**
24		**goes with a letter signed by me**. In that letter it says
25		that, "please be open to go to any place in the Region."
26	*Paula:*	These scientists are ready[the ones that will participate
27		in the activity]; do you have a list?
28	*Alexandra:*	The list is here. That's the one you had to ask Panchi [last
29		year's assistant for this activity], it's in a in a file.
30	*Paula:*	Yes, in a file.
31	*Alexandra:*	And in that file there are even the e-mails and everything.
32	*Paula:*	OK.
33	*Alexandra:*	OK. Then, they are the same from last year. But apart
34		from that, **we have also to look for and to send the**
35		**form, the form to all the people who work, that are**
36		**professors of the University**, be it 2,000, it doesn't
37		matter.
38	*Paula:*	OK.
39	*Alexandra:*	At least send it to—**send the nomination—the letter**.
40		We have to worry about sending the letter and the form
41		to the deans, OK, to the department directors,
42		requesting them to participate in this activity. The letter
43		that I send serves as the heading. OK.
44	*Paula:*	OK.
45	*Alexandra:*	That's it—and also send an e-mail to all these people. I
46		already sent you a form that I received.
47	*Paula:*	No.
48	*Alexandra:*	No? OK, then I'm going to send it to you.

The meeting is triggered by Paula when she asks for information, but also expressing a time limit to this discussion ("I must leave now," line 1–2). Consequently, Alexandra's explication will focus on what needs to be done for organizing this activity. Instead of a plain description of 1,000 Scientists, 1,000 Classrooms we have, in this sequence, a list of prescriptions, what we could already call a scripted trajectory, as taken in its common sense (i.e., the line from A to B).

This scripted trajectory is particularly presented in Alexandra's program of actions as she indicates the tasks that the different actors involved in this activity have to complete (Paula, the academics, the other institutions, and so forth). It is noteworthy that Alexandra focuses primarily on the 1,000 Scientists, 1,000 Classrooms' form to articulate this program of action (line 3: "Here is a form for the 1,000 Scientists"). From the beginning of this interaction—and, I would contend, through the overall organization of this activity—this form indeed appears to play a crucial role. As Alexandra explains in lines 6 and 12 to 13, this form is supposed to be filled out by the academics who will participate in the activity in which they "put a title to their meeting [with students]; they indicate whether they have any preferences" (lines 12–13).

By completing this form—personal data, conference information, and special requirement—the academics are not only entering the information required to coordinate this activity, they are also *committing themselves* to participate. In this sense, the form not only acts as a material trace of a personal engagement, a kind of organizational contract between the academics and Explora, but also *commits* its signatories to completing specific tasks for Explora. It is even explicitly written in the form's heading: "Participation commitment: 1,000 Scientists, 1,000 Classrooms, Tuesday, October 3, 2006." By giving a material character to this engagement, the form commits the academics by embodying their accountability vis-à-vis Explora with respect to this activity. In signing the form they are subscribing to the scripted trajectory presented by Explora (through Alexandra's speech and through the form) and can now be held accountable for it. In most organizational contracts this is meant to work both ways. However, in this case, since the form is only filled out by the academic, Explora can be said to be exempt from fulfilling its part of the contract (there are, though, other accountability instruments that do commit Explora's participation).

Still, for this form to be able to act as a contractual agent, it has to be associated with others in order to perform the required tasks of 1,000 Scientists, 1,000 Classrooms' scripted trajectory. By focusing on the form, Alexandra positions it as articulating these tasks. The scientists have to fill it out (line 6), Paula and Alexandra have to send it to all the professors of the university—to those who participated last year, to the deans, and to the department chairs (lines 40–42). In this case, the form acts as an *obligatory passage point* (Callon, 1986), what can also be understood as a point of intersection of multiple and diverse trajectories. All the information related to 1,000 Scientists, 1,000 Classrooms must pass through this form to be collected, classified, diffused, coordinated, and managed. In this sense, it plays an important role in aligning those multiple and simultaneous trajectories to a scripted story—a narrative of ordering "recursively told, embodied, and performed in a series of different materials" (Law, 1994, p. 259).

This story is the one Alexandra is projecting in her program of action based on her experience and on the specific goals and demands established by Explora's central committee. It is important to note here that the work of alignment is not only projected in the sequence of action presented in Alexandra's narrative but also already taking place in the actual interaction with Paula. As we can see in the excerpt, Paula aligns with Alexandra's program of action as she completes her sentences (lines 11 and 19) and agrees with her (lines 5, 17, 32, 38, 44). However, the story as it unfolds in this interaction not only refers to the things to do, it also includes the things not to do or to avoid (line 14).

Specifically, in this case, Alexandra instructs Paula to avoid special requirements from the academics (lines 12–16). Here, instead of including these requirements in the scripted trajectory, there is a specific instruction to omit it. The academics' preferences must not be part of the story if Explora's demands and goals are to be met. Again, there is a textual agent—the letter, signed by Alexandra that presents the activity and serves as the form's heading—mobilized to enforce this instruction. In reference to how the form is to be filled out, the letter explicitly says:

> If you have any preferences for a specific school and/or you have [already] committed your participation to a [particular] school, **we understand that the coordination of the activity will be your own responsibility** [bold in original]. In any case, communicate this information to us so that we can incorporate it in the activity's register and send the participation certificate.

The letter does not overtly deny the possibility of choosing a specific school. Instead, it frames the argument in terms of responsibility. By doing so, the letter clearly traces the boundaries between Explora's area of responsibility and what can be considered the professor's personal enterprise.

Ironically (and for the record), the letter also specifies that even if the coordination of these special cases is not taken care of by Explora, the information will be incorporated in the final report. Note here how boundaries are fluid as they constantly shift through Explora's discourse (as presented in Alexandra's program of action or in the letter) by defining an inside and outside. This process of boundary setting is not neutral. As we can see in the excerpt, it responds directly to specific criteria and standards. As Clegg and Kornberger (2006) contend, the manifestation of boundaries is the simplest and most basic way of organizing space, which is in fact a fundamental exercise of power. In the excerpt we can see that power is spatially exercised through the distinction of boundaries and also in the association of multiple and heterogeneous agents.

In associating the letter to the form and to Paula, Alexandra is aligning these agents so as to multiply their power of action (Latour, 1986a). By signing this letter, she is also materially authorizing this association and the specific actions that will be taken in this context by her "agents." We can also say that these agents—in association—represent Alexandra (and, furthermore, Explora). Through this *presentification* (Cooren, Brummans, & Charrieras, 2008), she is being incarnated, embodied into diverse materials. This way she is able to travel to different places simultaneously and successively. As a single individual, Alexandra would not possibly be able to meet every professor of the University to invite him or her to participate in this activity. She then has to delegate this work to other agents that will act in her name (and in Explora's name), that will follow her program of action, and will help her "virtually" meet those professors. However, for representation to be possible and effective, Alexandra has not only to authorize her delegates, but also be recognized as a legitimate author. This is possible now—and it was not the case 10 years before when Explora was just becoming known at the University—because of the intensive work of positioning Explora in the academic's agenda and also because of an institutional recognition of Explora's activities in the university and the scholar environment.

Here is Explora's first spatial and temporal movement concerning the 1,000 Scientists, 1,000 Classrooms activity: the dissemination of the form-with-the-letter "to all the people who work, that are professors at the University" (lines 35–36). We can see how this movement implies a great amount of work in enrolling and aligning actors, in intersecting and avoiding multiple trajectories and in defining specific boundaries. Now let's see what other spatial movements are about in a sequence that follows the previous one.

78	*Paula:*	Is that everything that there is to do? I mean, it's a lot but
79		what I'm saying is=
80	*Alexandra:*	=One moment.
81	*Paula:*	Oh, OK.
82	*Alexandra:*	That is, **on one side, then comes the other side**, that is
83		the coordinators.
84	*Paula:*	The schools, where the kids go.
85	*Alexandra:*	In fact, **she is preparing a form, Carla, get in touch**
86		**with Carla** … and get organized so that the teachers
87		indicate what **topics they would be interested in and**
88		**the grade of the students and how many students**
89		**there would be, what grade and the number of**
90		**students.**
91	*Paula:*	Then the topic they would be interested in, which course
92		(She repeats the information while taking notes.)
93	*Alexandra:*	Yes. **And the number of people.**

94		(Paula takes note)
95	*Alexandra:*	OK. So **collect on one side that information and after**
96		**[you cross them**=
97	*Paula:*	[I cross them
98	*Alexandra*	= *OK?*
99		(Paula moves her hands and crosses them).
100	*Alexandra:*	And it is necessary to assign each one and then=
101	*Paula:*	= The one closest to
102	*Alexandra:*	Exactly. So, there, after we have to=
103	*Paula:*	=To coordinate the date, the place
104	*Alexandra:*	Give them sufficient notice
105	*Paula:*	Of course
106	*Alexandra:*	And all that, OK. Now I'm going to send you the form
107		with the letter.
108	*Paula:*	OK
109	*Alexandra:*	When can we meet again the two of us to see this thing
110		of the system and how you think and to see the list you
111		have of what you collected from last year, OK, and all
112		that stuff? (While speaking, she takes out her day
113		planner.)
114	*Paula:*	Friday?
115	*Alexandra:*	At least the names. I know that Maria has them, those
116		from last year because of the certification, or maybe not.
117		It seems that Panchi also did that.
118	*Paula:*	**And how much is your—is your expectation?**
119	*Alexandra:*	**To beat last year's—that it seems to me they were**
120		**like 120.**
121	*Paula:*	**120, 120 is the minimum.**
122	*Alexandra:*	**We should have a minimum of 120 people.**
123	*Paula:*	**OK.**
124	*Alexandra:*	**OK. Now they can be 120 academics and like,**
125	*Paula:*	**Less schools.**
126	*Alexandra:*	**No, 150 conferences.**
127	*Paula:*	I mean that.
128	*Alexandra:*	Because sometimes we get some of them that are willing
129		to do two
130	*Paula:*	That is what I wanted to say.

Two important moments can be highlighted in this excerpt. The first one follows the logic presented previously; that is, Alexandra presenting her program of action and Paula aligning to it. Alexandra is now referring to "the other side" (line 82) of this program, which concerns the schools where the academics will go to present their conferences—the 1,000 classrooms part of this activity's equation. From lines 97 to 105, Paula aligns with Alexandra's explanations as she completes each utterance and finally marks a closure with an "of course" (line 105). This second part—"the other side"—is briefly explained, as both Alexandra and Paula appear to agree about the tasks that have to be carried out: assigning a conference to each school, coordinating the date and the place, and giving participants sufficient notice of the dates they will be expected to work with students. As in the first excerpt, it implies a spatial and temporal movement that is taking place outside the University and throughout the Region. There is also a space-time movement in the crossing of information, the intersection of two main trajectories—those of the academics and those of the school teachers—that have to be coordinated by Paula in order to create those encounters.

Again, we see how the tasks related to this program of action are articulated through a textual agent, another form that Carla is preparing (line 86) for the teachers of the participating schools to complete. There are then three new agents involved in the organization of this activity (at least according to Alexandra's story): Carla, the teachers' form, and the teachers themselves. It is worth noting that in this case the form is not associated with an explicit commitment; it is presented as a material trace to retrieve information about the topic of interest; that is, the number of students that will participate and their grade levels (lines 88–89). Alexandra thus defines Paula's tasks as simply 'collecting information and crossing it' but in fact, there is much more involved in these "accounting practices" (Quattrone, 2004).

Indeed, the filling-out of the form is not a neutral inscription of data. It enacts and reproduces the institution's ideology—which is understood as a complex work of compromise among political and social instances (Quattrone, 2004) as it embodies specific standards and criteria. In this sense, it is noteworthy that the form that Carla is preparing for the teachers corresponds to a part of the project that Explora Sur is presenting to Explora's central committee in order to obtain the budget for the different activities of the NSTW. As a translation of the NSTW project, the teachers' form embodies the central committee's requirements and expectations as well as those of the regional branch, which are strongly aligned. In fact the form functions as a projection of the activity as the teachers have to inscribe the estimated number of participants but once it is completed, it works as a control tool. In filling out the form, the teachers are implicitly engaging themselves to fulfill these standards (and Explora Sur is doing the same thing in completing the NSTW project).

As we can see in the excerpt, this accounting logic is also present in the interaction between Alexandra and Paula especially when, at line 110, Alexandra is fixing a date for a next update-meeting with Paula. This corresponds to the second important moment of this interaction that I would like to highlight. Here, Alexandra is making Paula accountable for the tasks that she is responsible for. In Alexandra's program of action—this scripted trajectory—there is also an accounting schedule through these weekly update-meetings to monitor Paula's advances. Even if Alexandra specifies the task that has to be accomplished at that time (lines 110–113), Paula anticipates a sanction in the overall goal of this activity: "And how much is your—is your expectation?" (line 118).

As we can see, Paula associates the activity's goal with Alexandra's expectation (not with Explora Sur or the central committee). This can be explained since Alexandra—as a project manager and as Explora Sur's regional coordinator—is held responsible for the NSTW, which includes the 1,000 Scientists, 1,000 Classrooms activity. Her expectations are then subsumed to Explora's central committee's goals (another scripted trajectory). We must remember that the activity's name is 1,000 Scientists, 1,000 Classrooms, which a priori presupposes a quantifying goal. Furthermore, this specific regional coordination has traditionally been very active in participating in this activity. Consequently, the goal for this year is determined with respect to last year's performance (line 120–126): minimum 120 academics or 150 conferences.

What is presented as Alexandra's personal expectation is in fact a collective one, in which Explora Sur's previous experiences and performance, as well as the central committee's standards are aligned. But it is not only a question of numbers; it also has do to with Explora being *present* everywhere in the region (and in the country) through this activity. Let us recall that Explora proudly refers to this activity as being The (with a big T) moment in the year when one thousand scientists get out of their research laboratories to travel, from North to South, to one thousand classrooms to talk about science and technology. Explora Sur also mobilizes this quantified and geographical argument, as is well illustrated in the opening paragraph of the form that academics receive:

> The participation of the region in this activity is **characterized by its great popularity and geographical range** [emphasis added], which implies at the moment of signing on that [scientists] accept the commitment to leave [the capital city of the Region] to meet with students.

Meeting these goals (number and geographical presence), as we will see next, will be the most important issue related to the organization of this activity (as it turns out, they will only be able to hold 80 conferences in 25 of the 45 cities of the region). The quantification of the activity will be, in fact, the guideline of the story-so-far told in this context and every program of action will be subsumed to this trajectory for it to become a success story.

In the following excerpt, which corresponds to an update meeting held one month after the meeting previously analyzed, Paula informs Alexandra that she has received only 12 forms from academics who are willing to participate in the 1,000 Scientists, 1,000 Classrooms activity. This unexpected incident triggers a series of adjustments to the initial program

presented by Alexandra at the first meeting. To be able to follow the
scripted trajectory, Alexandra and Paula now have a very limited period
in which to develop alternative strategies for enrolment. This constrain-
ing event brings to the fore quantification and time as important issues in
meeting the activity's goals.

1	*Alexandra:*	OK. Put this over there because I don't want to have
2		more things here (She gives Paula some papers and puts
3		other material on her desk such as books in order)
4	*Paula:*	(She opens a folder in which she has archived the
5		inscription forms received at the moment for the
6		activity.) I have received **twelve.**
7	*Alexandra:*	**Twelve?** (She stops putting her desk in order and looks
8		Paula straight in the eye.)
9	*Paula:*	Forms **at this moment.**
10	*Alexandra:*	You must now begin **to make telephone calls.**
11	*Paula:*	Phone calls, yes.
12	*Alexandra:*	Yes, that is question one. Second, send them **a reminder**
13		**e-mail.**
14	*Paula:*	OK.
15	*Alexandra:*	OK. To all the people, to **all the people** that you sent
16		[forms to], send them a second e-mail that says that you
17		have **extended the deadline** because the deadline has
18		passed.
19	*Paula:*	No, no, no, it's until **next Friday, the deadline.**
20		(…)
36	*Alexandra:*	OK.
37	*Alexandra:*	OK. Behind, please (She is referring to the papers she
38		gave Paula at the beginning of the meeting to put on
39		the table behind her). **Paula, this is, is urgent.**
40	*Paula:*	Yes, yes.
41	*Alexandra:*	Because we need to, to cross-file the information, also.
42	*Paula:*	But I haven't received any information from the other
43		side, or only two responses.
44	*Alexandra:*	That's because we are going to receive it on the 7th, Paula.
45		It was not requested before, OK.
46	*Paula:*	Hmm, hmm.
47	*Alexandra:*	**But, but what we need, we need to reach 100. That**
48		**means you are at 10%.**
49	*Paula:*	Yes.
50	*Alexandra:*	**OK, therefore you have to see a way, I don't know**
51		**how, but see a way for this to work, OK?**
52		(Paula nods)

As in the first meeting, Paula's presentation is straightforward. From her first intervention (lines 7 and 9) she frames the situation (and the overall interaction) in terms of numbers ("12") and time ("at this moment"). We can see, from the beginning, how the quantification and the timeline of the activity are enacted in the interaction as the guidelines of the 1,000 Scientists 1,000 Classrooms *story-so-far;* then as they are presented as the problem to be managed in order to meet the activity's goals. By framing this interaction (and the following ones) in these terms, a main trajectory is projected for the actors to follow to the letter. There is no questioning, for example, about the reason why so few professors responded to their call, or about the efficiency of the strategies used for enrolment.

After Alexandra's surprised (but brief) reaction in line 7, they rapidly engage in a task-oriented logic (very similar to the one analyzed in the first meeting) based on series of prescriptions to solve this arising problem: call by telephone (line 10), send a reminder e-mail (lines 12 and 13), extend the deadline (line 17–18). We could say that Alexandra and Paula are obliged to follow (are "under") a script (Latour, 2007; chapter 3)—the scripted trajectory, but a script they created and negotiated in their first meeting—when they were *over* it—but that is now actually framing their interaction, *telling them what to do*, so to speak. As Latour argues, this is the originality of an organizational script (as opposed to a novel, for example): "the situation changes completely and we are suddenly made to be the ones who insert instructions *into* the script" (Latour, chapter 3, p. 7).

Note that in this script the quantification and temporal frameworks are firmly associated, as they do not make sense on their own. There is the projected goal ("reach 100," line 47) that has to be met before the end of this project (the first Tuesday of October). There is the actual state of advance ("12 responses," lines 6–7), which represents only 10% of the expected goal (line 48). Consequently, the situation is being defined as urgent (lines 39) considering both the number of forms received at that moment and the project's timeline. The association of goals and deadlines is a crucial feature in scripts. This punctuates the rhythm of the coordination of the activity. In this case, the need to sign up 100 professors at the time of the event is what provides a rhythm for the interaction. In this passage, we can see how Alexandra and Paula use this spatiotemporal framework to position themselves before or after the script: "*I* have received *12* ... forms *at this moment*" (Paula, lines 7 and 9); "*You* must *now* begin to make telephone calls" (Alexandra, line 9); "*you* have *extended the deadline* because the *deadline has passed*." (Alexandra, lines 16–18); "No, no, no, *it's until next Friday*, the deadline" (Paula, line 19); "*we* need to reach *100*" (Alexandra, line 47), "*you* are at *10%*" (Alexandra, line 48). This positioning also implies the setting of boundaries of responsibility (especially in lines 48 to 51) as Alexandra positions herself and Paula (and both of them together) with respect to the main trajectory. We can see here an inclusion/exclusion dynamic: "*we* need to reach 100", "*you* are at 10%," "*you* have to see a way [to get this done]," "*I* don't know." As in the previous meeting, we can see that the enactment of boundaries is fluid as the actors are sometimes positioned inside or outside the scripted trajectory.

Spacing is here at work through a particular organizational mode of being, that of a *project* that has the capacity to control us once we have designed or created it (Latour, 2013). It is this spacing dynamic that we can see in this excerpt through three types of movements: to be over/under, before/after, and in/out the scripted trajectory. In this excerpt (as in the previous ones), these movements appear to be associated mostly to discursive strategies enacted in interaction: framing, positioning, accounting, and so forth. In the following excerpt, we can actually see how those spacing practices are physically embodied and how this materiality does make a difference (or at least that is what Alexandra believes) in enrolling new participants in the 1,000 Scientists, 1,000 Classrooms activity.

Alexandra and Paula now coconstruct alternative strategies of enrolment following the unexpectedly weak response to the call to participate in the 1,000 Scientists, 1,000 Classrooms activity. Let us recall that in order to encourage the academics to participate in this activity, an invitation letter, signed by Alexandra, was sent by Paula via e-mail with a participation form. Now, this association of the letter-with-the-form, authorized by Alexandra (through the signing) as a legitimate spokeobject seems to have not been sufficiently powerful to fulfill its task. Interestingly, a strategy that had worked in past years appears in this case to be ineffective. Alexandra thus proposes to develop a new strategy—what she calls "door-to-door"—to physically hand the form to the academics. This time, it is not the letter that will introduce the form; it is Paula who will travel with the form to the academics' offices in order to obtain their collaboration. Furthermore, Paula will have to find an ally from the department where she is doing the "door-to-door" strategy to introduce her to the professors. It is then the ally-with-Paula-with-the-form that are now authorized by Alexandra as spokespersons to represent her (and Explora) by making themselves physically present (in time and space) in the academics' offices. The "door-to-door" strategy is based in the embodiment of the organization in this actor-network that has the particularity of being physically/materially present (in a more corporal and "aggressive" way than in the case of e-mail).

The following excerpts show Paula, Andrés (her ally in the Chemistry Department), and the form in their first attempt to persuade a professor to participate in 1,000 Scientists, 1,000 Classrooms. We will see next that there is much more implicated in acting out the scripted trajectory. Paula will have to justify her presence (even mine and the camera's), validate the door-to-door strategy, and defend herself as a legitimate spokesperson and this without even leaving with the form duly completed by the academic.

1	*Andrés:*	(He approaches an open door. He looks in to see if there
2		is someone inside and looks back to Paula.) He is there,
3		let's go.
4		(Paula follows Andrés. Andrés knocks the door.)
5	*Andrés:*	Professor?
6	*Prof.:*	Hello
7	*Andrés:*	**Can I bother you for a moment?**
8	*Prof.:*	Sure, yes, come in.
9		(Andrés enters the professor's office. Paula stays near the
10		door.)
11	*Andrés:*	**What happens is that I come from Explora** (He points
12		towards Paula, she steps in timidly.) and this is the
13		person in charge of the 1,000 Scientists, 1,000 Class-
14		rooms program and she would like to talk to you.
15	*Paula:*	(She steps forward a little more) Can you give me a
16		minute, professor?
17	*Prof.:*	Yes, come in.
18		(Paula enters the office. Andrés looks at me. I remind
19		him that he and Paula have to ask the professor for
20		permission for me to film this conversation.)
21	*Andrés:*	Prof. (this informal way to say Professor is commonly
22		used by students in Chile), does it **bother you** if …
23		comes in (He points toward me. I go in.)
24	*Paula:*	If the camera comes in? We are doing—she is doing a
25		PhD study (She turns toward me.) from the University of
26		Canada and needs to film what I am going to say. Does
27		it bother you? If it does, we turn off the camera.
28	*Prof.:*	No. (He shakes his head.)
29	*Paula:*	OK. **What happens is that I'm here to make you an**
30		**invitation**.
31	*Prof.:*	Let's see.
32	*Paula:*	**(She takes out a form from a folder**.) The folder is blue
33		and has the logo of the University. **What happens is**
34		**that in October it is going to be Science Week.**
35	*Prof.:*	Yes.
36	*Paula:*	OK. **I don't know if you have heard about the activity**
37		**1,000 Scientists, 1,000 Classrooms?**
38	*Prof.:*	Hmm, hmm.
39	*Paula:*	**I've come to** see if you would like to participate, if you
40		are interested in participating (She looks down to the
41		form.) This activity is on October 3, only that day.
42	*Prof.:*	**And why do they do this through you and not the**
43		**person in charge here in our Faculty? It's Rafael, I**
44		**think**? *(He looks toward Andrés to confirm this*
45		*information.)*

46	*Paula:*	**What happens is that** Alexandra Valderrama talked,
47		hmm, she asked for the permission for us to do the
48		subject of
49	*Prof.:*	Ah, OK.
50	*Paula:*	To do the door-to-door. **What happens is that every**
51		**year we need to have at least 100 professors**
52		participating and going to the cities here in the region.
53	*Prof.:*	Hmm, hmm.
54	*Paula:*	And, in fact, now **we have a deficit of 70%.**
55	*Prof.:*	Aaah!
56	*Paula:*	So we are developing alternative strategies.
57	*Prof.:*	Hmm, hmm.
58	*Paula:*	For us to have **engaged professors**, OK. Because it's
59		**very important that the professors go, from the**
60		**University they go**
61	*Prof.:*	No, [I understand
62	*Paula:*	[go, go to the classrooms and that
63	*Prof.:*	Yes
64	*Paula:*	They **make the university closer.**
65	*Prof.:*	Yes.
66	*Paula:*	for the elementary school students.
67	*Prof.:*	Yes.

The first lines of this excerpt give us the tone of the whole interaction: Paula and Andrés (especially at the beginning) have to justify their presence. Andrés—as Paula's ally—is the designated person in charge of introducing her and Explora to each professor. Interestingly, in this case, he frames their presence as something that bothers his interlocutor (line 7)—he repeats a similar statement in asking for permission to film the interaction—and then starts explaining the reason why we are there. To an unusual situation is associated a justification. Note that he uses the expression "what **happens** is that" (line 11). Paula also uses this same expression several times throughout this interaction (lines 29, 33, 46). The door-to-door strategy is being presented both by Andrés and Paula as a happening, something unusual, an event that asks for some form of rationalization/justification. Now we can see that this event is being rationalized by Paula and Andrés in invoking and mobilizing different agents that they represent and doing so is intended to authorize them to be there at that moment.

Let's take, for example, Andrés's utterance at line 11: "What happens is that I come from Explora" and the he points at Paula. In mobilizing Explora, Andrés is actually presenting himself and Paula as Explora's spokespersons. We see how he is invoking the organization as a rationale for justifying their presence. Following the same logic he presents Paula as the person in charge of 1,000 Scientists, 1,000 Classrooms, the spokesperson for this activity. Paula invokes the power of other types of agents in order to justify her presence. She introduces a series of facts: "What happens is that in October it is going to be Science Week" (lines 33, 34), "I don't know if you have heard about the activity 1,000 Scientists, 1,000 Classrooms?" (lines 36–37). Note that between these two utterances, Paula takes out from the folder a participation form (just after she says that she comes to make an invitation). The form is being mobilized as a material support of the invitation. It legitimizes the facts that Paula is invoking to justify her presence.

In both cases, one could contend that Paula and Andrés present the facts or the organization in their discourse as a spacing mechanism to justify their presence. Ironically, the "door-to-door" strategy, which is based on the spokesperson's physical presence, can only start working once this presence is accounted for or justified. In this case, the justification consists of mobilizing Explora itself and all the activities it organizes. Explora and all these activities are supposed to authorize/justify/account for Paula and Andrés's presence. In this case, these accounting practices are key in acting out the scripted trajectory. To space the organization, Paula, Andrés, and the form must account for whom/what they represent.

What is particularly interesting in this passage is Paula's confrontation as a legitimate spokesperson. We can deduce that the organizational and factual arguments (presented in their discourse and supported by the form) were not really persuasive in justifying or accounting for Paula and Andrés's presence. At line 42, the professor overtly questions Paula as a legitimate spokesperson and by doing so a priori rejects the way she justifies or accounts for her presence in his office. This triggers another series of arguments (lines 43–54) that Paula frames again as facts ("What happens is that …"). Even in invoking Alexandra, Explora's regional director and a well-known professor at the University, Paula *presents* her in the context of asking permission for the "door-to-door" strategy. Paula then mobilizes the projected goal for this activity and the actual situation. The scripted trajectory is this time mobilized as a justification argument.

Finally, Paula invokes the University's mission of being closer to society and emphasizes the professor's status and responsibilities in this mission. In this passage, we see how Paula invokes different agents to defend herself as a legitimate spokesperson: the dean's permission, a recognized person (with a higher status than hers), a projected goal with its actual deficit, the professor's status and his responsibilities as well as a social principle. In fact, we could contend that it is not only Paula, Andrés, and the form (and me with the camera) that have entered the professor's office. It is a cluster of different and heterogeneous agents that are being made present here and now in the name of Explora, whose capacity to travel (and to be here and there at the same time) relies on these heterogeneous associations as well as Paula's power to legitimate herself as spokesperson and to justify her presence. In looking at the professor's response (especially in line 55 when he exclaims "Aaah") we can say that Paula's strategy was apparently effective.

Discussion

The purpose of this analysis has been to look for the spacing practices involved in the organization of 1,000 Scientists, 1,000 Classrooms, an activity organized by Explora, a Chilean government program of science and technology diffusion, in the context of National Science and Technology Week. With the analysis of these three episodes, I intended to illustrate how through these spacing practices an organization—in this case Explora—can move, be transported, translate itself to be here and there at the same time.

Following the definition of space-time discussed in the conceptual framework, we can find in this illustration two kinds of spacing practices. The first one refers to the developing or strengthening of a network of agents that will act in the name of the organization—and by doing so, will multiply its presence in space and time (by as many spokespersons as the organization has). In this case, we saw how the project manager associates various actors—her assistant, a form, a letter—and authorizes them to represent Explora in the task of inviting the academics to participate in the 1,000 Scientists, 1,000 Classrooms activity. This spacing practice of enrolment is intimately related to an ordering work of alignment, a scripted trajectory presented in the project manager's program of action in terms of what to do and also of what to avoid. We have analyzed this work of alignment as the intersection (and nonintersection) of multiple *stories-so-far* subsumed to the scripted trajectory. This corresponds to the second type of spacing practices through which the simultaneity of different trajectories is captured and ordered into one main story.

In this context, we saw how nonhuman agents—specifically in this case, the form—have an important and active role to play in enacting the scripted trajectory. They act as articulators of dissimilar trajectories when placed as obligatory passage points. They also act as agents of accountability by materially inscribing commitment and therefore committing its signatories. In considering both of these spacing practices—the hybrid association of spokespersons (and *spokesobjects*) and the intersecting (and nonintersecting) of trajectories—space is being created (but not an empty space, one filled with heterogeneous actors and diverse trajectories), and the 1,000 Scientists, 1,000 Classrooms activity is being constructed. Then in spacing organization there is both a geographical notion of space as many individuals and objects are enrolled to act in the name of Explora, and a four-dimensional definition of space as many stories are intersecting (while others are not). There is a successive displacement, from one place to another, from one time to another, but there is also a simultaneous displacement in all the coexistent stories related to the 1,000 Scientists, 1,000

Classrooms activity being told at the same space-time. Therefore, *spacing organization implies both a movement of succession and of simultaneity.*

This dynamic of succession and simultaneity is what explains the organizational mode of being here and there at the same time. Spacing is about being able to move sequentially and simultaneously thereby assuring continuity, which renders the organization and management of the project even more complex. The *here-and-thereness* of an organization constitutes a major dilemma precisely because the organization's spokespersons (which are, as we saw, multiple and heterogeneous), will evolve and, as they do, the continuity of the organization—the coherence of *then-and-nowness*—may be threatened. To preserve and maintain the organization's continuity an ad hoc mode of accounting must be developed.[6] As illustrated in the analysis, the actors assumed that they had to account for their presence and legitimate themselves as spokespersons. At the end of the road, it always seems to be a question of (re)presentation. Indeed, representation is the basis for understanding the organization's capacity to be here and there at the same time. Yet it is also what endangers its coherence and continuity and this explains the continuous need to justify or account for it.

In this analysis, we saw that scripted trajectories are important in maintaining this coherence as they align the different *stories-so-far* in one main story. In the case we studied, a scripted trajectory (negotiated and coconstructed in the first meeting) provided the guidance for the subsequent actions and interactions as the organizational actors acted it out (not without some improvisational skill) to fulfill their tasks. In this acting out of the script we can find three spatiotemporal movements as actors are being positioned under/above, before/after, and in/out the script. In the case we studied, these spatiotemporal movements respond to a particular mode of being of organization, that of a project, which has the capacity to create a before and an after by scheduling deadlines and appointments through the alignment of diverse means (Latour, 2013). Through this case we also saw that the actors were sometimes under the project—when it told them what to do—and sometimes over it—when they discussed it, questioned it, and adjusted it. The scripted trajectory framed their action but was also mobilized by the actors to set boundaries: inside/outside, before/after, and over/under the script.

This process of boundary setting is the simplest and most basic way of organizing as it enfolds and encloses some activities and excludes others (Clegg & Kornberger, 2006). In the case we studied, the delimitation of boundaries was guided by the meeting of a specific goal: a number of conferences to attain (around 100) in a specific timeline. By framing this story in terms of quantification and time, it subsumed and put aside all other possible stories that could have been told. As Paula, the assistant of the 1,000 Scientists, 1,000 Classrooms activity expresses it: "The success of this activity will be measured in how many conferences we were able to coordinate but if the students learned something or if the academics where pleased by this encounter, we will never know."

We saw, through these spacing practices how space is fundamental in any exercise of power. As Foucault (1984) argues in referring to the relation between space and power, discipline proceeds from the distribution of individuals in space. Now, Foucault focuses primarily on architectural space (as in the Panopticon) but we can transpose his arguments to a four-dimensional interactional space. As we showed in this analysis, the positioning of different agents in space and time above/under, in/out, and before/after a script plays a similar disciplinary role.

Notes

1. Tarde (1899/1999) and Whitehead(1929/1978) have argued that anything can be considered as a society. We have animal societies, solar societies, molecular societies, and so forth; what changes is the composition of the elements of the society under study.

2. The work of Law (Hetherington & Law, 2000)— and Law and Singleton (2005)— can be considered an exception. Also inspired by actor-network theory, he introduces topology—a branch of mathematics that explores the character of multiple spaces enacted by the movement of multiple shapes—to answer to the ontological dilemma of what is an object. Law (2002) overtly explores this topic spatially arguing that, "the making of objects has spatial implications and that spaces are not self-evident and singular, but that there are multiple forms of spatiality" (p. 92). His starting point can be found in Latour's (1987) notion of an immutable mobile—something that moves around but also holds its shape—which Law associates to what he calls a network-space. Following the same logic he presents an array of spatial possibilities. These include, along with networks, regions, fluid, and fire spaces; all related to different objects.

3. This ethnographic study was funded by the Fonds de Recherche sur la Société et la Culture du Québec and the Social Science and Humanities Research Council of Canada titled: "Espacer l'organisation: trajectoires d'un projet de diffusion scientifique au Chili" [Spacing organization: Trajectories of a diffusion science project in Chile].

4. In general, shadowing is defined as a research technique, which implies following a person as his or her shadow, walking in his or her footsteps while taking many field notes. Similar to participant observation, shadowing is used over a relatively long period of time, the researcher's objective being to follow the person throughout his or her different activities over the course of a day (McDonald, 2005). I discussed elsewhere the methodological implication of this technique to follow the hybrid character of action by engaging in a critical reviewing of contrasting uses of shadowing in the organizational literature (Meunier &Vásquez, 2008).

5. It is worth noting that since Chile has a large but narrow territory, the expression used to mean "all of the country" considers only North and South (and not East and West). In fact, there is a Chilean expression "from Arica to Punta Arena," which are the most northerly and most southerly cities of Chile, respectively.

6. These reflections arise from an e-mail exchange with James Taylor after the preconference, "What is an Organization? Materiality, Agency and Discourse," Montreal, May 2008.

9 Restructuring Identity through Sectorial Narratives

Isabelle Piette

For over 20 years, researchers in organization theory have wrestled with the idea of organizational identity. Various explanations of the stable or changing (Chreim, 2005), objectal or processual (Ravasi & van Rekom, 2003), cognitive or emotional (Oliver & Roos, 2007), macro or micro (Brickson, 2000) nature of identity have been discussed, classified, and commented upon. Our goal is to contribute to this debate by presenting the results of a discursive study of organizational identity. Many studies have used conversations, biographical narration, letters to shareholders, and organizational reports to shape the discursive perspective (Beech & Johnson, 2005; A. Brown & Humphreys, 2006; Humphreys & Brown, 2002). However, few studies have developed a theory of organizational identity born of the environmental narrative.

Thus, the present study will look at organizational identity through sectorial narratives and will consider its discursive construction as embedded in a worldview. Regarding the legislative reform case of the brewing industry, we study a ministry's change in narrative identity. We examined the production, transmission, and textual structure of two sectorial narratives produced in 2004 and 2006. Using a literary study approach, we analyzed and compared both documents as intentional acts and structural artifacts created within a social context. Our research indicates that sectorial narratives provide a deep structure, comparable to a scene, which allows the members of an organization to affirm an identity, legitimize a role, and stabilize a social position. By negotiating a new social structure, sectorial narratives become a strategic resource for the Quebec Ministry for Economic Development (QMED).

In the first part of this article, we will define the concept of organizational identity and, more specifically, the concept of narrative identity. Next, we will outline the case in question and the research problem. In the third section, we will present the analytical methodology and framework, followed by the results of the analysis. Finally, we will discuss these results and the contribution of the research.

Organizational Identity

There are many definitions of organizational identity. Some researchers define it as a distinctive and fundamental attribute tied in with organizational values, culture, performance, and products (Elsbach & Kramer, 1996). Others describe it as a collective understanding of the distinctive values and characteristics of the organization shared by the employees and the stakeholders (Hatch & Schultz, 1997). Finally, some define organizational identity as that which is fundamental, enduring, and distinctive in an organization (Whettent & Godfrey, 1998). These definitions are founded on the concept of the organization as an entity with objective characteristics, specific components, and relative stability. The organization's ontological status, its origins, and behavior are not questioned. Unlike this concept, we view the organization as the unstable result of organizing processes, a kind of social dynamic in a constant state of flux. The organization is created out of interactions, interpretations, mechanisms of power, texts, and discourses. For many years now, several researchers have viewed the organization as a social construct built by "everyday life" interactions, knowledge processes, and situations (A. Brown & Humphreys, 2006; Kärreman & Alvesson, 2001; Taylor & Van Every, 2000). In this framework, identity is seen as an institutionalized social expression instead of a set of beliefs, intentions, and shared attitudes (Whettent & Mackay, 2002). It reverts to a social construct as opposed to a core essence (Corley et al., 2006).

Organizational identity is shaped and modified by the interactions between the organization's members (Humphreys & Brown, 2002; Kärreman & Alvesson, 2001) and stakeholders (Chreim, 2005; Hardy, Lawrence, & Grant, 2005; Hardy, Palmer, & Phillips, 2000). It evolves through habits and practices that affect their worldview, values, and conventions. Organizational identity is the result of continuous construction by the participants in relationship with the organization and the environment. In this context, identity is a social construct that is both a catalyst for action and the social result of this action (Hardy, Palmer, & Phillips, 2000). Therefore, it is rooted in interaction, the acquisition of knowledge, and the discursive process.

According to (Czarniawska-Joerges, 1994), organizational identity is a metaphor of organization to which actors adhere in conjunction with the organization. As such, the organization becomes a *superperson*, an institutionalized entity capable of having an impact on the world. This explains why many researchers (Kornberger & Browns, 2007; Taylor & Van Every, 2000) believe that organizational identity is a kind of discursive interface similar to a hub of mediation where the results of negotiations between employees, management, and other stakeholders are briefly fixed. From this perspective, communicational practices organize the organizational identity (Ainsworth & Hardy, 2004; Hardy, Lawrence, & Grant, 2005; Taylor & Van Every, 2000).

The research associated with this trend shows the importance of narration as a discursive process in the development of identity. Many researchers (Ainsworth & Hardy, 2004; Chreim, 2005; Czarniawska, 1997; Giroux, 2006; Humphreys & Brown, 2002) touch on the concept of "narrative identity" by citing the works of Ricoeur (1990), Giddens (1991), and Bruner (1991). In this context, identity is a narrative construction (Chreim, 2005; Czarniawska-Joerges, 1994) to self-expression within a reflexive, operative, and semantic process (Ricoeur, 1990). Identity is formed and transformed through the creation, expression, and reception of the narrative. The narrative acts as a hermeneutic framework, which allows a person to find a place within the worldview, act with purpose, develop a rationale, make sense of and justify the established order of things, and proclaim its self-existence (Ainsworth & Hardy, 2004; Ezzy, 1998).

The narrative identity implies formulation, editing, and legitimacy. It requires a speaker and a receiver interacting in a narrative process (Czarniawska, 1997; Czarniawska-Joerges, 1994). Thus, whether we are considering the product of conversations between different actors (Hardy, Lawrence, & Grant, 2005) or official acts of communication (Chreim, 2005), the narrative is an action that mobilizes and creates social, symbolic, and political constructs (Ainsworth & Hardy, 2004; Humphreys & Brown, 2002). It is a process that uses symbolic and discursive resources (Hardy, Palmer, & Phillips, 2000) along with rhetorical techniques to generate a structured and structuring text. This allows the narrative to create a temporary image of the self and of the world, which gives meaning to events and a means to interact with the world.

Chreim (2005) has noted that the narrative identity of the organization differs from the narrative identity of the individual. Because of their collective nature, organizations have multiple authors and stakeholders who may produce several and different narrative identities at any point in time. An organizational narrative identity reflects power positions and authorial preferences (p. 570).

In this way, the narrative identity of an organization shapes not only the organization's identity, but also that of the employees (Humphreys & Brown, 2002) and of other organizations (Davis & Harré, 1990). It makes sense of the events that affect the organization and of its relationships with its stakeholders. This narrative identity must conform to society's expectations of rationality, consistency, and unification (Bourdieu, 2000). Therefore, the organization's narrative identity grows out of negotiations, interactions between internal and external stakeholders, as well as legitimization (Czarniawska, 1997).

This construct clearly shows the unstable nature of organizational identity. In fact, the narrative identity will evolve according to the context, the knowledge, the authors, and the audience (Giddens, 1991; Giroux, 2006). Not only does the narrative of identity define the organization from several perspectives, it also positions the organization within a changing landscape. Ricoeur (1990) says that it exposes an *idem/ipse* dialectic. In other words, the narrative identity is an adaptive continuity that allows an organization to remain "true" to itself while continuing to metamorphose. Chreim (2005) studies this paradox by illuminating the process of continuity and change that maintains an organization's identity through periods of flux. Other researchers offer different explanations of the changing nature of organizational identity such as (a) the use of symbolic and discursive resources to change the perception of the organization's stakeholders, its position, and its possibilities for expression (Hardy, Lawrence, & Grant, 2005), (b) imposing new categories and meanings on the organization's employees (Brown & Humphreys, 2006; Humphreys & Brown, 2002), (c) creating conversational practices that instantiate the organization in new contexts (Kärreman & Alvesson, 2001), or (d) the development of social categorization processes that reposition the organization within its environment (Lewellyn, 2004).

Few studies explain the organization's changing narrative identity in terms of the environmental narrative. In fact, we have noticed that a sectorial portrayal and dissemination of an apperception of the industry to the stakeholders have rarely been studied in the context of understanding the changes in an organization's narrative identity. Yet, Giddens (1991), Czarniawska (1997), and Charles Taylor (1998) tell us that the narrative identity has meaning only from the perspective of the subject embedded in its time and social space. Giroux (2006) says that: "Identity positions and defines the individual with respect to an alter ego either to confirm the similarity (belonging to a social group) or to delineate the difference (marginality, unique characteristic)" (p. 45). In this context, we believe that the creation of sectorial narratives constitutes an interesting basis from which to study the organization's changing narrative identity. In fact, the sectorial narratives illustrate the means by which the organization becomes embedded in society, the roles and status of the organization and its stakeholders in the world, as well as the forces that give direction to the quest for organizational identity. Therefore, the purpose of this paper is to explore the different sectorial narratives of the organization and to follow the evolution of its narrative identity. The empirical portion of this manuscript will begin with the presentation of the case study that will enable us to pursue our research problem.

Legislative Prereform of the Brewing Industry

The Quebec brewing industry experienced a veritable transformation after the liberalization of the market, the arrival of microbreweries, and the restructuring of the food and beverage stores. In the early 2000s, the

Quebec government reassessed the brewing industry following lobbying by local brewers, complaints from small merchants, and pressure from the *new public governance*. In 2002, the Alcohol, Racing, and Gambling Agency[1] (ARGA) began a process of legislative reform. Approximately 20 government agents were called upon to provide individual input into the proposed reform. The Quebec Ministry for Economic Development[2] (QMED) which, along with the ARGA and the Quebec Alcohol Board[3] (QAB), is responsible for the laws governing alcoholic beverages, was particularly affected by these consultations. In fact, the ARGA questioned QMED's reason for being. In 2003, the recommendations retained by the ARGA marginalized QMED's position within the brewing industry.

In early 2004, QMED invited the ministries and agencies of the brewing industry to an "in-depth examination" of the economic impact of the reform in order to identify problems and measures that could become the object of a government consensus. Another government consultation was undertaken, and QMED's representatives, who were responsible for coordinating the consultative process, attempted to reestablish the legitimacy of QMED's position within the brewing industry. Throughout 2004, the problems associated with the distribution and marketing of beer were discussed and addressed by a dozen stakeholders and the interministerial committee developed a unified vision of the brewing industry. In light of this vision, the committee met with both public and private sector stakeholders in closed meetings to establish a common diagnostic and to determine the topics for consideration. A status report of the brewing industry was written and presented to government officials in 2004. The committee members attested to the importance of the financial impact of the reform, proposed an exhaustive analysis of the industry, and a revision of the functions attributed to each of the government bodies. In 2005, following the introduction of the report, a second study of the brewing industry was undertaken by QMED's representatives, and a new document was submitted to QMED in March 2006 detailing the state of the industry, its stakeholders, and the competitive environment. This report was subsequently presented to several other government agencies including the QAB and the ARGA.

Thus, two reports were produced by QMED's representatives: the first one in November 2004 and the second in March 2006. While both of these documents paint a portrait of the brewing industry, there is a clear shift in the narrative. In fact, both official documents rest on different narrative tracks; the facts and the data are virtually identical, but the way in which they are presented has changed. Furthermore, we have noted that these changes coincide with the numerous disruptions taking place within QMED over the same period. In fact, the name of the QMED work group, the director, the employees, the mandate, and even the offices occupied by the group changed between 2004 and 2006. In this framework, we will explore the transformation of the narrative identity within the context of legislative reform. Our goal is to understand how the change in sectorial narrative from 2004 to 2006 reflects QMED's quest for an identity.

Methodology

The goal of this paper is to understand the change in narrative identity. To this end, we will examine two sectorial narratives (the reports) produced by QMED in 2004 and 2006 for the purpose of (a) exposing the organization's representations and environment, (b) recounting the interactions between the organization and its stakeholders, (c) identifying QMED's challenges and objectives, (d) understanding narratives' system of internal significance, and (e) retracing the enunciative modalities used to legitimize the organization's purpose and position within its industry. Through the comparison of these two sectorial narratives, we will trace the evolution of QMED's narrative identity. From this perspective, we have adopted an approach that regards the narrative as both acts of expression (discourses) and as artifacts (texts).

Many authors have developed narrative methods based on literary studies (e.g., Boje, 2001; Czarniawska, 1998). In this same vein, the methodology used in this research rests on French sociocritical literary studies (Bourdieu, 1991; Dubois, 1992; Duchet, 1979). Our research postulates that narratives are the social, political, and symbolic result of a drafting process and are guided by intention, context, rules, and references. The sociality of the narrative is determined by the context in which it is produced, and the text may have an impact on society (Dubois, 1992; Pelletier, 1991). Therefore, we examined the narratives within an analytical framework that considers the context, the process, and the textual structures.

Analytical Framework of Sectorial Narratives

This research is inspired by Ricoeur's (1986) analytical approach and is based on a strategy of critical hermeneutic analysis. This analytical framework has been used by Phillips and Brown (1993) and by Prasad and Mir (2002) to analyze the meaning and relationship of the organization interacting with its environment. The critical hermeneutic approach used in this research allows us to connect different levels of narrative interpretation through the *hermeneutic circle*, which integrates the parts into the whole and the whole into its parts. Furthermore, this analytic framework allows the narrative to be studied within its *hermeneutic horizon*, in other words, embedded within its culture, its authors, and its interpretation. To this end, it fuses divergent data, analytical techniques, and interpretive systems into a coherent approach. The analytical framework we employed is broken down into three steps with specific objectives, data, and analytical techniques.

The first step of our analysis relates to the narrative context and production process. At this stage, we will illuminate the purpose and the intended project of each of the narratives produced in 2004 and 2006, as well as the drafting process. Our research employed many sources including a 2-hour semidirected interview with a member of the organization that participated in the drafting of the report, a validation interview, and close to 20 ministerial notes and work documents used during the drafting process.

The second step of our analysis deals with the textual structures of the narratives. The purpose of this step in the analysis is to delve into the content, depictions, and enunciative modalities of these sectorial narratives from 2004 and 2006. This step mixes two complementary analysis techniques: (a) Greimas's (1983) actantial model, which analyzes the narrative's content, and (b) Gourdeau (1993) and Genette's (1983) narratological analysis, which looks at the way in which the narration is told.

Greimas's (1983) actantial model analyzes the narrative's content through its actions and the interactions of the actants (human, animal, or object). According to Greimas, all narratives are a *hero's quest* for a *valuable objective*. The hero's quest is motivated by a cause and has a clear outcome. The *sender* is the element that establishes the *junction* between the quest and the hero. The *receiver* is the element that benefits from the quest. In addition, the quest is hindered by at least one obstacle that pits the hero and his *helpers* against an *opponent*. To fulfill the quest, the hero must follow a *narrative program* (a method by which the objective is attained) that leads him to accomplish a *principal performance* (the central action required to compete the quest) with the help of a *modal performance* (secondary action). In this section, the actantial model will allow us to identify several actants playing various parts, to see the relationship between the actants, to define QMED's representation and that of its environment, and finally, to identify the actions retained to reach the objective. A table will be used to compare the analysis of both narratives.

The narratological analysis put forth by Gourdeau (1993) and Genette (1983) looks at the way in which the narration is told. According to Genette (1983), all writings are a verbal representation (narrative) that recounts a story (series of events and actions) through an act of creation (narration). The author enters into an implicit narrative contract with the audience that predetermines the logic of the story. From this perspective, the narration opens a fictional space (the narrative) where a story told to an audience by a *narrator* unfolds. Therefore, the narratology analysis studies the story in terms of the *enunciative grammar* (Benveniste, 1966). It categorizes the story into time of narration, narrative voice, and narrative perspective (Gourdeau, 1993). Time of narration places the time of the narration in relation to the time of the story. This duality brings out the length of the story with respect to the length of the text. It allows us to consider the relative importance of the narrative (discourse) compared to that of the story (content). Narrative voice examines the relationship between the story and the *narrator* (the storyteller). It considers the *narrative time* and the *narrative levels*. The narrative time looks at the moment when the events are recounted. Is the story taking place in the past, present, or future, or at the same time as the narration? Narrative levels consider the narrator's position in relation to the story. Is the narrator inside the story (*intradiegetic*) or outside of it (*extradiegetic*)? Does the narrator participate in the story (*homodiegetic*) or not (*heterodiegetic*)? Finally, narrative perspective examines the way in which the narrator perceives the story and the fictional space. It clarifies the narrator's point of view and his or her access to information. Is the narrator omniscient or is his or her perspective limited to immediate knowledge? Analysis of the narrative structure through time, voice, and perspective allows us to uncover the modalities of QMED's representation and the enunciative strategies used. A table will be used to compare the analysis of both narratives.

The third step of the analysis synthesizes all the elements to examine QMED's narrative identity. In this section, the results of the previous steps contribute to developing an understanding of QMED's identity as it was expressed in 2004 and 2006. To this end, we will apply Czarniawska's (1997), Giddens's (1991), and Ricoeur's (1990) concepts, which consider narrative identity in terms of (a) the coherence of the subject's experience and the way in which it is expressed, (b) the subject's memory, which ensures the continuity of its identity and expresses the change, and (c) the statement of the subject's *subjectivity* in relation to the situation. At this point, we will retrace the elements that support the coherence of QMED's experience as the hero or secondary actant in the narratives. We will identify and explain the processes that ensure the continuity of and the changes in QMED's identity. To conclude, we will evaluate and describe the extent of QMED's commitment in the narratives. A table will be used to compare both narrative identities.

Results

First Stage: Production of the Sectorial Narrative

The first narrative was written in the context of a consultative approach within the brewing sector. Three QMED advisors coordinated and drafted a report examining the economic problems and issues of the industry. From January to November 2004, QMED's advisors created an interministerial committee to look at the brewing industry, to negotiate with stakeholders from other ministries and agencies, to organize private consultations with the brewing industry's associations, and to provide statistical analyses for the purpose of drafting a document. In 2004, a 38-page confidential report was submitted. This report was divided into five parts:

the introduction (3% of the document), the context (29%), the problems (47%), the recommendations (5%), and the appendices (16%).

The goal of the report was to legitimize QMED's role within the brewing industry's legislative reform project and to position the ministry as the principal agent of economic development in the industry. To this end, QMED, in conjunction with the QAB, wrote a ministerial memo to emphasize that:

> [QMED] believes that it is important to revise the jurisdiction and responsibilities of the M/A [ministries and agencies] to ensure that those required for the economic development of the industry are clearly assigned. [QMED] believes that it is important for one agency, preferably a ministry—probably [QMED]—be responsible for the economic development of the alcoholic beverages sector. (memos, January 24, 2004)

At this time, QMED's group of representatives responsible for the brewing sector's economic development also tried to consolidate its position within the ministry. Michel, an advisor for QMED, explained, "I told Jacques [the director]: 'We have to take this [the economic development] in hand; that's our mandate.' Jacques had no choice but to say so. At one point, we had the whole consultation and the reports to do; it was huge" (Interview, August 15, 2006). The assertion of QMED's legitimacy within the project of legislative reform of the brewing industry represented an important case and an opportunity to promote the team's know-how.

The second narrative was written in answer to the recommendations made in the 2004 report. In fact, the report concluded, "The Quebec government should complete the gathering of strategic information … as this would allow us to complete the analysis of the situation regarding the manufacturing and distribution of beer" (MDERR, 2004, pp. 31–32). However, this second report involved solely the members of QMED and was not intended to be kept strictly confidential. It was closely tied to the internal pressures and changes of QMED. In fact, its purpose was to grow QMED's strategic vision in the sector. According to Michel, a QMED advisor, "the deputy minister said: each group responsible for a sector should develop its strategy … we had to have one too" (Interview, November 22, 2007). Throughout 2005 and 2006, a newly hired advisor supervised new information gathering, and analyzed and drafted an exhaustive portrait of the industry with the help of two QMED advisors and a few stakeholders from other ministries and agencies. The 39-page document submitted in 2006 was divided into five sections: the introduction (3% of the document), the context (21%), the structure of the industry (64%), the diagnostic and the strategies (10%), and the conclusion and recommendations (2%). Subsequently, the report was presented to the Quebec ministries and agencies.

The document was drafted under difficult circumstances, during conflicts between the members of the group responsible for the brewing industry and pressures that brought about a restructuring of the group. The director was replaced, the mandate revised, the workspace reduced and reorganized. Members of the group retired, new advisors were hired, and the group was officially renamed. In this context, the creation of the 2006 report represents an important accomplishment for the group and for the ministry.

Second Stage: Analysis of the Sectorial Narrative

The Actantial Model.   Analysis of the actantial models shows that the narratives from 2004 and 2006 develop different constructs for the brewing industry and for QMED. The actantial model of the 2004 narrative centers on the Quebec government's quest for riches. The report begins with an observation on the incompatibility between the legal framework and the business practices of the brewing industry. This issue led the government to reevaluate the legislative provisions. The narrative states that:

> The two-fold purpose of Quebec's new beer marketing strategy put in place in 1992 … was to open up the Quebec market … [and to allow] the Quebec brewing industry to adjust to its new competitive environment. However, the partial information gathered by the inter-ministerial work group on beer … justifies a comprehensive review of the legislative, regulatory, and administrative provisions. (Ministère du Développement économique et régional et de la Recherche [MDERR], 2004, p. 1)

In this context, the government's helpers battle the opponents who are attempting to divert economic wealth away from Quebec. To obtain this wealth by legitimate means, the ARGA was commissioned by the government to revise the permit system, at which point QMED supported the ARGA by imparting its knowledge and know-how.

The actantial model of the 2006 narrative is also centered on the Quebec government's quest for riches. The report also begins with the disparity between the legislative system and industry practices. In the 2006 narrative, however, new, more diffuse, helpers and opponents make their appearance. Another notable difference is that the government called upon QMED to remedy the situation, as it is responsible for the activities that promote economic development. In this case, the ARGA supported QMED in revising the legal framework. Table 9.1 shows the results of the analysis using the actantial model.

Table 9.1 Comparison of the Actantial Structures of the Sectorial Narratives

Elements	2004 narrative	2006 narrative
Sender	Inefficiency of the marketing system established in 1992 Official acknowledgement of illegal marketing practices Cumbersomeness and incoherence of the legal framework	Outsourcing and relocation of production activities overseas Restructuring of the industry Development models for the brewing industry
Hero	ARGA	QMED
Object	Economic wealth	Economic wealth
Receiver	People of Quebec	People of Quebec
Helpers	Ministries and agencies Quebec micro-breweries Major Quebec breweries Quebec retailers	Ministries and agencies Quebec micro-breweries Major Quebec breweries Quebec retailers Consumers Technology
Opponents	Major Quebec breweries Foreign superstores operating in Quebec Trade agreements Canadian provinces	Major Quebec breweries Large grocery chains Trade agreements Canadian provinces Neo-liberal ideology Technology
Narrative program	Create a new legislative system	Adopt and implement economic measures
Principal performance	Revise the entire permit system	Understand the dynamics of the industry's economy in order to implement effective measures
Modal performance	Understand the dynamics of the economy	Revise the legislative framework

We can see that the quest of both sectorial narratives is essentially the same and reveals a similar account of a relationship of desire (see Table 9.1). However, the actantial model shows that this "relationship of desire" (Greimas, 1983) is created through different worldviews, senders, and value systems. First, we observed that the initial states of the narratives present divergent perceptions of the industry. The 2004 narrative emphasizes the history of the brewing market and of Quebec's system for marketing beer. The legal framework determines the roles and conditions of the actants, and indeed, of the competitive environment.

> All of the provincial and state governments of Canada and the United States carefully manage their beer markets in order to maximize profits and tax benefits, and to minimize negative social impacts. The modalities, constraints and restrictions of the Quebec marketing sys-

tem for foreign beer is comparable to the systems in place in the other Canadian provinces and in the United States. (MDERR, 2004, p. 11)

By contrast, the initial state that is described in the 2006 narrative shows intervening factors in the competitive structure and dynamics of the market. The narrative depicts not only the legal context, but also the demographic, political, economic, and financial makeup of the industry. It focuses on the latitude afforded the actants and on the economic forces at work. Thus, the narrative defines the industry as a place of economic games, negotiations, and strategic allegiances operating under the pressures of globalization.

In keeping with Quebec's other industries, the brewing sector is increasingly polarized. On the one hand, we have the large international brewing companies who have divided up the market share both locally and internationally. On the other hand, we have the local micro-breweries that must contend with the conditions negotiated between the large brewers, distributors, and retailers. (Ministère du Développement économique, de l'Innovation et de l'Exportation [MDEIE], 2006, p. 37)

Therefore, we can observe that the initial state in the 2004 narrative rests on a legislative equilibrium, while the initial state of the 2006 narrative rests on an economic one. Consequently, the senders that initiate the quest are different.

In the 2004 narrative, the apparent inefficacy of the marketing system, the uncompetitive practices, the merging of the major Quebec breweries with foreign businesses, and the lobbying of the companies led to the quest. In fact, it is the impact caused by the marketing system that launches the action. "The situation created by the new Quebec marketing system for beer and the interpretation of some of its modalities ... spurred a reevaluation of our legislative, regulatory, and administrative measures, and their underlying direction with regard to beer" (MDERR, 2004, p. 13).

By comparison, the quest described in the 2006 narrative is initiated by "the outsourcing of production and/or the relocation of production activities" (MDEIE, 2006, p. 38). According to the document, "National business[es] have a tendency to disappear for the benefit of global entities, and the various governments must develop policies that favor the growth or the maintenance of the current economic activity" (MDEIE, 2006, p. 33).

In this context, the heroes are defined with respect to their role and place in the industry. In the 2004 narrative, the ARGA, as the entity responsible for the development and enforcement of the marketing system, is the principal actant. In the 2006 narrative, QMED becomes the hero because its "mandate is to develop strategies and action plans that promote the brewing industry's economic development" (MDEIE, 2006, p. 1). We conclude, therefore, that the perception of the initial state of the industry affects the *communication of the quest* (Greimas, 1983) and the identification of the hero.

Furthermore, Jouve (1997) postulates that this stage of the narrative elucidates the values and norms that propel the hero. In the document from 2004, the ARGA appears to conform to the norms and laws of the governing body. The hero begins to quest not only in response to market pressures, but also to reestablish the legitimacy of the Quebec government. To this end, the 2004 narrative states, "Several stakeholders highlighted that the current competitive conditions in the Quebec beer market have become inequitable and counterproductive. They must be revised…. Therefore, these stakeholders invite the Quebec government to clean up its market" (MDERR, 2004, p. 17). The 2004 narrative indicates that the accumulation of wealth originates in reestablishing the Quebec government's authority and in compliance with the laws. However, the 2006 narrative refers to economic intervention, innovation, and industry collaboration as the catalyst. Faced with the globalization of brewing activities, QMED, "must implement policies" (MDERR, 2004, p. 33) and "business retention programs and attractive conditions" (MDERR, 2004, p. 38). The hero conforms to business norms (managing innovation, information, and intangible assets) to improve the sector's and the province's competitiveness. In 2006, wealth is accumulated for the people through "proposed strategies and action plans" (MDEIE, 2006, p. 1).

The quest of each narrative unfolds through distinct power relationships. Regulations, norms, and trade agreements govern the relationship between the helpers and the opponents in the 2004 narrative (see Table 9.1). The legislative framework and economic norms define the relationship between the actants. The power issue is the result of incoherence, deficiencies, or contradictions within the legal framework and from the clash of the laws with the business practices. Therefore, power resides in the ability to create regulation, "manage" business norms, and influence public opinion.

In the case of the 2006 narrative, the focus is on Quebec's penetrable borders and the threat of globalization. It defines a larger number of helpers and opponents (see Table 9.1) that form alliances. "The partnership between the large brewers and distributors should intensify because they need each other" (MDEIE, 2006, p. 35). This scenario creates some ambiguity about the relationship between helpers and opponents: "Instead of competing in similar markets, with similar products, using similar marketing tools, they will have to develop strategic alliances to streamline their activities, increase their negotiating power, and maintain their shelf space" (MDEIE, 2006, p. 36). In the 2006 narrative, power resides in the ability to create and manage strategic alliances.

From this perspective, the two texts offer different narrative programs on the quest for economic wealth. The narrative program of the 2004 text focuses on establishing a new marketing and distribution system for beer. This program rests on the ARGA's principal performance, that is, "a comprehensive review of the legislative, regulatory, and administrative measures…, and their underlying direction" (MDERR, 2004, p. 1) as well as on the modal performance to develop its knowledge of the industry. This knowledge is "essential [and] must be obtained directly from the industry prior to initiating any reform" (MDERR, 2004, p. 1). On the other hand, the narrative program of the 2006 report emphasizes, "establishing cooperative measures that will reconcile corporate interests with the socioeconomic development of society as a whole" (MDEIE, 2006, p. 34). To support this program, QMED must understand the dynamics of the industry and its development models. In this way, the 2006 narrative attempts to "formulate a diagnostic" (MDEIE, 2006, p. 1) of the structure and "development models of the brewing industry" (MDEIE, 2006, p. 29).

The actantial models of the narratives show different content in terms of the perception of the industry, the actants, the values, the power relationships, and the narrative programs. More specifically, an examination of the content reveals differing perceptions of QMED within the brewing industry and varying possible interactions with the actants. In the 2006 narrative, QMED is a hero with the ability to act in the industry, while the 2004 narrative shows QMED as a secondary actant.

Narratological Analysis.   Analysis of the narrative structures reveals distinct narrative modalities in terms of time, voice, and perspective. Table 9.2 compares the results of the analysis for both texts. The span and temporal order of the 2004 and 2006 narratives differ (see time in Table 9.2). The 2004 narrative covers a greater time span than the one from 2006, and the temporal forms used to narrate the story create distinct temporal orders. The timeframe of the 2004 narrative is also more complex than that of the 2006 text. In fact, the narrative structure from 2004 is divided between the *context* section and the *problems* section. The report begins with the *context* section, which provides an overview of the industry's history and actants. The narration recounts important events by moving back and forth through time. This allows the narrator to show the impact of historical events on the present situation. Verb tenses move from present, to past perfect, to imperfect, then back to present. However, this narrative structure changes in the following section, the *problems*. At this stage, there is a lengthy pause in the narration to present four issues divided into 28 discussion topics. In this section, the discourse becomes omnipresent, and the history and actants of the industry are no longer at the forefront. The verb tenses employed here are the present and imperfect.

Table.9.2 Comparison of Narratological Components of the Sectorial Narratives

Components	2004 narrative	2006 narrative
Time	Time span of the story: 1944–2004 Narrative forms: summary and pause	Time span of the story: 1986–2008 Narrative form: scene
Voice	Several narrative voices Time of narration: past and present Narrative level: homodiegetic and intradiegetic	Single narrative voice Time of narration: present and future Narrative level: homodiegetic and intradiegetic
Perspective	Diegesis mode Limited knowledge or narrator Internal perspective of the government	Mimesis mode Omniscient narrator External perspective

The narrative structure of the 2006 document, by comparison, presents a series of scenes that justify the discourse in the introduction, the diagnostic and strategies, and the conclusion and recommendations. The story is told mostly in the present tense with a few elements told in the past. The actions and interactions of the actants are elucidated through the description of the industry. Thus, the dominant "narrative form" is the scene where the unit of discourse equates to a unit of story (Gourdeau, 1993).

Furthermore, we observed that the narrative voice differs from one document to the other. The narrative produced in 2004 uses several narrative voices, while the one from 2006 employs a single voice (see Table 9.2). In the 2004 narrative, the expressive acts are explicit and are accentuated with temporal and spatial indicators (*deictics*) such as *until now, today, currently, here, In Quebec*, and by the use of the pronoun *we* (Benveniste, 1966). In addition, we discerned a multiplicity of voices which allows for many perspectives on the industry, many different demands, and many different interpretations. These voices relate to the stakeholders in the brewing industry. They are compared and contrasted: *we, our partners, this work group* against *them, the permit holders, the other Canadian provinces and the American states*. These voices are structured and recorded through a collective narrator: the interministerial work group. They are not directly referenced. Instead, *we* and *us* are used in the narration of the debate. The report is peppered with *many stakeholders question, many stakeholders put forth, the small retailers request, the QAB favors, Canadian brewers would like*. Thus, the narration in the story (intradiegetic) and in the fictional space (homodiegetic) uses the time of narration to elucidate the present and debate sectorial issues.

In the narrative from 2006, a single voice tells the story and discusses the challenges facing the industry. This lone voice of the narrator is present in the story (intradiegetic) and in the fictional space (homodiegetic). The narrator is present in the introduction, diagnostic and strategic, and conclusion and recommendation sections through the use of the pronoun *we*, the present tense, and temporal and spatial indicators such as *At the present time* and *here* (Benveniste, 1966). We observed, however, that 85% of the text showed few enunciative markers (deictics), that it is written in the third person, and that it uses the present and future tenses for narration. This is done to convey a sense of neutrality and objectivity (Benveniste, 1966).

Finally, the narratives rely on opposing narrative perspectives (see Table 9.2). On the one hand, the 2004 narrative is narrated as a *diegesis mode* (Genette, 1983) where the presence of the narrator is not hidden. On the other, the 2006 narrative is primarily narrated as a *mimesis mode* where the story seems to show itself without outside intervention (Genette, 1983). In the narrative from 2004, the story is told and publicized by several voices that debate the issues, question the knowledge, and provide justifications. As a result, the understanding of the industry appears subjective and incomplete (Ducrot, 1984). For example, from the outset, the narrator notes "the absence and ambiguity of some information" (MDERR, 2004, p. 1). In this sentence, the narrator presents openly the interministerial group's limited understanding.

In 2006, by contrast, the narrative reduces and mitigates subjective remarks by using single voice, common and established knowledge, tables, statistics, graphs, diagrams, and many details. By doing so, the narrator creates *real effects* (Barthes, 1982) or a *referential fallacy* (Riffaterre, 1978). He appears omniscient; he understands the issues, the needs, the aspirations, and even the future of the actants. Thus, the 2006 report explains the major brewers' strategy for the coming years by stating, "this group's own gravitational force will end its mutation ..." (MDEIE, 2006, p. 34). These enunciative modalities objectify this perception of the industry to create a sense of objectivity.

The narratology analysis reveals that QMED's commitment to the narration is greater in 2006 than in 2004. In truth, the 2004 narrative denotes a complex composition of voices debating the roles and issues of the industry. QMED is just a voice among many. However, the 2006 narrative shows QMED as authoritative and omniscient. This voice imposes its perception of the industry and determines the purport, roles, and condition of every actant.

Third Stage: Elucidating the Narrative Identity

Studying the production of the narratives and their textual structures reveals that the sectorial narratives bear the marks of QMED's narrative identity. By applying Czarniawska's theories (1997), we are able to reconstruct QMED's narrative identity in terms of coherence, continuity, and commitment to the experience. Table 9.3 shows the comparison between identity elements of both QMED narratives.

Table 9.3 Comparison of the Elements of QMED's Narrative Identities

Elements	2004 Narrative	2006 Narrative
Coherence	Function of the State within the industry QMED's position within the government Legislative reform of the brewing industry Consultative process Compliance with and respect for laws and authority Use of several voices coordinated by a collective narrator Diegesis narrative perspective Limited knowledge justifies negotiations	Function of the State within the industry QMED's position within the government Desire for economic balance Economic intervention, innovation, and collaboration are valued Globalization issues and collaborative strategy Models for the development of the brewing industry Narrative form: scene Omniscient narrator
Continuity	Constancy of the State and its laws Historical context of the industry and its legal framework Constancy of the same government and business stakeholders Temp span of the story and narrative level of the report	Constancy of the state and of trade agreements Context of legislative reform Historical context of the legal framework Constancy of the businesses Temp span of the story and narrative level of the report Mimesis narrative perspective
Commitment	QMED's role as an expert in economic development Narration from an internal perspective Opportunity to participate in the industry's negotiations by organizing the consultative process in 2004	QMED's key position as an agent for economic development Strategic planning process in the industry and tabling of measures Objective narration of the structure and functioning of the industry Narration from an external perspective

In 2004, QMED organized a consultative process and produced a sectorial narrative. Through the production and publication of this narrative, QMED experiments with an intervention from inside the brewing industry. This experience occurred within the context of a legislative reform initiated by the ARGA at the beginning of the 2000s. Through its expertise in economic development, QMED is enlisted into the ARGA's project. We observe several elements which contributed to the coherence of this experience (see Table 9.3); first, the importance attributed to the growth and development of the legal framework within the industry, and QMED's position within the government. Next, the coherence is rooted in compliance to and respect for laws and authority.

The narrative is driven by a desire to create, manage, and influence the norms and regulations that form the basis for the negotiations. From a narratological perspective, the use of several voices in the narration and the diegesis mode further complement the cohesion between the production process and the narrative. The continuity of QMED's experience rests on the constancy of the State, as well as on the historical context of the industry and the legislation (see Table 9.3). The narration gains legitimacy through the continuity afforded by the frequent use of flashbacks. Finally, we notice that QMED's commitment is rooted to his role in the creation of the narrative (the organization of the consultative process and the drafting of the report) and in the structure of the narrative. The actantial model and the narrative track reveal QMED to be a secondary government stakeholder, an expert in economic development; a key player in the process of reform and a member of the collective narrator of the narrative (see Table 9.3).

By comparison with the 2004 narrative, the 2006 narrative is based on QMED's experience with strategic planning in 2005 and 2006. In this context, the narrative's coherence is rooted in QMED's official mandate, which is to ensure economic development without hindering the social equilibrium (see Table 9.3). The narrative is further supported by values of economic intervention, innovation and collaboration. The narrative also confirms its coherence through the issue of globalization, the strategies adopted by the stakeholders and the development models that followed. QMED attempts to clarify them to better focus its actions. Therefore, the narrative form and narrator's omniscience make the strategic planning of collaboration inevitable. In addition, continuity relies on the constancy of the State and of the trade agreements (see Table 9.3). The historical contexts of the legal framework and the legislative reform form a backdrop for the changes made within the coherent continuity. In the 2006 narrative, QMED's commitment is evidenced by its role as an active participant and visionary in its unilateral definition of the industry. In fact, the narrative produced in 2006 defines the industry, delineates it and qualifies it formally and officially. From this perspective, it occupies a key position: that of narrator and of *hero-protector*; QMED is the point of reference for economic development.

Both narratives appear to create different organizational identities for QMED. In fact, they do not elucidate the same coherence, continuity, or commitment (see Table 9.3). Their narrations refer to divergent portrayals of QMED as actant, distinctive ways to express his experience (in 2004 narrative QMED is a voice among many versus in 2006 narrative QMED is the single authoritative and omniscient voice) and different understandings of the course of events. QMED's identity is more established in 2006 than in 2004, and it inserts itself into a more stable, less ambiguous perception of the industry. In the 2006 narrative, QMED is able to act on the world and bring about significant change. The value system on which its actions are based rests on its own quest. Therefore, in these narratives, we can clearly see a desire for expression that is in keeping with the changes experienced by the group responsible for the brewing industry at QMED in 2005 and 2006. In fact, the new team has greater influence both within QMED and with the other ministries and agencies. As Michel, an advisor for QMED, says "we have a little more elbow room and we're taken more seriously" (Interview, November 22, 2007). We can conclude that these different sectorial narratives reflect a change in QMED's narrative identity.

Discussion

The Strategic Narratives

Our results reveal that the members of the group responsible for the brewing industry's economic development within QMED officially and formally changed their narrative identity from 2004 to 2006. How? And why? Many researchers (Ainsworth & Hardy, 2004; Hardy, Palmer, & Phillips, 2000; Taylor & Van Every, 2000) suggested that narrative identity is linked to a worldview and is established in collaboration with the stakeholders. Hardy, Palmer, and Phillips (2000) noted that individuals can change organizational identity by engaging to discursive activity to intervene through the production of concepts, objects, and subject positions. In this perspective, transformation of organizational identity represents the enactment of particular strategies (Hardy, Palmer, & Phillips, 2000). From Czarniawska's (1997) point of view, organizational actors used several textual strategies and rhetoric to express their organizational identity. They used a set of devices to claims their social position, improve their credibility or justify their worldview to other actors in or outside organization (Czarniawska, 1997). Thus, change of narrative identity implies introduction of new statement, receptivity of stakeholders, use of rhetoric, and *textualization process*.

In this context, it appears that the change in narrative identity of QMED came from negotiations with stakeholders which establish a collective understanding of the industry, better means of expression and new structures to make sense of industry. As demonstrated in the third stage of analysis, the organizational identity of QMED is transformed as a result of the publication of the narrative on the brewing industry. In 2004, QMED's advisors attempted to legitimize their position in the industry in the face of ARGA legislative reform. In order to defend its position, QMED organized and coordinated a consultative process and drafted a report. In this way, QMED's advisor introduced a new discursive statement through the use of narratives which influences their stakeholders. Michel, an advisor for QMED, explained that after the 2004 was submitted, the ARGA was more aware of the economic impacts, and it was like a cold shower for them. It put the brakes on their fervor to change everything. They realized that they couldn't do whatever they wanted without first analyzing the impact. (Interview, November 22, 2007)

The consultative process changed ARGA's plans and created a new understanding of the industry. The 2004 narrative formalized the debate and structured a collaborative vision. Indeed, we saw that the diegesis mode of narrative formalized the collective narrator and consensual construct around the worldview (see p. 264). From this perspective, the narrative, and the process through which it was created, strengthened QMED's position and its mandate. In fact, it appears that the 2004 sectorial narratives became a strategic resource for QMED members to reinforce and proclaim their organizational identity (Hardy, Palmer, & Phillips, 2000).

From Taylor, Cooren, Giroux, and Robichaud's (1996) point of view, the narration process of QMED is similar to a textualization process. Conversations and negotiations of the consultative process are transformed and fixed into an official and published text. The text objectifies the perception of the industrial sector and the position of organizations in a *distanciation process*. According to Taylor et al. (1996):

> [D]istanciation is a consequence of the dialectic of speaking and writing. By writing the discourse down—"fixing" it—discourse is objectified (and hence "sheltered from destruction"). It becomes part of a practice, the object of a technology, "a material to be worked upon and formed." As an object, it is decontextualized, distanced from its origins, made accessible to an "unlimited set of reading." (pp. 23–24)

Therefore, narrative as artifact acts as a social structure and gives meaning and explanation. In this way, the impact of the 2004 narrative allowed QMED's advisors to develop a new narration with a more defined narrative identity. In 2005, QMED's advisors began drafting a new sectorial narrative. Indeed, since the publication of the 2004 narrative, they have benefited from a renewed legitimacy, greater powers of expression and an acknowledgement of their expertise. This allowed them to draft a new narrative in which QMED was the hero of the industry and the single omniscient narrator. According to our study, we affirm that sectorial narratives allowed QMED's advisors to change the ministry's identity through a narrativization of the industry. Through narrativization meaning is negotiated, new structure is created, and a legitimate figured world is constructed.

Conclusion

The goal of our study was to understand the transformation of narrative identity through sectorial narratives. To this end, we analyzed and compared two sectorial narratives produced by QMED in 2004 and 2006, during the legislative prereform in the brewing industry. The results of this research showed that production of sectorial narratives implies a hidden autobiographical act and highlighted the importance of the dissemination of a worldview for the assertion of an organization's identity and the consolidation of its position. It reveals that the creation of sectorial narrative acts as a strategic resource.

Thus, our study contributes to the discursive perspective of organizational identity in a few ways. First, it proposes to analyze identity in a sectorial narration and negotiated construction of a worldview. Second, it develops an analytical framework which examines narrative as both acts of expression and artifacts. Third, this paper shows empirical evidence that demonstrates the *distanciation process* of the text (Ricoeur, 1986; Taylor, Cooren et al., 1996) in the context of interorganizational relations.

These observations lead us to suggest several research avenues. The conceptual framework presented in this paper has demonstrated that there are many future avenues and implications for further research. Our findings emphasize a certain necessity to bridge a gap between narratives as artifact and narrative as a situated action. In addition, other study of sectorial narrative from market reports or strategic planning could be done to develop a deeper understanding the narrativization impact on interorganizational relations.

Note

1. The Alcohol, Racing and Gambling Agency's French name is Régie des alcools, des courses et des Jeux (RACJ). In 2004, the French title of the Quebec Minister of Economic Development was "Ministère du Développement économique et régional et de la Recherche" (MDERR). However, in 2006, the same minister changed his title to "Ministère Développement économique, de l'Innovation et de l'Exportation" (MDEIE). The Quebec alcohol board's French name is Société des alcools du Québec (SAQ).

10 Organization by Debate

Exploring the Connections between Rhetorical Argument and Organizing

Mathieu Chaput

What is an organization? Much interest has been generated among social scientists in their attempts to answer that question. However, it can be said that the ways of dealing with this *ontological problematic* have been modified considerably in recent years. For a long time, the main metastrategies have included postulating "prior definitions" (Durkheim) or "ideal-types" (Weber) of what an organization *is* (or should be), ultimately resulting in dominant product or entitylike conceptualizations. Organization was then conceived as an always and already present reality, in which various social phenomena were accomplished and could be neutrally observed.[1]

That particular view, while still existing today, is nonetheless being increasingly challenged from a variety of perspectives, including those held by the growing field of organizational communication. By successively undertaking what may be referred to as "interpretive" (Putnam & Pacanowsky, 1983), "discursive" (Alvesson & Kärreman, 2000a,b; Grant, Hardy, Oswick, & Putnam, 2004; Mumby & Clair, 1997; Putnam & Fairhurst, 2001), and potentially "interactional" (Cooren, 2007) turns, scholars in that field have gradually transformed organizations from an *explanandum* to an *explanans*; that is, from what constitutes the source of explanation to what should be accounted for and explained (Latour, 2005; Taylor & Van Every, 2000). Thus, we can note an important and undergoing change in the various ways that communication is linked to organization. This relationship can no longer be recognized strictly as a *containment* type, where communication is what circulates within a reified and a priori organizational structure; nor is it limited to a *production* type of relationship, where communication and organization are said to produce one another but with the remaining "chicken and egg" problem of identifying which one first came into being; but it is also instantiated as an *equivalence* type of relationship, which implies that communicating and organizing are one and the same phenomenon (Fairhurst & Putnam, 1999, 2004; Putnam, Phillips, & Chapman, 1996; Smith, 1993; J. R. Taylor, 1995).

Subsequently, since the early 2000s the research agenda in organizational communication scholarship has been focused, among other things, on an enduring interest in the question of organizational ontology and the ensuing role of communication. This focus is not limited to the study of communication *in* organizations, but is also devoted to understanding how organizations are constituted *through* communication (Putnam & Nicotera, 2009). And obviously, there is not one prevalent manner available to deal with this question. Consequently, propositions to address this question of "what is an organization?" have often taken the form of full perspectives on communication, with the likes of postpositivism, social constructionism, structuration theory, critical theory, and feminism (Corman & Poole, 2000; May & Mumby, 2005). In other instances, responses have been developed as more specific communication practices or modes of discourse, including narratives (Czarniawska, 1997), speech acts (Cooren, 2000), and conversational sequences (Boden, 1994).

The present essay addresses what could be identified as one potential but often neglected communication practice linked with the process of organizing. More explicitly, it tries to explore how the practice of argumentation can be associated with the "communicative constitutive question" of organizational ontology; that is, with "how organizations are discursively constituted through language and interaction processes" (Fairhurst, 2004, p. 336). This exploration will proceed through three phases. First, we briefly review the initial rejection of argumentative discourse as an acceptable model of organizational communication. Then, we propose to reframe this discussion by putting forward three perspectives on argumentation with subsequent connections to the organizing phenomenon, arguing for the potential contribution of a rhetorical view on argument. In the third section, we provide an illustration of such a rhetorical perspective through the detailed description of an episode of deliberations, undergoing between delegates of a recently born political party. Throughout this case analysis, we try to summarize the relevance and implications of rhetorical argumentation as a practice and method to account for the question of "what is an organization."

Argumentation in Organizations: The Initial Rejection

To highlight the connections between argumentation and the study of organizations, one would have to start in principle by reviewing the appropriate literature in order to infer some generalized comments on the state of the art in that precise area of research. However, before we come to this point, we consider it more meaningful to begin with an elaborate case *against* the relevance of argumentation as a method for the study of organizational life, as it seemed mostly depreciated as a mode of discourse at the time when the "interpretive turn" was undertaken in the field of organizational communication.

This critical moment was first initiated at the beginning of the 1980s, with the introduction by Walter R. Fisher (1984) of his theory of human communication as narration, anchored in a conception of *homo narrans*, or humans as "essentially storytellers" (p. 7). His proposal was built around a distinction between what he presented as two incommensurable modes of thinking and speaking, identified as the rational and the narrational paradigms. The former had its roots in philosophical rationalism, valued rationality, technical knowledge, and posited argument as its main genre of discourse. Fisher would state that within the rational world paradigm, "argument as product and process is *the* means of being human, the agency of all that humans can know and realize in achieving their *telos*" (p. 4).

In contrast to universal standards of validity and truth, narration was presented by Fisher (1984) as operating through the production of "good reasons" of real-life actors, and judged accordingly by criteria of *narrative probability* (i.e., as coherent stories), and *narrative fidelity*, as whether similar to or plausible in relation to lived experiences. One important contribution of the narrative paradigm, according to Fisher, lies in its greater sensibility to context, which implies that what can be evaluated as good reasons vary according to dimensions such as situation, media, and genres. It also contributes to reconnecting persuasion with aesthetics, *logos* with *mythos*, discourse and reason with stories (Fisher, 1985). In addition, his model contained not only epistemological but political implications as well, recognizing the natural capacity of beings to tell meaningful stories. In opposition to the rational world paradigm where experts and specialized fields of arguments reign, the transition to stories and to a *logic of good reasons* encompassed values and motives in the public sphere, making them decisive in the conduct of public moral arguments.

While mostly intended for the field of rhetorical theory and criticism, Fisher's dual paradigms provided solid theoretical foundations for the narrative analysis of organizations. And nowhere is this influence more palpable than in Karl Weick and Larry Browning's (1986) influential essay on models of organizational communication. Introduced as a review essay, the article rapidly transformed into a call for conceptual innovations, deploring that, at the time, "[t]he current study of organizational communication ha[d] too much organization and too little communication" (p. 244). In opposition to the predominant transmission view of communication, Weick and Browning proposed to introduce and evaluate the alternative models of argument and narration but, faithful to Fisher's (1984, 1985) paradigms, they quickly dismissed the former in favor of the later.

They claimed that argumentation was not differentiated enough to capture the richness of organizational life. Comparatively, they argued that narration supplies an "emphasis on meaning, interpretation, and understanding" (p. 248). According to them, the practice of argumentation should be associated with a "mechanistic view" of organization (Weick, 1987), favoring technicality and hierarchy as opposed to the interactivity and flexibility of stories (Browning, 1992) that not only maintain but also create organizational cultures. In short, their *partis pris* in favor of narrative analysis can be summarized by the assertion that "most models of organization are based on argumentation rather than narration ..., yet most organizational realities are based on narration" (Weick, 1995, p. 127). Argumentation was thus rejected in terms of the study of organizational communication, being presumed insufficient to grasp the full richness of organizational life.

While these consequences can be difficult to measure directly against Weick and Browning's (1986) promotion of the narrative paradigm, any dedicated observer is able to measure the exponential interest regarding stories and storytelling in organizational settings during that era. And recent reviews indicate that narrative analysis covers a wide range of theoretical perspectives, from the functional stance to the interpretive and from critical theory to postmodern approaches (Gabriel, 2004; Giroux & Marroquìn, 2005; Rhodes & Brown, 2005). By contrast, the study of argumentation in organizational settings has received considerably less attention, although qualitatively significant. To a lesser extent, it can also be mentioned here that although traditional study of argumentation was subsumed under the broader field of rhetoric, contemporary developments in organizational rhetoric have largely appropriated the Burkean tradition, which places emphasis on identification rather than persuasion and on the unconscious rather than deliberation and argument (Cheney, 1983a, 1983b, 1991; Cheney, Christensen, Conrad, & Lair, 2004; Cheney & Lair, 2005; Meisenbach & McMillan, 2006).

So, where can we go from here if we now wish to make the case *for* the argumentative study of organizations? An initial, but somewhat expected reaction would imply challenging all assumptions underlying the distinction between the rational and narrational paradigms. Consequently, we could pinpoint the many inconsistencies and even contradictions within the theory (Warnick, 1987), or we might plead for a critical confusion between genres of discourse and paradigms (Rowland, 1987). We could also mention here the rather problematical polarization between reason and narrative (McGee & Nelson, 1985), as well as the limited application of the model to discourses that are not stories (Rowland, 1989). At a different level, we could arguably cast doubts on the whole relevance of paradigms to account for communication practice and theoretical differences in the domain of social sciences (Giddens, 1989). But in choosing this path, we would remain stuck with the whole paradigmatic confrontation, not to mention the risk of facing the conventional rejoinder by the author, claiming that most criticisms are misplaced or based on partial understanding of the theory (Fisher, 1987, 1989).

A second possible reaction would involve mobilizing the "straw person argument" (cf. Miller, 2000) as a fallacy, thereafter rejecting the partial reading of argumentation proposed by Weick and Browning (1986) and others in favor of a "purer" depiction of what argumentation should be.

But this would equate here with the production of another fallacy, the *argumentum ad verecundiam*, or argument from authority. A third solution would be to envision the different possible answers to the question of "what is argument?" That way, we would be able to the grasp various perspectives on argument in order to better explore how they can connect with the process of organizing. This third way is the one we will now turn to in the next section.

Organization in Argumentation: Three Different Perspectives

To raise the question of "what is argument?" could be as complex and misleading as the quest for organizational ontology, for there is today considerable and differentiated approaches to the study of argumentation, in communication studies but also in linguistics, informal logic, or philosophy (for a comprehensive review, see van Eemeren, Grootendorst, Snoeck Henkemans, et al., 1996). Efforts have been made to search for a common theoretical core beyond the diversity of views, and many scholars relied on the classical paradigm of argumentation, systematized for the first time by Aristotle in his *Organon* (literally, "instrument," "tool," sharing a common root with the word *organization*) and *Rhetoric*. The Athenian philosopher distinguished between the art of reasoning to pursue truths and discover knowledge with *analytical logic*, the art of dialogue to address critically questions of a general interest with *dialectic*, and the art of speaking well in civic discourse across the genres of the judiciary, the deliberative, and the epidictic with *rhetoric*. This foundational classification remained relatively unchanged throughout the centuries, and still serves today as an organizing principle for different perspectives, identifying argument as a *product*, argumentation as a *procedure*, and arguing as a *process* (Brockriede, 1978; Habermas, 1984; Tindale, 1999; Wenzel, 1990, 1992; Zarefsky, 2001). Accordingly, each perspective implicitly supports a specific notion of organization related to argumentative discourse.

The Logical Perspective

First, argument considered as a *product* can be defined as a set of statements, a network of premises and conclusions, or of claims and supporting reasons, "by which someone chooses to represent 'meanings' abstracted from the ongoing processes of communication" (Wenzel, 1992, p. 125). This perspective thus emphasizes the structure of the text making coherent links amongst a constellation of propositions. From this view, an argument must be distinguished from a narration or a description, since it has a typical and recognizable form.

Concerns for organization in argument production are related to the progression among various statements of a text, enabling a transformation of a state of affairs by means of induction, deduction, or abduction.

Analysis and evaluation of arguments thus acknowledge the underlying importance of the arrangement of the various elements of the argumentative texts. This discourse analyst notes: "A central problem for the analysis of arguments concerns their underlying organization: Are they sequences of logically related steps? Why do some propositions allow the deduction of others? Which inference steps result in fallacious reasoning?" (Schiffrin, 1985, p. 36). Single models of arguments like the syllogism, the example, or the enthymeme can be traced to this product perspective on argumentation, as with the famous Toulmin model of the layout of arguments, built around an initial *claim*, supported by *data*, and linked together through a general but field-dependent *warrant*, specified through a *qualifier*, and attenuated by possible *rebuttals*, but further justified by additional *backing* of the warrant (Toulmin, 1958/2003). In short, organization operates in the argumentation as product perspective by authorizing or limiting certain associations between statements in the composition of texts.

Argumentation as Dialectical

Second, argumentation as *procedure* affiliates itself with the dialectical stance on critical debate and focuses on the regulative conventions that organize the conduct of agents in specific settings, like courtrooms, academic journals, or legislative assemblies. Argument is seen here as a "methodology for bringing the natural process of arguing under some sort of deliberate control" (Wenzel, 1992, p. 124). Therefore, disagreements can lead to dialogue and quarrels, discussions or conflicts, and dialectical arguments propose rules and norms to regulate the management of disputes, to reach decisions, or to enhance mutual understanding.

From this view, organization acquires a relatively different meaning. Its concern here is on the various procedural elements that participate in the accomplishment of argumentative encounters. Arguments as products focus on the composition of texts, but arguments as procedure attribute a greater importance to contexts. Accordingly, what may be said and how is largely a matter of particular settings and environments. But besides context-specific norms of discourse, changing across "argument spheres" (Goodnight, 1999) or "argument fields" (Zarefsky, 1992), one can find approaches establishing a more general set of norms to achieve the resolution of disagreements. In the case of the pragma-dialectics, participants must adhere to an inherent standard of rationality, adopt alternate roles of questioning and defending a contested viewpoint, accomplish various stages of the critical discussion through the production of certain types of speech acts, and follow a series of rules, stating for instance that parties must not prevent the expression of viewpoints, must retract their contested propositions if unsuccessfully defended, as well as trying to avoid unclear or ambiguous formulations (van Eemeren & Grootendorst, 2003). This framework serves both as a method for the analysis of argument and as a guide for the participants. Others have adopted and expanded this model to other types of dialogue, including negotiation, deliberation, or eristic, each one organized by different initial situations, main goals, or functions, and with the possibility of shifts from one type of dialogue to another (Walton, 1992, 1998; Walton & Krabbe, 1995).

A Rhetorical View on Argument

Third, arguing as a *process* subscribes to a rhetorical perspective that stresses the natural communication phenomena by which agents address themselves to each other in an effort to win their adherence and accomplish persuasion. This perspective is highlighted by its preference for the analysis of arguments in natural settings, as a "rule-governed method people use for managing certain conversational event" (Jackson & Jacobs, 1992, p. 681). Arguments thus exist initially as a particular form of interaction, in which "two or more people maintain what they construe to be incompatible positions" (Willard, 1989, p. 42).

Here, the possible connection of arguments with a notion of organization appears to be less obvious, even problematic. This may be explained by the idea that from a rhetorical perspective, argument seems to be an open-ended construct, in the sense that "there is no way to specify *a priori* what counts as an argument" (Wenzel, 1987, p. 106). It may nonetheless be identified as a communicational performance, and as an embodied activity implying that "arguments are not in statements but in people" (Brockriede, 1992, p. 73). Consequently, the process view accepts the idea that argument may refer to whatever communication vehicles one can find in polemic interactions: "serial predication, claiming, and reason-giving as well as proxemic, paralinguistic, gestural, and facial clues" (Willard, 1989, p. 92). And by further adopting a constitutive model of rhetorical effectivity, any social practice could be then translated as an argument (Greene, 1998).

This suggests that rhetorical argumentation emerges as a method and practice in absence of any institutionalized methods, where only insufficient evidence or truths are available, or when established rules and norms do not already prevail. It may further be depicted as a temporary breach in authority and the ordinary conduct of affairs. In other words, it emerges and exists solely in the realm of the contingent, during situations where decisions have to be made and acted upon, but where agents must rely on probabilities rather than on certainties.

From this aspect, it bears resemblance to, but is also distinct from dialectics. For while the study of dialectics "centers on contradictions or the ways that oppositional forces create situations that are 'both-and' or 'either-or'" (Putnam, 2003, p. 40), rhetoric applies to cases that even contest the realm of an already identifiable problematic. Similarly conceived as a contextualized and interactive practice, rhetoric and dialectic differ regarding the overall degree of uncertainty, since it might be argued that "[r]hetoric is viewed as the counterpart (*antistrophos*) of dialectic, primarily because Aristotle realized that not all problematics dissolve differences into reliable univocal categories" (Farrell, 1993, p. 26; see van Eemeren & Houtlosser, 2002, for alternate views associating dialectic to rhetoric).

Accordingly, we would argue that rhetorical argumentation is subsumed into the realm of the *preorganizational*, or at least in the domain of the lesser organized practice related to judgment and decision, and could therefore be explored as a *preferred site of observation for the process of organizing through communication*. In other words, interest for rhetorical arguments in organizational settings could contribute, as a *method*, to illuminate the ways by which actors construct and negotiate, through their argumentative *practice*, the important question of organizational ontology.

Argumentation in Organizational Communication Studies

To the best of our knowledge, however, such a perspective has not yet been pursued in the broader field of organizational communication. We mentioned earlier, as was also noticed by Weick and Browning (1986) that attention to argument in organizations has never been quantitatively very important, although we can discover that some very instructive insights have emerged from that modest literature.

Most reviewed works have in fact adhered to an argument as product perspective, connecting the structure and form of arguments with organizational phenomena. Exemplar studies of this type have combined Simon's (1947) notion of decision premises with Aristotle's model of the enthymeme in order to account for how organizations influence the way that their members make decisions, create identification, and exert unobtrusive forms of control (Cheney & Tompkins, 1987). Another line of studies, affiliated with structuration theory, explored in detail the ways that group members appropriate and reproduce some underlying argument structures in the course of decision making (see McPhee, Corman, & Iverson, 2007, for a more recent illustration; see Meyers & Seibold, 1990; Seibold & Myers, 2006, for a review of these works). Others have been interested in the types of arguments produced by organizational members, whether using ethnographic observations (Watson, 1995) or interviews (Hamilton, 1997).

Some scholars also have associated arguments with a more global stance on organizations: either by defining organizations as "texts" or bodies of discourse consisting primarily of arguments (Tompkins, Tompkins, & Cheney, 1989), by adopting a metaphor of organization as argument to account for processes of integration, progression, multivocality, and contextualization (Sillince, 2005), or else by proposing a vision of organizations as arguments initially grounded in a claim or thesis, with other organizations existing as counterclaim or antithesis (Clair, 2007).

As for the procedural view, it could be associated to various studies on negotiations and bargaining, where arguments are used by agents as persuasive tactics, invention, or issue development, with various frequency and success according to stages or types of policy deliberations (see Putnam & Fairhurst, 2001, pp. 104–106, for more related references; Putnam & Jones, 1982; Putnam & Wilson, 1989; Putnam, Wilson, & Turner, 1990; Roloff, Tutzauer, & Dailey, 1987).

On a broader level, we could mention here the definition of organization as "a set of procedures for argumentation and interpretation as well as for solving problems and making decisions" (Cohen, March, & Olsen, 1976, p. 25). And in spite of his criticism of that definition, we could also include here Weick's (1995) own reflections on arguing as an instance of sensemaking. He indeed emphasized the procedure of meetings as an important occasion for expression and confrontation of majority and minority voices in organizations, a vision anchored in what has come to be defined as the "Protagoras maxim," following the remark of this famous Sophist that there are always two sides to every question" (Billig, 1996).

But then, what could a rhetorical perspective on organizational arguments look like? That will be the object of this chapter's next section, when we witness an episode of passionate discussions about the place of *collectives* in the recently born political party Québec solidaire.

Organizing through Rhetorical Argument: Collectives in Québec Solidaire?

The sequence presented here is based on a transcription of filmed interactions that occurred in September of 2006 during the second national assembly of Québec solidaire, a political party in the Canadian province of Québec inaugurated only 8 months earlier. Justified by the project of "uniting the forces of the Left," its creation had been the result of a merger between an enduring coalition of smaller parties, bonded under the label of the Union des forces progressistes (UFP), with a political movement, identified as Option citoyenne (OC), emerging mainly out of women's organizations. While evaluated by most members as a critical success, this merger nonetheless resulted in the need to "manag[e] multiple identities" (Cheney, 1991). This was especially the case since one of the founding organizations, the UFP, had succeeded in maintaining a certain level of internal cohesion and external unity by authorizing *collectives*, a collection of opinion groups whose members were simultaneously members of the wider organization. This unique experience was to be translated into the newly founded party, and accordingly, a "recognition policy for collectives" was to be adopted during that particular gathering in September 2006. Many readers will notice a predominant familiarity with the problem of organizational identification, but this issue will have to be addressed elsewhere because the focus here is on the process by which some actors try to constitute, through argumentation, what defines their organization, and accordingly, how they should act.

Approaching the end of a full day of work, divided between formal deliberations and small-group sessions, and following in-depth discussions about electoral, financial, and mobilization strategies, delegates of Québec solidaire who were participating at that assembly were planning to adopt a recognition policy for collectives, enabling four specific groups to have information tables during the party's future meetings. However, evoking a lack of time, a perceived climate of general fatigue, and considering the decisive importance of the issue at hand, the elected chair of the meeting first proposed that delegates postpone the debate about the recognition of collectives until the next assembly the following November. In the meantime, he proposed that the four groups that had already filed demands for recognition, Socialisme international, Parti communiste du Québec, Gauche socialiste, and Masse critique, should temporarily be allowed to establish information tables for the next meeting, until the policy could be appropriately discussed and voted. The chair then invited delegates to comment on this proposal.

The delegates were facing a difficult choice, and repeated demands were held for a break during which delegates of every local association in the province could discuss the issue informally before taking an official position on the floor of the assembly. Following a 5-minute interruption, the chair once again invited delegates to the two standing microphones (yellow and rose), alternatively giving the floor to women and men as a way to incarnate the party's foundational principle of feminism. Although speaking with a polite and relatively measured tone, the first few interventions highlighted a sustained impression of polarization amongst delegates, characterized by the anxiety of some and the exasperation of others (all transcripts originally in French):

Chair: Thank you. I'm sure that the collectives have noted that. (.) Yellow microphone, a woman.

Delegate 1: So, hmm, ((Names herself)) from Saguenay, hmm, Dubuc. If we postpone, we postpone, and I don't see the second part, that there should be tables and also that the name of Québec solidaire should be there, in their information, since it has not been discussed. And also, as for myself, I think that we must discuss it, and discuss it in depth. It's important. We are a *young* party, and people do not know what to expect from us. So if they have Québec solidaire feminist, communist, socialist, they won't understand, so I think that it brings *much* confusion, and if somebody is a party *outside* of Québec solidaire, and then comes here, *in* Québec solidaire to hold a table, then I don't understand. That's it.

Chair:	Thank you. So, I, I interpret your question as a demand to vote both points separately, and so we will vote separately the two parts of the proposition. So, hmm, rose microphone, a man please.
Delegate 2:	((Names himself)) from Québec Saint-Jacques. My intervention goes in the same direction as what has just been said, a moment ago, hmm, by the other person at the same microphone. Hmm, like I said earlier, I have in my possession a sheet which has been distributed during a public assembly two days ago, where Masse critique presents itself as a collective belonging to Québec solidaire. Well, sure it's not written that it is recognized, but I would like to make sure that we are going to debate this question, as to its merit and dispose of it. And that we are not going to, may I say, see people intervene here and there, claiming affiliation to Québec solidaire, playing on the terms *known, unknown, recognized*. It seems to me that it is not this way that we begin to *develop* collectives in an organization like ours or any others. Let's have a discussion, let's take dispositions, so then we can agree. But then, to hide between the sheets and between the lines, saying that we have not written "recognized" in our document, personally I do not think that it's a good way to render sympathetic the proposition to constitute collectives. That's one point. Another point, I would not want that what we all say, me like the others, only represent the will of some speakers at this assembly. So if we adopt a resolution about this, and we state who will be authorized to make interventions through literature tables, for instance during our assemblies, then if that is what's authorized it's *that*. Not that and other sorts of things that in the meantime have not been restricted.
Chair:	Thank you. Yellow microphone, a woman.
Delegate 3:	I think that =
Chair:	= Identification
Delegate 3:	Yes, hmm ((Names herself)), Mercier, and collective who intend to be recognized, Socialisme International. I think that it is important to remind all members of the history behind Québec solidaire, behind the UFP, which is the unity of the forces of the Left. The UFP was formed *by* at least *two* of the collectives that filed a demand to be recognized today. So, it's not just members coming out of somewhere or parties that now want to belong. *We are part* of Québec solidaire. That is the reality, in the first place. In the second place, it was stated by the national directive that collectives who filed demands have the right to hold information tables. We are

collectives, until we are recognized we are collectives, and at that moment, we will be recognized collectives. But they are not parties coming out of nowhere, these are parties at the *foundation* of Québec solidaire. So, I remind you of this today. As for the proposition to postpone, hmm, I feel that there is going to be another proposition made, which I will support, to postpone it until tomorrow morning. So, I think it's important to recognize *already* the right for collectives to hold tables, but it's been, it's going to be one year next February that the party is formed, and we still don't have a recognition policy. So, we would like things to go a little bit faster. Thank you.

Despite its considerable length, this excerpt enables us to better capture the argumentative process of deliberations than, say, a description exclusively limited to premises and conclusions. And although space limitations constrain us from providing an in-depth analysis, various aspects can be noted here in order to help us grasp how rhetorical arguments contribute to the constitution of organizations.

Presence and Presentification

First, the transcript shows the diversity of elements of justification brought up by the three delegates in support of the acceptance or refusal of the chair's two propositions. That is, speakers act to make different things present in their discourse, thus representing differently what their party really *is*, which in turn promotes a distinct course of action. The first person to intervene here (Delegate 1) will evoke the novel character of the party, the various labels and identifications, as well as the potential expectations from public opinion, justifying prudence and control as opposed to a quickly made decision. Interesting to note is also the definite role played by physically absent actors who are made discursively present in this intervention; that is, the people outside Québec solidaire whose support justifies the party's existence, illustrating the "blurring quality of organizational boundaries" (Cheney & Christensen, 2001). As for the second delegate who intervenes (Delegate 2), we see him defending his position by stating a case of "textual agency" (Cooren, 2004) involving a document that acted to publicly associate a collective with Québec solidaire, raising subsequently the risk that the name of his party be appropriated by various people or groups. In the case of the third delegate (Delegate 3), however, different things are being made present, notably the history of the party itself, and the active role played by some collectives in that process.

Competing efforts by actors to make things present in a certain way can be traced to the point that, contrary to logical demonstration, rhetorical argumentation implies a prior selection of facts and values, expressed through a particular description and with a specific language, according to the importance given by the speaker (Perelman, 1982). Thus, according to Perelman and Olbrechts-Tyteca (1969), the creation of presence—depicted as "the displaying of certain elements on which the speaker wishes to center attention in order that they may occupy the foreground of the hearer's consciousness" (p. 142)—is one important role of argumentation. It also contributes to the constitution of organizations, if we accept the notion that what an organization is depends on the various agencies by which it is made present or "presentified" (Brummans, Cooren, & Chaput, 2009; Cooren, 2006; Cooren, Brummans, & Charrieras, 2008). A rhetorical perspective adds to that view that the ontological question is always potentially contested and negotiated, as illustrated by the actor's discourses. Here we can see that the party is either depicted as new and unfamiliar for many, therefore necessitating prudence and control over whose voices compose the organizational voice, or as a new phase on an enduring historical project of unification, characterized by the ever present plurality of different voices. A rhetorical view on *presentification* would then help to account for the always potentially disputed and negotiated character of organizational ontology. That is, what an organization essentially "is" is constantly subject to debate between members, adversaries, and third-parties like researchers and journalists, hence the necessity for that organization to always be made present in a persuasive way.

Audience and the Problem of "Scaling Up"

Rhetorical discourse is distinct from logic and dialectic by being *addressed* to particular audiences (Burke, 1950/1969), not usually restricted to the physically present individuals but encompassing *"the ensemble of those whom the speaker wishes to influence by his argumentation* [emphasis in original]" (Perelman & Olbrechts-Tyteca, 1969, p. 19). Considering the excerpt once again, we observe that while Delegate 1 addresses herself to the other delegates and observers of the assembly, she seems to judge that the preferred audience should be the ambiguously defined and generalized notion of the "people," possibly referring to all electors and citizens of the province. Delegate 2 also pleads for a wider notion of audience to judge the question of collectives, claiming that "I would not want that what we all say, me like the others, only represent the will of some speakers at this assembly." Discourse by Delegate 3 directly appeals to *"all members,"* arguing in favor of a shared vision of the party and of its history. In all three cases, we can note an effort to transcend particular groups and move beyond divisions in order to embrace a generalized vision of what *Québec solidaire* is and should be. This appeal to a wider conception of audience, based either on the respect of the democratic process of discussion and decision or on the respect of past agreements, claims for a general rule of justice.

Even though the full implications of this assertion cannot be discussed here, it could be argued that claims to generalization and construction of something similar to a "universal audience" (Perelman & Olbrechts-Tyteca, 1969) is a practice used by actors to transform *individual* into *organizational* discourse, thus grasping the problem of "scaling up" from interactions to organization (Taylor & Van Every, 2000). By evoking the respect of democratic procedures or the founding principles of Québec solidaire, actors reiterate in a sense what is, or should be, *constitutive* of their organization beyond particular cases. In other words, even without being authorized as official spokespersons of the organization they simultaneously produce and reproduce what the "organizational voice" of Québec solidaire could sound like. Consequently, observing how actors justify themselves by evoking wider notions of justice—in the sense of what can be *justified*—could become an alternate path to finding the organization in communication without having to struggle with the "micro-macro gap" (see Boltanski & Thévenot, 1999; 2006, for theoretical developments in that direction).

Transformation of the Rhetorical Situation

The deliberative process thus evolved through successive efforts by delegates to associate or dissociate the party from collectives, by valuing unity against pluralism as the favored mode of organizing. The polarization of positions grew more visible through voice tones and body gestures. The chair's proposition to postpone debate had resulted in establishing a debate of its own. As we will observe here, tensions reached a climax when accusations of censorship were addressed, succeeding in bringing the chair to step out of his role as moderator and to enter in the debate:

Chair: =Rose microphone.
Delegate 4:   Hello, my name is ((names himself)), I'm on the Québec solidaire national coordination committee, responsible for media relations. I'm also a founding member of Masse critique, a civic education collective, formed in great part by students from UQAM [University of Québec at Montreal]. Not exclusively, but many of us study at UQAM. I strongly oppose postponing this debate once *again* that had been deferred too often, which gives rights to various trends in our party, implying that people can group themselves to work on common objectives, whatever they are, or to share ideas together. It would be a minimum, like ((names Delegate 3)) mentioned, to recognize that collectives have already existed for a long time, throughout the history of the Left, and of the UFP also, that we are here, we already act, we already work, we distribute information sheets, we discuss. And I

notice here that we want to constrain, people from *speaking* inside our party about shared ideas, especially regarding the second point. That is censorship, which I strongly oppose. I also oppose various strategies of deferring and delays, the aim of which is to reject this debate once again.

Chair: Mister ((names Delegate 4)), [I authorize myself to interrupt you

Delegate 4: [So you will understand that I'm against=

Chair: =It's not a matter of censorship or anything else of that range, it's a proposition brought forward by the presidency of the assembly, who *judges* that the importance of the debates involving the recognition of collectives does not justify that we do that "too quickly, a Saturday evening, when everybody is tired." So I think it's a matter of *respect*, and for delegates and for the importance of the subject on the table, that a proposition to postpone is subjected to debate=

Delegate 4: =Mister ((names the chair)), I was=

Chair: =I invite you to discuss the proposition to postpone please.

Delegate 4: Mister ((names the chair)), I was referring to the arguments=
((Moderate applause from a segment of the audience, following the chair's energetic comments))

Delegate 4: =that I heard on the floor today and not to the content of your proposition because I was out of the room when it was announced. I was referring to the arguments brought up on the floor today.
((Moderate applause from another segment of the audience, following Delegate 4's intervention))

Chair: Yellow microphone, please.

Delegate 5: Yes, ((names himself)), Party spokesperson. Hum, I, I simply invite to maybe consider a position, I, I propose to reject this proposition in its totality and instead simply postpone until tomorrow morning, to begin the discussion around eight thirty=
((Important applause coming from the audience))

Delegate 5: =in the spirit of giving it a try. It's possible that at the end of an hour's exercise, or three quarters of an hour, I think, it could enable us to reconcile [this issue] with the agenda for tomorrow. Hum, if we succeed, sometimes we are surprised by the quality of interventions, by their concision, by their- Well. If we are able to emerge a- a- a vicropote which responds to the demands of those who have interrogations, then it will be done, otherwise tomorrow, well we will postpone at that time, but to give ourselves a chance, to demonstrate a minimum of concern, hmm, let's say, of loyalty to the agreement that we had, which led to unity, and which

should, at a certain point, give a clear answer for the status of hmm. So my proposition is, it's to defeat that proposition, to hold a 45 minutes debate starting at 8:30 tomorrow morning.
((Massive applause by the audience, following Delegate 5's calmly expressed proposition))

Once again, it is necessary to include substantial excerpts of the interaction sequence so that we can witness and comprehend the dynamic evolution of this argumentative process. Of particular interest here is the way Delegate 5 accomplishes a notable transformation of the situation by rallying the diverse positions into a coherent solution.

As we can observe at the beginning of this sequence, Delegate 4 proposes his own version of the party's ontology, with the subsequent role of collectives. He starts by framing the debate on collectives as a right for pluralism, then reiterates the story of the collectives as already playing a considerable part within the party, and providing a description of various activities to emphasize his point. This argumentation progressively leads him to conclude that opposition to recognition equates with a denial of freedom of speech and association, thus condemning it as censorship. The ongoing debate seems at that point to reach a higher level of antagonism, translated into *argumentum ad hominem* or personal attacks against a segment of the assembly. This perceived case of injustice expressed by Delegate 4 leads to another, and we see the chair transgressing his role of moderator to take part in the debate, arguing against such accusations by restating his previous justifications. Once again, we are facing two different notions of justice, which tend, however, to derive more exclusive or divided conceptions of who or what elements compose the organization. The gradual shift in the interaction toward antagonism can be observed in part by noting the frequent interruptions in the actor's turns of talk, but also by the responses of the audience following the chair's and Delegate 4's interventions. Applause coming from different parts of the actual audience further suggests the emergence of factions out of this confrontation, not even reluctant to take sides explicitly about the issue at hand at the risk of causing more divisions. And as will later be accounted by another delegate (Delegate 6), debates had never been as emotional as during that day, "reflecting the fact that there is something latent, more or less latent ever since the beginning of negotiations for the creation of Québec solidaire" (not included in the excerpts).

Another transformation is operated in the argumentation process, when a new speaker grabbing the microphone raises an alternative proposition for the debate, spontaneously generating applause from a considerable part of the audience. He further develops his argument to support his position, culminating in a general approval from the people present. It is now a widely accepted idea that a discourse acquires a rhetorical quality by responding to situations of certain kinds (Bitzer, 1968/1995), by judging by the spontaneous approval and subsequent acceptance of the proposition, it can be asserted that the response here was appropriate. It provides a reachable short-term solution that momentarily would stop the increasing tension between members of collectives and nonmembers, conciliating demands from a majority to spend more time discussing this critical issue.

Viewed from a rhetorical perspective, this performance can be praised for its timely character or *kairos*, defined as the quality to say the right thing at the right moment, and for its use of practical wisdom or *phronesis*, "judgment that is embodied in action," "consummated in the efficacy of good *praxis*" (Beiner, 1983, p. 74). Perhaps more significantly for us, it well illustrates a conception of argumentation as organizing in at least two different ways. First of all, because of its performative character as a type of situated speech act that instantiate for all members a way to act collectively, a program for future action. The declaration is then accomplished perlocutionary, as members will manifest their approval through applause and voting. In that case, argumentation produces transformation, changing the world by acting on it. It thus allows a speaker *to induce or increase the mind's adherence to the theses presented for its assent* [emphasis in original]" (Perelman & Olbrechts-Tyteca, 1969, p. 4).

But this argumentative discourse not only organizes by transforming immediate orientations of action, but also by proving a reassertion; that is, a different reading of Québec solidaire's organizational ontology. He discursively operates an integration of both disputed positions, claiming both the importance of discussion before reaching judgment and loyalty for historical agreements with collectives. His rhetorical argumentation thus succeeds also in accomplishing the dialectical transformation of synthesis, offering a new but coherent view of what the party *is*, and how members should *act* accordingly. This "organizing effect" of rhetorical discourse is further enhanced by the subtle but significant shift in the way deliberation sets a way for an epidictic praise of members, valuing their capacity for good and concise interventions and for being loyal toward pluralism.

Unfortunately for the assembled delegates, this rhetorical success was short lived. The next morning, following an explicative lecture from the president of the party, brief interventions by members from collectives, and the anticipated period of debate, a common agreement could not be reached, the two votes that were held ended in no resolution being reached. This "undecidability" was maintained for more than a year, until all collectives were ultimately recognized as parts of Québec solidaire.

Concluding Remarks

In this essay, we presented what could be qualified as a rationale for the joint exploration of argumentative practices and the process of organizing, illustrated by an account of a passionate debate within a political organization with its constitutive implications. As such, we hope that it will convince researchers of the relevance of studying argumentation as an organizing practice and as a method of inquiry in analyzing organizational phenomena of all kinds. With a focus on the details of actual interactions, the perspective presented here differs from previous efforts to propose a general model of argument as organizational communication, likely to include such notions as decisional premises (Cheney & Tompkins, 1987; Tompkins, Tompkins, & Cheney, 1989), argumentation repertoires (Sillince, 1999), or arguments as the raison d'être of an organization (Clair, 2007). Much more modest in its scope, the view depicted in this paper invites analysts to view arguments as one of many unique processes through which organizations can be made, unmade, or rebuilt, constituting in this way a valuable trail to comprehend the question of organizational ontology. Consequently, arguments should be considered as "unique discourse events" that contribute to illuminating the way in which actors construct their world, like "lightning flashes that momentarily expand our horizon. They summon explanation and reason-giving, attack and defence, and thus provide glimpses of the tacit world behind the routine" (Willard, 1996, p. 218).

To acknowledge this eventful and often ephemeral character of rhetorical argumentation does not necessarily undermine its potential to explain how an organization gets created and sustained in time through communication. First, future research could be devoted to explore and expand linkages between perspectives of argumentative and organizational discourses, for instance by distinguishing the rhetorical and procedural modalities in the organizing property of communication (see Cooren & Taylor, 1999) or by identifying types of statements that either qualify as true, acceptable, or persuasive in a given organizational setting. Argumentative analysis could therefore help to grasp the assumptions on which organizations are built and maintained.

Second, concerns for Aristotelian and other classical conceptions of argument could help researchers and practitioners alike discover (or rediscover) anterior practices of judgment and deliberation in situations of contingency, as well as particular abilities and virtues such as prudence or phronesis (see Flyvbjerg, 2006, for a discussion on phronetic organizational research). Adhering to such a rhetorical perspective could provide an alternative lens and critical tool to the more economically oriented models of decision making in organizations.

Our third and final concern here relates to Maurice Charland's (1999) assumption that argument would simply be one type of persuasive discursive configuration, by which he emphasizes that "much rhetorical force is pre- or extra-argumentative" (pp. 467–468). That remark could stimulate scholars of organizational communication and rhetoric to consider how various kinds of rhetorical practices intersect within the communicative constitution of an organization. Particularly appealing here are the ways by which argumentative interactions by the delegates of Québec solidaire contributed to enact, transform, and unsuccessfully stabilize a shared narrative about the party's existence, history and values. This narrative form, which provides its members with a collective identity and motivation to act beyond internal differences, shares some poignant similarities with Charland (1987)'s own work on the "constitutive rhetoric" of the Peuple Québécois, that is, the constitution of a collective subject and audience through narrative form. Thus, future research could develop some junctions between arguments and constitutive narratives instead of positioning them as opposite discursive modes or paradigms, without reminding us of the complex dialectic of text and conversation innovatively elaborated by James R. Taylor to explain how organizations emerge from communication.

Note

1. I would like to thank François Cooren for his insightful comments and for linguistic corrections on earlier versions of this chapter. It goes without saying that I am solely responsible for any remaining errors in the text.

11 Constituting the Temporary Organization

Documents in the Context of Projects

Viviane Sergi

Introduction: A Popular Practice

Nowadays, projects and project management are enjoying a considerable popularity: glamorized as a mode of work organization that offers flexibility and that is associated with change and innovation, they seduce organizations from all sectors of activity (Ekstedt, Lundin, Söderholm, & Wirdenius, 1999). Consequently, this form of temporary organizing is increasingly adopted by a wide variety of organizations. The number of people getting certified as project managers (mostly by the most influential professional organization in this field, the Project Management Institute) continues to grow.[1]

Still, despite this growing interest, little is known about the work being done while projects are in progress. For some, this situation is linked to the fact that most of the field is still concentrating on project management, and has yet to move to project research (Söderlund, 2005). For others, this relative absence of research on the work and the social phenomena taking place "inside" projects is attributable to the fact that the field is dominated by a functionalist and instrumental approach based on rationalist assumptions about project management (Cicmil, 2006; Cicmil & Hodgson, 2006; Engwall, 2003; Thomas, 2000). However, this view of project management is giving rise to more and more questions. Critics have stressed the prescriptive nature of most of the knowledge in project management; they have also underlined that project planning and control are still the main focus of most of what is published on this topic (Packendorff, 1995; Söderlund, 2005). Concerned with the standardization of project management, this approach overlooks the actual work being done in projects and does not consider its social dimensions, nor the contribution of objects to action. So far, in-depth qualitative studies that devote their attention to the nature and distinctive features of "doing projects" are lacking (Söderlund, 2004). Adopting such a qualitative approach, our study focuses on the material dimension of project work and management.

In the field of project management, some researchers are now advocating an alternative to this dominant approach, which can be seen as a "qualitative turn" in the study of projects. This turn implies putting in action temporary organizing processes and social dynamics at the forefront of the inquiry (Packendorff, 1995; Söderlund, 2005). This perspective considers that projects are enacted (Kreiner, 1995) and that greater attention should be paid to what Cicmil, Williams, Thomas, and Hodgson (2006) have identified as the "actuality" of project, by "focussing on *social process* and how practitioners *think in action* [emphasis original], in the local situation" (p. 676). In this respect, qualitative studies of project work and organization are on the increase. Yet, there is still a lack of studies on tools used in project work and management. Because the contribution of objects to action and organizing abound in projects, we believe that projects offer an untapped opportunity for study. Although their presence has been recognized by some, they have mainly been examined by two kinds of studies. On the one hand, some studies, based on surveys, identify the tools used by firms and try to link this use to other variables (such as the size of the firm or its sector; e.g., Besner & Hobbs, 2005; White & Fortune, 2002). On the other hand, studies adopting a critical stance develop a radically different viewpoint: for Hodgson (2002), Räisänen and Linde (2004), and Styhre (2006), amongst others, tools such as project methodology and documentation are "simply" an extension of the control mechanisms and disciplining techniques that compose project management. With some exceptions, tools have rarely been investigated beyond these two stances (Papadimitriou & Pellegri, 2007; Sapsed & Salter, 2004).

More to the point, in this age of collaborative tools and mobile devices, one kind of object seems to get less attention: documents. Still, documents are profusely present in projects. In fact, when reading mainstream literature on project management (articles and bestselling books such as the PMBOK* Guide, 2004), one realizes that the production of documents throughout the duration of a project is an integral part of project management and work. Project plans, requirements, charts, checklists, reports, and summaries have to be produced in order to plan and control the project. One popular practitioner-oriented book (Berkun, 2005) even underlines both the usefulness of writing and the importance of writing well in the context of projects. Document production and circulation is so present in project management that some researchers have stated that this field is on the verge of becoming bureaucratic (Styhre, 2006). But despite the fact that documents occupy such a significant place in projects, their nature and their roles are taken for granted and thus remain unquestioned. We ask ourselves, wanting as we do to open the black box of documents in the context of projects: what do documents do for project management and work?

From Passive Means to Active Contributors

In order to be able to answer this question, one cannot simply rely on how tools are usually defined. Tools are generally reified, viewed as "mere objects," as passive and as neutral support to action. Tools are thus seen as instrumental in getting universal results: having been designed to meet some predefined ends, they "just" have to be implemented and the promised results will be obtained. Once designed, it is believed that tools are ready to be put to use in any context. Deterministic in essence, this perspective establishes a direct and causal relationship between tools and their consequences. In this view, tools are never problematic: when the expected results are not produced, this situation is mainly attributed to its users. In this conceptualization, explanations are asymmetric (Latour, 1987, 2005): successes are attributed to the tools and failures, to the individuals using the tools.

The field of information systems (IS) and information technology (IT) research is a good representative of this perspective and also of the alternatives that were developed in order to question this view. During the period of intense adoption of new technologies and software solutions (such as e-mail, groupware, and ERPs) in the 1980s and 1990s, studies documented that the gains in productivity expected from the introduction of these new technologies (supposed to be considerable) varied greatly from context to context (see Pinsonneault & Rivard, 1998, for a presentation of the mixed results of studies on the link between IT and productivity); most of this variation was attributed to the employees' resistance to the newly introduced technology. Dissatisfied with this view and with its explanations, some researchers opted for a different perspective on these tools, rooted in social constructionism. Numerous qualitative studies were conducted on what was happening with and around the technologies. Most notably, works by researchers such as Barley (1986), Orlikowski (1992, 1996, 2000), and Robey and Sahay (1996) illustrate that technologies are shaped by values and interests and that they are open to different interpretations; that their introduction is often accompanied by a period of negotiation, conflicts, and adaptation; that they are closely linked to and influenced by the cultural, social, and organizational context in which they are deployed; that their outcomes are related to the local use and context, more than to their properties; and that their recurrent use leads to appropriation, a process in which their proprieties can be modified, modestly or substantially. Globally speaking, by looking closely at the social processes by which people make sense, configure, adapt, transform, and, ultimately, use (or not!) IT, these studies have contributed to debunk the dominant and deterministic view on technological tools. But IS and IT researchers are not the only ones who have taken a different look at tools: scattered in the social sciences, we can find a number of studies which, taken together, provide a much more active portrait of other tools, a strong and clear departure from the passive and neutral one that is usually painted. Such a portrait is the cornerstone of our study.

Some studies have demonstrated that tools are part of the organizational dynamics (e.g., Bechky, 2003; Lacoste, 2000). *Object* is an equivocal term. Lacoste (2000) underlines the point that such a word is used to designate tools, technologies, instruments, and devices. To this list, we can also add texts, writings, documents, graphs, and images—even though, as Geisler (2001) points, we are reluctant to treat writings as objects. When conceived from a social constructionism viewpoint, objects are often seen as mediators; as such, they are defined as material, technical, *and* social artifacts: "As an integral part of work processes, objects help us to accomplish tasks, but not in a merely technical manner. Artifacts, subject to interpretation, participate in the constitution of the social dynamics of organizations" (Bechky, 2003, p. 746). In her work, Akrich (1987, 1990) shows that technical objects can be seen as scripts that define a space, roles, and rules of interaction; she also puts forward the idea that objects and social organization cannot be understood separately: objects need the social organization to be stabilized, and the social organization cannot hold without a number of objects. Our definition of objects comprises all the elements underlined by Lacoste, Bechky, and Akrich: their sociotechnical nature, the mediation processes they trigger and sustain, their imbrication in the social fabric, and their participation to the social dynamic.

This mediating role played by objects is at the core of another, yet related, perspective on tools. In this perspective, tools are conceived as boundary objects, helping people to work together, to coordinate their actions, and to communicate (e.g., Carlile, 2002; Star & Griesemer, 1989). As the name implies, boundary objects are located at the articulation point between different groups that have to collaborate. These objects are flexible enough to meet the needs of the different groups that have to use them; at the same time, they are sufficiently robust to remain unmodified by this diversity of uses and interpretations. Amongst others, prototypes (Carlile, 2002), sketches, and drawings (Bechky, 2003), project management methodologies and tools (Sapsed & Salter, 2004), and temporal artifacts (Yakura, 2002) have been recognized as boundary objects. These studies illustrate that the cooperation and communication processes between people who, despite their differences, have to collaborate are more than facilitated by these objects: "Boundary objects are the practical artifacts that allow diverse groups to work together. They provide a locus for communication, conflicts, and coordination" (Yakura, 2002, p. 968). Moreover, these tools can help in negotiations between groups.

Tools have also been studied for what they carry and stand for. For example, Berg (1997) considered a category of objects that he labeled formal tools. Reflected in the structure of these tools is a model of the work that has to be conducted with them. Moreover, these tools establish rules regarding the actions and their timing. Methodologies, protocols, standards, expert systems, and medical records are formal tools because they prescribe what has to be done: in doing so, they organize and guide the execution of work. Like boundary objects, these tools mediate action, since the model of work on which they are based directly influences the steps taken to accomplish the work. Even though she does not use the expression "formal tools," Suchman (1995) discusses the political implications of tools that are built upon an abstract model of work. While considering the representation of work that informs tools like business process reengineering and workflow modeling, she reminds us that representations are never neutral. By including and excluding elements, they serve the interests of the group that elaborated them in the first place.

Generally speaking, recognizing the agency of objects has been one of the major contributions of actor-network theory (Latour, 1987, 2005). In his work, Latour has promoted the idea that agency is not only a property of humans, and that objects (or nonhumans) fully intervene in human phenomena; for him, "things" make relationships more durable. He contends that separating material and social dimensions is fruitless, and that we should always ask ourselves what makes the action possible. The answer to this question often involves, as his work on laboratories shows, objects of various kinds.

Taken together, the conclusions of these studies contribute to a reconceptualization of objects and tools. This perspective has been adopted for the study of documents by some researchers. We use the word *document* to designate everything that can adopt a paper form in organizational settings and that is used to convey content; for example, texts, writing devices (such as forms), drawings, spreadsheets, sketches, and instrument traces that are printed. A document can combine many of these forms; for example, a text may be accompanied by a few drawings. No one will dispute the fact that documents, especially those produced in organizational settings, convey information: but they do more. Winsor (1998) notes that documents are memory extenders: Their content exhibits a form of fixity (Levy, 2003), but they can be easily moved around (Winsor, 1998); they are, as Latour (1986b) labeled them, immutable mobiles.

Furthermore, documents also structure, organize, and coordinate work, management, and relationships between individuals (Callon, 2002; Fraenkel, 2001; Henderson, 1991; Prior, 2003; Sellen & Harper, 2002); they influence and shape work practices (Sellen & Harper, 2002); they create order and provide meaning (J. S. Brown & Duguid, 2000; Latour, 1986b; Levy, 2003); and they support the understanding of the reality in which individuals are evolving. Overall, they have a stabilizing power over the collective (J. S. Brown & Duguid, 2000; Geisler, 2001; Levy, 2003; Winsor, 2006). They can be used to make others act (Winsor, 2006). These conclusions are in line with the conception of objects presented earlier. But despite the equivocal formulations, most of these studies do not attribute a clear agency to documents. Some authors, like Fraenkel (2001) and Winsor (2006) hint at the idea that documents can accomplish actions, but do not investigate this possibility any further. Only Henderson (1991) and Cooren (2004) acknowledge it. Adopting the ideas of Latour on the agency of objects, Cooren clearly proposes that they perform actions and thus "make a difference"; in this respect, he contends that the textual agency of documents should be studied. Building on these insights, our research aims precisely to illustrate how documents participate in the realization of a specific project, and, more importantly, contribute to the constitution of this temporary endeavor.

Context and Methods

We conducted an ethnographic case study of a development project in a Montréal software firm (Soft-A).[1] A software company was chosen because of the prevalence of project organizing in this sector. Founded in the early 1980s, Soft-A is a well-established company, whose commercial activities are based around five specialized software solutions built on powerful algorithms developed in-house for clients located worldwide. Their software solutions consist of various modules that can be tailored to the specific needs of each client. The size of Soft-A's software is colossal: each of them consists of millions of code lines. Because it offers very specialized software, Soft-A enjoys durable relationships with its clients. Although Soft-A produces an enriched and updated version of all the modules of its software every year, its clients usually keep their version for many years before upgrading their software. Consequently, Soft-A's software has a long operating life. In this respect, how each change or new application is developed has to be carefully documented. If some projects revolve around the development of novel applications and modules, most of the projects at Soft-A consist in working on code that has been previously written. And since all applications in every module of each type of software are intertwined, making changes is no small business.

In this light, it is not surprising that questions pertaining to work organization, formalization of procedures and documentation, and methodologies and other tools development have always been a dominant concern at Soft-A. Such a concern ensures that work at Soft-A is considered by managers and employees alike to be structured and formalized. All projects have to follow the company's methodology, and a number of documents have to be produced along the way. When writing code, programming standards have to be respected. Every employee has, in the form of binders, a copy of the methodology and the list of standards. This list is updated and expanded on a regular basis. Templates of the documents that have to be produced have been developed. Contrary to what other researches have reported on the low or lack of use in practice of formalized methods and tools in software projects (Fitzgerald, 1998; Riemenschneider, Hardgrave, & Davis, 2002; Truex, Baskerville, & Travis, 2000), at Soft-A, these tools are not only used by the employees, but they are appreciated by most of them. They are regarded as useful and necessary to accomplish the complex work that has to be done. Also contributing to this high degree of use is the fact that these tools were developed in close collaboration with the employees who would later have to work with them. Such a collaborative process ensured that the tools produced would fit their daily needs and practices.

The design of the research builds on the ethnographic tradition (Laplantine, 1996; van Maanen, 2001). In order to explore what people do and how they work when they are involved in a project, and in an effort to get closer to the objects used in projects, we followed a development project at Soft-A, the Graph project. The Graph project consisted in the rewriting of an application used to produce graphics (named Graph, hence the name of the project) in one of the modules of Soft-A's main software. The project was completed in 2005, between the months of January and November. Eighteen persons contributed to the project; most of them were interviewed at least once. Because of its technical complexity, Graph was seen as a big project at Soft-A. Graph was considered by the interviewees to be representative of the projects done at Soft-A; it was also viewed as an overall success, despite the overruns it experienced. We observed 22 meetings related to the project and conducted interviews with the members of the project team. The observations were particularly important, since the meetings were the main site of the collective work done on the project. Observing the meetings allowed us to look at the interactions between the team members, to witness the various activities in which they participated as the project progressed, and to study how the documents intervened in practice. We also collected various documents, such as plans, analyses, reports, records, and e-mails; 80 documents directly related to the project were gathered and analyzed.

A detailed narrative of the project was developed in order to present its main episodes, standard procedure in all ethnographies. Following the chronology of the project, this narrative combined the documents that we collected and the meetings that we attended. The interviews, transcribed and analyzed using N'Vivo software, also served to develop this narrative and the analysis of the observations, since they offered details on the project and on the company's history and practices. In this narrative, each document that we received was described—e-mail, analysis, report, section of freshly written code, or Excel spreadsheet used in the planning. The close examination of their contents (what was written), of their purposes (why, by whom, and when they were produced), and of their influence on the team (what they did for the team and the project) led us to identify their roles and the action they performed on the Graph project. The view we developed on objects structured our examination. The next sections will detail how this examination revealed that documents were, in the case of the Graph project, inseparable from the work that needed to be done to complete the project and that they greatly influenced the processes that constituted the project. We thus discovered that documents had the capacity to act, influencing group thinking and decision making, stimulating sensemaking, understanding, and idea generation, and help-ing to create and maintain the various individuals making up the team.

Documenting the Action of the Documents

Work on the Graph project, as in any projects at Soft-A, alternated between team work (mostly done during the team meetings) and individual work. Documents and meetings were closely linked since no meeting took place before a document was produced and circulated; documents were present at each and every meeting we observed. Meetings thus were based on the documents previously produced, and most of the discussions happening during the meetings revolved around the documents' content. Since keep-ing track of what was modified, discussed, or decided upon during the meeting was important, documents were usually updated after the meet-ing. This dynamic is represented in Figure 11.1.

As stated by most of the interviewees, documents abound at Soft-A. Because Soft-A's products adopt a written form and numerous documents have to be produced in the course of ongoing projects, so writing occupies a significant place in the daily activities of development team members. In the case of the Graph project, most of the documents can be divided into two broad categories: management documents and technical docu-ments. Management documents present the plans and the organization of work (like assignment of work and time estimates), where technical documents expose the work done on parts of the code of Graph (be it new code written or modifications to existing code). The individuals inter-viewed all confirmed that all documents required by Soft-A's standards were produced, and all tools were used according to their formal roles. For example, the project followed the steps prescribed by the development methodology. So while the documents were carrying out the specific tasks they had been developed for (e.g., expose the needs that justify the project; present a detailed view of the architecture of the new Graph that had to be done), they also *performed* a variety of actions, which can each be captured by a verb. In all cases, it was the documents that were in charge of accom-plishing these actions; these acts were significant for the unfolding of the project and had consequences for the team members. Each intervention of the documents contributed to push forward the project. Moreover, if

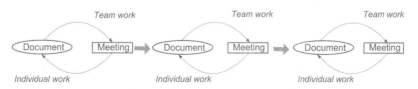

Figure 11.1 Work dynamic in Graph project.

Table 11.1 Categories of Actions Performed by Documents

Category	Actions	Consequences	Basis of Performance
Visibilizing actions	Expose Keep visible	Make visible elements that would otherwise be difficult to see	Degree of detail that can be conveyed
Structuring actions	Structure collective work Guide individual work Assign	Shape what was either done in group or alone; give orders or indications that have to be followed	Duration of support
Articulating actions	Bring together Connect Link past and future	Establish relationships	Capacity to go over space and time limits
Sense making actions	Stimulate reflection Trigger talk Explain Compare Suggest	Encourage exchanges, develop collective understanding, generate ideas, open options to consideration, and help construct solutions	Richness
Signaling actions	Affirm Announce Warn Remind	Send messages to team members regarding decisions, precisions, and priorities	Persistence of signals

any of these actions could have been done by a member of the project team (and were, in fact, at times), in all instances, documents proved to be *better*—more efficient, more powerful or more successful—in achieving what was expected or desired with such an action.

Table 11.1 lists all the actions that the documents performed for the project. Some of the actions that were identified during the analysis of the documents had a common basis, and were thus grouped. This table also presents the main consequences (the results) produced by the actions of the documents, and the characteristics of the documents that contributed to render their action more effective than that of their human counterparts. The following sections describe what is summarized in Table 11.1.

Visibilizing Actions

Two actions performed by the documents belong to this category: to expose and to keep visible. In both cases, documents contributed to making visible what would otherwise have been difficult to see as precisely. Compared to humans, documents can convey information and offer details on what they are covering in a more economic way. For example, one of the actions that most documents performed was to expose, to present.

Considering the written nature of the work at Soft-A, it was the documents that were in charge of revealing the details of what each team member, especially the developers, had done for the project. Without the documents, the various sections of code composing the parts of the Graph window simply could not have been efficiently communicated. Most of the documents that were exposing code were voluminous; without a document it would have been impossible for a developer to present his or her work on a section of code to fellow team members. Furthermore, at Soft-A, every section of code written is subjected to a walkthrough, a technical meeting where every person invited comments on what has been produced. This discussion can get extremely precise; for example, in one meeting, one team member noted the absence of a capital letter in one line of code amongst thousands![2] More generally speaking, by exposing the code, some documents revealed the product that the team was working on.

Since the team could not build a prototype, as is the case in other design projects, such as engineering and architecture, and that their work was, until the last months of the project when they assembled all the modified sections of code, intangible, documents *were* the product for a long period of time of the project. The documents that exposed the code embodied, materialized, the product that was the raison d'être of the project. Other documents—the bugs sheets—contributed to exposing yet another facet of the development: its errors and shortcomings. By listing all the known bugs of the development, the imperfections of the work were fully highlighted. They had to be exposed in detail, since they had to be, for the most part, corrected before the end of the project; but finding solutions to these problems proved to be, in many cases, troublesome. The documents helped in this complicated task by giving to the team members as much detail as possible on the bugs. However, exposing was not limited to technical documents. In this regard, the plans prepared by the project leader unveiled to the team members the tasks that had to be completed, the duration of these tasks, and the overall progress of the project. As was the case for the technical dimension of the project, it would have been exhausting for the project leader to communicate all these information; an Excel page could do the job more easily. The management of the project also materialized thanks to the documents.

By considering the content of the documents and the notes from the meetings' observations, we realized that documents were responsible for keeping visible a number of elements that could have been neglected or even forgotten without their intervention. Technical possibilities that were rejected had to be inscribed in formal documents because of the work they entailed and the decision taken to exclude an element from the project. These elements could have become invisible by having been eliminated from the project. Once invisible, they could have created confusion, dissatisfactions, or even conflicts later on; by saying that such and such possibility would be realized in a future project, the documents prevented questions or negative comments on the absence of some elements in the final product. Without the documents, it would have been much more difficult for humans doing the project to disclose this information.

Structuring Actions

Documents actively structured the project in three ways: by structuring the collective work, by guiding the individual work, and by assigning the work. In all three cases, the documents offered the team members a form of support that was long-lasting, because this support was anchored in an object rather than in a person, who could be unavailable when needed or could be less consistent in his or her choice of words. All structuring actions contributed to giving shape to the project and to delineating the path the project would follow.

First of all, they structured the collective work done during the meetings. Some meetings observed were clearly oriented by the documents that had been sent a few days earlier. People commented on their content following the order of the document; comments were made on the basis of this order, and not on the basis of the hierarchical position of the various team members or on the swiftness of the persons. Documents defined, for the team members, what they would be discussing and the order in which these discussions would take place. At times, the project leader provided a general overview of the meetings; however, if the reasons why they were meeting up and the nature of what would happen during this collective episode were announced by the project leader, it was done very quickly. No other formal agenda was presented. In this respect, documents structured the meetings and by doing so, they focused the attention of the team members.

When the team members were working on their separate tasks, documents played a role akin to the one they performed during the meetings: they guided their work by offering markers regarding each task that had to be done. Documents in this sense supported the developers, who could rely on them to be guided while executing the work they had been assigned. Because the work accomplished in the Graph project was complex, developers often had to go back to the documents to verify that they were on the right track. More generally speaking, several individuals we interviewed declared that one of the main challenges they faced in their work was to know when to stop working on the code. The very nature of the work they are performing explains why it is never easy for them to stop: most them are auto-declared perfectionists who would like to produce code that is not only technically impeccable, but also elegant. Furthermore, all of them are interested in developing new options, in using new technologies: experimenting is, for them, part of the fun they have while completing their tasks. Their technical imagination is thus constantly running. And finally, as some respondents told us, it is always possible, in software engineering, to push things forward; the line where to stop is never neatly drawn. In this context, to have clear reference points helped the developers by indicating the direction that had to be followed.

In a more precise fashion, documents also structured the work of the team members by allocating the work and assigning tasks to each of them. By designating who was responsible for which tasks, documents took over the work of the project leader. This allocation was always a topic of discussion during the meetings; all the decisions where negotiated within group. But when the team dispersed, each person still had the documents in hand to know exactly what was expected of them. By attributing the tasks, these documents clarified the work. Guiding and assigning are actions that can be distinguished by their relative degree of precision. While guiding is indicating the general parameters of the technical work, assigning is linked to organizing, since it corresponds to identifying the specific tasks and the individuals in charge of completing them. Both of these actions took place outside of the meetings.

Articulating Actions

To bring together, connect, and link past and future: these are actions that illustrate the capacity that documents possess to articulate and link elements that are otherwise separated or disconnected. These actions are performed well by documents because they can go over spatial and time boundaries. At Soft-A, most projects have to gather people from different groups inside the organization, people who would not be working together without a specific project. This gathering effect of the project is helped by the documents. In this respect, one of the significant actions accomplished by the documents was to bring together all the individuals who had been assigned to the Graph project. In all instances, the episodes of collective work would simply not have happened if a document had not been produced and transmitted. This document justified that a meeting was held because it sent the message that some collective work had to be done. Without either a managerial or a technical document the meeting would have been baseless. As explained earlier, this is typical of the dynamic at Soft-A: documents *declared* when episodes of team work (the meetings) would take place. But in doing so, documents gathered individuals from different departments of the organization: they established a temporary link between these otherwise disconnected persons. Moreover, documents were also sent to people who would not attend to the meeting. For example, although many sales representatives were concerned by the Graph project, not all of them were present during the meetings. Technical documents were also regularly sent to the members of the software quality assurance group that were involved in Graph. In both cases, these individuals did not all need to attend all meetings, especially those happening during the execution phase of the project. By including them (and sometimes, directly referring to them in the text), the documents kept those persons involved in the project despite their physical absence.

Corollary to this action, documents also connected individuals. While bringing together was an action which led to the formation of a group, connecting established a relationship between individuals. This capacity of the documents enabled them to create an exchange between persons who were not necessarily communicating face to face. This is a fundamental property of documents. For example, since Graph was a graphical interface, one of Soft-A's experts on graphical interfaces was a member of the project team. Toward the end of the project, developers needed his input. But at that time, this expert was very sought after. Since he did not have the gift of ubiquity, he prepared a detailed description of each of his comments. His comments were circulated and discussed thoroughly during a meeting from which he was absent. Because this document connected them, he was able to explain his opinions even though he was physically somewhere else.

Finally, documents also contributed to articulating what constituted the project by linking past and future. By referring directly to past projects (for example, by recalling reasons for certain technological choices being made) and by mobilizing these references in the current decisions that had to be taken, documents helped to maintain the continuity of the Graph application: it ensured that its future was in line with its past. In the context of Soft-A, whose products are mature, such continuity is important. But it has to be created and re-created: and in order to do so, the past has to be made known to the team member of the project, so that the choices they are making today take into account choices made in the past.

Sensemaking Actions

Documents helped the project's team members to reflect on, to understand, and to develop the newly designed Graph application. In all cases, the richness of the documents set in motion the imagination of the project team members. First of all, during individual and collective work documents stimulated team members' thinking processes. This stimulation stemmed from the act of reading the content of the document: this content triggered the team members to think about what they were reading. At times, documents even appealed to specific persons, by asking them to give special consideration to a particular aspect of the project, by questioning them, by calling for their comments and ideas. Especially during collective work episodes, many documents appeared to have the capacity to trigger talk and conversations. Because reading the documents provoked reactions, and the goal of the meetings was to share these reactions, documents sparked off most of the discussions: they led the team members to express themselves. Often, we noticed that people made explicit references to the documents in the opening sentence of their comment. But since these discussions aimed at improving the documents also revolved around unresolved issues, documents could also stimulate the team members' thinking processes while they were meeting and trigger spontaneous verbal interventions. Like exposing and getting together, stimulating thinking and triggering talk have been the most common actions by the documents in the project we studied.

Furthermore, documents offered explanations to the people who read them. Their content was not only exposed: in many instances, this exposition was complemented with additional information that helped the readers to understand what was presented. For example, in technical documents, the new sections of code were often preceded by explanations regarding the choices made by the developer. By explaining what they were exposing, the documents clarified the work on the Graph development and encouraged a smooth development process. Documents also compared elements, such as options, possibilities, and ideas, which were shown side by side. By establishing comparisons, documents brought out the options' similarities and differences. And by doing so for their readers, documents invited them to reflect on the possibilities, to consider them, and to ultimately take sides, which were then collectively discussed during the meetings. Documents compared options easily: readers were able to get at a glance the commonalities and the differences. Finally, documents also made suggestions, regarding paths that could be followed, alternatives to what was being done, or to what appeared as the obvious choice. In these cases, documents remained open and never indicated any preference: their intervention gave ideas to team members, ideas that had to be considered while on the team.

Signaling Actions

Affirm, announce, warn, and remind: all the actions making up this last category sent a message to the project team members. The documents made affirmations, when decisions had been agreed upon, or when faced with an inescapable reality (like the number of remaining days in the project), the intention was to use the documents to inform the team members. For example, some documents showed the progress (in percentages) of each of the correction tasks that had to be done on the development: by doing so, these documents *stated*. By presenting what was under way or what was about to be initiated, other documents *announced*, which led them to lay down the foundations of the work to come. Documents could also clearly *warn* the team members: they made specific persons aware of elements that they had to look after or that they should not lose sight of. On other occasions, these warnings were directed to all the team members. Finally, by reiterating what had been said during the meetings, documents reminded the team members what was important and what they had decided. This was done in order to limit the negative consequences that could have come from any oversight. By repeating significant elements, documents underlined the project's priorities at the time. Because they had been established and negotiated during the meetings, priorities were well-known to the team members; but by repeating them, the documents contributed to keeping clear and obvious what was capital and to distinguish it from what was trivial. The persistence of the documents' message was useful to the team members: since documents could be consulted and referred to when each team member was working on his or her own, these important signals were still unaltered.

Discussion and Conclusion: Constituting the Project

Packendorff (1995) has proposed that our understanding of projects could benefit from a move from seeing projects as tools to achieve a defined end to conceiving them as "a temporary organization, an aggregate of individuals temporarily enacting a common cause" (p. 326). This move would lead researchers to study "temporary organizing processes, i.e. the deliberate social interaction occurring between people working together to accomplish a certain, inter-subjectively determined task" (Packendorff, 1995, p. 328). This perspective is fruitful, especially in a field dominated by a strong functionalist and instrumental conception of projects; however, various studies on objects and tools, like those we presented, have underlined the fact that these elements are indispensable to make things happen, in any work setting. Project work and project management are no exception to this idea.

In this line of thought, we proposed and illustrated that all the processes and interactions in project settings profit from the presence of various objects and tools, like documents. The different actions summarized in Table 11.1 demonstrate the importance of documents in the case of the Graph project. Being deeply involved in creating what is happening in the project, the documents contributed by constituting it, giving it a constitution. The production, circulation, manipulation, discussion, and correction of the documents significantly shaped the work of the team members and the management of the project. Even more, through the responsibilities that were delegated to them, the documents performed actions that held together the project. We can even say that documents served the project by helping it to take shape. Projects are by definition temporary: being time-limited, they have little time to address conflicts and tensions that could arise during action and to develop mechanisms to limit or correct them. They have "to hold," despite the fact that people from different departments have to collaborate in a context were the work is complex and abstract. In this respect, projects have a need for a relative stabilization, a stabilization that makes this arrangement work while it has to. Such a temporary durability is not only the result of the willingness of the individuals involved in the project: it is also created and maintained by the action of the documents. In the project we studied, documents did make a difference. Work and management practices, interactions, and their results in the form of a new piece of software would have been more difficult to accomplish and obtain if documents had not been part of the scene. What was delegated to documents—the possibilities to make visible, to structure, to articulate, to make sense, and to signal—is directly linked to the properties of textual objects. Because of the degree of detail that they can convey, their physical durability, their capacity to cross spatial and temporal limits, the richness they can reveal, and the persistence of their messages, documents did better than humans in actions where these properties were useful. And the actions that were facilitated by these properties are precisely those that make projects happen: materializing the product, the work, the collective, exposing and explaining what had been done, delineating the path to follow, sparking off thought and talk, organizing work, and warning and reminding team members of priorities and constraints.

The repertoire that we elaborated from our fieldwork is far from exhaustive. By studying other projects in the same company and other contexts, other actions played by documents could be uncovered. For example, in the case of the Graph project, documents did not accomplish clear legitimizing actions. Still, this role has been documented by various studies on texts and rhetoric (e.g., Winsor, 1998, 2006). Our research is a first step in developing such a repertoire, and more qualitative studies are needed.

Recently, Orlikowski (2007) has argued that the materiality of organizing has been neglected in organization theory and has proposed "that we recognize that *all* [emphasis in original] practices are always and everywhere sociomaterial, and that this sociomateriality is constitutive, shaping the contours and possibilities of everyday organizing" (p. 1444). The focus on situated action and practice advocated by Packendorff (1995) and by Cicmil et al. (2006) to study projects is more than welcome and will help scholars and practitioners alike better understand what happens while being involved in projects. However, in following this line of inquiry, we claim that we should not lose sight of the objects. As our research shows, their contribution to the actuality of projects is considerable and should be better recognized.

Acknowledgement

This research was made possible by a grant from the Social Sciences and Humanities Research Council of Canada. The author would like to thank Line Bonneau for her helpful comments.

Notes

1. Some details regarding the company and the persons interviewed have been disguised or modified to ensure confidentiality.
2. This is not a trivial remark, since the use of upper vs. lower case letters is defined by the company's programming standards. Capital and lower case letters represent different elements: it is thus crucial that they are used according to what they are supposed to designate.

12 Organizational Communication at the Crossroads

James R. Taylor

At a Crossroads?

The study of organization, seen from a communicational perspective, now stands at a crossroads. Organizational communication has been at a crossroads before, to be sure. The first time was in the 1960s when Charles Redding, Lee Thayer, and Phil Tompkins, drawing on an accumulation of research, announced the birth of a new field bearing the name it now does, "Organizational Communication" (not, incidentally, "Communication *in* Organization" nor "Communication *and* Organization"; the distinction is fundamental). They were soon backed up by a new generation of American scholars: Peter Monge, Linda Putnam, Leonard Hawes, George Cheney, Stan Deetz, Bob McPhee, Scott Poole, Cynthia Stohl, Ted Zorn, Eric Eisenberg, Charlie Conrad, Gail Fairhurst, Larry Browning, Dennis Mumby, Kathy Krone, and many others.

We arrived at a second crossroads in 1981, at the historic summer conference at Alta, Utah, when some of these young Turks led the equivalent of a palace revolt (Putnam & Pacanowsky, 1983). This was when the field began to shake itself free from the stifling dominance of positivism inherited from psychology and sociology in the 1960s. The Alta manifesto was inspired by innovators such as Karl Weick, Anthony Giddens, and Michel Foucault and opened up the field by encouraging alternative modes of research, more interpretative and more critical than those that had been deemed acceptable before.

We arrived at a third crossroads in the 1990s. The defining moment, for me, was Ruth Smith's ICA presentation in 1993 to the annual conference of the International Communication Association (ICA), based on her doctoral research at Purdue University. Her findings reported on how people in our field had conceptualized the communication-organization relationship, since its inception. She based her analysis on the images or metaphors that authors used to describe the relationship. Most people (about 70% of all authors) reified organization by treating it as if it were a natural phenomenon like any other: In essence, a "house" for communication to occur in. By making the organization into a container to be filled with communication, the researchers were offered the convenience of being able to concentrate on the communication process. The downside, however, was that in doing so they were obscuring the basis of the organization *in those self-same communication processes*. When Smith tried to imagine an alternative metaphor that would better explain the roots of organization in communication, however, she drew a blank: Production, maybe? If so, which produces which? Equivalence? That's a stretch, as she herself conceded. Maybe, from a retrospective view, they were the wrong questions.

It was Ruth Smith who reminded us that, to paraphrase Gertrude Stein speaking about Oakland, California, and as Bruno Latour has persuasively argued in this book (chapter 3), in the case of the organization "there is no THERE *there*." The THERE is in fact HERE, in our own communication: forever *both* here *and* there.

I was stimulated to explore the possibility of an alternative image to that of communication-in-organization in an article published in 1995 (Taylor, 1995b). I built my argument around Maturana and Varela's (1987) concept of *autopoiesis*, a theory that treats the cell as a closed, self-reproductive system. It postulates a reflexive loop by means of which the communicative and other productive processes in the cell manufacture themselves and their own boundary, the cell's wall. I took from the notion of autopoiesis the principle that the human organization, as a society, must be also, in its way, reflexively self-reproducing. As Klaus Krippendorff (2008) has observed, social organizations are distinguished from machines, "whose parts are permanently in place or engaged," because the former are "organisms that must maintain uninterrupted autopoiesis" (p. 8). Like Maturana (1997), however, I do *not* see the human organization as a replica of the cell: far from it. The logic may be similar in some respects but the processes are different, and the end product is quite another thing. Such metaphors mask, in particular, the role of human communication in establishing agency (more on that later).

As the chapters of this book attest, we have left that 1990s crossroads behind us. We have ceased to think of communication as merely something going on *in* an organization. It is time to concentrate on the flip side of that coin: why it is, and how, and when, that organization emerges *in* and *through* communication.

We have, however, now arrived at a new crossroads. We need to break with another tradition, this time one that goes all the way back to 17th century thinkers such as Leibniz and Descartes, and indeed well before that. It is a tradition that automatically takes the *individual* as the starting point of theory building and analysis. This prejudice is enshrined in the whole history of Western thought. We have built a carpenter's shed full of methods that impel us to always start with the individual as the unit of analysis: *experiments*, focused on individuals and their reactions; *surveys*, sampling individual respondents drawn from a "population"; *interviews* that probe individual perspectives. Such methodology encourages micro-macro thinking. Communication theory, also, as it has been too long conceived, has assumed messages sent from one person, a sender, to another person, a receiver. Accumulations of messaging produce networks: Micro-macro again.

These shibboleths no longer have the upper hand they once did (although they have not vanished). There is a great deal of fascinating research now going on, much of it modeled on ethnography-inspired studies of social formation or on conversational process. I find this work very exciting, and was delighted to see it well represented in this volume. But I think it is the case that we still do not have, as Bob Craig (Craig & Muller, 2007) has reminded us, an explicit, well-conceived theory of communication. What I am going to outline in these concluding remarks are some of the things we need to get clear in order to free ourselves from the all too well-engrained habit, that is encrusted in tradition, of going back to the individual as the social unit: what Elizabeth Van Every (personal communication) calls the "default assumption." If communication is a difficult science to master, theoretically and empirically, it is because it runs counter to—indeed *contradicts*—this long-established prejudice.

The Importance of Relationship

If the individual is not the basic unit of analysis then what is? To cite Barbara Czarniawska, network theory has traditionally assumed "the existence of actors, who forge connections" (chapter 1). The alternative approach, that she calls "action net," assumes instead the primacy of *organizing*. Rather than privilege individual actors, she writes, "action net reverts this assumption, suggesting that connections between and among actions, when stabilized, are used to construct the identities of actors." Actors and organizations are "outcomes rather than inputs of organizing" (p. 13). As she observes, you can only become a publisher by publishing, and publishing is already a web of connections—relationships.

One of the best teachers I ever had was at the University of London. A linguist, she emphasized something I have never forgotten. When children learn to speak it is not the *words* they start with. They master the *rhythmic patterns* of speech before they can handle words. They learn, moreover, to use language in context—a *relational* context. When you watch parents teaching their children to speak, as she did, you see that what the latter are absorbing is attitude. They were, after all, born into a situation, and had to learn how to swim in a pool of relationships if they were to thrive. This means that they had to know the right sound patterns and gestures to register their needs, and who to address themselves to. They had mastered these skills well before they could mouth a single word intelligibly: one of the first ones typically being, as every parent knows, "*NO!!!*."

I therefore propose a new slogan: It All Begins and Ends as a Relationship, in a Context.

It was Harvey Sacks (1992) who pointed out that identities do not come packaged individually. They are grouped into sets: mother-daughter, uncle-niece, employer-employee, master-servant, doctor-patient, lawyer-client, and so on. Relationships! As Goffman in his 1959 book put it, we put on a face, try out a line, and depending on how well things go, we *establish* an identity, *in* a context. The famous "identity crisis" that so many young people traverse as they grow up is mainly a quest to find a relational context in which to flourish and grow. The other crisis, the midlife crisis, is the downside of that quest: it indexes dissatisfaction with the matrix of relationships in which one has become embedded over the years.

This is not to deny the reality of the individual experience. It is just to set our priorities straight. In Valérie Carayol's words, "the initial entities are not substances, but rather events and relationships. They therefore play a fundamental role in the construction of reality" (Carayol, 2008, p. 164). Similarly for Barbara Czarniawska, it is the *connections* that construct identities rather than the other way around.

Actor? Agent? Actant?

A concept that has preoccupied a number of contributions to this volume is that of agent, and its related notions of actor and agency. I would like to take a minute to add my own reading of these terms. Take the concept of actor. To level the playing field, and to give nonhuman entities their just status as contributors to the unfolding of action, Bruno Latour introduced the term *actant*. He was clear about the rationale, and the source (Latour, 1994, p. 33). The reason for introducing the term was to avoid having to use the term *actor* for nonhumans, because to do so would be, as he put it in his 1994 article, an "uncommon" use of the word. It would be "confusing." The term *actant,* he then wrote, is "a borrowing from semiotics." Which semiotics he had in mind is also an open secret—"*un secret de Polichinelle.*" It was Algirdas Julien Greimas. It was Greimas, a semiotician who specialized in the analysis of narrative, who proposed the distinction between actor and actant.

Greimas justified the basis for his neologism in this way, as "between *actants*, having to do with narrative syntax, and *actors*, who are recognizable in the particular discourses in which they are manifested" (Greimas, 1987, p. 106). *Actants*, in other words, are defined by their place in the syntactic structure of narrative. Their eventual physical manifestation is, at that level of abstraction, immaterial. *Actors*, however, are recognizable as real people. For Greimas, an *actant*, as in actor-network theory, is not necessarily a human being, but it must nevertheless manifest the quality of what Greimas called an "anthropomorphic classeme." What he meant by that mouthful is that an actant is an expression of agency, whatever its materialization, *because we can detect in it the presence of a human attitude.* To borrow a term from van Vuuren and Cooren (2008), it is *attitude* that transforms a connection of actions, human and otherwise, into a relationship: makes it, to use Greimas's term, *anthropomorphic.* For example, again citing Greimas, a rule may "require" someone to do something (or, more likely, *not* to do something). The rule communicates an attitude: signs that say "No right turn," "No smoking," "Please close the door."

Actor-network theory has borrowed the term *actant* but it has sometimes tended to downplay the communicative logic of human motive behind it. For Greimas, actants are agents because they are components in a relationship that is *narratively* defined. To be more precise, the actant is defined by what Greimas called a *communication schema.* Communication in turn is grounded in a *structure of exchange* (Greimas, 1987, p. 77); it is two-way, not unidirectional.

It is the embedding in a communicative relationship that makes the actant meaningful to us as conveying attitude. Whatever the materialization of the agency, *provided it is grounded in and expresses human motive* (i.e., is "anthropomorphic"), it qualifies as an actant. If it fails that test, the actant no longer works. Imagine the consequence, for example, if you were told that all the signs in a building had been randomly moved around over Hallowe'en, or on April Fools' Day. You wouldn't trust them any longer. The human agency inscribed in them would be wrong. As Kirsch and Neff (2008) have put it, the artifacts that sustain organizational communication—the lifeblood of an organization, as they describe it—are those that are "inscribed with instrumental, symbolic, and aesthetic meanings." They serve as "the conceptual link among disparate and sometimes conflicting groups within organizations" (p. 3).

Actor-network theory sometimes tends, on my reading, to play down the *2-way, reciprocal,* and *associational* machinery of communication. The meaning of an act is not located in the written or spoken words themselves, nor in the persons who speak them, but *in the fact that the act which they materialize is already embedded within and reconstructs a relationship.* Again it is not so much a question of connections as of *relationships.*

As John Austin (1962) pointed out, if there is no uptake of an act of speech it fails. A text has no intrinsic meaning of its own. Its meaning is established in a communicative sequence that indexes or establishes a relationship (Robichaud, 2006). ANT has retained the connectivity, but has sometimes obscured the punctuation that communication *as a reciprocal relationship* introduces into a sequence of speech acts. Instead, ANT too often offers us an explanation of action that is linear. The result, in some cases, is to evacuate action of its communicative sense and patterning. Worse, it is to lose sight of the basis of organization in communication: grounded in the patterns of exchange, the negotiation of transactions, and the formation of relationships that are thereby implied.

What *Is* An Organization?

The problem presented by this marginalizing of the basis of communication in exchange is that an organization is not "out there" any more than a person is "in here." As Bruno Latour has put it in his contribution to this book (chapter 3), "there never is any 'sui generis' corporate body.... Organizations ... remain always *immanent* to the instrumentarium that brings them into existence ... an organization is not and will never be a superorganism, a whole superior to its parts, a corporate body, a moral entity made up of its many individual constituents" (p. 49). I subscribe fully to that view.

If we wish the relational basis of communication out of existence, however, then I think that, inevitably, part of the road kill will be organization. And we all know that organizations *are* real, a crucial part of our 21st century environment. If, however, you accept the ontological primacy of relationship, I now mean to argue, the nature of organization ceases to be a mystery. Like any other set of relationships it is embedded in a temporary accommodation, still under negotiation.

This being said, we have to be careful. As Anne Nicotera (chapter 5) points out, we have tended to be so focused on process, on organization as a *verb* (an "organizing"), that we have obscured the other side of the coin, organization as a *noun*. As she points out, an organization is an agent. But then how can it be an agent if it is not also an *entity* that is capable of acting? This raises in turn the question of what kind of entity it *is*. If not, as Bruno Latour put it, a "superorganism," then what is it?

Organization as Entity?

Nicotera answers her own question by citing some remarks she overheard on campus at George Mason University where she teaches. One person said, "I like the way *we* are starting to integrate writing instruction across the campus." At another time Nicotera heard this: "I don't get why *the university* wants me to teach composition." As she points out, the difference lies in the pronoun. The first person said "we." She "cast herself," Anne writes, "as a member of a collective agent." The second person said "the university" but she could as easily have substituted "it" or "they." In other words, she was separating herself from *it*, the university, and *they*, its spokespersons, and, in the same breath, she was ascribing agency both to *it* and to *herself*.

First person plural ("we") versus third person ("it," "they"): The relational framing has shifted from associational (*we* as a linking of cooperating agents) to dissociational (*they* or *it* as *not we*, someone else who is imposing on us, in this case). The crucial difference is that in the first instance authority is equitably shared. In the second, it is skewed in a way that attributes to one agent, an "it," a greater authority than "I" or "we."

It is the university that "wants" its members to follow a certain policy, not the other way around. She has in effect anthropomorphized the organization: made it a person as if it had a human form. She attributes attitude and intention to *it*. By doing so she has implicitly, notice, also established a hierarchy of actants: university, its spokespersons, its members. In effect, there is no *we* in the absence of an *it* or a *they*, any more than there is, as George Herbert Mead many years ago argued, a *me* in the absence of a *you*.

I think Nicotera has hit upon the defining characteristic of organization: a skewed distribution of authority that makes one actant, the organization, *one-up*, to use an expression borrowed from Watzlawick, Beavin, and Jackson (1967), while others, namely the people who work for the organization, are *one-down*. Think of a soldier in the army. He or she executes the orders of superior officers. They, in turn, express the intention of their commanders. They, however, represent the army. The army is a wing of government, and supports the commander-in-chief, the civilian who heads up the government, which in theory must channel the will of the people. The responsibility for deciding (and the attribution of attitude) keeps being pushed upward—*en amont*—with the consequence that the delegation of authority to act is pushed further and further downward— *en aval*. The sense of personal responsibility risks being evacuated as the chain becomes extended.

The resulting disconnect is well documented, historically, in its effects: on the one hand, what might be called the post-World War II Nuremberg effect ("I only did what I was told to do therefore I am innocent"); on the other, the Abu Ghraib syndrome, where no one above the rank of sergeant is indicted on the grounds that the abuses were due to a few "bad apples"—those who "exceeded" their authority. Why do we humans do this, since the implication, as Stan Deetz (2008) reminds us, is an inequality of agencies that is an open invitation to abuse?

The Hybrid Character of Agency

Here is another place where I think we can put Bruno Latour's (chapter 3) incisive analysis to work. His point is that any actant is a hybrid construction: both human and material. One of his ways to illustrate the hybrid character of acting has been to refer to the endless debate in North America about the need for government action to control the sale and distribution of handguns (see also Latour, 1994). Advocates of total absence of regulation, like the National Rifle Association in the United States, contend that guns don't kill, people do. Those who favor gun control argue roughly the opposite, that it is the widespread availability of guns that explains the extraordinarily high rate of murders in that country, compared with others having more restrictive legislation. Actor-network proposes that it is neither the gun, in isolation, nor the shooter. It is the *fusion* of shooter and gun that is enabled to act (and thereby incidentally transforms the gun into an expression of attitude). Others are surreptitiously being enabled as well, of course: legislators, lobbies, gun manufacturers, merchant associations, and on and on.

Now let us look at a different case, that of the organization. Who is the "it" that is insisting on the need to "teach composition" in Nicotera's example? The university, obviously. How do we describe the *actant* in that case? If we take actor-network theory logic to heart we would have to say that the university-as-actant is born in the fusion of university and teacher (not to mention a few other things like classrooms, textbooks, alumni, departments of education, and of course students!). The university cannot act on its own, because *it is not that kind of entity*. It is not a person: an *actor*. It is, following Greimas's (1987) reasoning, an actant. It is not going to be doing the teaching itself, because it cannot. On the other hand, the teachers *are* actors, but in joining the university as its agents, they also became actants; they are now *university* teachers, an intermediary linking the university to its students.

There is, however, a problem if we take the Greimas definition of actant seriously. Remember, for it to qualify as an actant it must be a member of the class that he calls, in his jargon, anthropomorphic. It must, that is, have *human* characteristics. It is too big a stretch—what do you think?—to attribute intrinsic feelings, desires, an attitude, a passion, an intention to the rifle locked up in the gun rack on the wall (something, incidentally, that Bruno Latour has meticulously avoided doing). To paraphrase van Vuuren and Cooren (2008) it is a little hard to claim that it was the *gun's* attitude that "made it do" what it did. It is the person with the gun in his or her hand that attributes to the act of killing an anthropomorphic attitude. From this perspective the gun is a means, an agency, a transmitter of attitude, but it is not where the attitude originated. To use Gibson's famous term (1979), the gun is an *affordance*, a vehicle of attitude.

The case of organization is different from the gun. It too is an entity, in a way. But it is not like a gun. It has no intrinsic materiality (nor indeed any intrinsic agency). And nevertheless we easily, and daily, attribute anthropomorphic characteristics to it, without blinking an eye. In today's newspaper, on one page alone, I read that *Washington* has "snubbed" Ottawa, that the *U.S. Securities and Exchange Commission* has "announced" talks, that *it* has "chosen" Australia over Canada, that *it* does not "want" to try forging an agreement, that *the world's biggest banks* have "rebuffed" calls for stricter rules, and so on and on. Thus organizations are actants in a way that objects like guns are not. In the case of an organization it is the people who *represent* it who are the affordances. This is true even though there is no real entity—and here I am in total agreement with Bruno Latour—that we can ever point to and say that's it, *there* is the organization. *Unlike* the gun it is an entirely fictitious, totally immaterial construction. It just happens, however, that it is also a powerful actant *because we attribute an attitude to it* as we do with signs. This is how it becomes real, materialized in its agents. An organization, in other words, has many heads and multiple hands but no mind of its own, and assuredly no heart. It is Callon and Latour's (1981) *Leviathan*.

The Rationale for Attributing Agency to an Immaterial Actant: Organization

Why do we need organizations? Very simply, because their existence lends to our own actions, as their representative agents, a greatly increased power to exert an influence on the world. Because those teachers Anne Nicotera was overhearing represented—were an extension of—the university, they could count on access to classrooms, and all the accoutrements that go with them, libraries and bookstores, and on and on. They had acquired a status, a credibility, and an identity that enabled them to function effectively in their relations with peers, with students, with administration, and with others in their nonuniversity communities. There were also, of course, tangible rewards, including a salary.

There is, however, a price to be paid for this delegation of attitudes to another entity that we have invented through our own communicative practices. In doing so we have incarnated a relationship of authority where our own intentions and attitudes have to take the backseat. But the reward in enhanced authority, identity, and *prestige* in dealing with other organizational and nonorganizational agents is also considerable, even at the cost of becoming one-down within the organizing context itself.

It is a curious trade-off that we humans seem to have invented. It is a deal we have naturalized, most blatantly by reifying the organization in our own discourse: critical theorists as much as positivists, by the way. The "deal," however, is fragile: as Nicotera puts it, even to survive its infancy, "the organization's raison d'être must remain primary in the agentic activities of the individuals, collectives, and nonhuman agents that continually and recursively presentify and incarnate it" (chapter 5, p. 78). That is tenuous.

If the concept of emergence is to be sustainable, an entity generated by a process, then we must not see the side effects of organizing as merely an aberration or a deformation of what Habermas (1976/1979) calls "authentic" communication—something that is due to bigness and the games of power it encourages. We must recognize the same effects as always potentially present even in the simplest of human encounters.

Nicotera's anecdote about overhearing colleagues' chatter offers one clue: the pronouns. If I say "you and I" I refer to two human actors. But the collective "we" is *not* an actor, because it does not refer to any single person. It is already an *actant*: the result of a fusion, a connection, a relationship. As such, it is indefinitely extensible. It might mean only you and me. Or "we" might be the gang at the office, or an organizational division, or the organization itself. Or it might be a whole nation, or a coalition of countries (NATO, for example), or humanity. The logic is associative. When, however, the speaker counterposes "I" against "it" or "they" she is *dissociating* herself from the actant: it is the *university* ("it," "they") who wants "me" to "teach composition."

We use pronouns such as *I, we, you, it, he, she, and they* with great skill to communicate to others our associative and dissociative preferences. As we do, we are continually establishing our own identity, as well as that of the actants we relate to, *including that of the organization*.

Robert Swieringa (2008) develops a similar theme in his analysis of a regular seminar at a research laboratory in entomology. In his account the dynamic of talk is one where students must develop a chronicle that describes, and offers an account of, their current research projects. Their interlocutor is the lab head. Not only is her authority established in these dialogues but the identity of the group itself, and its members, is talked into being. The participants, the author reports, "identify themselves as belonging to 'the' community." By doing so, they come to rely on "a definable substantive perception of relations between individuals and among them as contributing to a collective." The reporting process is described by the author as a "discursive space" that encourages them to "enact their agency as members of the lab and collectively maintain the laboratory as an environment suitable for undertaking activities relevant to their own developing trajectories and the lab's 'organization'" (pp. 2–3). Can we generalize from this analysis to the larger sphere of the whole network of communities of practice that make up an organization? I think we can.

The Interplay of Conversation and Text

Nicotera uses our 1996 article (Taylor, Cooren, Giroux, & Robichaud, 1996), to lay out a roadmap that explains how the ongoing object-oriented conversations of many communities of practice finally crystallize into an entity that people recognize as an "organization." The crucial step, in her (and our) analysis, is the construction of a text that both expresses the attitude of this strange new entity, the organization, and is recognized by people inside the organization as doing so because they also find themselves and their activities mirrored in it. I see this as an extension of the dynamic described by Swieringa: a community that takes shape in the reporting activities of its members, as they account for what they are doing, as individuals, and as a community of practice to which they belong and where they establish their identity. What is added is the construction of a text that will communicate identity beyond the boundaries of any single conversation.

Nicotera calls this translation of talk into text "reification." She describes a process that starts as an inscription, first verbally, then turns up in text, like the minutes of a meeting, or someone's report, and is finally transmuted into a rainbow of other physical manifestations. Thinking, for example, of McPhee and Zaug's (2009) work (see also Putnam & Nicotera, 2009) this is how the organization is made visible to those both outside it, and inside it.

We have often glorified the strategic role of top management, as if managers alone wrote the text. But as Benoît Cordelier (2008) pointed out, there never actually is a "unifying managerial vision that would tune up organizational representations and facilitate actors' cooperation" (p. 1). Leadership should not be thought of as a property of individuals, as Fairhurst and Cooren (2008) make clear in their contribution. Authority is not *some*where, but *every*where.

The 1996 paper Nicotera cites laid out a notion of conversations that generate texts, and through the continuing negotiation of many such texts, the result is finally a definitive text, that which states the attitude and strategy of the organization itself. What we did not do in the 1996 paper, as Nicotera points out, was to ask, "What then?" If Benoît Cordelier (2008) is right, the game has only just begun. We got the players out on the field in our article, but then we kind of went off to congratulate ourselves, and have a beer. We almost missed the game itself.

We've been trying to make up for our earlier want of diligence ever since. But what is truly exciting in this conference is to see that we are now part of a much larger community of similarly motivated searchers. Asmuss and Thomsen (2008), for example, remind us that organizational strategy is not a one-shot war. Strategy becomes, to cite them, "meaningful as it is talked into being." The relationship between company strategy and the conversational encounters that characterize the many discourse communities of the organization is, as they put it, "a dynamic two-way relation." Viviane Sergi (chapter 11) maps the process of planning in a similar way. Isabelle Piette (chapter 9) also sees the emergence of an organizational identity as a work in progress. She describes the organization "as the unstable result of organizing processes, a kind of social dynamic in a constant state of flux" (p. 151). For her, the identity of the organization is a narrative construction. As she puts it, the "narrative acts as a hermeneutic framework, which allows a person to find a place within the worldview, act with purpose, develop a rationale, make sense of and justify the established order of things, and proclaim its self-existence." But the narrative is never more that "a temporary image of the self and the world" that for the moment "gives meaning to events and a means to interact with the world." It is continually being reconstructed "according to the context, the knowledge, the authors, and the audience."

Conclusion

For me it has been an uncanny experience to meet up with the ghost of Jim Taylor past (like Scrooge's old partner Marley in Dickens's *Christmas*

Carol). Steffen Blashke (2008) describes a fictitious conversation between Luhmann and Taylor (I should read up on them one day, they sound interesting, I thought). According to Boris Brummans (chapter 6) Jim Taylor is a Buddhist? I didn't know that; people are always surprising you, aren't they? Jim Taylor a magician? I like that! thank you, Mark van Vuuren (van Vuuren & Cooren, 2008). Reading and hearing about myself this way I think I finally get what Derrida was driving at. I have been encountering a *restance* of myself: a residue, a trace, an artifact—or maybe an avatar? Whichever, I don't always agree with this guy. Sometimes I don't even recognize him. That's what time does: you end up arguing with yourself or not even realizing it is *you*. But then, *is* it? Could, perhaps, *I* be actually a *him* who has been invented by others, or, even more alarming, a *me* still to be constructed (Mead, 1934)?

To conclude this modest reflection on the current state of our field, I would like to reflect a bit on my reaction to the fine-grained and incisive analysis of my thinking by several contributions in the volume, notably Linda Putnam (chapter 2), Boris Brummans (chapter 6), Anne Nicotera (chapter 5), but also Tim Kuhn (2008), Bill Buxton (2008), Stephen Blaschke (2008), and Bob McPhee (2008). What all these authors perceived in my writings over the years is that whatever body of theory and research I have managed to produce reflects, on the surface, the influence of seemingly contradictory ideas. It is, they think, marked as much by ambiguity as by perceptiveness (an accusation to which I plead guilty: I have often myself felt I was confronting the ambiguous).

The most probing and perceptive of these analyses is that of Putnam (chapter 2), who sees in not only my own work, but also that of the community of scholars with which I identify, a dialectical tension. As she notes in passing, *dialectic* is not a word I would use, because of its Hegelian overtones, but of course she is right. The reason, however, is to be found in my conviction that, to use terms invented by the English philosopher of language John Austin, communication is both *constative* and *performative*. There is no shortage of articles and books that emphasize the constative dimension of language use: the current vogue of writing on knowledge invention, diffusion, and management, especially in the literature of management studies, illustrates what I mean. But there is correspondingly a dearth of writing on the performative dimension of language use, at least in the literature that is focused on communication and organization (Fauré, Brummans, Giroux, & Taylor, 2010). To be performative, to me, means to establish authority and precedence through communicating, both of people and of knowledge. The construction of authority is essential to the emergence of organization in the first place, because if it is not authored in performance it cannot exist. The authoring of the organization, however, cannot be accomplished without a determination of who and what has precedence over what and whom: hierarchy, in other words. In that everyone has an interest in sustaining the reality of organization—it is where they find their own identity—then everyone has a common goal. But since a ladder of precedence is the inevitable consequence of attaining this end their interests cease to be convergent. Linda Putnam has, I think, gone to the heart of this "dialectic" in that she recognizes the consequence. As she writes, "these contests of moments of struggle among the unitary and competing communities of practice also give rise to new collectives and macro-actors. This conception also locates power not as a property of the macro-actor but in the network of people or in the alliance for whom the actor speaks" (chapter 2, p. 31). Again *power* is not a word I much use, but she is right.

Both Nicotera (chapter 5) and McPhee (2008) have questioned my consistency of perspective on the ontological status of organization, in its relation to communication. As I have already said, Nicotera wonders about the entity status of organization and I have tried to explicate my view on the question. McPhee, for his part, is preoccupied with the issue of "equivalence" (a notion no more than briefly sketched in Smith's 1993 paper). He suspects that my colleagues and I harbor, without ever admitting it, a predilection for this view of the link between communication and organization: if not an equivalence, exactly, a "near" equivalence. He associates this dangerous tendency with the conversation-text interplay that has indeed figured centrally in my own work. He thinks, I suspect, that I am again downplaying the substantiality of organization. So perhaps it is worth seeing how, if I can, to clarify my position.

The issue turns on the question of identity. Earlier theorists such as Mead, Goffman, and Garfinkel subscribed to the view, which I share, that identity is something to be continually established, in a context, confronted by a situation, in interaction with others. All we have done is to extend this view in two ways. First, we have argued that it is not only the individual whose identity is thus constructed communicatively but that of the organization as well. Within the bounds of the communicative process, this is the only way the entity status of both people and collectives could be established.

The second move that we have made is to emphasize the role of agency in this ongoing negotiation of identity. When an ex-president of the United States meets the supreme leader of North Korea, for example, both are *agents* who represent their respective governments (and perhaps even their populations). But agency can be (and is) expressed in a multitude of ways: an aircraft carrier in the Japan Sea, a bomb test, an ultimatum sent via the diplomatic mail, a speech or a meeting. Unless this were so, organization would not exist, as an entity, because it could never itself function as its own agent, since it lacks materiality in and of its own person. And yet we know that organization *does* exist, multiply materialized: as offices, factories, stores, networks, located here, there and everywhere. It is *present* in our lives. Only through agency could this be accomplished.

Strictly speaking, there is no answer to the question of the equivalence of communication and organization. My dictionary defines the word *organization* as (a) organizing or being organized, but also as (b) an organic structure, (c) a unified group or systemized whole, such as a club or union, and (d) the administrative structure of a business or political party. I certainly see communication and getting organized as equivalent (I cannot imagine how organizing could be accomplished other than in and through communication). I equally, however, do not understand communication as a "unified group," including not merely clubs and union, but corporations and government agencies. I think that administration is a consequence of communicative practices of a certain kind, but that is not to make communication equivalent to the resulting "organic structure." It is fair to ask in what ways communication and organizing are equivalent. But to try to pin down the relationship once and for all is fruitless: that is not how language works.

One associated issue is the interplay of text and conversation, if only because, as Wittgenstein argued, words mean what they do when people use them to communicate. Words have families of meanings, as my dictionary recognizes, and they depend on how people use them, in what context. I share the view of the linguist M. A. K. Halliday (1970/2002) that speech as well as writing is mediated by the production and interpretation of text. There would be no conversation without text. Text, therefore, is our agent: literally *that which acts*, as well as *acting for* us. Practically speaking, however, it is more useful to restrict the term *text* to its more usual connotation of an inscription, on paper or whatever medium will serve to preserve the words and disseminate them beyond the boundaries of the thought processes or conversations where they were first produced. All human conversation organizes. But if the organization is to transcend the boundaries of any single conversation it must mobilize text in this latter sense. So I see organization as existing in the small as well as the large. But this does not trivialize the study of large organization because the means by which text acts in these contrasting contexts are transformed as a consequence of scale.

Finally, a word in response to Boris Brummans's intriguing analysis (chapter 6). No Boris, I am not a Buddhist (he knows that). But yes it is true that I think our analyses of human organization are too often imprisoned in worn-out habits of thought. I do not indeed, as I have tried to make clear, think there is any essence that we could think of as organization-in-and-of-itself. It is, as he puts it, empty at the core. Here I think we should become more conscious of the transformation that has befallen the ancient science of physics over the course of the past century. Once Einstein had formulated his law $E=MC^2$, the world changed. Matter, he was making clear, is merely frozen energy. I suggest we need to make some kind of similarly transformative move, by recognizing that organization is a material construction only in the sense that it is a frozen configuration of agency, both human and nonhuman. The bonding agents that hold the particles of matter together are, however, not as fragile, nor are they the same as those of human organization. We need to understand them in a new way.

Hari Tsoukas (chapter 4) intimated something similar in his contribution to the dialogue. He described "the inherently indeterminate" character of all human experience. In this respect, I was strongly struck, in reading his chapter, how closely it parallels the reasoning of one of my most treasured sources, Charles Sanders Peirce (1955). What Tsoukas, citing Castoriadis (1997), calls *magma* (the matter out of which "ensidic" organizations are derived) corresponds, to me, to Peirce's "firstness." As Peirce put it, in describing firstness, "For as long as things do not act upon one another there is no sense of meaning in saying that they have any being, unless it be that they are such in themselves that they may perhaps come into relation with others" (Peirce, 1903/1940, p. 76). Like Peirce as well, Tsoukas sees meaning arising in the "punctuation into nameable units" as the indispensable condition—the sine qua non—of understanding. Tsoukas calls this punctuation *ensemblizing*; Peirce uses a different term, *thirdness*. The idea, however, seems to me to be the same. Tsoukas then uses this conceptualization to explain the foundation of organization in the meaningful (literally meaning-*full*) practices of the people who participate in its construction.

This is a complex but revealing analysis with which I am greatly in sympathy. What it still lacks (and I would say the same for Peirce) is the dimension of reflexivity which is the essence of communication. I too recognize that "organization is the ensemblizing of magmatic being as the latter is self-constituted within practices." What I wish Hari had made clearer was that the embedding of practices within practices is, as I believe, the essence of communication (and of organization). Communication does not merely enable practice; *it* is also a practice.

These are the conceptual puzzles that now confront us. This is the threshold we stand on. This defines our crossroads. It means more than coming up with new theory. If we are to become a serious science we must also understand the conduct of inquiry itself in ways that break new ground. Our own practice, after all, is merely one more way of "ensemblizing," of "constituting magmatic being."

Bibliography

Acker, J. (1994). The gender regime of Swedish banks. *Scandinavian Journal of Management, 10*(2), 117–130.

Ainsworth, S., & Hardy, C. (2004). Discourse and identities. In D. Grant, C. Hardy, C. Oswick, & L. L. Putnam (Eds.), *The SAGE handbook of organizational discourse* (pp. 153–173). London, England: Sage.

Akrich, M. (1987). Comment décrire les objets techniques? [How may technical objects be described?]. *Techniques et culture, 9*, 49–64.

Akrich, M. (1990). De la sociologie des techniques à une sociologie des usages" L'impossible intégration du magnétoscope dans les réseaux câblés de première génération [Techniques of sociology to a sociology of uses" The impossible integration of video cable networks in the first generation]. *Techniques et culture, 16*, 83–110.

Allport, F. H. (1954). The structuring of events: Outline of a general theory with applications to psychology. *Psychological Review, 64*, 3–30.

Allport, F. H. (1962). A structuronomic conception of behavior: Individual and collective. *Journal of Abnormal and Social Psychology, 64*, 3–30.

Alvesson, M., & Kärreman, D. (2000a). Taking the linguistic turn in organizational research: Challenges, responses and consequences. *Journal of Applied Behavioral Science, 36*, 136–158.

Alvesson, M., & Kärreman, D. (2000b). Varieties of discourse: On the study of organizations through discourse analysis. *Human Relations, 53*, 1125–1149.

Ashcraft, K. L. (2004). Gender, discourse and organization: Framing a shifting relationsip. In D. Grant, C. Hardy, C. Oswick, & L. L. Putnam (Eds.), *The Sage handbook of organizational discourse* (pp. 275–298). London, England: Sage.

Ashcraft, K. L., Kuhn, T., & Cooren, F. (2009). Constitutional amendments: "Materializing" organizational communication. *The Academy of Management Annals, 3*(1), 1–64.

Asmuss, B., & Thomsen, C. (2008, May). *Conversations in organizations: The role of internal conversations for doing leadership.* Paper presented at the conference What is an organization? Materiality, agency and discourse. Montréal, Québec, Canada.

Atlan, H. (1979). *Entre le cristal et la fumée* [Between crystal and smoke]. Paris, France: Éditions du Seuil.

Austin, J. L. (1962). *How to do things with words.* Cambdrige, MA: Harvard University Press.

Bakhtin, M. M. (1981). *The dialogic imagination: Four essays by M. M. Bakhtin* (C. Emerson & M. Holquist, Trans.). Austin, TX: University of Texas Press.

Bannerman, C., Massey, D., Boddington, G., Layzell, R., Lee, R., Miller, G., Wallen, E. (2005, January). *Making space* [Seminar Transcript]. London, England: Royal Institute of British Architects. Retrieved from http://www.rescen.net/archive/images/Making_Space_05_Trans.pdf

Barley, S. R. (1986). Technology as an occasion for structuring: Evidence from observations of CT scanners and the social order of radiology departments. *Administrative Science Quarterly, 31*(1), 78–108.

Barnard, C. (1968). *The functions of the executive*. Cambridge, MA: Harvard University Press. (Original work published 1938)

Barnes, B. (1995). *The elements of social theory*. London, England: UCL Press.

Barnes, J. (1984). *Flaubert's parrot*. London, England: Picador.

Barret, F. J., Thomas, G. F., & Hocevar, S. P. (1995). The central role of discourse in large-scale change: A social constructionist perspective. *Journal of Applied Behavioral Science, 31*, 352–372.

Barthes, R. (1982). L'effet de réel [The effect of the real]. In G. Genette & T. Todorov (Eds.), *Littérature et réalité* [Literature and reality] (pp. 81–90). Paris, France: Seuil.

Bateson, G. (1972). *Steps to an ecology of mind*. New York, NY: Ballantine Books.

Bateson, G. (1979). *Mind and nature*. Toronto, Canada: Bantam.

Baxter, L. A., & Montgomery, B. M. (1996). *Relating: Dialogue and dialectics*. New York, NY: Guilford Press.

Bechky, B. A. (2003). Object lessons: Workplace artifacts as representations of occupational jurisdiction. *The American Journal of Sociology, 109*(3), 720–752.

Beech, N., & Johnson, P. (2005). Discourses of disrupted identities in the practice of strategic change. *Journal of Organizational Change Management, 18*(1), 31–47.

Beer, S. (1973). The surrogate world we manage. *Behavioral Science, 18*, 198–209.

Beiner, R. (1983). *Political judgement*. Chicago, IL: University of Chicago Press.

Benveniste, É. (1966). *Problèmes de linguistique générale* (Vol. 1) [Problems in general linguistics]. Paris, France: Gallimard.

Berg, M. (1997). Of forms, containers and the electronic medical record: Some tools for a sociology of the formal. *Science, Technology and Human Values, 22*, 403–433.

Berger, P. L., & Luckmann, T. (1966). *The social construction of reality; A treatise in the sociology of knowledge*. Garden City, NY: Doubleday.

Berkun, S. (2005). *The art of project management*. Sebastopol, CA: O'Reilly.

Besner, C., & Hobbs, B. (2005). An empirical investigation of project management practice: In reality, which tools do practitioners use? In D. P. Slevin, D. I. Cleland, & J. K. Pinto (Eds.), *Innovations: Project management research 2004* (pp. 337–351). Newton Square, PA: Project Management Institute.

Billig, M. (1996). *Arguing and thinking: A rhetorical approach to social psychology* (2nd ed.). Cambridge, UK: Cambridge University Press.

Bitzer, L. F. (1995). The rhetorical situation. In C. R. Burgchardt (Ed.), *Readings in rhetorical criticism* (pp. 58–67). State College, PA: Strata. (Original work published 1968)

Blashke, S. (2008, May). *What is organizational communication? A fictitious discourse between Luhmann and Taylor*. Paper presented at the conference What is an organization? Materiality, agency and discourse. Montréal, Québec, Canada.

Boden, D. (1994). *The business of talk: Organizations in action*. Cambridge, England: Polity Press.

Boje, D. M. (2001). *Narrative methods for organizational and communication research*. London, England: Sage.

Boltanski, L., & Thévenot, L. (1999). The sociology of critical capacity. *European Journal of Social Theory, 2*(3), 359–377.

Boltanski, L., & Thévenot, L. (2006). *On justification.* Princeton, NJ: Princeton University Press.

Borges, J. L. (1999). *Selected non-fictions* (E. Allen, S. J. Levine, & E. Weinberger, Trans.). New York, NY: Viking.

Bourdieu, P. (1991). Le champ littéraire [The literary field]. *Actes de la recherche en sciences sociales, 89*, 3–46.

Bourdieu, P. (2000). *Pascalian meditations* (R. Rice, Trans). Cambridge, England: Polity Press.

Bragd, A. (2002). *Knowing management.* Gothenburg, Sweden: BAS.

Bragd, A., Christensen, D., Czarniawska, B., & Tullberg, M. (2008). Discourse as the means of community creation. *Scandinavian Journal of Management, 24*(3), 199–208.

Brickson, S. (2000). Exploring identity: Where are we now? *Academy of Management Review, 25*(1), 147–148.

Brockriede, W. (1978). Argument as epistemological method. In D. A. Thomas (Ed.), *Argumentation as a way of knowing* (pp. 128–134). Annandale, VA: Speech Communication Association.

Brockriede, W. (1992). Where is argument? In W. L. Benoit, D. Hample, & P. J. Benoit (Eds.), *Readings in argumentation* (pp. 73–78). New York, NY: Foris.

Brown, A., & Humphreys, M. (2006). Organizational identity and place: A discursive exploration of hegemony and resistance. *Journal of Management Studies, 43*(2), 231–257.

Brown, J. S., & Duguid, P. (2000). *The social life of information.* Boston, MA: Harvard Business School Press.

Brown, R. H. (1977). *A poetic for sociology.* New York, NY: Cambridge University Press.

Brown, S. L., & Eisenhardt, K. M. (1998). *Competing on the edge.* Boston, MA: Harvard Business School Press.

Browning, L. D. (1992). Lists and stories as organizational communication. *Communication Theory, 4*, 281–302.

Browning, L. D., & Beyer, J. M. (1998). The structuring of shared voluntary standards in the U.S. semiconductor industry: Communicating to reach agreement. *Communication Monographs, 65*, 220–243.

Browning, L. D., Beyer, J. M., & Shetler, J. C. (1995). Building cooperation in a competitive industry: SEMATECH and the semiconductor industry. *Academy of Management Journal, 38*, 113–151.

Brummans, B. H. J. M. (2006). The Montreal School and the question of agency. In F. Cooren, J. R. Taylor, & E. J. Van Every (Eds.), *Communication as organizing: Empirical and theoretical explorations in the dynamic of text and conversation* (pp. 197–211). Mahwah, NJ: Erlbaum.

Brummans, B. H. J. M., Cooren, F., & Chaput, M. (2009). Discourse, communication, and organizational ontology. In F. Bargiela (Ed.), *The handbook of business discourse* (pp. 53–65). Edinburgh, Scotland: Edinburgh University Press.

Brummans, B. H. J. M., Cooren, F., & Charrieras, D. (2007). *To be or not to be: The question of organizational presence.* Paper presented at the 57th International Communication Association Conference. San Francisco, CA.

Bruner, J. (1986). *Actual minds, possible worlds.* Cambridge, MA: Harvard University Press.

Bruner, J. (1991). The narrative construction of reality. *Critical Inquiry, 18*, 1–21.

Bruner, J. (1996). The narrative construal of reality. In *The culture of education* (pp. 130–149). Cambridge, MA: Harvard University Press.

Bruni, A. (2005). Shadowing software and clinical records: On the ethnography of non-humans and heterogeneous contexts. *Organization, 12*(3), 357–378.

Burke, K. (1969). *A rhetoric of motives.* Berkeley: University of California Press. (Original work published 1950)

Burns, T., & Stalker, G. M. (1961). *The management of innovation.* Oxford, England: Oxford University Press.

Burns, T., & Stalker, G. M. (1994). *The management of innovation* (Rev. ed.). New York, NY: Oxford University Press.

Butler, S. (2009) *Life and habits.* Cambridge, England: Cambridge University Press. (Original work published 1878)

Buxton, W. J. (2008, May). *Enacting civilization: Organizational dynamics in Harold Innis's early writings on the railway.* Paper presented at the conference What is an organization? Materiality, agency and discourse. Montréal, Québec, Canada.

Callon, M. (1986). Some elements of a sociology of translation: Domestication of the scallops and the fishermen of Saint Brieuc Bay. In J. Law (Ed.), *Power, action and belief* (pp. 196–223). London, England: Routledge.

Callon, M. (1991). Techno-economic networks and irreversibility. *The Sociological Review* [Monograph], *38*, 132–161.

Callon, M. (2002). Writing and (re)writing devices as tools for managing complexity. In J. Law & A. Mol (Eds.), *Complexities: Social studies of knowledge practices* (pp. 191–217). Durham, NC: Duke University Press.

Callon, M., & Latour, B. (1981). Unscrewing the big leviathan: Or how actors macro-structure reality and how sociologists help them to do so. In A. V. Cicourel & K. Knorr-Cetina (Eds.), *Advances in social theory and methodology: Toward an integration of micro and macro-sociologies* (pp. 278–303). London, England: Routledge.

Callon, M., Millo, Y., & Muniesa, F. (Eds.). (2007). *Market devices* (Sociological Review Monographs). Oxford, England: Wiley-Blackwell.

Canary, H. (2007). *The communicative creation of policy knowledge: A structurating-activity approach.* Tempe: Arizona State University.

Candea, M. (2010) *The social after Gabriel Tarde: Debates and assessment.* London, England: Routledge.

Capra, F. (1988). *Uncommon wisdom.* London, England: Fontana.

Carayol, V. (2008, May). *Human and non-human relations in organizational communication.* Paper presented at the conference What is an organization? Materiality, agency and discourse. Montréal, Québec, Canada.

Carlile, P. (2002). A pragmatic view of knowledge and boundaries: Boundary object in new product development. *Organization Science, 13*(4), 442–455.

Carroll, L. A., & Arneson, P. (2003). Communication in a shared governance hospital: Managing emergent paradoxes. *Communication Studies, 54*, 35–55.

Castoriadis, C. (1987). *The imaginary institution of society* (K. Blamey, Trans.). Cambridge, England: Polity Press. (Original work published 1975)

Castoriadis, C. (1997). The logic of magmas and the question of autonomy (D. Ames Curtis, Trans.). In D. Ames Curtis (Ed.), *The Castoriadis reader* (pp. 308–309). Oxford, England: Blackwell.

Chandler, A. D. (1990) *Scale and scope. The dynamics of industrial capitalism.* Cambridge, MA: Harvard University Press.

Charland, M. (1987). Constitutive rhetoric: The case of the peuple Québécois. *Quarterly Journal of Speech, 73*(2), 133–150.

Charland, M. (1999). Rehabilitating rhetoric: Confronting blindspots in discourse and social theory. In J. L. Lucaites, C. M. Condit, & S. Caudill (Eds.), *Contemporary rhetorical theory: A reader* (pp. 464–473). New York, NY: Guilford.

Cheney, G. (1983a). On the various and changing meanings of organizational membership: A field study of organizational identification. *Communication Monographs, 50,* 324–362.

Cheney, G. (1983b). The rhetoric of identification and the study of organizational communication. *Quarterly Journal of Speech, 69,* 143–158.

Cheney, G. (1991). *Rhetoric in an organizational society: Managing multiple identities.* Columbia: The University of South Carolina Press.

Cheney, G., & Christensen, L. T. (2001). Organizational identities: Linkages between internal and external communication. In F. M. Jablin & L. L. Putnam (Eds.), *The new handbook of organizational communication: Advances in theory, research, and methods* (pp. 231–269). Thousand Oaks, CA: Sage.

Cheney, G., Christensen, L. T., Conrad, C., & Lair, D. J. (2004). Corporate rhetoric as organizational discourse. In D. Grant, C. Hardy, C. Oswick, & L. L. Putnam (Eds.), *The Sage handbook of organizational discourse* (pp. 79–104). Thousand Oaks, CA: Sage.

Cheney, G., & Lair, D. J. (2005). Theorizing about rhetoric and organizations: Classical, interpretive and critical aspects. In S. May & D. K. Mumby (Eds.), *Engaging organizational communication theory and research: Multiple perspectives* (pp. 55–84). Thousand Oaks, CA: Sage.

Cheney, G., & Tompkins, P. K. (1987). Coming to terms with organizational identification and commitment. *Central States Speech Journal, 38,* 1–15.

Chia, R. (2000). Discourse analysis as organizational analysis. *Organization, 7,* 513–518.

Chia, R. (2005). The aim of management education: Reflections on Mintzberg's "Managers not MBAs". *Organization Studies, 26*(7), 1090–1092.

Chia, R. C. H. (1996). *Organizational analysis as deconstructive practice.* New York: Walter de Gruyter.

Chitgopekar, A. (2007). *Communal and personal identity structuration: An examination of Asian Indian Marathi identity.* Tempe: Arizona State University.

Chreim, S. (2005). The continuity-change duality in narrative texts of organizational identity. *Journal of Management Studies, 42*(3), 567–593.

Christensen, D. (2007). *Meningsfullt arbeite via "solidariska" chefer* [Meaningful work through "solidarity" managers.]. Gothenburg, Sweden: BAS.

Cicmil, S. (2006). Understanding project management practice through interpretative and critical research perspectives. *Project Management Journal, 37*(2), 27–37.

Cicmil, S., & Hodgson, D. (2006). Making projects critical: An introduction. In D. Hodgson & S. Cicmil (Eds.), *Making projects critical* (pp. 1–28). New York, NY: Palgrave.

Cicmil, S., Williams, T., Thomas, J., & Hodgson, D. (2006). Rethinking project management: Researching the actuality of projects. *International Journal of Project Management, 24,* 657–686.

Clair, R. P. (2007). *Organizations as arguments: A case of monitoring sweatshops.* Paper presented at the Annual Conference of the National Communication Association. Chicago, IL.

Clegg, S., & Kornberger, M. (2006). Organising space. In S. Clegg & M. Kornberger (Eds.), *Space, organizations and management theory* (pp. 143–162). Copenhagen, Denmark: Copenhagen Business School Press.

Coase, R. (1937). The nature of the firm. *Economica, 4*(16), 386–405.

Cohen, M. D., March, J. G., & Olsen, J. P. (1972). A garbage can model of organizational choice. *Administrative Science Quarterly, 17*(1), 1–25.

Cohen, M. D., March, J. G., & Olsen, J. P. (1976). People, problems, solutions and the ambiguity of relevance. In J. G. March & J. P. Olsen (Eds.), *Ambiguity and choice in organizations* (pp. 24–37). Bergen, Norway: Universitetsforlaget.

Coleman, J. (1982). *The asymmetrical society.* Syracuse, NY: Syracuse University Press.

Connerton, P. (1989). *How societies remember.* Cambridge, England: Cambridge University Press.

Cook, S. D., & Yanow, D. (1996). Culture and organizational learning. In M. D. Cohen & L. S. Sproull (Eds.), *Organizational learning* (pp. 430–459). Thousand Oaks, CA: Sage.

Cooper, R. (1992). Formal organization as representation: Remote control, displacement and abbreviation. In M. Reed & M. Hughes (Eds.), *Rethinking organization* (pp. 254–272). London, England: Sage.

Cooper, R., & Law, J. (1995). Organization: Distal and proximal views. *Research in the Sociology of Organizations, 13*, 237–274.

Cooren, F. (2000). *The organizing property of communication.* Philadelphia, PA: Benjamins.

Cooren, F. (2001). Translation and articulation in the organization of coalitions: The Great Whale River case. *Communication Theory, 11*, 178–200.

Cooren, F. (2004). Textual agency: How texts do things in organizational settings. *Organization, 11*, 373–393.

Cooren, F. (2006). The organizational world as a plenum of agencies. In F. Cooren, J. R. Taylor, & E. J. Van Every (Eds.), *Communication as organizing: Practical approaches to research into the dynamic of text and conversation* (pp. 81–100). Mahwah, NJ: Erlbaum.

Cooren, F. (Ed.). (2007). *Interacting and organizing: Analyses of management meeting.* Mahwah, NJ: Erlbaum.

Cooren, F. (2008). Between semiotics and pragmatics: Opening language studies to textual agency. *Journal of Pragmatics, 49*, 1–16.

Cooren, F. (2010) *Action and agency in dialogue.* Philadelphia, PA: John Benjamins Pub.

Cooren, F., Brummans, B. H. J. M., & Charrieras, D. (2008). The coproduction of organization presence: A study of Médecins sans frontières in action. *Human Relations, 61*(10), 1339–1370.

Cooren, F., & Fairhurst, G. T. (2002). The leader as a practical narrator: Leadership as the art of translating. In D. Holman & R. Thorpe (Eds.), *Management and language: The manager as a practical author* (pp. 85–103). London, England: Sage.

Cooren, F., & Fairhurst, G. T. (2009). Dislocation and stabilization: How to scale up from interactions to organization. In L. L. Putnam & A. M. Nicotera (Eds.), *Building theories of organization: The constitutive role of communication.* Mahwah, NJ: Erlbaum.

Cooren, F., Fox, S., Robichaud, D., & Talih, N. (2005). Arguments for a plurified view of the social world: Spacing and timing as hybrid achievements. *Time & Society, 14*, 263–280.

Cooren, F., Matte, F., Taylor, J. R., & Vásquez, C. (2007). A humanitarian organization in action: Organizational discourse as an immutable mobile. *Discourse & Communication, 1*, 153–190.

Cooren, F., & Taylor, J. R. (1997). Organization as an effect of mediation: Redefining the link between organization and communication. *Communication Theory, 7*, 219–260.

Cooren, F., & Taylor, J. R. (1999). The procedural and rhetorical modes of the organizing dimension of communication: Discursive analysis of parliamentary commission. *The Communication Review, 3*(1–2), 65–101.

Cooren, F., Taylor, J. R., & Van Every, E. J. (Eds.). (2006). *Communication as organizing: Practical approaches to research into the dynamic of text and conversation.* Mahwah, NJ: Erlbaum.

Cordelier, B. (2008, May). *Between symbolic and regulationist transaction: For a new praxeology around the technical object.* Paper presented at the conference What is an organization? Materiality, agency and discourse. Montréal, Québec, Canada

Corley, K., Harquail, C. V., Pratt, M., Glyn, M. A., Fiol, C. M., & Hatch, M. J. (2006). Guiding organizational identity through aged adolescence. *Journal of Management Inquiry, 15*, 85–99.

Corman, S. R., & Poole, M. S. (Eds.). (2000). *Perspectives on organizational communication: Finding common ground.* New York, NY: Guilford.

Craig, R. T., & Muller, H. L. (2007). *Theorizing communication.* Thousand Oaks, CA: Sage.

Crang, M., & Thrift, N. (2000). *Thinking space.* New York, NY: Routledge.

Cyert, R. M., & March, J. G. (1963). *A behavioral theory of the firm.* New York, NY: Routledge.

Czarniawska-Joerges, B. (1994). Narratives of individual and organizational identities. *Communication Yearbook, 17*, 193–221.

Czarniawska, B. (1997). *Narrating the organization: Dramas of institutional identity.* Chicago, IL: University of Chicago Press.

Czarniawska, B. (1998). *A narrative approach to organization studies.* London, England: Sage.

Czarniawska, B. (Ed.). (2006). *Organization theory.* Cheltenham, England: Edward Elgar.

Czarniawska, B. (2008). *A theory of organizing.* Cheltenham, England: Edward Elgar.

Czarniawska, B. (2008, May). *Organizations as obstacles to organizing.* Paper presented at the conference What is an organization? Materiality, agency and discourse. Montréal, Québec, Canada.

Czarniawska, B. (Ed.). (2009). *Organizing in the face of threat and risk.* Cheltenham, UK: Edward Elgar.

Czarniawska, B., Diedrich, A., Engberg, T., Eriksson-Zetterquist, U., Gustavsson, E., Lindberg, K., … Zackariasson, P. (2007). *Organisering kring hot och risk.* [Organizing around threats and risk]. Lund, Sweden: Studentlitteratur.

Czarniawska, B., & Hernes, T. (Eds.). (2005). *Actor-network theory and organizing.* Malmö, Sweden: Liber.

Davis, B., & Harré, R. (1990). Positioning: The discursive production of selves. *Journal for the Theory of Social Behaviour, 20*(1), 43–63.

Debaise, D. (2006) *Un empirisme spéculatif: Lecture de Procès et Réalité de Whitehead* [A speculative empirism: A study of Whitehead's process and reality]. Paris, France: Vrin.

Deetz, S. (2008, May). *The open organization: Governance, stakeholder involvement and new communication models.* Paper presented at the conference What is an organization? Materiality, agency and discourse. Montréal, Québec Canada.

Derrida, J. (1976). *On grammatology* (G. C. Spivak, Trans.). Baltimore, MD: John Hopkins University Press.

Derrida, J. (1986). *Memoires for Paul de Man* (C. Lindsay, J. Culler, & E. Cadava, Trans.). New York, NY: Columbia University Press.

Derrida, J. (1988). *Limited Inc.* Evanston, IL: Northwestern University Press.

Dewey, J. (1954) *The public and its problems.* Athens: Ohio University Press. (Original work published 1927)

Diamond, M., Allcorn, S., & Stein, H. (2004). The surface of organizational boundaries: A view from psychoanalytic object relations theory. *Human Relations, 57,* 31–53.

DiMaggio, P. J., & Powell, W. W. (1991). The iron cage revisited: Institutional isomorphism and collective rationality in organization fields. In W. W. Powell & P. J. DiMaggio (Eds.), *The new instituionalism in organizational analysis* (pp. 63–82). Chicago, IL: University of Chicago Press. (Original work published 1983)

Dionysiou, D. (2007). *Resistance to stability: Identifying the barriers to the emergence of organization.* Glasgow, Scotland: University of Strathclyde.

Dionysiou, D., & Tsoukas, H. (2008, May). *Resistance to stability: Identifying the barriers to the emergence of organization.* Paper presented at the conference What is an organization? Materiality, agency and discourse. Montréal, Québec, Canada.

Dreyfus, H. (1991). *Being-in-the-world.* Cambridge, MA: MIT Press.

Dubois, J. (1992). *Le roman policier ou la modernité* [The police procedural or modernity]. Paris, France: Nathan.

Duchet, C. (1979). *Sociocritique* [Sociocriticism]. Paris, France: Nathan.

Ducrot, O. (1984). *Le dire et le dit* [The saying and the said]. Paris, France: Minuit.

Eisenberg, E. M. (1990). Jamming: Transcendence through organizing. *Communication Research, 17,* 139–164.

Ekstedt, E., Lundin, R. A., Söderholm, A., & Wirdenius, H. (1999). *Neo-industrial organizing: Action, knowledge formation and renewal in a project-intensive economy.* London, England: Routledge.

Elsbach, K., & Kramer, R. (1996). Members response to organizational identity threats: Encountering and countering the Business Week rankings. *Administrative Science Quarterly, 41,* 442–476.

Engwall, M. (2003). No project is an island: Linking projects to history and context. *Research policy, 32*(5), 789–808.

Erlingsdottir, G., & Lindberg, K. (2005). Isomorphism, isopraxism, and isonymism: Complementary or competing processes? In B. Czarniawska & G. Sevón (Eds.), *Global ideas: How ideas, objects and practices travel in the global economy* (pp. 47–70). Malmö, Sweden: Liber.

Evans-Wentz, W. Y. (2000). *The Tibetan book of the great liberation: The method of realizing nirvana through knowing the mind* (2nd ed.). Oxford, UK: Oxford University press. (Original work published 1954)

Ezzy, D. (1998). Theorizing narrative identity, symbolic interactionism and hermeneutics. *The Sociological Quarterly, 39*(2), 239–252.

Fairclough, N. (1995). *Critical discourse analysis: The critical study of language.* London, England: Longman.

Fairclough, N. (2005). Discourse analysis in organization studies: The case for critical realism. *Organization Studies, 26*(6), 915–939.

Fairhurst, G. T. (2004). Textuality and agency in interaction analysis. *Organization, 11*(3), 335–353.

Fairhurst, G. T., & Cooren, F. (2008, May). *Charismatic leadership as the hybrid production of presences.* Paper presented at the conference What is an organization? Materiality, agency and discourse. Montréal, Québec, Canada.

Fairhurst, G. T., Cooren, F., & Cahill, D. J. (2002). Discursiveness, contradiction, and unintended consequences in successive downsizings. *Management Communication Quarterly, 15*, 501–540.

Fairhurst, G. T., & Putnam, L. L. (1999). Reflections on the organization-communication equivalency question: The contributions of James Taylor and his colleagues. *The Communication Review, 3*(1–2), 1–19.

Fairhurst, G. T., & Putnam, L. L. (2004). Organizations as discursive constructions. *Communication Theory, 14*, 5–26.

Fairhurst, G. T., & Sarr, R. A. (1996). *The art of framing: Managing the language of leadership*. San Francisco, CA: Jossey-Bass.

Farrell, T. B. (1993). *Norms of rhetorical culture*. New Haven, CT: Yale University Press.

Fauré, B., Brummans, B. H. J. M., Giroux, H., & Taylor, J. R. (2010). The calculation of business, or the business of calculations: Accounting as organizing through everyday communication. *Human Relations, 63*, 1249–1273.

Feldman, M., & Pentland, B. (2003). Reconceptualizing organizational routines as a source of flexibility and change. *Administrative Science Quarterly, 48*, 94–118.

Fisher, W. R. (1984). Narration as a human communication paradigm: The case of public moral argument. *Communication Monographs, 51*, 1–22.

Fisher, W. R. (1985). The narrative paradigm: In the beginning. *Journal of Communication, 35*(4), 74–89.

Fisher, W. R. (1987). *Human communication as narration: Toward a philosophy of reason, value, and action*. Columbia: University of South Carolina Press.

Fisher, W. R. (1989). Clarifying the narrative paradigm. *Communication Monographs, 56*, 55–58.

Fitzgerald, B. (1998). *An empirically-grounded framework for the information systems development process*. Paper presented at the International Conference on Information Systems, Helsinki, Finland.

Fletcher, J. K. (1999). *Disappearing acts: Gender, power and relational practice at work*. Cambridge, MA: MIT Press.

Flyvbjerg, B. (2006). Making organization research matter: Power, values, and phronesis. In S. Clegg, C. Hardy, & W. R. Nord (Eds.), *The Sage handbook of organization studies* (pp. 357–382). Thousand Oaks, CA: Sage.

Fordham-Hernandez, T., & McPhee, R. (1999). *Cognitive maps of organization narratives and processes: Differences across levels of an organizational hierarchy*. Paper presented at the Annual Conference of the International Communication Association, San Francisco, CA.

Foucault, M. (1984). *The Foucault reader*. London, England: Penguin.

Foucault, M. (1995). *Discipline and punish: The birth of the prison*. New York, NY: Vintage.

Fox-Keller, E. (2000) *The century of the gene*. Cambridge, MA: MIT Press.

Fraenkel, B. (2001). La résistible ascension de l'écrit au travail [The resistible rise of the written work]. In A. Borzeix, B. Fraenkel, & J. Boutet (Eds.), *Langage et travail: Communication, cognition, action* [Language for work: Communication, cognition and action].Paris, France: CNRS.

Freeland, R. F. (2001). *The struggle for control of the modern corporation: Organizational change at General Motors, 1924–1970*. Cambridge, England: Cambridge University Press.

Gabriel, Y. (2004). Narratives, stories and texts. In D. Grant, C. Hardy, C. Oswick & L. L. Putnam (Eds.), *The Sage handbook of organizational discourse* (pp. 61–77). Thousand Oaks, CA: Sage.

Gadamer, H.-G. (1980). Practical philosophy as a model of the human sciences. *Research in Phenomenology, 9,* 74–85.

Garfinkel, H. (2002). *Ethnomethodology's program: Working out Durkheim's aphorism* (A. Warfield Rawls, Ed.). Lanham, MD: Rowman & Littlefield.

Geisler, C. (2001). Textual objects: Accounting for the role of texts in the everyday life of complex organizations. *Written Communication, 18*(3), 296–325.

Genette, G. (1983). *Nouveau discours du récit* [New discourse of narrative]. Paris, France: Seuil.

Gibson, J. (1979). *The ecological approach to visual perception.* Boston, MA: Houghton Mifflin.

Giddens, A. (1979). *Central problems in social theory: Action, structure and contradiction in social analysis.* Berkeley, CA: University of California Press.

Giddens, A. (1984). *The constitution of society: Outline of the theory of structuration.* Cambridge, England: Polity Press.

Giddens, A. (1987). Time and social organization. In *Social theory and modern sociology* (pp. 140–165). Stanford, CA: Stanford University Press.

Giddens, A. (1989). The orthodox consensus and the emerging synthesis. In B. Dervin, L. Grossberg, B. O'Keefe, & E. Wartella (Eds.), *Rethinking communication" Vol. 1. Issues* (pp. 53–65). Newbury Park, CA: Sage.

Giddens, A. (1991). *Modernity and self-identity: Self and society in the late modern age.* Stanford, CA: Stanford University Press.

Giroux, N. (2006). Vers une narration réflexive? [Towards a reflexive narration?] In E. Soulier (Ed.), *Le Storytelling* [Storytelling] (pp. 37–65). Paris, France: Hermès Science.

Giroux, N., & Marroquín, L. (2005). L'approche narrative des organisations [An approach to the narrative of organizations]. *Revue française de gestion, 31*(159), 15–42.

Glassman, R. B. (1973). Persistence and loose coupling in living systems. *Behavioral Science, 18,* 83–98.

Goffman, E. (1959). *The presentation of self in everyday life.* Garden City, NY: Doubleday Anchor.

Goffman, E. (1997). The interaction order. In *The Goffman reader* (C. Lemert & A. Branaman Eds., pp. 233–261). Malden, MA: Blackwell. (Original work published 1983)

Goleman, D. (2003). *Destructive emotions, how can we overcome them? A scientific dialogue with the Dalai Lama.* New York, NY: Bantam Dell.

Gonzalez, V., & Mark, G. (2005). Managing Currents of Work: Multi-tasking Among Multiple Collaborations. In H. Gellersen et al. (eds.), *ECSCW 2005: Proceedings of the Ninth European Conference on Computer-Supported Cooperative Work, 18–22 September 2005, Paris, France* (pp. 143–162). Dordrecht, Netherlands: Springer.

Goodnight, G. T. (1999). The personal, technical, and public spheres of argument: A speculative inquiry into the art of public deliberation. In J. L. Lucaites, C. M. Condit, & S. Caudill (Eds.), *Contemporary rhetorical theory: A reader* (pp. 251–264). New York, NY: Guilford.

Gourdeau, G. (1993). *Analyse du discours narratif* [An analysis of narrative discourse]. Boucherville, Quebec: G. Morin.

Grant, D., Hardy, C., Oswick, C., & Putnam, L. L. (Eds.). (2004). *The Sage handbook of organizational discourse.* Thousand Oaks, CA: Sage.

Gray, G. W. (1964). The founding of the Speech Association of America: Happy birthday. *Quarterly Journal of Speech, 50,* 342–345.

Greene, R. W. (1998). The aesthetic turn and the rhetorical perspective on argumentation. *Argumentation and Advocacy, 35*(1), 19–29.

Greimas, A. J. (1983). *Du Sens: Vol. 2. Essais sémiotiques* [On meaning Vol. 2: Semiotic essays]. Paris, France: Seuil.

Greimas, A. J. (1987). *On meaning: Selected writings in semiotic theory* (P. J. Perron & F. H. Collins, Trans.). London, England: Frances Pinter.

Groleau, C., & Taylor, J. R. (1996). Toward a subject-oriented worldview of information. *Canadian Journal of Communication, 21*, 243–265.

Güney, S. (2006). Making sense of a conflict as the (missing) link between collaborating actors. In F. Cooren, J. R. Taylor, & E. J. Van Every (Eds.), *Communication as organizing: Empirical and theoretical explorations in the dynamic of text and conversation* (pp. 19–35). Mahwah, NJ: Erlbaum.

Gyatso, T., the 14th Dalai Lama of Tibet. (2005). *Four essential Buddhist commentaries.* Dharamsala, India: Library of Tibetan Works and Archives. (Original work published 1982)

Gyatso, T., the 14th Dalai Lama of Tibet. (2004). *Dzogchen: Heart essence of the grat perfection* (T. Jinpa & R. Barron, Trans., 2nd ed.). Ithaca, NY: Snow Lion. (Original work published 2002)

Habermas, J. (1979). *Communication and the evolution of society* (T. McCarthy, Trans.). Boston, MA: Beacon Press. (Original work published 1976)

Habermas, J. (1984). *The theory of communicative action: Vol. 1. Reason and the rationalization of society.* Boston, MA: Beacon Press.

Hage, J. (1965). An axiomatic theory of organizations. *Administrative Science Quarterly, 10*, 289–320.

Halliday, M. A. K. (2002). *On grammar.* New York, NY: Continuum. (Original work published 1970)

Hamilton, P. M. (1997). Rhetorical discourse of local pay. *Organization, 4*(2), 229–254.

Hannah, M., & Freeman, J. (1989). *Organizational ecology.* Cambridge, MA: Harvard University Press.

Hardy, C., Lawrence, T. B., & Grant, D. (2005). Discourse and collaboration: The role of conversations and collective identity. *Academy of Management Review, 30*(1), 58–77.

Hardy, C., Palmer, I., & Phillips, N. (2000). Discourse as a strategic resource. *Human Relations, 53*(9), 1227–1248.

Harré, R., & Gillett, G. (1994). *The discursive mind.* Thousand Oaks, CA: Sage.

Harré, R., & Secord, P. F. (1972). *The explanation of social behaviour.* Oxford, England: Blackwell.

Hatch, M., & Schultz, M. (1997). Relation between organizational culture, identity and image. *European Journal of Marketing, 31*, 356–365.

Hawes, L. C. (1974). Social collectivities as communication: Perspective on organizational behavior. *Quarterly Journal of Speech, 60*, 497–502.

Heath, C., & Luff, P. (1992). Media space and communicative asymmetries. Preleminary observations of video mediated interactions. *Human Computer Interaction, 7*, 315–346.

Hegel, G. W. F. (1949). *The phenomenology of mind* (J. B. Baillie, Trans., 2nd ed.). London, England: George Allen & Unwin. (Original work published 1807)

Henderson, K. (1991). Flexible sketches and inflexible data bases: Visual communication, conscription devices, and boundary objects in design engineering. *Science, Technology and Human Values, 16*(4), 448–473.

Heracleous, L. (2004). Boundaries in the study of organization. *Human Relations, 57*, 95–103.

Herman, D. (2002). *Story logic: Problems and possibilities of narratives*. Lincoln, NE: University of Nebraska Press.

Hernes, T. (2004). Studying composite boundaries: A framework of analysis. *Human Relations, 57*, 9–29.

Hetherington, K., & Law, J. (2000). Materialities, globalities, spatialities. In J. Bryson, P. Daniels, N. Henry, & J. Pollard (Eds.), *Knowledge, space, economy* (pp. 34–49). London, England: Routledge.

Hirschman, A. O. (1967). *Development projects observed*. Washington, DC: Brookings Institution.

Hodgson, D. (2002). Disciplining the professional: The case of project management. *Journal of Management Studies, 39*(6), 803–821.

Hodgson, G. (1996). Williamson, Oliver. In M. Warner (Ed.), *The handbook of management thinking* (pp. 748–751). London, England: International Thomson Business Press.

Hopwood, A. G., & Miller P. (Eds). (1994) *Accounting as social and institutional practice*. Cambridge, England: Cambridge University Press.

Howard, L. A., & Geist, P. (1995). Ideological positioning in organizational change: The dialectic of control in a merging organization. *Communication Monographs, 62*, 110–131.

Humphreys, M., & Brown, A. (2002). Narratives of organizational identity and identitifcation: A case study of hegemony and resistance. *Organization Studies, 23*(3), 421–448.

Hutchins, E. (1995). *Cognition in the wild*. Cambridge, MA: MIT Press.

Iverson, J. O., & McPhee, R. D. (2008). Communicating knowing though communities of practice: Exploring internal communicative processes and differences among CoPs. *Journal of Applied Communication Research, 36*(2), 176–199.

Jackson, S., & Jacobs, S. (1992). Structures of conversation argument: Pragmatic bases for the enthymeme. In W. L. Benoit, D. Hample, & P. J. Benoit (Eds.), *Readings in argumentation* (pp. 681–706). New York, NY: Floris.

James, W. (1950). *The principles of psychology*. New York, NY: Dover. (Original work published 1890)

James, W. (1996) *A pluralistic universe*. London, England: University of Nebraska Press. (Original work published 1909)

Jameson, J. K. (2004). Negotiating autonomy and connection through politeness: A dialectical approach to organizational conflict management. *Western Journal of Communication, 68*, 257–277.

Johnson, M. (1993). *Moral imagination*. Chicago, IL: University of Chicago Press.

Jouve, V. (1997). *La poétique du roman* [The poetics of the novel]. Paris, France: SEDES.

Kallinikos, J. (1996). *Technology and society*. Munich, Germany: Accedo.

Kärreman, D., & Alvesson, M. (2001). Making newsmakers: Conversational identity at work. *Organization Studies, 22*(1), 59–89.

Katambwe, J. M., & Taylor, J. R. (2006). Modes of organizational integration. In F. Cooren, J. R. Taylor, & E. J. Van Every (Eds.), *Communication as organizing: Empirical and theoretical explorations in the dynamics of text and conversation* (pp. 55–77). Mahwah, NJ: Erlbaum.

Katz, D., & Kahn, R. L. (1966). *The social psychology of organizations*. New York, NY: Wiley.

Keown, D. (2004). *Oxford dictionary of Buddhism*. Oxford, England: Oxford University Press.

Kephart, K., & Schultz, C. (2001). *Shedding light on shadowing: An examination of the method*. Paper presented at the Annual meeting of the American Educational Research Association. Seattle, WA.

Kernochan, R. A., McCormick, D. W., & White, J. A. (2007). Spirituality and the management teacher. *Journal of Management Inquiry, 16*, 61–75.

Kirby, E. L., & Krone, K. J. (2002). "The policy exists but you can't really use it": Communication and the structuration of work-family leave. *Journal of Applied Communication Research, 30*, 50–77.

Kirsch, D., & Neff, G. (2008, May). *Artifacts and the constitution of organizations*. Paper presented at the conference What is an organization? Materiality, agency and discourse. Montréal, Québec, Canada.

Kocolowski, L. (1986). Crown pension fund makes "ethical" investments. *National Underwriter, 90*(43), 6.

Kögler, H. (1996). *The power of dialogue*. Cambridge, MA: MIT Press.

Kornberger, M., & Browns, A. D. (2007). Ethics as a discursive ressource for identity work. *Human Relations, 60*(3), 497–518.

Kreiner, K. (1995). In search of relevance: Project management in drifting environments. *Scandinavian Journal of Management, 11*(4), 335–346.

Krippendorff, K. (2008, May). *Organizations as networks of conversations and stakeholders*. Paper presented at the conference What is an organization? Materiality, agency and discourse. Montréal, Québec, Canada.

Kuhn, T. (2008a, May). *A communicative theory of the firm: Discursive practices, text, objects, and consent formation in organizing*. Paper presented at the conference What is an organization? Materiality, agency and discourse. Montréal, Québec, Canada.

Kuhn, T. (2008b). A communicative theory of the firm: Developing an alternative perspective on intra–organizational power and stakeholder relationships. *Organization Studies, 29*, 1227–1254.

Kuhn, T., & Ashcraft, K. L. (2003). Corporate scandal and the theory of the firm: Formulating the contributions of organizational communication studies. *Management Communication Quarterly, 17*, 20–57.

Kunda, G. (1992). *Engineering culture*. Philadelphia, PA: Temple University Press.

Lacoste, M. (2000). Les objets et le travail collectif [Objects and collective work]. In P. Delcambre (Ed.), *Communications organisationnelles: objets, pratiques, dispositifs* [Organizational communication: Objects, practices, devices] (pp. 23–33). Rennes, France: Presses Universitaires de Rennes.

Lakoff, G. (1987). *Women, fire, and dangerous things*. Chicago, IL: University of Chicago Press.

Lamoreux, N. R. (2004). Parnerships, corporations, and the limits on contractual freedom in U.S. history: An essay in economics, law and culture. In K. Lipartito & D. B. Sicilia (Eds.), *Constructing corporate America: History, politics, culture* (pp. 29–65). New York, NY: Oxford University Press.

Laplantine, F. (1996). *La description ethnographique* [Ethnographic description]. Paris, France: Nathan.

Lascoumes, P., & Le Galès, P. (Eds.). (2002). *Gouverner par les instruments* [Governed by the instruments]. Paris, France: Presses de l'Institut National des Sciences Politiques.

Latour, B. (1986a). The power of associations. In J. Law (Ed.), *Power, action and belief: A new sociology of knowledge?* (pp. 264–280). London, England: Routledge.

Latour, B. (1986b). Visualisation and cognition: Thinking with eyes and hands. In H. Kuklick (Ed.), *Knowledge and society: Studies in the sociology of culture past and present* (Vol. 6, pp. 1–40). Greenwich, CT: JAI Press.

Latour, B. (1987). *Science in action*. Cambridge, MA: Harvard University Press.

Latour, B. (1993). *We have never been modern* (C. Porter, Trans). Cambridge, MA: Harvard University Press.

Latour, B. (1994). On technical mediation—Philosophy, sociology, genealogy. *Common Knowledge, 3*(2), 29–64.

Latour, B. (1996). On interobjectivity. *Mind, Culture, and Activity, 2*(4), 228–245.

Latour, B. (1998). *Artefaktens återkomst* [Artifact's return].Stockholm, Sweden: Nerenius & Santérus.

Latour, B. (1999). On recalling ANT. In J. Law & J. Hassard (Eds.), *Actor network theory and after* (pp. 15–50). Oxford: Blackwell.

Latour, B. (2002). Gabriel Tarde and the end of the social. In P. Joyce (Ed.), *The social in question: New bearings in history and the social sciences* (pp. 117–132). London, England: Routledge.

Latour, B. (2003) What if we were talking politics a little? *Contemporary Political Theory, 2*, 143–164.

Latour, B. (2005). *Reassembling the social: An introduction to actor-network-theory*. Oxford, England: Oxford University Press.

Latour, B. (2007). A textbook case revisited: Knowledge as mode of existence. In E. Hackett, O. Amsterdamska, M. Lynch, & J. Wacjman (Eds.), *The handbook of science and technology studies* (3rd ed., pp. 83–112). Cambridge, MA: MIT Press,.

Latour, B. (2009). *The making of law: An ethnography of* the *Conseil d'Etat*. London, England: Polity Press.

Latour, B. (2010). Coming out as a philosopher. *Social Studies of Science, 40*, 599–608.

Latour, B. (2011). *On the cult of the factish gods followed by iconoclash*. Durham, NC: Duke University Press.

Latour, B. (2013). *An inquiry into modes of existence*. Cambridge, MA.: Harvard University Press.

Latour, B., & Hernant, É. (1998). Paris ville invisible [Paris the invisible city]. Paris, France: Éditions la Découverte.

Latour, B., & Weibel, P. (Ed.). (2005). *Making things public. Atmospheres of democracy.* Cambridge, MA: MIT Press.

Law, J. (1994). *Organizing modernity.* Oxford, England: Blackwell.

Law, J. (2000). Materialities, spatialities, globalities. Retrieved from http://www.comp. lancs.ac.uk/sociology/papers/Law-Hetherington-Materialities-Spatialitiers-Globalities.pdf

Law, J. (2002). Objects and Spaces. *Theory, Culture & Society, 19*(5–6), 91–105.

Law, J., & Singleton, V. (2005). Object lessons. *Organization, 12*(3), 331–355.

Lawrence, P. R., & Lorsch, J. W. (1967). *Organization and environment: Managing differentiation and integration.* Boston, MA: Harvard University Press.

Lawrence, T., Zilber, T., & Leca, B. (Eds.) (2010). *Organization studies*: Special issue on 'Institutions and Work', *31*(8).

Levy, D. M. (2003). *Scrolling forward: Making sense of documents in the digital age.* New York, NY: Arcade.

Lewellyn, N. (2004). In search of modernization: The negotiation of social identity in organization reform. *Organization Studies, 25*(6), 947–968.

Lewin, K. (1951). *Field theory in social science; selected theoretical papers*. New York, NY: Harper & Row.

Lewis, L. K. (2006). Collaboration: Review of communication scholarship and a research agenda. In C. Beck (Ed.), *Communication yearbook 30* (pp. 197–247). Thousand Oaks, CA: Sage.

Lewontin, R. C. (1995). Genes, environments and organisms. In R. B. Silvers (Ed.), *Hidden histories of science* (pp. 115–140). New York, NY: New York Review of Books.

Lorde, A. (1981). The master's tools will never dismantle the master's house. In C. Moraga & G. Anzaldua (Eds.), *The bridge called my back: Writings by radical women of color* (pp. 98–101). New York, NY: Kitchen Table: Women of Color Press. (Original work published 1979)

Luhmann, N. (1995). *Social systems*. Stanford, CA: Stanford University Press.

Lundberg, C. C. (1982). An open letter to Karl Weick. *Journal of Applied Behavioral Science, 18*(1), 113–117.

MacIntyre, A. (1985). *After virtue* (2nd ed.). London, England: Duckworth.

Malone, T. W., & Crowston, K. (1994). The interdisciplinary study of coordination. *ACM Computing Surveys, 26*(1), 87–119.

March, J. G., & Olsen, J. P. (Eds.). (1976). *Ambiguity and choice in organizations*. Bergen, Norway: Universitetsforlag.

March, J. G., & Olsen, J. P. (1989). *Rediscovering institutions. The organizational basis of politics*. New York, NY: Free Press.

March, J. G., & Simon, H. A. (1993). *Organizations*. New York, NY: Wiley. (Original work published 1958)

March, J. G., Simon, H. A., & Guetzkow, H. S. (1993). *Organizations* (2nd ed.). Malden, MA: Blackwell.

Marroquín, L., & Vásquez, C. (2008, May). *At the crossroad of conversation and text: Juggling with outcome and process*. Paper presented at the conference What is an organization? Materiality, agency and discourse. Montréal, Québec, Canada.

Martin, J. (2002). *Organizational culture: Mapping the terrain*. Thousand Oaks, CA: Sage.

Maruyama, M. (1974). Paradigms and communication. *Technological Forecasting and Social Change, 6*(3–32).

Massey, D. (1993). Politics and space/time. In M. Keith & S. Pile (Eds.), *Place and the politics of identity* (pp. 140–165). New York, NY: Routledge.

Massey, D. (1994). *Space, place, and gender*. Minneapolis: University of Minnesota Press.

Massey, D. (1999). Space–time, "science" and the relationship between physical geography and human geography. *Transactions of the Institute of British Geographers, 24*, 261–276.

Massey, D. (2001). Talking of space-time. *Transactions of the Institute of British Geographers, 26*, 251–261.

Massey, D. (2003). Some times of space. In S. May (Ed.), *Olafur Eliasson: The weather project*. London, England: Tate Modern.

Massey, D. (2004). Geographies of responsibility. *Geografiska Annaler, 86 B*(1), 5–18.

Massey, D. (2005). *For space*. Thousand Oaks, CA: Sage.

Maturana, H. R. (1997). *La objetividad: Un argumento para obligar* [Objectivity: A compelling argument]. Santiago, Chile: Dolmen.

Maturana, H. R., & Varela, F. J. (1987). *The tree of knowledge*. Boston, MA: Shambhala.

May, S., & Mumby, D. K. (Eds.). (2005). *Engaging organizational communication theory and research: Multiple perspectives*. Thousand Oaks, CA: Sage.

Mayer, S., Grosjean, S., & Bonneville, L. (2008, May). *(Re)thinking the organization as a heterogenous network: The case of Net art.* Paper presented at the conference What is an organization? Materiality, agency and discourse. Montréal, Québec, Canada.

McDonald, S. (2005). Studying actions in context: A qualitative shadowing method for organizational research. *Qualitative Research, 5*(4), 455–473.

McGee, M. C., & Nelson, J. S. (1985). Narrative reason in public argument. *Journal of Communication, 35*(4), 139–155.

McKenzie, D. A., Muniesa, F., & Siu, L. (Eds.). (2007). *Do economists make markets? On the performativity of economics.* Princeton, NJ: Princeton University Press.

McPhee, R. D. (1985). Formal structure and organizational communication. In R. D. McPhee & P. K. Thompkins (Eds.), *Organizational communication: Traditional themes and new directions* (pp. 149–177). Beverly Hills, CA: Sage.

McPhee, R. D. (1988). Vertical communication chains: Toward an integrated view. *Management Communication Quarterly, 1,* 455–483.

McPhee, R. D. (2004). Text, agency, and organization in the light of structuration theory. *Organization, 11,* 355–371.

McPhee, R. D. (2008, May). *A structurational critique of some central Montreal School schemata.* Paper presented at the conference What is an organization? Materiality, agency and discourse. Montréal, Québec, Canada.

McPhee, R. D., Corman, S. R., & Iverson, J. O. (2007). "We ought to have … Gumption …": A CRA analysis of an excerpt from the videotape *Corporation: After Mr. Sam.* In F. Cooren (Ed.), *Interacting and organizing: Analysis of a management meeting* (pp. 133–161). Mahwah, NJ: Erlbaum.

McPhee, R. D., Habbel, D., & Fordham Habbel, T. (1987). *Process theories of organizational structure.* Paper presented at the Annual Conference of the International Communication Association, Montreal, Canada.

McPhee, R. D., & Iverson, J. O. (2006). *Agents of constitution in Communidad: Constitutive processes of communication in organizations.* Paper presented at the 56th Annual Conference of the International Communication Association. Dresden, Germany.

McPhee, R. D., & Iverson, J. O. (2009). Agents of constitution in Communidad: Constitutive processes of communication in organization. In L. L. Putnam & A. M. Nicotera (Eds.), *Building theories of organization: The constitutive role of communication* (pp. 21–48). Mahwah, NJ: Erlbaum.

McPhee, R. D., & Trethewey, A. (2000). [Review of *The emergent organization: Communication as its site and surface* by J. R. Taylor & E. J. Van Every]. *Management Communication Quarterly, 14,* 238–334.

McPhee, R. D., & Zaug, P. (2000). *The communicative constitution of organizations: A framework for explanation, 10.* Retrieved from http://www.cios.org/getfile/McPhee_v10n1200

McPhee, R. D., & Zaug, P. (2009). The communicative constitution of organizations: A framework for explanation. In L. L. Putnam & A. M. Nicotera (Eds.), *Building theories of organization: The constitutive role of communication* (pp. 21–48). New York, NY: Routledge.

Mead, G. H. (1934). *Mind, self and society from the standpoint of a social behaviorist.* Chicago, IL: University of Chicago Press.

Meisenbach, R. J., & McMillan, J. J. (2006). Blurring the boundaries: Historical developments and future directions in organizational rhetoric. *Communication Yearbook, 30,* 99–141.

Melville, D. R. (1987). Social vision is still a vital component of leadership. *Business Month, 11*(5), 36–38.

Merchant, C. (1995). *Earthcare: Women and the environment.* New York, NY: Routledge.

Meunier, D., & Vásquez C. (2008, July). On shadowing the hybrid character of action: A communicational approach. *Communication Methods and Measure, 2*(3), 167–192.

Meyers, R. A., & Seibold, D. R. (1990). Perspectives on group argument. *Communication Yearbook, 13,* 268–302.

Miller, K. I. (2000). Common ground from the post–positivist perspective: From "straw person" argument to collaborative coexistence. In S. R. Corman & M. S. Poole (Eds.), *Perspectives on organizational communication: Finding common ground* (pp. 46–67). New York, NY: Guilford.

Miller, K. I. (2005). *Communication theories: Perspectives, processes, and contexts.* (2nd ed.). Boston, MA: McGraw–Hill.

Ministère du Développement économique, de l'Innovation et de l'Exportation (MDEIE). (2006). *L'industrie brassicole au Québec* [The brewing industry in Quebec]. Montreal, Canada: Author.

Ministère du Développement économique et régional et de la Recherche.(MDERR). (2004). *Le régime québécois de commercialisation de la bière* [The Quebec commercialization of beer]. Montreal, Canada: Author

Mintzberg, H. (1989). *Mintzberg on management.* New York, NY: Free Press.

Monge, P. R., & Contractor, N. (2003). *Theories of communication networks.* New York, NY: Oxford University Press.

Monge, P. R., & Pool, M. S. (2008). The evolution of organizational communication. *Journal of Communication, 58,* 679–692.

Mumby, D. K. (2005). Theorizing resistance in organization studies: A dialectical approach. *Management Communication Quarterly, 19,* 19–44.

Mumby, D. K., & Clair, R. P. (1997). Organizational discourse. In T. A. van Dijk (Ed.), *Discourse studies: A Multidisciplinary Introduction: Vol. 2. Discourse as social interaction* (pp. 181–205). Thousand Oaks, CA: Sage.

Myers, K. K. (2005). *Organizational knowledge and assimilation in high reliability organizations.* Arizona State University.

Newcomb, T. (1953). An approach to the study of communicative acts. *Psychological Review, 60,* 393–404.

Norbu, C. N. (2000). *The crystal and the way of light: Sutra, Tantra and Dzogchen.* Ithaca, NY: Snow Lion.

November, V., Camacho, E.,& Latour, B. (2010). The territory is the map—Space in the age of digital navigation. *Environment and Planning D: Society and Space, 28,* 581–599.

O'Barr, W. M., & Conley, J. M. (1992). *Fortune and folly. The wealth and power of institutional investing.* Homewood, IL: Irwin.

Oliver, D., & Roos, J. (2007). Beyond text: Constructing organizational identity multimodally. *British Journal of Management, 18,* 342–358.

Orlikowski, W. J. (1992). The duality of technology: Rethinking the concept of technology in organizations. *Organization Science, 3*(3), 398–427.

Orlikowski, W. J. (1996). Improvising organizational transformation over time: A situated change perspective. *Information Systems Research, 7*(1), 63–92.

Orlikowski, W. J. (2000). Using technology and constituting structure: A practice lens for studying technology in organizations. *Organization Science, 11*(4), 404–428.

Orlikowski, W. J. (2007). Sociomaterial practices: Exploring technology at work. *Organization Studies, 28*(9), 1435–1448.

Orr, J. (1996). *Talking about machines: An ethnography of a modern job.* Ithaca, NY: ILR Press.

Packendorff, J. (1995). Inquiring into the temporary organization: New directions for project management research. *Scandinavian Journal of Management, 11*(4), 319–333.

Papa, M. J., Auwal, M. A., & Singhal, A. (1995). Dialectic of control and emancipation in organizing for social change: A multitheoretic study of the Grameen Bank in Bangladesh. *Communication Theory, 5*, 189–223.

Papadimitriou, K., & Pellegri, C. (2007). Dynamics of a project through Intermediary Objects of Design (IODs): A sensemaking perspective. *International Journal of Project Management, 25*, 437–445.

Parsons, T. (1968). *The structure of social action: A study in social theory with special reference to a group of recent European writers.* New York, NY: Free Press.

Paulsen, N., & Hernes, T. (Eds.). (2003). *Managing boundaries in organizations.* Basingstoke, England: Palgrave Macmillan.

Peach, L. (1985). Managing corporate citizenship. *Personnel Management, 17*(7), 32–35.

Peirce, C. S. (1940). *The philosophy of Peirce: Selected writings* (J. Buchler, Ed.). New York, NY: Dover. (Original work published 1903)

Peirce, C. S. (1955). *Philosophical writings of Peirce.* New York, NY: Dover.

Peirce, C. S. (1960). *Collected papers.* Cambridge, MA: Belknap Press of Harvard University Press.

Pelletier, J. (1991). *Le roman national: Essais néo–nationalistes et roman québécois contemporain* [The national novel: Neonationalist essays on the contemporary Quebec novel]. Montreal, Canada: VBL.

Pepper, S. (1942). *World hypotheses.* Berkeley, CA: University of California Press.

Perelman, C. (1982). *The realm of rhetoric.* Notre Dame, IN: University of Notre Dame Press.

Perelman, C., & Olbrechts-Tyteca, L. (1969). *The new rhetoric: A treatise on argumentation.* Notre Dame, IN: University of Notre Dame Press.

Perrow, C. (1986). *Complex organizations: A critical essay* (3rd ed.). New York, NY: McGraw Hill.

Perrow, C. (1991). A society of organizations. *Theory and Society, 20*, 725–762.

Philipsen, G. (1975). Speaking "like a man" in Teamsterville: Cultural patterns of role enactment in an urban neighborhood. *Quarterly Journal of Speech, 61*, 13–22.

Phillips, N., & Brown, J. L. (1993). Analyzing communication in and around organizations: A critical hermeneutic approach. *Academy of Management Journal, 36*(6), 1547–1576.

Phillips, N., Lawrence, T. B., & Hardy, C. (2004). Discourse and institutions. *Academy of Management Review, 29*, 635–652.

Pickering, A. (1995). *The mangle of practice.* Chicago, IL: University of Chicago Press.

Pinsonneault, A., & Rivard, S. (1998). Information technology and the nature of managerial work: From the productivity paradox to the Icarus paradox? *MIS Quarterly, 22*(3), 287–311.

Pipan, T., & Porsander, L. (2000). Imitating uniqueness: How big cities organize big events. *Organization, 21*(1), 1–27.

PMI. (2004). *A guide to the Project Management Body of Knowledge* (PMBOK® Guide; 3rd ed.). Newton Square, PA : Project Management Institute.

Polanyi, M. (1962). *Personal knowledge.* Chicago, IL: University of Chicago Press.

Polanyi, M., & Prosch, H. (1975). *Meaning.* Chicago, IL: University of Chicago Press.

Poole, M. S., & Van de Ven, A. H. (1989). Using paradox to build management and organizational theories. *Academy of Management Review, 14,* 562–578.

Powell, W. W., & DiMaggio, P. J. (Eds.). (1991). *The new institutionalism in organizational analysis.* Chicago, IL: University of Chicago Press.

Powers, R. (1998). *Gain.* New York, NY: Farrar, Starus & Giroux.

Prasad, A., & Mir, R. (2002). Digging deep for meaning: A critical hermeneutic analysis of CEO letters to shareholders in the oil industry. *Journal of Business Communication, 39*(1), 92–116.

Prigogine, I. (1992). Beyond being and becoming. *New Perspectives Quarterly, 9,* 22–28.

Prigogine, I. (1997). *The end of certainty.* New York, NY: Free Press.

Prigogine, I., & Stengers, I. (1984). *Order out of chaos.* London, England: Fontana.

Prior, L. (2003). *Using documents in social research.* London, England: Sage.

Pugh, D. S., & Hickson, D. J. (1964/1996). *Writers on organizations* (5th ed.). London, England: Penguin.

Putnam, L. L. (2003). Dialectical tensions and rhetorical tropes in negociations. *Organization Studies, 25*(1), 35–53.

Putnam, L. L., & Boys, S. (2006). Revisiting metaphors of organizational communication. In S. R. Clegg, C. Hardy, T. B. Lawrence, & W. R. Nord (Eds.), *The Sage handbook of organisational studies* (2nd ed., pp. 541–576). London, England: Sage.

Putnam, L. L., & Fairhurst, G. T. (2001). Discourse analysis in organizations: Issues and concerns. In F. M. Jablin & L. L. Putnam (Eds.), *The new handbook of organizational communication: Advances in theory, research, and methods* (pp. 78–136). Thousand Oaks, CA: Sage.

Putnam, L. L., & Jones, T. S. (1982). Reciprocity in negotiations: An analysis of bargaining interactions. *Communication Monographs, 49*(3), 171–191.

Putnam, L. L., & Nicotera, A. M. (Eds.). (2009). *Building theories of organization: The constitutive role of communication.* New York, NY: Routledge.

Putnam, L. L., & Pacanowsky, M. E. (Eds.). (1983). *Communication and organization: An interpretive approach.* Beverly Hills, CA: Sage.

Putnam, L. L., Phillips, N., & Chapman, P. (1996). Metaphors of communication and organization. In S. R. Clegg, C. Hardy & W. R. Nord (Eds.), *Handbook of organization studies* (pp. 375–408). London, England: Sage.

Putnam, L. L., & Wilson, S. R. (1989). Argumentation and bargaining strategies as discriminators of integrative outcomes. In M. A. Rahim (Ed.), *Managing conflict: An interdisciplinary approach* (pp. 121–141). New York, NY: Praeger.

Putnam, L. L., Wilson, S. R., & Turner, D. B. (1990). The evolution of policy arguments in teachers' negotiations. *Argumentation, 4,* 129–152.

Quattrone, P. (2004). Accounting for God: Accounting and accountability practices in the Society of Jesus (Italy, 16th–17th centuries). *Accounting, Organizations and Society 29,* 647–683.

Quattrone, P., Thrift, N., McLean, C., & Puyou, F.-R. (2010). *Imagining business: Performative imagery in organizations.* London, England: Routledge.

Quinn, R. W., & Dutton, J. E. (2005). Coordination as energy-in-conversation. *Academy of Management Review, 30,* 36–57.

Räisänem, C., & Linde, A. (2004). Technologizing discourse to standardize projects in multi-project organizations: hegemony by consensus? *Organization, 11*(1), 101–121.

Ravasi, D., & van Rekom, J. (2003). Key issues in organizational identity and identification theory. *Corporate Reputation Review, 6,* 118–132.

Real, K., & Putnam, L. L. (2005). Ironies in the discursive struggle of pilots defending the profession. *Management Communication Quarterly, 19*, 91–119.

Reed, M. I. (2000). The limits of discourse analysis in organizational analysis. *Organization, 7*, 524–530.

Rhodes, C., & Brown, A. D. (2005). Narrative, organizations and research. *International Journal of Management Reviews, 7*(3), 167–188.

Rice, A. K. (1987). *Productivity and social organization: The Ahmedabad experiment.* London, England: Tavistock. (Original work published 1958)

Ricoeur, P. (1973). The model of the text: Meaningful action considered as a text. *New Literary History, 5*(1), 91–117.

Ricoeur, P. (1984). *Time and narrative* (Vol. 1). Chicago, IL: University of Chicago Press.

Ricoeur, P. (1986). *Du texte à l'action: Essais d'herméneutique,* Vol. 2 [From text to action. Essays on hermeneutics]. Paris, France: Seuil.

Ricoeur, P. (1990). L'identité narrative [Narrative identity]. *Revue des sciences humaines, 221*, 35–47.

Riemenschneider, C. K., Hardgrave, B. C., & Davis, F. D. (2002). Explaining software developer acceptance of methodologies: A comparison of five theoretical models. *IEEE Transactions on Software Engineering, 28*(12), 1135–1144.

Riffaterre, M. (1978). The referential fallacy. *Columbia Review, 57*(2), 21–35.

Ritzer, G. (2008). *The McDonaldization of society.* (5th ed.). Los Angeles, CA: Pine Forge Press.

Robertson, T. (1997, September 7–11). *Cooperative work and lived cognition: A taxonomy of embodied actions.* Paper presented at the Fifth European Conference on Computer-Supported Cooperative Work, Lancaster, England.

Robey, D., & Sahay, S. (1996). Transforming work through information technology: A comparative case study of geographic information system in county government. *Information Systems Research, 7*(1), 93–110.

Robichaud, D. (2006). Steps toward a relational view of agency. In F. Cooren, J. R. Taylor, & E. J. Van Every (Eds.), *Communication as organizing: Empirical and theoretical explorations in the dynamic of text and conversation* (pp. 101–114). Mahwah, NJ: Erlbaum.

Robichaud, D., Giroux, H., & Taylor, J. R. (2004). The metaconversation: The recursive property of language as a key to organizing. *Academy of Management Review, 29*(4), 617–634.

Rogers, R. A. (1998). Overcoming the objectification of nature in constitutive theories: Toward a transhuman, materialist theory of communication. *Western Journal of Communication, 62*, 244–272.

Roloff, M., Tutzauer, F., & Dailey, W. (1987). *The role of argumentation in distributive and integrative bargaining contexts: Seeking relative advantage but at what cost?* Paper presented at the First International Conference of the Conflict Management Group, Fairfax, VA.

Rosch, E. (1999). Reclaiming concepts. In R. Núñez & W. J. Freeman (Eds.), *Reclaiming cognition: The primacy of action, intention and emotion* (pp. 61–77). Thorverton, England: Imprint Academic.

Rosch, E. (2004). "If you depict a bird, give it space to fly": On mind, meditation, and art. In J. Baas & J. Jacobs (Eds.), *Buddha mind in contemporary art* (pp. 37–47). Berkeley, CA: University of California Press.

Rosch, E. (2007). More than mindfulness: When you have a tiger by the tail, let it eat you. *Psychological Inquiry, 18*(4), 258–264.

Rosch, E. (2008). Beginner's mind: Paths to the wisdom that is not learned. In M. Ferrari & G. Potworowski (Eds.), *Teaching for wisdom: Cross-cultural perspectives on fostering wisdom* (pp. 135–162). New York, NY: Springer.

Rowland, R. C. (1987). Narrative: Mode of discourse or paradigm. *Communication Monographs, 54*, 264–275.

Rowland, R. C. (1989). On limiting the narrative paradigm: Three case studies. *Communication Monographs, 56*, 39–54.

Rudd, G. (1995). The symbolic construction of organizational identities and community in a regional symphony. *Communication Studies, 46*, 201–221.

Rudd, G. (2000). The symphony: Organizational discourse and the symbolic tension between artistic and business ideologies. *Journal of Applied Communication Research, 28*, 117–143.

Ryle, G. (1963). *The concept of mind*. London, England: Penguin.

Sachs, P. (1993). Shadows in the soup: Conceptions of work and nature of evidence. *The Quarterly Newsletter of the Laboratory of Comparative Human Cognition, 15*(4), 125–133.

Sacks, H. (1992). *Lectures on conversation*. Oxford, England: Blackwell.

Saludadez, J. A., & Taylor, J. R. (2006). The structuring of collaborative research networks in the stories researchers tell. In F. Cooren, J. R. Taylor, & E. J. Van Every (Eds.), *Communication as organizing: Empirical and theoretical explorations in the dynamic of text and conversation* (pp. 37–54). Mahwah, NJ: Erlbaum.

Sampson, A. (1995). *Corporate man. The rise and fall of the corporate life*. London, England: HarperCollins.

Sapsed, J., & Salter, A. (2004). Postcards from the edge: Local communities, global programs and boundary objects. *Organization Studies, 25*(9), 1515–1534.

Sawyer, K. R. (2003). *Improvised dialogues*. Westport, CT: Ablex.

Scarry, E. (1985). *The body in pain: The making and unmaking of the world*. New York, NY: Oxford University Press.

Schauer, E. (1991). *Playing by rules*. Oxford, England: Clarendon Press.

Schiffrin, D. (1985). Everyday argument: The organization of diversity in talk. In T. A. van Dijk (Ed.), *Handbook of discourse analysis: Vol. 3. Discourse and dialogue* (pp. 35–46). London, England: Academic Press.

Schwartzman, H. B. (1993). *Ethnography in organizations* (Vol. 27). Newbury Park, CA: Sage.

Scott, C. R., Corman, C. R., & Cheney, G. (1998). Development of a structurational model of identification in the organization. *Communication Theory, 8*, 298–336.

Scott, W. R. (1987). *Organizations: Rational, natural and open systems*. Englewood Cliffs, NJ: Prentice-Hall.

Searle, J. R. (1969). *Speech acts: An essay in the philosophy of language*. Cambridge, England: Cambridge University Press.

Seibold, D. R., & Myers, K. K. (2006). Communication as structuring. In G. J. Shepherd, J. S. John, & T. Striphas (Eds.), *Communication as … Perspectives on theory* (pp. 143–152). Thousand Oaks, CA: Sage.

Seidl, D., & Becker, K. H. (Eds.). (2005). *Niklas Luhmann and organization studies*. Malmö, Sweden: Liber.

Sellen, A. J., & Harper, R. H. R. (2002). *The myth of the paperless office*. Cambridge, MA: MIT Press.

Selznick, P. (1949). *TVA and the grass roots: A study in the sociology of formal organizations*. New York, NY: Harper & Row.

Seo, M. G., & Creed, W. E. D. (2002). Institutional contradictions, praxis, and institutional change: A dialectical perspective. *Academy of Management Review, 27,* 222–247.

Seo, M. G., Putnam, L. L., & Bartunek, J. M. (2004). Dualities and tension of planned organizational change. In M. S. Poole & A. H. Van de Ven (Eds.), *Handbook of organizational change and innovation* (pp. 73–107). New York, NY: Oxford University Press.

Shantideva. (1997/1999). *The way of the Bodhisattva: A translation of the Bodhicharyavatara* (Padmakara Translation Group, Trans.). Boston, MA: Shambhala Dragon.

Sheldrake, R. (1999). *Dogs that know when their owners are coming home and other unexplained powers of animals.* New York, NY: Random House.

Shenhav, Y. (2003). The historical and epistemological foundations of organization theory: Fusing sociological theory with engineering discourse. In H. Tsoukas & C. Knudsen (Eds.), *The Oxford handbook of organization theory. Meta-theoretical perspectives* (pp. 183–209). Oxford, England: Oxford University Press.

Shotter, J., & Katz, A. M. (1996). Articulating a practice from within the practice itself: Establishing fromative dialogues by the user of a "social poetics." *Concepts and Transformation, 1,* 213–237.

Sillince, J. A. A. (1999). The organizational setting, use and institutionalization of argumentation repertoires. *Journal of Management Studies, 36*(6), 795–830.

Sillince, J. A. A. (2005). *A theory of organizational communication: Organization as rhetoric.* Bordeaux, France: Centre de recherche de Bordeaux—École de gestion.

Silverman, D. (1970). *The theory of organisations: A sociological framework.* London, England: Heinemann Educational.

Silverman, D. (1994). On throwing away ladders: Re-writing the theory of organizations. In J. Hassard & M. Parker (Eds.), *Towards a new theory of organizations* (pp. 1–23). London, England: Routledge.

Simon, H. A. (1947). *Administrative behavior.* New York, NY: Macmillan.

Smith, R. C. (1993). *Images of organization: Root-metaphors of the organization–communication relation.* Paper presented at the Annual Conference of the International Communication Association, Washington, DC.

Söderlund, J. (2004). Building theories of project management: Past research, questions for the role and practice of project management. *International Journal of Project Management, 22,* 183–191.

Söderlund, J. (2005). What project management really is about: Alternative perspectives on the role and practice of project management. *International Journal of Technology Management, 32*(3/4), 371–387.

Sotirin, P., & Gottfried, H. (1999). The ambivalent dynamics of secretarial "bitching": Control, resistance, and the construction of identity. *Organization, 6,* 57–80.

Spencer–Brown, G. (1979). *Laws of form.* New York, NY: Dutton.

Spooner, L. (1986). Community relations calls for a new kind of giving. *Savings Institutions, 107*(5), 70–75.

Star, S. L., & Griesemer, J. R. (1989). Institutional ecology, "translations" and boundary object: amateurs and professionals in Berkeley's museums of vertebrate zoology, 1907–1939. *Social Studies of Science, 19,* 387–420.

Starbuck, W. H. (2003). The origins of organization theory. In H. Tsoukas & C. Knudsen (Eds.), *The Oxford handbook of organization theory: Meta–theoretical perspectives* (pp. 143–182). Oxford, England: Oxford University Press.

Stohl, C., & Cheney, G. (2001). Participatory practices/paradoxical practices: Communication and the dilemmas of organizational democracy. *Management Communication Quarterly, 14*, 349–407.

Styhre, A. (2006). The bureaucratization of the project manager function: The case of the construction industry. *International Journal of Project Management, 24*(3), 271–276.

Suchman, L. (1995). Representations of work: Making work visible. *Communications of the ACM, 38*(9), 56–64.

Suchman, L. (2000). Organizing alignment: A case of bridge-building. *Organization, 7*(2), 311–327.

Swieringa, R. C. (2008, May). *"Reporting" the laboratory: Collective discursive practice as organizing and manifesting community.* Paper presented at the conference What is an organization? Materiality, agency and discourse. Montréal, Québec, Canada.

Tarde, G. (1999) *Monadologie et sociologie* [Monadology and Sociology]. Paris, France: Les empêcheurs de penser en rond. (Original work published 1895)

Tarde, G. (2000) *Social laws: An outline of sociology* (H. C. Warren, Trans.). Kitchener, ON, Canada: Batoche Books. (Original work published 1899). Retrieved from http://socserv.mcmaster.ca/~econ/ugcm/3ll3/tarde/laws.pdf

Taylor, C. (1985a). *Human agency and language* (Vol. 1). Cambridge, England: Cambridge University Press.

Taylor, C. (1985b). *Philosophy and the human sciences* (Vol. 2). Cambridge, England: Cambridge University Press.

Taylor, C. (1991). The dialogical self. In D. R. Hiley, J. F. Bohman, & R. Shusterman (Eds.), *The interpretive turn* (pp. 304–314). Ithaca, NY: Cornell University Press.

Taylor, C. (1993a). Engaged agency and background in Heidegger. In C. Guignon (Ed.), *The Cambridge companion to Heidegger* (pp. 317–336). Cambridge, England: Cambridge University Press.

Taylor, C. (1993b). "To follow a rule…". In C. Calhoun, E. LiPuma & M. Postone (Eds.), *Bourdieu: Critical perspectives* (pp. 45–59). Cambridge, England: Polity Press.

Taylor, C. (1995a). *Philosophical arguments.* Cambridge, MA: Harvard University Press.

Taylor, C. (1998). *Les sources du moi: La formation de l'identité moderne* [Sources of the self. The formation of modern identity]. Montreal, Canada: Boréal.

Taylor, J. R. (1993c). *Rethinking the theory of organizational communication: How to read an organization.* Norwood, NJ: Ablex.

Taylor, J. R. (1995b). Shifting from a heteronomous to an autonomous worldview of organizational communication: Communication theory on the cusp. *Communication Theory, 5*(1), 1–35.

Taylor, J. R. (1999). What is "organizational communication"? Communication as a dialogic of text and conversation. *Communication Review, 3*, 21–64.

Taylor, J. R. (2000a). Apples and orangutan[g]s: The worldviews of organizational communication. *Saison Mauve, 3*, 45–64.

Taylor, J. R. (2000b). *What is an organization?* Retrieved from www.cios.org/www.ejc/v10n200.htm

Taylor, J. R. (2001a). *The role of text in conversation: Saussure revisited.* Paper presented at the Annual conference of the International Communication Association. Washington, DC.

Taylor, J. R. (2001b). Toward a theory of imbrication and organizational communication. *American Journal of Semiotics, 17*(2), 1–29.

Taylor, J. R. (2005). Engaging organization through worldview. In S. May & D. K. Mumby (Eds.), *Engaging organizational communication theory and perspectives: Multiple perspectives* (pp. 197–221). Thousand Oaks, CA: Sage.

Taylor, J. R. (2006). Coorientation theory: A conceptual framework. In F. Cooren, J. R. Taylor, & E. J. Van Every (Eds.), *Communication as organizing: Empirical explorations of the dynamic of text and conversation* (pp. 141–156). Mahwah, NJ: Erlbaum.

Taylor, J. R. (2009). Organizing from the bottom up? Reflections on the constitution of organization in communication. In L. L. Putnam & A. M. Nicotera (Eds.), *Building theories of organization: The constitutive role of communication* (pp. 153–186). New York, NY: Routledge.

Taylor, J. R. (2011). Communication is *not* neutral: "Worldview" and the science of organizational communication. In C. Chandlin & S. Sarangi (Eds.), *Handbook of communication in organizations and professions* (pp. 103–120). Berlin: Mouton de Gruyter.

Taylor, J. R., & Cooren, F. (1997). What makes communication "organizational"? How the many voices of collectivity become the one voice of organization. *Journal of Pragmatics, 27,* 409–438.

Taylor, J. R., & Cooren, F. (2006). Making worldview sense: And paying homage, retrospectively, to Algirdas Greimas. In F. Cooren, J. R. Taylor & E. J. Van Every (Eds.), *Communication as organizing: Practical approaches to research into the dynamic of text and conversation* (pp. 115–136). Mahwah, NJ: Erlbaum.

Taylor, J. R., Cooren, F., Giroux, N., & Robichaud, D. (1996). The communicational basis of organization: Between the conversation and the text. *Communication Theory, 6*(1), 1–39.

Taylor, J. R., & Giroux, H. (2005). The role of language in self–organizing systems. In G. Barnett & R. Houston (Eds.), *Self-organizing systems* (pp. 131–168). New York, NY: Hampton Press.

Taylor, J. R., Groleau, C., Heaton, L., & Van Every, E. J. (2001). *The computerization of work: A communication perspective.* Thousand Oaks, CA: Sage.

Taylor, J. R., & Gurd, G. (1994). Contrasting perspectives on nonpositivist communication research. In L. Thayer (Ed.), *Organization <——> Communication. Emerging perspectives* (Vol. 3, pp. 32–73). Norwood, NJ: Ablex.

Taylor, J. R., Gurd, G., & Bardini, T. (1997). The worldviews of cooperative work. In G. Bowker, L. Gasser, S. L. Star, & W. Turner (Eds.), *Social science research, technical systems and cooperative work* (pp. 379–413). Mahwah, NJ: Erlbaum.

Taylor, J. R., & Robichaud, D. (2004). Finding the organization in the communication: Discourse as action and sensemaking. *Organization, 11,* 395–413.

Taylor, J. R., & Van Every, E. J. (1993). *The vulnerable fortress: Bureaucratic organization and management in the information age.* Toronto: University of Toronto Press.

Taylor, J. R., & Van Every, E. J. (2000). *The emergent organization: Communication as its site and surface.* Mahwah, NJ: Erlbaum.

Taylor, J. R., & Van Every, E. J. (2011). *The situated organization. Case studies in the pragmatics of communication research.* New York, NY: Routledge.

Thévenot, L. (2006). *L'action au pluriel: Sociologie des régimes d'engagement* [The action in the plural: Sociology of commitment schemes]. Paris, France: La Découverte.

Thomas, J. (2000) Making sense of project management. In R.A. Lundin and F. Hartman (Eds.), *Projects as business constituents and guiding motives* (pp. 25–43). Boston. MA: Kluwer Academic.

Thompson, J. D. (1967). *Organizations in action: Social science basis of administrative theory.* New York, NY: McGraw–Hill.

Thondup Rinpoche, T. (2002). *The practice of Dzogchen* (3rd ed.). Ithaca, NY: Snow Lion. (Original work published 1989)

Thondup Rinpoche, T. (2001). *Enlightened journey: Buddhist practice as daily life.* Boston, MA: Shambhala. (Original work published 1995)

Thrift, N. (2005). *Knowing capitalism.* London, England: Sage.

Tindale, C. W. (1999). *Acts of arguing: A rhetorical model of argument.* Albany, NY: State University of New York Press.

Tompkins, E. V. B., Tompkins, P. K., & Cheney, G. (1989). Organizations as arguments: Discovering, expressing, and analyzing the premises for decisions. *Journal of Management Systems, 1*(2), 35–48.

Toulmin, S. E. (2003). *The uses of argument.* Cambridge, England: Cambridge University Press. (Original work published 1958)

Tracy, S. J. (2004). Dialectic, contradiction, or double bind? Analyzing and theorizing employee reactions to organizational tension. *Journal of Applied Communication Research, 32*, 119–146.

Trethewey, A. (1999). Isn't it ironic: Using irony to explore the contradictions of organizational life. *Western Journal of Communication, 63*, 140–167.

Truex, D., Baskerville, R., & Travis, J. (2000). A methodical systems development: The deferred meaning of systems development methods. *Accounting, Management and Information Technologies, 10*, 53–79.

Tsoukas, H. (1996). The firm as a distributed knowledge system: A constructionist approach. *Strategic Management Journal, 17*, 11–25.

Tsoukas, H. (2005). *Complex knowledge.* Oxford, England: Oxford University Press.

Tsoukas, H., & Chia, R. (2002). On organizational becoming: Rethinking organizational change. *Organization Science, 13*, 567–582.

Tsoukas, H., & Hatch, M. J. (2001). Complex thinking, complex pratice: The case for a narrative approach to organizational complexity. *Human Relations, 54*, 979–1013.

Tullberg, M. (2000). *Växelsång. Om organisering för förändring på SJ* [Singing nail. On organising for change in the Swedish Rail]. Gothenburg, Sweden: BAS.

Urgyen Rinpoche, T. (1995). *Rainbow painting: A collection of miscellaneous aspects of development and completion* (E. P. Kunsang, Trans.). Hong Kong, China: Rangjung Yeshe.

Van de Ven, A. H., & Poole, M. S. (2005). Alternative approaches for studying organizational change. *Organization Studies, 26*, 1377–1404.

van Eemeren, F. H., & Grootendorst, R. (2003). *A systemic theory of argumentation: The pragma-dialectical approach.* Cambridge, England: Cambridge University Press.

van Eemeren, F. H., Grootendorst, R., Johnson, R. H., Plantin, C., Willard, C. A. (1996). Fundamentals of argumentation theory: A handbook of historical backgrounds and contemporary developments. Mahwah, NJ: Erlbaum.

van Eemeren, F. H., & Houtlosser, P. (Eds.). (2002). *Dialectic and rhetoric: The warp and woof of argumentation analysis.* Dordrecht, Netherlands: Kluwer Academic.

van Maanen, J. (2001). Afterword: Natives "R" Us: Some notes on the ethnography of organizations. In D. Gellner & E. Hirsch (Eds.), *Inside organizations: Anthropologists at work* (pp. 233–261). Oxford, England: Berg.

van Vuuren, M., & Cooren, F. (2008, May). *"My attitude made me do it": Considering attitudes as actants.* Paper presented at the conference What is an organization? Materiality, agency and discourse. Montréal, Québec, Canada.

Varela, F. J. (1999). *Ethical know-how: Action, wisdom, and cognition.* Stanford, CA: Stanford University Press.

Varela, F. J., Thompson, E., & Rosch, E. (1992). *The embodied mind: Cognitive science and human experience.* Boston, MA: MIT Press.

V'asquez, C., Brummans, B., & Groleau, C. (2012). Notes from the field: Organizational shadowing as framing. *Qualitative Research in Organizations and Management: An International Journal, 7*(2), 144–165. doi: 10.1108/17465641211253075

Vaughn, M., & Stamp, G. H. (2003). The empowerment dilemma: The dialectic of emancipation and control in staff/client interaction at shelters for battered women. *Communication Studies, 54,* 154–168.

Vimalamitra, A. (2000). *The stages of meditation* (L. Jamspal, Trans.). Leh, India: Ladakhratnashridipika.

von Bertalanffy, L. (1950). An outline of general system theory. *British Journal for the Philosophy of Science, 1,* 139–164.

von Bertalanffy, L. (1951). General system theory—A new approach to unity of science. *Human Biology, 23,* 303–361.

von Foerster, H. (1981). *On cybernetics of cybernectics and social theory.* Frankfurt, Germany: Campus Verlag.

Vyner, H. M. (2002). The descriptive mind science of Tibetan Buddhist psychology and the nature of the healthy human mind. *Anthropology of Consciousness, 13,* 1–25.

Vyner, H. M. (2004a). *The healthy mind interviews: Khenpo Nyima Wangyal.* Khatmandu, Nepal: Vajra.

Vyner, H. M. (2004b). *The healthy mind interviews: Khenpo Tsewang Gyatso.* Kathmandu, Nepal: Vajra.

Vyner, H. M. (2005). *The healthy mind interviews: Lopon Tegchoke.* Kathmandu, Nepal: Vajra.

Waldo, D. (1961). Organization theory: An elephantine problem. *Public Administration Review, 21,* 210–225.

Walton, D. N. (1992). *Plausible argument in everyday conversation.* Albany, NY: State University of New York Press.

Walton, D. N. (1998). *The new dialectic: Conversational contexts of argument.* Toronto, Canada: University of Toronto Press.

Walton, D. N., & Krabbe, E. C. W. (1995). *Commitment in dialogue: Basic concepts of interpersonal reasoning.* Albany, NY: State University of New York Press.

Warnick, B. (1987). The narrative paradigm: Another story. *Quarterly Journal of Speech, 73,* 172–182.

Watson, T. J. (1995). Rhetoric, discourse and argument in organizational sense making: A reflexive tale. *Organization Studies, 16*(5), 805–821.

Watzlawick, P., Beavin, J. H., & Jackson, D. (1967). *Pragmatics of human communication: A study of interaction patterns, pathologies, and paradoxes.* New York, NY: Norton.

Weber, M. (1920). Bureaucracy (F. Elwell, Trans.). *Wirtschaft und Gesellschaft* [Economy and society] (pp. 650–678). Retrieved from http://www.faculty.rsu.edu/-felwell/Theorists/Weber/Whome.htm

Weick, K. E. (1969). *The social psychology of organizing.* Reading, MA: Addison-Wesley.

Weick, K. E. (1976). Educational organizations as loosely coupled systems. *Administrative Science Quarterly, 21,* 1–19.

Weick, K. E. (1977). Enactment processes in organizations. In B. M. Staw & G. R. Salancik (Eds.), *New directions in organizational behavior* (pp. 267–300). Chicago, IL: St. Clair Press.

Weick, K. E. (1979). *The social psychology of organizing.* Reading, MA: Addison-Wesley.

Weick, K. E. (1987). Theorizing about organizational communication. In F. M. Jablin, L. L. Putnam, K. H. Roberts, & L. Porter (Eds.), *Handbook of organizational communication: An interdisciplinary perspective* (pp. 97–122). Newbury Park, CA: Sage.

Weick, K. E. (1990). The vulnerable system: An analysis of the Tenerife air disaster. *Journal of Management, 16*(3), 571–593.

Weick, K. E. (1993). The collapse of sensemaking in organization: The Mann Gulch disaster. *Administrative Science Quarterly, 38*(4), 628–652.

Weick, K. E. (1995). *Sensemaking in organizations.* Thousand Oaks, CA: Sage.

Weick, K. E. (1996). Drop your tools: An allegory for organization studies. *Administrative Science Quarterly, 21*(1–19).

Weick, K. E. (1998). Improvisation as a mindset for organizational analysis. *Organization Science, 9*(5), 543–555.

Weick, K. E. (1999). Sensemaking as an organizational dimension of global change. In D. L. Cooperrider & J. E. Dutton (Eds.), *Organizational dimensions of global change* (pp. 39–56). Thousand Oaks, CA: Sage.

Weick, K. E. (2006). Faith, evidence, and action: Guesses in an unknowable world. *Organization Studies, 27,* 1723–1736.

Weick, K. E., & Browning, L. D. (1986). Argument and narration in organizational communication. *Yearly Review of Management of the Journal of Management, 12,* 243–279.

Weick, K. E., & Putnam, L. L. (2006). Organizing for mindfulness: Eastern wisdom and Western knowledge. *Journal of Management Inquiry, 15,* 514–524.

Weick, K. E., & Roberts, K. (1993). Collective mind in organizations: Heedful interrelating on flight decks. *Administrative Science Quarterly, 38,* 357–381.

Weick, K. E., & Sutcliffe, K. M. (2006). Mindfulness and the quality of organizational attention. *Organization Science, 17,* 514–524.

Weick, K. E., Sutcliffe, K. M., & Obstfeld, D. (2005). Organizing and the process of sensemaking. *Organization Science, 16,* 409–421.

Wendt, R. F. (1998). The sound of one hard clapping: Counterintuitive lessons extracted from paradoxes and double binds in participative organizations. *Management Communication Quarterly, 11,* 323–371.

Wenzel, J. W. (1987). The rhetorical perspective on argument. In F. H. van Eemeren, R. Grootendorst, J. A. Blair, & C. A. Willard (Eds.), *Argumentation: Across the lines of discipline. Proceedings of the Conference on Argumentation in 1986* (pp. 101–109). Dordrecht, Netherlands: Foris.

Wenzel, J. W. (1990). Three perspectives on argument: Rhetoric, dialectic, logic. In J. Schuetz & R. Trapp (Eds.), *Perspectives on argumentation: Essays in honor of Wayne Brockeriede* (pp. 9–26). Prospect Heights, IL: Waveland.

Wenzel, J. W. (1992). Perspectives on argument. In W. L. Benoit, D. Hample, & P. J. Benoit (Eds.), *Readings in argumentation* (pp. 121–143). New York, NY: Foris.

Whettent, D., & Godfrey, P. (1998). *Identity in organizations.* Thousand Oaks, CA: Sage.

Whettent, D., & Mackay, A. (2002). A social actor conception of organizational identity and its implications for the study of organizational reputation. *Business and Society, 41,* 393–414.

White, D., & Fortune, J. (2002). Current practice in project management—An empirical study. *International Journal of Project Management, 20*(1), 1–11.

Whitehead, A. N. (1978) *Process and reality. An Essay in Cosmology.* New York, NY: Free Press. (Original work published 1929)

Wiener, N. (1948). *Cybernetics: Or the control and communication in the animal and the machine.* Cambridge, MA: MIT Press.

Wiley, N. (1988). The micro–macro problem in social theory. *Sociological Theory, 6,* 254–261.

Willard, C. A. (1989). *A theory of argumentation.* Tuscaloosa, AL: University of Alabama Press.

Willard, C. A. (1996). *Liberalism and the problem of knowledge: A new rhetoric for modern democracy.* Chicago, IL: University of Chicago Press.

Winsor, D. (1998). Rhetorical practices in technical work. *Journal of Business and Technical Communication Quarterly, 12*(3), 343–370.

Winsor, D. (2006). Using writing to structure agency: An examination of engineers' practice. *Technical Communication Quarterly, 15*(4), 411–430.

Witmer, D. (1997). Communication and recovery: Structuration as an ontological approach to organizational culture. *Communication Monographs, 64,* 324–349.

Wittgenstein, L. (1953). *Philosophical investigations.*(G. E. M. Anscombe, Trans.). Oxford, England: Blackwell.

Wittgenstein, L. (1979). *On certainty.* (D. Paul & G. E. M. Anscombe, Trans.). Oxford, England: Blackwell.

Wittgenstein, L. (1980). *Remarks on the philosophy of psychology* (Vol. 2, C. G. Luckhardt & M. A. E. Aue, Trans.). Chicago, IL: University of Chicago Press.

Woodward, J. (1965). *Industrial organization: Theory and practice.* Oxford, England: Oxford University Press.

Yakura, E. K. (2002). Charting time: Timelines as temporal boundary object. *Academy of Management Journal, 45*(5), 956–970.

Yates, J., & Orlikowski, W. J. (1992). Genres of organizational communication: A structurational approach to studying communication and media. *Academy of Management Review, 17,* 299–326.

Ybema, S., Yanow, D., Wels, H., & Kamsteeg, F. (Eds.) (2009). *Organizational ethnography: Studying the complexities of everyday life.* London, England: Sage.

Zarefsky, D. (1992). Persistent question in the theory of argument fields. In W. L. Benoit, D. Hample, & P. J. Benoit (Eds.), *Readings in argumentation* (pp. 417–436). New York, NY: Floris.

Zarefsky, D. (2001). Argumentation. In T. O. Sloane (Ed.), *Encyclopedia of rhetoric* (pp. 33–37). Oxford, England: Oxford University Press.

Index